Fodor's
Romania

Fodor's Travel Publications, Inc.
New York and London

Fodor's Rome

Editor: Thomas Cussans
Area Editor: Barbara Walsh Angelillo
Editorial Contributors: Eliana Cosimini, Leslie Gardiner,
Andrew Heritage, Roger Jones
Art Director: Fabrizio La Rocca
Cartographer: David Lindroth
Illustrator: Karl Tanner
Cover Photograph: Michael Norcia

Design: Vignelli Associates

Contents

Foreword

It is not the geographical site—the famed and now almost obliterated Seven Hills, embraced by the serpentine progress of Father Tiber—that has made Rome the lodestone for countless generations. In fact, the location of the city conspired against Rome for centuries, centuries during which the Pontine Marshes bred malaria, the disease that some historians claim was the real reason for the fall of the Roman Empire.

Rome's eminence is due to human genius. People from all over the world crowd into the city to see the traces of the men and women who have lived and worked here at key periods in the past. It is a place not just of religious pilgrimage, but of artistic and historical pilgrimage, a place made fascinating by its associations with creative inspiration, with the lust for power, with the development of empire, and with the worship of gods, either one or many. It is Rome's identification with the best and the basest in mankind that has made it a magnet.

This is an exciting time for Fodor's, as it begins a three-year program to rewrite, reformat, and redesign all 140 of its guides. Here are just a few of the exciting new features:

★ Brand-new computer-generated maps locating all the top attractions, hotels, restaurants, and shops

★ A unique system of numbers and legends to help readers move effortlessly between text and maps

★ A new star rating system for hotels and restaurants

★ Restaurant reviews by major food critics around the world

★ Stamped, self-addressed postcards, bound into every guide, give readers an opportunity to help evaluate hotels and restaurants

★ Complete page redesign for instant retrieval of information

★ FODOR'S CHOICE—Our favorite museums, beaches, cafés, romantic hideaways, festivals, and more

★ HIGHLIGHTS '89—An insider's look at the most important developments in tourism during the past year

★ TIME OUT—The best and most convenient lunch stops along the shopping and exploring routes

★ A 10-page Traveler's Menu and Phrase Guide in all major foreign guides

★ Exclusive background essays create a powerful portrait of each destination

★ A minijournal for travelers to keep track of their own itineraries and addresses

We wish to express our gratitude to Barbara Walsh Angelillo for her expertise and tireless efforts in helping construct this guide.

While every care has been taken to ensure the accuracy of the information in this guide, the passage of time will always bring change, and consequently, the publisher cannot accept responsibility for errors that may occur.

All prices and opening times quoted here are based on information available to us at press time. Hours and admission fees may change, however, and the prudent traveler will avoid inconvenience by calling ahead.

Fodor's wants to hear about your travel experiences, both pleasant and unpleasant. When a hotel or restaurant fails to live up to its billing, let us know and we will investigate the complaint and revise our entries where the facts warrant it.

Send your letters to the editors of Fodor's Travel Publications, 201 E. 50th Street, New York, NY 10022. European readers may prefer to write to Fodor's Travel Publications, 30–32 Bedford Square, London WC1B 3SG, England.

Highlights'89 and Fodor's Choice

Highlights '89

The major change in Rome in 1988 was the closure of large areas of the center to most traffic, including tour buses. With the disappearance of the once-legendary congestion of the city's narrow streets, walking around Rome has become significantly less arduous. City buses and taxis are making better time, too. Just as important, the chronic pollution from car exhausts, which has done so much damage to monuments and buildings, is on the wane. Cleaning of buildings has begun in earnest, revealing pale beige and rose-colored masterpieces in place of the dark and solemn structures known for so long.

Restorations of many of the city's major monuments continue. Predicting just what work will be finished and when is a chancy business at best. But 1989 should see the wraps come off **Trajan's Column,** the **Arch of Constantine,** and the **column of Marcus Aurelius** in Piazza Colonna. It's hoped that restorations on the **Arch of Septimius Severus** will be completed in 1989, but don't be surprised to find the arch still under its protective covering. The biggest restoration project in the city—the cleaning of Michelangelo's **Sistine Ceiling**—is also scheduled for completion in 1989. The work, which began in 1982, has caused widespread controversy—is the cleaning damaging Michelangelo's awesome ceiling irreparably, or is it returning it to its pristine state?—but most experts now seem to agree that the brilliant coloring of the restored ceiling is much as the artist painted it. An almost equally ambitious cleaning program of Michelangelo's **Last Judgment** in the Sistine Chapel should begin late in 1989. The project's director expects this to last some years, but won't be drawn to say when he hopes to finish.

The extensive restoration work at the **Galleria Borghese** will continue through 1989. The first-floor sculpture galleries will remain open during the work, but the second-floor picture collection will stay closed till 1990.

The program of expansion at the **Museo Nazionale Romano** is gradually coming to an end. Parts of the museum's archaeological collection—all of which has been hidden for years—will be on view in 1989. The newly renovated **Palazzo Massimo** across the square from the museum is being converted into an annex. It will house much of the museum's substantial collection of classical sculptures. It's hoped that work will be completed some time in 1989. Similarly, what was once the neighboring city planetarium will open in late 1988 as a showcase for sculptural decorations from the Baths of Diocletian, Trajan's Baths, and the Baths of Caracalla. Finally, the long-awaited new wing of the **Galleria d'Arte Moderna** opened in 1988.

Following a series of on-again, off-again decisions as to whether or not to proceed with the ambitious excavations under Mussolini's grandiose **Via dei Fori Imperiali,** it seems likely that the project will now go ahead, though on a considerably smaller scale than originally projected some years back. Just how much digging will take place is hard to say.

Forecasts of exchange rates through 1989 can't be made with any certainty, but there seems reason to believe that the relatively weak dollar may continue. This at any rate is the view taken by Italian tourist authorities, who are accordingly stressing the value for money that Italy and Rome offer. Equally, they are hoping that the trend toward greater sophistication among U.S. visitors—to get off the beaten track and do more than see the main sights—will continue. There may be no shortage of great sights in Rome, but there is an equal abundance of lesser-known attractions, too. Those who take the trouble to seek them out will always be rewarded.

On the hotel front, at least one new luxury hotel is slated to open in 1989: the **Minerva** opposite Santa Maria Sopra Minerva. There's been a hotel here since at least the 17th century, and, in its former manifestation, it was one of downtown Rome's most atmospheric places to stay. The new hotel will come under the management of Holiday Inns. The **Sole al Pantheon,** just by the Pantheon, is also being refurbished.

Foodwise, the most conspicuous development has been the explosion of fast-food outlets. Younger Romans enthusiastically have taken to the "eat-and-run" lifestyle. Gourmets shouldn't despair, however: There are still numerous traditional eating places throughout the city, where good value and authentically Roman fare are on the menu. Chinese restaurants are becoming noticeably more popular although many complain that their standards are not as high as they might be.

Rome's nightlife scene is getting livelier by the month, or so it sometimes seems. More and more discos, clubs, and late-night cafés are opening to cater for a burgeoning youth culture, La Dolce Vita reborn, perhaps. The classiest new neighborhood is the **Via del Governo Vecchio** area, where cafés, wine bars, upscale shops, and health-food stores are proliferating. The old, working-class neighborhood of **Testaccio** shows signs of following suit. Theaters and chic cafés are opening, and more and more Romans are discovering the joys of the area's traditional sawdust-on-the-floor trattorias. Authentic Roman cooking at low prices is still available here, but signs are that prices surely will rise soon. Plans to transform the former slaughterhouse in Testaccio into an arts and exhibition center to rival the Beaubourg in Paris have, however, shown a typically Roman reluctance to progress beyond the drawing board.

Lovers of music received a serious setback in 1988 with the announcement by ecclesiastical authorities that henceforth strict limitations would be placed on concerts in churches. For many years, the lack of suitable concert venues in the city has been at least partially compensated for by concerts in Catholic churches. Now, however, only religious works may be performed. Promoters and performers are reeling, too, with the simultaneous announcement that admission must be free. The few Protestant churches in the city have predictably been deluged with requests that concerts be allowed to take place there.

Conspicuous security measures are still in force, especially at Leonardi da Vinci airport. The police presence is highly visible throughout much of the city, too. This hasn't had much effect on the bands of gypsies, mainly young children, who beg aggressively on many streets. Be wary of them. They are frighteningly adept at picking pockets. Purse snatchers continue to be a nuisance. Be careful on crowded buses, especially those most used by tourists such as the 64 bus from Termini Station to St. Peter's.

Construction work around the sports stadium at **Foro Italico** will continue through 1989 as Rome prepares to host the 1990 World Cup Soccer Championships. Other major construction projects include the long-awaited rail link between Leonardo da Vinci airport and the city's Ostinese train station. Officially, services should begin in late 1989, but Romans have learned to take announcements like this skeptically.

As of 1988, it's easier to keep in touch with events in the USA. The Monte Carlo television station, which is received in Rome, now broadcasts the previous night's CBS newscast the next morning at 8. Those who feel the need to watch Dan Rather while drinking their breakfast *caffelatte* need no longer smuggle the stuff back home.

Fodor's Choice

No two people will agree on what makes a perfect vacation, but it's fun and helpful to know what others think. We hope you'll have a chance to experience some of Fodor's Choices yourself in the Eternal City. For detailed information about each entry, refer to the appropriate chapters in Exploring Rome.

Special Moments

Piazza Navona at dawn
The Capitoline at dusk
Your first sight of the dome of St. Peter's
Rome in the fall, especially October
The Forum in the snow
An aperitif in the Caffè Greco

Works of Art

The Sistine Ceiling
Pietro da Cortona's ceiling in Palazzo Barberini
The head of Constantine in the Capitoline Museums
Canova's sculpture of Pauline Borghese in Villa Borghese
Raphael's Stanze in the Vatican
The Apollo Belvedere in the Vatican Museums

Churches

San Clemente
San Andrea al Quirinale
Santa Maria Maggiore
Sant' Ivo alla Sapienza
San Giovanni in Laterano
St. Peter's

Monuments

Bernini's Tomb of Urban VII in St. Peter's
Pyramid of Gaius Cestius
Pantheon
Colosseum
Monument to Vittorio Emanuele
Ara Pacis

Classical Sites

Trajan's Forum
Foro Romano
Hadrian's Villa
Temple of Vesta
Baths of Caracalla
Arch of Septimius Severus

Museums

Etruscan Collections at Villa Guilia
National Gallery of Modern Art
Collections at Palazzo Barberini
Vatican Museums

Walks

Villa Borghese and the Pincio
Along the Janiculum
Villa Celimontana
Anywhere in Old Rome early on a Sunday
Along the Via Appia Antica

Off the Beaten Track

The excavations under St. Peter's
The state apartments of the Doria Pamphili palace
The Ghetto
The Protestant cemetery
The church of Santi Quattro Coronati

Hotels

Eden *(Very Expensive)*
Hassler *(Very Expensive)*
Forum *(Expensive)*
Valadier *(Expensive)*
Carriage *(Moderate)*
Internazionale *(Moderate)*
Ausonia *(Inexpensive)*
Suisse *(Inexpensive)*

Restaurants

Le Restaurant of the Grand Hotel *(Very Expensive)*
El Toulà *(Very Expensive)*
Andrea *(Expensive)*
Alberto Ciarla *(Expensive)*
Ranieri *(Expensive)*
Romolo *(Moderate)*
Vecchia Roma *(Moderate)*
Baffetto *(Inexpensive)*
L'Eau Vive *(Inexpensive)*

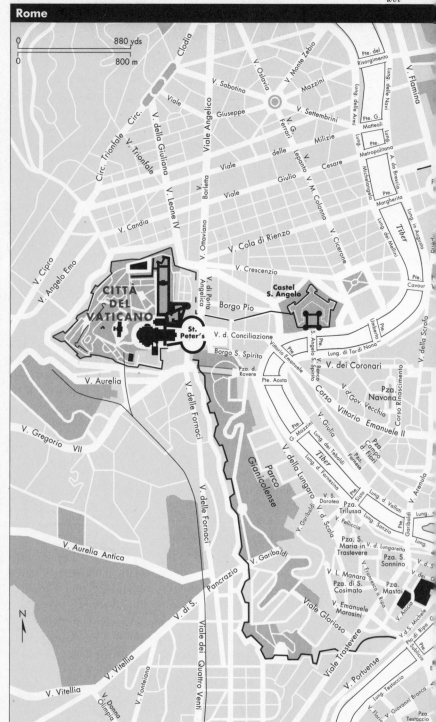

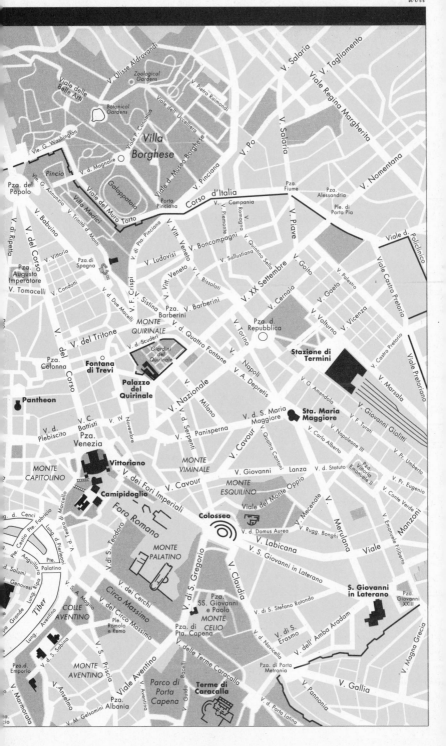

World Time Zones

Numbers below vertical bands relate each zone to Greenwich Mean Time (0 hrs.).
Local times frequently differ from these general indications,
as indicated by light-face numbers on map.

Auckland, **1**	Denver, **8**	New York City, **16**	Rio de Janeiro, **23**
Honolulu, **2**	Chicago, **9**	Washington, DC, **17**	Buenos Aires, **24**
Anchorage, **3**	Dallas, **10**	Miami, **18**	Reykjavik, **25**
Vancouver, **4**	New Orleans, **11**	Bogotá, **19**	Dublin, **26**
San Francisco, **5**	Mexico City, **12**	Lima, **20**	London (Greenwich), **27**
Los Angeles, **6**	Toronto, **13**	Santiago, **21**	Lisbon, **28**
Edmonton, **7**	Ottawa, **14**	Caracas, **22**	Algiers, **29**
	Montreal, **15**		Paris, **30**
			Zürich, **31**

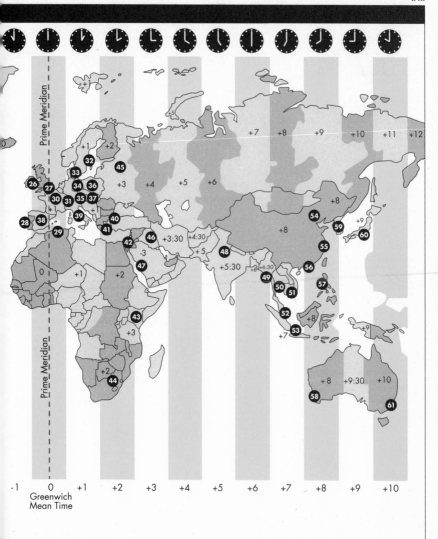

Introduction

by Leslie Gardiner

A free-lance writer and broadcaster, Leslie Gardiner's knowledge of Italy dates from 1942 when, as an escaped prisoner of war, he walked from the Alps to Sicily, a journey he has repeated on foot and by road and rail many times since. He has gained numerous awards for his travel articles.

Coming off the autostrada at Roma Nord or Roma Sud, you know by the convergence of heavily trafficked routes that you are entering a grand nexus: All roads lead to Rome. And then the interminable suburbs, the railroad crossings, the intersections—no wonder they call it the Eternal City.

Nearer the center, Rome begins to have the air of a city socially divided. On one side, compact masses of old tenements crowd above mean streets. On the other, soaring yellow-washed apartment blocks, five stories high with inner courtyards, are geometrically aligned. Poor or not-so-poor, your Roman likes living in a crowd, in the thick of things. The residential suburb, out at Monte Sacro or Garbatella, has little appeal for him.

In the urban sprawl a few features that match your expectations of Rome begin to take shape: a bridge with heroic statues along its parapets; a towering cake of frothy marble decorated with allegorical figures in extravagant poses; a piazza and an obelisk under an umbrella of pine trees; a fountain pitted with age, bearing the notice *ACQUA NON POTABILE*—which doesn't prevent street urchins from dashing up to drink at it. Street names touch a chord of schoolroom memories: Via Appia Nuova, Via Aurelia Antica. The very gratings and manhole covers are stamped SPQR, "The Senate and Populace of Rome," an expression that links the citizen with his ancestor of 22 centuries ago and gives the stranger the eerie feeling that the dust he stirs has been stirred by the togas of Cato, Cicero, and Seneca. In Rome, 22 centuries are just a few generations back.

You have arrived. You are in the city's heart. Your automobile is parked in the shadow of a stone she-wolf, along with automobiles which have ROMA on their license plates. Italian index letters are abbreviations of the vehicle-licensing towns, MI for Milan, GE for Genoa and so on—except in Rome. The Roman motorist wears ROMA, spelled out in full. Like the SPQR, that was Mussolini's doing. He reasserted the grandeur that was ROME. He made Romans understand that they were the children of heroes and demigods.

Up north, they tell us that Turin with its industry and Milan with its commerce are the true capital cities of Italy. Rome is badly planned, badly sited, too far south, too enervating in summer, a town of lawyers, civil servants, and tourists. But the Roman can smile at that. He knows he inhabits the fountainhead of the Western world, not solely of Italy. He knows that his town, and no other, collected the wisdom of Egypt and Greece, refined and enriched it, and supplied the nations which arose afterward with their laws, systems of government, religions, military arts, and the foundations of their language and literature. Those black-eyed urchins at the wall-fountain, that gross woman bawling from her tiny balcony, that grandfather snoring on a cane chair at street level, that white-robed child emerging from the side door of the church, that pallid waiter polishing the restaurant window with yesterday's newspaper —all can say, as their distant ancestors said, *Civis Romanus sum*—"I am a Roman citizen." If they should travel to other parts of Italy they will note without surprise that most main streets are called Via Roma; that every medieval walled town has its Porta Romana, the gate that faces Rome; and that, on posts beside every main road, the distance to Rome is recorded every tenth of a kilometer.

Rome was not built in a day, though much of superficial Rome was built in less than a century. The old city grew organically, and still grows, and its growth is chronicled in its stones. When you look into this city you see how, like Troy, it exists on several levels. Unlike the levels of Troy, these have each been a spiritual metropolis for whole societies of human beings, most of whom never set eyes on Rome. Under the swarming traffic lie traces of Etruscan Rome; ancient Veii and Caere, strongholds of Etruscan princes, are virtually part of modern Rome.

There is a Rome of the Republics and the Emperors, outcropping in unexpected places like barbershops, garage forecourts, and railroad sidings. There is an early-Christian Rome, tunneling away in the catacombs, and a Dark-Age Rome, when the pampered citizenry fled to Carthage and, on arrival, immediately wanted to know what was playing at the theater. Engineers working on sewers or boring for extensions to the metropolitana (the subway) run afoul of the relics. A constant war is waged between archaeology departments and the town planners.

There are gaps in history's stratification. In the Middle Ages the city was reduced to a rural slum on the banks of an evil-smelling Tiber, and the malarial heirs of imperial grandeur borrowed classical pillars to repair their hovels. There is also Rome of the Papacies, and Rome of a period when the Popes were hunted in and out like criminals. There is evidence of Byzantine Rome, of the dark little brick-and-tile churches which incorporated Rome's name in an architectural style (Romanesque), and of the sumptuous flowering of the later-Renaissance styles which are called Roman Baroque.

Rome, however, though rich in florid sculptures, intricate ornamental motifs, and neo-Classical effects, cannot show us galleries of famous paintings the way many provincial centers can. For a capital city, she lacks a capital display of national artists. The Italian heritage is spread over the whole country; all major cities and many small towns and villages have their share of the treasure.

Closer to the present day and to the surface of Rome lies the early-19th-century city, destination of Grand Tourists. That is the Rome of Gioacchino Belli, dialect poet and satirist, and of Goethe's and Stendhal's travel books. In the English quarter, at the foot of the Spanish Steps, the poet John Keats died and Mrs. Babington kept her teashop.

Students of the Risorgimento—the resurgence and reunification of Italy in the 19th century—know a Rome of Garibaldi and his insurgents. From a vantage point on the Janiculum, the hero on horseback surveys the terrain in bloody skirmishes and betrayals. Doves from St. Peter's Square love to fly up and perch on the saddle of that equestrian statue, so that it often looks as though Garibaldi is carrying the birds to market.

Toward the end of the last century, the Eternal City spread its wings. On September 20, 1870 (Via Venti Settembre is one of the most durable of Italian street names), General Cadorna's regiment of *bersaglieri* breached the Porta Pia, proclaimed Rome capital of Italy, and made Pope Pius IX the "prisoner of the Vatican." The gold rush of merchants and contractors from the north, the arrival of hordes of bureaucrats from Florence, briefly the former capital, and of poor immigrants from Naples and Calabria, doubled the population of 100,000 in days, and took it to half a million in months. The Via Nazionale and the Via Venti Settembre were christened and the city-center slums were cleared for public buildings more in keeping with Rome's dignity. But the new city council rejected Garibaldi's scheme for diverting the Tiber. Without the Tiber, floods and all, Rome would not have been Rome.

Much of modern Rome, therefore, went up in a few years in the 1880s, decade of the *gran febbre di Roma* ("great fever of Rome")—a fever that ended with the patient's total collapse. "Through greed and childish dreams," a newspaper said, "the bankers have promoted building in a manner devoid of all prudence. . . . Every stage of construction depended on promissory notes. . . . When foreign bankers refused to discount notes, the paper tower crumbed."

The so-called "building yard of Italy" in the later 1880s was a field of ruins among the classical ruins, infested by provincials whom the promise of work had drawn in by the thousand. Rome grew dirtier and more decrepit, littered with shacks and cardboard tents until well into the present century. Of the 1920 population of 800,000, it was reported that nearly one fifth of all citizens lived in "abusive dwellings." Then came fascism, which ruthlessly swept them away. Wreckers moved into Trastevere and the slums near the Capitol, homes of those who could most truly claim Roman citizenship. A new central thoroughfare, the broad Via dei Fori Imperiali, was laid down from Mussolini's Palazzo Venezia to the Colosseum of the Caesars. One human touch was the rebuilding of the old *rione* (district) fountains, the venerable sculpted wells of the different parishes—an important feature of tourist Rome today.

Monumental architecture of the past 50 years has not much disturbed the shabby but stylish buildings of central Rome. No skyscraper out-tops the 450-foot dome of St. Peter's. New-look architecture, by exponents of the school of Gio Ponti and Nervi, is almost wholly confined to the EUR complex, site of the aborted Universal Exposition of Rome in 1942 and Olympic venue of 1960—a suburb bigger than Florence. On the whole, modern buildings look pretentious and ephemeral, and they fall far short of tradition. Through the '50s and the '60s there was an uncontrolled expansion of building along the main exit roads, but this has now long since been checked and recent talk has been of planned satellite towns in the Alban and Sabine hills. Rome has once again her squatter settlements and gypsy encampments among the arches of the old aqueducts, especially on the eastern approaches, Via Casilina and the Cinecittà area. But it is decreed that the city herself—beautiful and pleasing in spite of everything—shall be confined within her present limits.

1 Planning Your Trip

Before You Go

Government Tourist Offices

Contact the Italian State Tourist Office for free information.

In the United States 630 Fifth Ave., New York, NY 10111, tel. 212/245–4822; 500 N. Michigan Ave., Chicago, IL 60611, tel. 312/644–0990; 360 Post St., Suite 801, San Francisco, CA 94108, tel. 415/392–6206.

In Canada 3 Place Ville Marie, Montreal, Quebec H3B 2E3, tel. 514/866–7667.

In the United Kingdom 1 Princes St., London W1R 8AY, tel. 01/408–1254.

Tour Groups

Tour groups are not just for beginners anymore. While whistle-stop express tours of all the famous sights are still available—and a good introduction for those making a first visit—there is a growing number of more specialized and sophisticated packages. In fact, considering the wealth of options available, the toughest part of your vacation may well be finding the tour that best suits your personal style. Listed below is a sampling of programs to give you an idea of what is available. For more information, contact your travel agent and/or the Italian State Tourist Office.

When considering a tour, be sure to find out: (1) exactly what expenses are included (particularly tips, taxes, side trips, additional meals, and entertainment); (2) ratings of all hotels on the itinerary and the facilities they offer; (3) cancellation policies for both you and for the tour operator; and (4) if you are traveling alone, what the single supplement is. Most tour operators request that bookings be made through a travel agent—there is no additional charge for doing so.

General-Interest Tours **American Express Vacations** (Box 5014, Atlanta, GA 30302, tel. 800/241–1700 or, in GA, 800/282–0800) is a veritable supermarket of tours: You name it, they've either got it packaged or will customize a package for you.
CIT Tours (666 Fifth Ave., New York, NY 10103, tel. 212/397–9300 or 800/223–7987) offers several popular packages backed by an extensive support network in Italy.
Central Holiday (206 Central Ave., Jersey City, NJ 07307, tel. 201/798–5777 or 800/526–6045) can be counted on for solid, reasonably priced tours.
Hemphill/Harris (16000 Ventura Blvd., Suite 200, Encino, CA 90024, tel. 818/906–8086 or 800/421–0454) is at the other end of the spectrum: Its 16-day "Best of Italy" and 22-day "Fantasia Italiana" are deluxe, and priced accordingly.
Other major operators to Italy include: **Cosmos/Globus Gateway** (150 S. Los Robles Ave., Suite 860, Pasadena, CA 91101, tel. 818/449–0919 or 800/556–5454); **Donna Franca Tours** (470 Commonwealth Ave., Boston, MA 02215, tel. 617/227–0237); **Perillo Tours** (577 Chestnut Ridge Rd., Woodcliff Lake, NJ 07675, tel. 201/307–1234 or 800/431–1515); and **Italiatour** (666 Fifth Ave., New York, NY 10103, tel. 212/765–2183 or 800/237–0517).

Special-Interest Tours There is a staggering wealth of art and architecture offered by **Rome and Esplanade Tours** (581 Boylston St., Boston, MA 02116, tel. 617/266–7465).

Trafalgar Tours (21 E. 26th St., New York, NY 10011, tel. 212/689–8977 or 800/854–0103) offers "Club 21–35," faster-paced tours for travelers unafraid of a little physical activity—whether it's bike riding or discoing the night away.

Dailey-Thorp Travel (315 W. 57th St., New York, NY 10019, tel. 212/307–1555) offers deluxe opera and music tours including "Opera Capitals of Italy" (Rome, Naples, Florence, Bologna, Milan). Itineraries vary according to available performances.

Package Deals for Independent Travelers

Italiatour's "Italian Honeymoon" series of tours will melt the heart of any romantic couple with candlelight dinners and a host of special treats. Italiatour, Alitalia airline's in-house tour operator, also has more traditional air/hotel packages, as do Central Holiday and CIT Tours (*see* General-Interest Tours for addresses).
TWA Getaway Vacations (800–GETAWAY) has a reasonably priced eight-day "Roman Holiday."
TourCrafters (30 S. Michigan Ave., Chicago, IL 60603, tel. 312/726–3886) offers city and self-drive tours of the countryside.

When to Go

The main tourist season in Rome starts at Easter (when the greatest number of visitors flock to the city) and runs through September. Spring and fall are the best seasons to visit: It's neither too hot nor too cold, there's usually plenty of sun, and the famous Roman sunsets are at their best. In July and August, come if you like, but learn to do as the Romans do—get up and out early, seek shady refuge from early afternoon heat, take a nap if you can, resume activities in the late afternoon, and stay up late to enjoy the evening breeze. During August many shops and restaurants close, and on the August 15 holiday Rome is a ghost town. Roman winters are relatively mild, with some persistent rainy spells.

The following are average daily maximum and minimum temperatures for Rome.

Jan.	52F	11C	May	74F	23C	Sept.	79F	26C
	40	5		56	13		62	17
Feb.	55	13	June	82	28	Oct.	71	22
	42	15		63	17		55	13
Mar.	59	15	July	87	30	Nov.	61	16
	45	7		67	20		49	9
Apr.	66	19	Aug.	86	30	Dec.	55	13
	50	10		67	20		44	6

Current weather information on 235 cities around the world—180 of them in the United States—is only a phone call away. Call 800–247–3282 to obtain the Weather Trak telephone number for your area. When you reach that number a taped message will tell you to dial the three-digit access code to any of the destinations. The code is either the area code (in the USA) or the first three letters of the foreign city. For a list of all access codes, send a stamped, self-addressed envelope to Cities,

Box 7000, Dallas TX 75209. For further information, phone 214/869–3035 or 800/247–3282.

National Holidays (1989) January 1 (New Year's Day); January 6 (Epiphany); March 26 and 27 (Easter Sunday and Monday); April 25 (Liberation Day); May 1 (May Day); June 2 (Republic Day); August 15 (Assumption, or Ferragosto); November 1 (All Saints); December 8 (Immaculate Conception); December 25 and 26 (Christmas).

Note that Rome has an additional holiday—June 29, St. Peter's Day—when many shops and businesses are closed.

Festivals and Seasonal Events

Contact the Italian State Tourist Office (*see* Government Tourist Offices) for exact dates and further information on all the festivals held in Rome.

Jan. 5–6 **Epiphany** is the eve on which the Piazza Navona's toy fair explodes in joyful conclusion, with much noise and rowdiness to encourage *Befana*, an old woman who brings toys to good children and pieces of coal (represented by similar-looking candy) to the naughty.

Feb. **Carnival** celebrations reach a peak of masquerading fun on the Sunday and Tuesday before Lent begins. On the evening of *Martedì Grasso* (Mardi Gras) many restaurants hold special carnival parties—you'll need to make reservations well in advance.

Apr. **Easter** is the big event of the month, preceded by the solemn rites of **Holy Week,** in which the Pope takes an active part. The Monday after Easter, known as *Pasquetta*, is traditionally a day for an outing into the country.

Late Apr. The Piazza di Spagna bursts into bloom, with the Spanish Steps covered with azaleas. Nearby, Via Margutta holds an outdoor art show.

Late Apr. to early May The **International Horse Show** brings sleepy Piazza di Siena, an amphitheater in Villa Borghese, to life with stirring competition and a chic crowd of spectators.

Early May The **Rose Show** opens at Valle Murcia on the slopes of the Aventine Hill overlooking the Circus Maximus and continues into June.

Mid-May An **antiques fair** is held in the beautiful old Via dei Coronari in Old Rome, when shops stay open late and the street is lit by torches.

Late May The Italian **International Tennis Tournament** is held at Foro Italico.

Mid-June to mid-July The **Festival of Baroque Music** is held in Viterbo. The **Pontine Music Festival** is held in the Caetani castle in Sermoneta and in the abbeys of Fossanova and Valvisciolo, all in the province of Rome.

June 23 On the eve of the **Feast of St. John the Baptist,** June 24, the neighborhood of San Giovanni bursts with festive activities, mainly gastronomic.

June 29 The **Feast of St. Peter's,** patron saint of Rome, is marked by solemn celebrations in the basilica; this is your chance to see the interior of the church ablaze with light.

Mid-June to late July	The **French Academy** at Villa Medici holds a festival of performing arts featuring leading French artists.
Mid-July	The **Festa di Noantri** in Trastevere combines religious processions with concerts of traditional Roman music and a sidewalk fair.
Aug. 5	The **Feast of the Madonna of the Snow** is marked in the Basilica of Santa Maria Maggiore by a high mass, during which rose petals are thrown to represent the miraculous August snowfall that indicated where the church should be built.
Aug. 15	**Ferragosto** marks the height of the summer vacation period. Most shops, restaurants, and museums are closed, public transport is at a minimum, and the city is the quietest it will ever be. There are special celebrations in the church of Santa Maria in Trastevere.
Late Sept. to early Oct.	A **Handicrafts Fair** brings torchlight, street stalls, and animation to Via dell'Orso.
Early Oct.	The **Grape Harvest Festival** in Marino, in the Castelli Romani area, features parades and fountains spouting wine, free to all comers.
Dec. 8	This is the day of the **Feast of the Immaculate Conception,** when the Rome Fire Department honors the Virgin Mary by replacing the garland on top of her statue in Piazza di Spagna.
Late Dec.	*Presepi* (Christmas crèches) go on display in many churches; some of them are antique and quite elaborate.
Dec. 24 and 25	**Christmas** is very much a family holiday in Rome. There are no public celebrations other than solemn religious rites, beginning on Christmas Eve; these are especially beautiful in the city's older churches and in St. Peter's, where the Pope officiates both at midnight mass and at the late-morning mass on Christmas Day, before imparting his blessing to the faithful in the square.

What to Pack

Pack light because baggage trolleys are scarce in airports and railroad stations. Luggage restrictions on international flights are tight, which will help limit what you take (for luggage regulations on airlines *see* Getting to Rome by Plane).

Rome has mild winters and hot, sticky summers. Take a medium-weight coat for winter and a lightweight jacket or sweater for summer evenings, which may be cool. Brief summer thunderstorms are common, so take a folding umbrella. Leave plastic raincoats at home; Rome's high humidity level in summer makes them extremely uncomfortable. Casual clothes are the general rule, especially during the summer, although jackets and ties are required in most deluxe restaurants and bars. Jeans are as popular in Rome as at home and are perfectly acceptable for sightseeing and informal dining. Wear sturdy walking shoes, preferably with crepe or rubber soles, for Rome's many cobblestone streets and the gravel paths that surround some of the historic buildings.

The dress codes are strict for visits to churches, cathedrals, and the Vatican museums: shorts for both men and women are taboo. Women must cover their bare shoulders and arms—a shawl will do—but no longer need to cover their heads. Although there are no specific dress rules for the huge papal audiences, you will be out of place in shorts or immodest outfits. The Vatican Information Office in St. Peter's Square will tell you the dress requirements for smaller audiences.

To protect yourself against purse snatchers and pickpockets, take a handbag with long straps that you can sling across your body, bandolier style, with a zippered compartment for your money and other valuables.

You'll need an electrical adapter for hairdryers and other small appliances. The current is 220 volts and 50 cycles. If you stay in budget hotels, take your own soap. Many do not provide soap or give guests one tiny bar per room.

Taking Money Abroad

Traveler's checks and major U.S. credit cards—particularly Visa—are accepted in Rome. You'll need cash for some of the smaller restaurants and shops. Although you won't get as good an exchange rate at home as abroad, it's wise to change a small amount of money into Italian lire before you leave to avoid long lines at airport currency exchange booths. Most U.S. banks will exchange your money into lire. If your local bank can't provide this service, you can exchange money through **Deak International.** To find the office nearest you, contact Deak at 630 Fifth Ave., New York, NY 10011, tel. 212/635–0515.

For safety and convenience, it's always best to take traveler's checks. The most widely recognized are **American Express, Barclay's, Thomas Cook,** and those issued through major commercial banks such as **Citibank** and **Bank of America.** Some banks will issue the checks free to established customers, but most charge a 1% commission fee. Buy some of the traveler's checks in small denominations to cash toward the end of your trip. This will save you from having to cash a large check and ending up with more foreign money than you need. You can also buy traveler's checks in lire, a good idea if the dollar is falling and you want to lock in the current rate. Remember to take the address of offices where you can get refunds for lost or stolen traveler's checks.

Banks and bank-operated currency exchange booths in airports and railroad stations are the best places to change money. Hotels and privately run exchange firms will give you a significantly lower rate.

Getting Money from Home

There are at least three ways to get money from home: (1) Have it sent through a large commercial bank with a branch in Rome. The only drawback is that you must have an account with the bank; if not, you'll have to go through your own bank and the process will be slower and more expensive. (2) Have it sent through **American Express.** If you are a cardholder, you can cash a personal check or a counter check at an American Express office for up to $1,000; $200 will be in cash and $800 in traveler's checks. There is a 1% commission on the traveler's checks. American Express has a new service that will be available in most major cities worldwide by January 1989, called American Express MoneyGram. Through this service, you can receive up to $5,000 cash. It works this way: You call home and ask someone to go to an American Express office or an American Express MoneyGram agent located in a retail outlet, and fill out an American Express MoneyGram. It can be paid for with cash or any major credit card. The person making the payment is given a reference number and telephones you with that number. The American Express MoneyGram agent calls an 800 number and authorizes the transfer of funds to an American Express office or participating agency in Rome. In most cases, the money is available immediately on a 24-hour basis. You pick it up by showing identification and giving the reference number. Fees vary according to the amount of money sent. For sending $300 the fee is $22; for $5,000, $150. To find out the American Express MoneyGram location nearest your home and the location of offices in Rome, call 800/543–4080. You do not have to be a cardholder to use this service. (3) Have it sent through Western Union (tel. 800/988–4726). If you have a MasterCard or Visa, you can have money sent for any amount up to your credit limit. If not, have someone take cash or a certified cashier's check to a Western Union office. The money will be delivered in two business days to a bank in Rome. Fees vary with the amount of money sent. For $1,000 the fee is $67; for $500, $57.

Italian Currency

The unit of currency in Italy is the lira. The bills are 100,000, 10,000, 5,000, and 1,000 lire. Coins are 500, 100, and 50 lire. At press time (mid-May) the exchange rate was about 1,249 lire to the U.S. dollar, 984 to the Canadian dollar, and 2,199 to the pound sterling.

What It Will Cost

A vacation in Rome may not be as expensive as you would imagine—it can easily cost less than a vacation in Paris or London, and less than a stay in other Italian cities, say, Milan or Venice. The weakening of the dollar has made a difference, of course, but, as the lira remains fairly stable, inflation within Italy is decreasing, hovering at around 6% annually. Transportation costs in Rome are steadily increasing and the cost of long-distance telephone calls is the highest in Europe, far higher than in the United States. When it comes to finding somewhere to eat and stay, though, you should have no difficulty in finding somewhere to suit your taste and your pocketbook. (For the prices of restaurants and hotels *see* Dining and Lodging chapters.)

Taxes A cover charge appears as a separate item in restaurant checks, as does the service charge, usually about 15%. Cover and service charges can add up to a considerable extra on your bill. Taxes are usually included in the rates quoted by hotels, though it is wise to check. There are several direct taxes in Italy that affect the traveler, such as the 18% IVA (VAT) tax on car rental.

Sample Costs A cup of espresso coffee, taken while standing at the bar, costs from 700 to 1,000 lire, depending on the type of establishment; you will pay triple for table service. A bottle of beer costs from 1,600 to 2,500 lire, a Coke costs 1,500 lire. A *tramezzino* (small sandwich) costs about 1,200 lire, a more substantial one about

2,000 lire. You will pay about 5,000 lire for a short taxi ride. Admission to a major museum is about 5,000 lire, a three-hour sight-seeing tour about 25,000 lire.

Passports and Visas

Americans All U.S. citizens require a passport to enter Italy. Applications for a new passport must be made in person; renewals can be obtained in person or by mail (see below). First-time applicants should apply well in advance of their departure date to one of the 13 U.S. Passport Agency offices. In addition, local county courthouses, many state and probate courts, and some post offices accept passport applications. Necessary documents include: (1) a completed passport application (Form DSP–11); (2) proof of citizenship (birth certificate with raised seal or naturalization papers); (3) proof of identity (driver's license, employee ID card, or any other document with your photograph and signature); (4) two recent, identical, two-inch square photographs (black and white or color); (5) $42 application fee for a 10-year passport (those under 18 pay $27 for a five-year passport). Passports are mailed to you in about 10 working days.

To renew your passport by mail, you'll need completed Form DSP–82, two recent, identical passport photographs, and a check or money order for $35.

Visa are not required for U.S. citizens visiting Italy for less than three months.

Canadians All Canadian citizens require a passport to enter Italy. Send the completed application (available at any post office or passport office) to the Bureau of Passports, Complexe Guy Favreau, 200 Dorchester W, Montreal, Quebec H2Z 1X4. Include $25, two photographs, a guarantor, and proof of Canadian citizenship. Applications can be made in person at the regional passport offices in Edmonton, Halifax, Montreal, Toronto, Vancouver, or Winnipeg. Passports are valid for five years and are non-renewable.

Visas are not required for Canadian citizens visiting Italy for less than three months.

Britons All British citizens require a passport to enter Italy. Applications are available from travel agencies or a main post office. Send the completed form to a regional Passport Office. The application must be countersigned by your bank manager, or by a solicitor, barrister, doctor, clergyman, or Justice of the Peace who knows you personally. In addition, you'll need two photographs and the £15 fee. The occasional tourist might opt for a British Visitor's Passport. It is valid for one year, costs £7.50 and is non-renewable. You'll need two passport photographs and identification. Apply at your local post office.

Visas are not required for British citizens visiting Italy for less than three months.

Customs and Duties

On Arrival Visitors to Italy who are not nationals of other EEC countries can bring into Italy duty-free: (1) 400 cigarettes, or 200 cigarillos, or 100 cigars, or 500 grams of tobacco; (2) one liter of alcohol or two liters of wine; (3) 50 grams of perfume and one-quarter liter of toilet water. Visitors to Italy who are nationals of other

EEC countries can bring in duty-free: (1) 300 cigarettes, or 150 cigarillos, or 75 cigars, or 400 grams of tobacco; (2) one and a half liters of alcohol, or three liters of sparkling wine and three liters of table wine; (3) 90cc of perfume. All visitors may bring in 10 rolls of still camera film and 10 reels of movie film duty-free. Other items intended for personal use are generally admitted, so long as the quantities are reasonable.

On Departure **U.S. residents** bringing any foreign-made equipment from home, such as cameras, will be wise to carry the original receipt with them or register it with U.S. Customs before they leave (Form 4457). Otherwise they may end up paying duty on their return. U.S. residents may bring home duty-free up to $400 worth of foreign goods, as long as they have been out of the country for at least 48 hours. Each member of the family is entitled to the same exemption, regardless of age, and exemptions can be pooled. For the next $1,000 worth of goods, a flat 10% rate is assessed; above $1,400, duties vary with the merchandise. Included for travelers 21 or older are one liter of alcohol, 100 cigars (non-Cuban), and 200 cigarettes. Only one bottle of perfume trademarked in the United States may be brought in. However, there is no duty on antiques and art over 100 years old. Anything exceeding these limits will be taxed at the port of entry, and may be taxed additionally in the traveler's home state. Gifts valued at under $50 may be mailed to friends or relatives at home duty-free, but not more than one package per day to any one addressee and not to include perfumes costing more than $5, tobacco or liquor.

Canadian residents have a $300 exemption and may also bring in duty-free up to 50 cigars, 200 cigarettes, two pounds of tobacco, and 40 ounces of liquor, provided these are declared in writing to customs on arrival and accompany the traveler in hand or checked-through baggage. Personal gifts should be mailed as "Unsolicited Gift—Value under $40." Request the Canadian Customs brochure, "I Declare," for further details.

British residents are faced with two levels of duty-free allowances: one for goods bought in a duty-free shop in the EEC; one for goods bought in the EEC but not in a duty-free shop. In the **first** category they may bring home: (1) 200 cigarettes, or 100 cigarillos, or 50 cigars, or 250 grams of tobacco; (2) two liters of still table wine, plus one liter of alcohol over 22% by volume, or 38.8 proof (most spirits), or two liters of alcohol under 22% by volume (fortified or sparkling wine), or a further two liters of still table wine; (3) 50 grams of perfume and a quarter liter of toilet water; (4) other articles up to a value of £32, but not more than 50 liters of beer. In the **second** category they may bring home: (1) 300 cigarettes, or 150 cigarillos, or 75 cigars, or 400 grams of tobacco; (2) five liters of still table wine plus one and a half liters of alcohol over 22% by volume, or 38.8 by proof (most spirits), or three liters of alcohol under 22% by volume (fortified or sparkling wine), or a further three liters of still table wine; (3) 75 grams of perfume and three-eighths liters of toilet water; (4) other articles up to a value of £250, but not more than 50 liters of beer.

Traveling with Film

If your camera is new, shoot and develop a few rolls before leaving home. Pack some lens tissue and an extra battery for your built-in light meter. Invest about $10 in a skylight filter; it will protect the lens and reduce haze.

Film doesn't like hot weather. If you're driving in summer, don't store film in the glove compartment or on the shelf under the rear window. Put it behind the front seat on the floor, on the side opposite the exhaust pipe.

On a plane trip, never pack unprocessed film in check-in luggage: If your bags get X-rayed, you can say goodbye to your pictures. Always carry undeveloped film with you through security and ask to have it inspected by hand. (It helps to isolate your film in a plastic bag, ready for quick inspection.) Inspectors at American airports are required by law to honor requests for hand inspection; abroad, you'll have to depend on the kindness of strangers. With modern airport scanning machines it should be safe to pass your film through the machine from five to 500 scans, depending on the speed of your film, though bear in mind that the effects are cumulative.

If your film gets fogged and you want an explanation, send it to the **National Association of Photographic Manufacturers,** 600 Mamaroneck Ave., Harrison, NY 10528. It will try to determine what went wrong. The service is free.

Staying Healthy

There are no serious health risks associated with travel to Italy. However, the **Centers for Disease Control** (CDC) in Atlanta warns that most of Southern Europe is in the "intermediate" range for risk of contracting traveler's diarrhea. Part of this may be due to an increased consumption of olive oil and wine, which can have a laxative effect on stomachs used to a different diet.

If you have a health problem that might require purchasing prescription drugs while in Rome, have your doctor write a prescription using the drug's generic name. Brand names vary widely from country to country. Some U.S. and U.K. medications may be available from the pharmacy in the Vatican (tel. 06/686–4146).

The International Association for Medical Assistance to Travelers (IAMAT) is a worldwide association offering a list of approved English-speaking doctors whose training meets British and American standards. For a list of Italian physicians and clinics that are part of this network contact, **in the United States,** IAMAT, 736 Center St., Lewiston, NY 14092, tel. 716/754–4883. **In Canada:** 188 Nicklin Rd., Guelph, Ontario N1H 7L5. **In Europe:** Gotthardstrasse 17, 6300 Zug, Switzerland. Membership is free.

Shots and Medications Inoculations are not needed for entering Italy. The American Medical Association (AMA) recommends Pepto Bismol for minor cases of traveler's diarrhea.

Insurance

Travelers may seek insurance coverage in three areas: health and accident, lost luggage, and trip cancellation. Review your existing health and home-owner policies; some health insurance plans cover health expenses incurred while traveling, some major medical plans cover emergency transportation, and some home-owner policies cover the theft of luggage.

Health and Several companies offer coverage designed to supplement ex-
Accident isting health insurance for travelers:

Carefree Travel Insurance (Box 310, 120 Mineola Blvd., Mineola, NY 11501, tel. 516/294–0220 or 800/645–2424) provides
coverage for medical evacuation. It also offers 24-hour medical
phone advice.

Health Care Abroad, International Underwriters Group (243
Church St. W, Vienna, VA 22180, tel. 703/281–9500 or 800/237–
6615), offers comprehensive medical coverage, including emergency evacuation, for trips of 10–90 days.

International SOS Insurance (Box 11568, Philadelphia, PA
19116, tel. 215/244–1500 or 800/523–8930) does not offer medical insurance but provides medical evacuation services to its
clients, which are often international corporations.

Travel Guard International, underwritten by Cygna (1100 Cen-
terpoint Dr., Stevens Point, WI 54481, tel. 715/345–0505 or
800/782–5151), offers medical insurance, with coverage for
emergency evacuation when Travel Guard's representatives in
the United States say it is necessary.

Lost Luggage Lost luggage is usually covered as part of a comprehensive
travel insurance package that includes personal accident, trip
cancellation, and sometimes default and bankruptcy insurance.
Several companies offer comprehensive policies:

Access America Inc., a subsidiary of Blue Cross-Blue Shield
(Box 807, New York, NY 10163, tel. 800/851–2800).

Near, Inc. (1900 N. MacArthur Blvd., Suite 210, Oklahoma
City, OK 73127, tel. 800/654–6700).

Travel Guard International (*See* Health and Accident Insurance
above.)

Trip Cancellation Flight insurance is often included in the price of a ticket when
paid for with American Express, Visa, and other major credit
cards. It is usually included in combination travel insurance
packages available from most tour operators, travel agents,
and insurance agents.

Renting and Leasing Cars

Renting If you're flying into Rome and planning to spend some time
there, it's best to arrange car rental before you leave. Save
money by arranging to pick up your car either in the city or at
the airport. You'll have to weigh the added expense of renting a
car from a major company with an airport office against the
savings on a car from a budget company with offices in town.
You could waste precious hours trying to locate the budget
company in return for only small financial savings and you may
find that the type of car you want is not available at short notice. If you're arriving and departing from different airports,
look for a one-way car rental with no return fees. If you're traveling to more than one country, make sure your rental contract
permits you to take the car across borders and that the insurance policy covers you in every country you visit. Be prepared
to pay more for a car with automatic transmission; they are not
as readily available as those with manual transmissions so reserve them in advance.

Rental rates vary widely, depending on size and model, number of days you use the car, insurance coverage, and whether
special drop-off fees are imposed. Rental companies usually
charge according to the exchange rate of the dollar at the time

the car is returned or when the credit card payment is processed. In most cases, rates quoted include unlimited free mileage and standard liability protection. Not included are Collision Damage Waiver (CDW), which eliminates your deductible payment should you have an accident, personal accident insurance, gasoline, and European value-added tax (VAT). The VAT in Italy is 18%.

Three companies with special programs to help you hedge against the falling dollar by guaranteeing advertised rates if you pay in advance are: **Budget Rent-a-Car** (3350 Boyington St., Carrollton, TX 75006, tel. 800/527–0700); **Connex Travel International** (983 Main St., Peekskill, NY 10566, tel. 800/333–3949); and **Cortell International** (770 Lexington Ave., New York, NY 10021, tel. 800/223–6626, or, in New York, 800/442–4481). Other budget rental companies serving Rome include **Europe by Car** (1 Rockefeller Plaza, New York, NY 10020, tel. 800/223–1516, or, in California, 800/252–9401); **Foremost Euro-Car** (5430 Van Nuys Blvd., Van Nuys, CA 91404, tel. 800/423–3111); and **Kemwel** (106 Calvert St. Harrison, NY 10528, tel. 800/678–0678). Finally, the big three U.S. agencies also rent cars in Rome: **Avis,** tel. 800/331–1212; **Hertz,** tel. 800/223–6472; or, in New York, 800/522–5568; and **National** or **Europcar,** tel. 800/Car–Rent.

Driver's licenses issued in the United States and Canada are valid in Italy. Non-EEC members must have Green Card insurance. You might also take out an International Driving Permit before you leave, to smooth out difficulties if you have an accident or as an additional piece of identification. Permits are available for a small fee through local offices of the **American Automobile Association** (AAA) and the **Canadian Automobile Association** (CAA), or from their main offices: **AAA,** 8111 Gatehouse Rd., Falls Church, VA 22047–0001, tel. 703/AAA–6000; **CAA,** 2 Carlton St., Toronto, Ontario M5B 1K4, tel. 416/964–3170.

Britons driving in Italy should have a valid driving license, supported by an Italian translation, obtainable from the Italian State Tourist Office, or from the RAC, tel. 01/686–2525, or AA, tel. 0256/20123, free of charge. Green Card insurance is a wise buy, though not compulsory for EEC nationals. All drivers must carry their car registration documents and a red warning triangle.

Leasing For trips of 21 days or more, you may save money by leasing a car. With the leasing arrangement, you are technically buying a car and then selling it back to the manufacturer after you've used it. You receive a factory-new car, tax-free, with international registration, and extensive insurance coverage. Rates vary with the make and model of car and length of time used.

Before you go, compare long-term rental rates with leasing rates. Remember to add taxes and insurance costs to the car rentals, something you don't have to worry about with leasing. Companies that offer leasing arrangements include **Europe by Car** and **Kemwel,** listed above.

Rail Passes

For those planning to do a lot of traveling by train, the **Italian RailPass** is excellent value as it covers the entire Italian system, including Sicily and Sardinia. The pass is available in first class for periods of eight days ($169), 15 days ($204), 21 days ($245), and 30 days ($295). In second class the prices for the same periods are $107, $130, $152, and $186. You must buy the pass before you leave for Italy, either through travel agents or through **Italian State Railways** (666 Fifth Ave., New York, NY 10103, tel. 212/397–2667).

The **EurailPass**, valid for unlimited first-class train travel through 16 countries, including Italy, is an excellent value if you plan on traveling around the Continent. The ticket is available for 15 days ($298), 21 days ($370), one month ($470), two months ($650), and three months ($798). For those 26 and under there is the **Eurail Youthpass**, for one or two months' unlimited second-class train travel, at $320 and $420. The EurailPass does not cover Great Britain, and is available only if you live outside Europe or North Africa. The pass must be bought from an authorized agent in the Western Hemisphere or Japan *before* you leave for Europe. Apply through your travel agent, or **Italian State Railways** (see above).

For travelers who want to spread out their train journeys, there is the new **Eurail Flexipass**. With this pass, travelers get nine days of unlimited first-class train travel, but they do not have to ride for nine consecutive days, as they can use the pass on any nine days in a 21-day period. The **Flexipass** costs $310.

Student and Youth Travel

The **International Student Identity Card** entitles students to youth rail passes, special fares on local transportation, Intra-European Student Charter flights, and discounts at museums, theaters, sports events, and many other attractions. If purchased in the United States, the $10 cost of the ISIC also includes $2,000 in emergency medical insurance, plus $100 a day for up to 60 days of hospital coverage. Apply to the **Council on International Educational Exchange** (CIEE), 205 E. 42nd St., New York, NY 10017, tel. 212/661–1414. **In Canada,** the ISIC is available for CN $10 from the **Association of Student Councils,** 187 College St., Toronto, Ontario M5T 1P7.

The **Youth International Educational Exchange Card** (YIEE), issued by the Federation of International Youth Travel Organizations (FIYTO), 81 Islands Brugge, DK-2300 Copenhagen S, Denmark, provides similar services to nonstudents under the age of 26. In the United States, the card costs $10 and is available from CIEE (address above), or from **ISE,** Europa House, 802 W. Oregon St., Urbana, IL 61801, tel. 217/344–5863. **In Canada,** the YIEE is available from the **Canadian Hostelling Association** (CHA), 333 River Rd., Vanier, Ottawa, Ontario K1L 8H9, tel. 613/476–3844.

An **International Youth Hostel Federation** (IYHF) membership card is the key to inexpensive dormitory-style accommodations in thousands of youth hostels around the world. Hostels provide separate sleeping quarters for men and women at rates ranging from $7 to $15 a night per person, and are situated in a variety of buildings, including converted farmhouses, villas, restored castles, and specially constructed modern buildings. IYHF membership costs $20 a year and is available in the United States through **American Youth Hostels,** Box 37613, Washington, DC 20013, tel. 202/783–6161. AYH also publishes an extensive directory of youth hostels around the world.

Economical **bicycle tours** for small groups of adventurous, energetic students are another popular AYH student travel service. For information on these and other AYH services and publications, contact the AYH at the address above.

Council Travel, a CIEE subsidiary, is the foremost U.S. student travel agency, specializing in low-cost charters and serving as the exclusive U.S. agent for many student airfare bargains and student tours. The 80-page *Student Travel Catalog* and "Council Charter" brochure are available free from any Council Travel office in the United States (enclose $1 postage if ordering by mail). Contact CIEE headquarters at 205 E. 42nd St., New York, NY 10017, tel. 212/661–1414, or Council Travel offices in Berkeley, La Jolla, Long Beach, Los Angeles, San Diego, and San Francisco, CA; Chicago, IL; Amherst, Boston, and Cambridge, MA; Portland, OR; Providence, RI; Austin and Dallas, TX; and Seattle, WA.

The **Educational Travel Center,** another student travel specialist worth contacting for information on student tours, bargain fares, and bookings, may be reached at 438 N. Frances St., Madison, WI 55703, tel. 608/256–5551.

Students who would like to work abroad should contact **CIEE's Work Abroad Department** (205 E. 42nd St., New York, NY 10017, tel. 212/661–1414). The council arranges various types of paid and voluntary work experiences overseas for up to six months. CIEE also sponsors study programs in Europe, Latin America, and Asia, and publishes many books of interest to the student traveler, including *Work, Study, Travel Abroad: The Whole World Handbook* ($8.95 plus $1 postage); *Work Your Way Around the World* ($10.95 plus $1 postage); and *Volunteer! The Comprehensive Guide to Voluntary Service in the U.S. and Abroad* ($5.50 plus $1 postage).

The Information Center at the **Institute of International Education,** 809 UN Plaza, New York, NY 10017, tel. 212/984–5413, has reference books, foreign university catalogues, study-abroad brochures, and other materials, which may be consulted by students and nonstudents alike, free of charge. The Information Center is open weekdays 10–4, Wednesday 10–7.

IIE administers a variety of grant and study programs offered by U.S. and foreign organizations, and publishes a well-known annual series of study-abroad guides, including *Academic Year Abroad, Vacation Study Abroad,* and *Study in the United Kingdom and Ireland.* The institute also publishes *Teaching Abroad,* a book of employment and study opportunities overseas for U.S. teachers. For a current list of IIE publications with prices and ordering information, write to Publications Service, Institute of International Education, 809 U.N. Plaza, New York, NY 10017. Books must be purchased by mail or in person; telephone orders are not accepted. General information on IIE programs and services is available from its regional offices in Atlanta, Chicago, Denver, Houston, San Francisco, and Washington, DC.

For information on the **Eurail Youthpass,** *see* Rail Passes above.

Traveling with Children

Publications *Family Travel Times* is an eight- to 12-page newsletter published 10 times a year by **TWYCH** (Travel with Your Children,

80 Eighth Ave., New York, NY 10011, tel. 212/206–0688). Subscription includes access to back issues and twice-weekly opportunities to call in for specific advice.

Hotels **CIGA Hotels** (reservations: tel. 800/221–2340), which welcomes families, has two Rome properties (both will arrange babysitting).

Villa Rentals **At Home Abroad, Inc.,** 405 E. 56th St., Suite 6H, New York, NY 10022, tel. 212/421–9165. **Hideaways, Inc.,** Box 1464, Littleton, MA 01460, tel. 617/486–8955. **Italian Villa Rentals,** Box 1145, Bellevue, WA 98004, tel. 206/827–3694. **Vacanze in Italia,** 153 W. 13th St., New York, NY 10011, tel. 212/242–2145 or 800/553–5405. **Villas International,** 71 W. 23rd St., New York, NY 10010, tel. 212/929–7585 or 800/221–2260.

Home Exchange See *Home Exchanging: A Complete Sourcebook for Travelers at Home or Abroad* by James Dearing (Globe Pequot Press, Box Q, Chester, CT 06412, tel. 800/243–0495, or, in CT, 800/962–0973).

Getting There On scheduled international flights, children under two years not occupying a seat pay 10% of the adult fare. Various discounts apply to children two to 12. Reserve a seat behind the bulkhead of the plane, which offers more leg room and can usually fit a bassinet (supplied by the airline). At the same time, inquire about special children's meals or snacks, offered by most airlines. (See TWYCH's "Airline Guide," in the Feb. 1988 issue of *Family Travel Times,* for a rundown on children's services offered by 46 airlines.) Ask airlines in advance if you can bring aboard your child's car seat. For the booklet, "Child/Infant Safety Seats Acceptable for Use in Aircraft," write **Community and Consumer Liaison Division,** APA–400 Federal Aviation Administration, Washington, DC 20591, tel. 202/267–3479.

Baby-sitting Services Check with the hotel concierge or maid for recommended childcare arrangements. Local agency: **A1 Circula Dei Bambini** (34 Via Ricci Curbastro, Rome, tel. 06/558–2916).

Pen Pals For names of children in Rome to whom your children can write before your trip, send a self-addressed, stamped envelope to **International Friendship League** (55 Mt. Vernon St., Boston, MA 02108, tel. 617/523–4273) or to **Student Letter Exchange** (308 Second St. NW, Austin, MN 55912).

Hints for Disabled Travelers

Italy has only recently begun to provide for disabled travelers, and facilities such as ramps, telephones, and toilets for the disabled are still the exception, not the rule. Seats are reserved for the disabled on public transportation, but vehicles have no lifts for wheelchairs. In many monuments and museums, even in some hotels and restaurants, architectural barriers make it difficult, if not impossible, for the disabled to get about. St. Peter's, the Sistine Chapel, and Vatican Museums are accessible to wheelchairs. The terminals of the new Fiumicino Airport–Rome Ostiense rail connection have elevators for wheelchairs.

Throughout Rome parking spaces near major monuments and public buildings are reserved for cars transporting the disabled. In the narrow streets of the city's center, parked cars hugging the buildings, the lack of sidewalks, and bumpy, uneven, cobblestone pavements make for hard going.

Sources of **The Information Center for Individuals with Disabilities** (20
Information Park Plaza, Room 330, Boston, MA 02116, tel. 617/727–5540)
offers useful problem-solving assistance, including lists of
travel agents that specialize in tours for the disabled.
Moss Rehabilitation Hospital Travel Information Service (12th
St. and Taber Rd., Philadelphia, PA 19141, tel. 215/329–5715)
provides information on tourist sights, transportation, and accommodations in destinations around the world. The fee is $5
for each destination. Allow one month for delivery.
Mobility International (Box 3551, Eugene, OR 97403, tel. 503/
343–1284) has information on accommodations, organized
study, etc. around the world.
The Society for the Advancement of Travel for the Handicapped
(26 Court St., Brooklyn, NY 11242, tel. 718/858–5483) offers
access information. Annual membership costs $40, or $25 for
senior travelers and students. Send $1 and a stamped, self-
addressed envelope.
The Itinerary (Box 1084, Bayonne, NJ 07002, tel. 201/
858–3400) is a bimonthly travel magazine for the disabled.

Hints for Older Travelers

The American Association of Retired Persons, or AARP (1909 K
St. NW, Washington, DC 20049, tel. 202/662–4850), has two
programs for independent travelers: (1) the **Purchase Privilege
Program,** which offers discounts on hotels, airfare, car rentals,
and sightseeing; and (2) the **AARP Motoring Plan,** which offers
emergency aid and trip routing information for an annual fee of
$29.95 per couple. The AARP also arranges group tours, in-
cluding apartment living in Europe, through two companies:
Olson-Travelworld (5855 Green Valley Circle, Culver City, CA
90230, tel. 800/227–7737) and **RFD, Inc.** (4401 W. 110th St.,
Overland Park, KS 66211, tel. 800/448–7010). AARP members
must be 50 or older. Annual dues are $5 per person or per cou-
ple.

Elderhostel (80 Boylston St., Suite 400, Boston, MA 02116, tel.
617/426–7788) is an innovative 13-year-old program for people
60 and older. Participants live in dorms on some 1,200 campuses
around the world. Mornings are devoted to lectures and semi-
nars; afternoons to sightseeing and field trips. The all-inclusive
fee for two- to three-week trips, including room, board, tuition,
and round-trip transportation, is $1,700–$3,200.

Travel Industry and Disabled Exchange, or TIDE (5435 Donna
Ave., Tarzana, CA 91356, tel. 818/343–6339) is an industry-
based organization with a $15 per person annual membership
fee. Members receive a quarterly newsletter and information
on travel agencies and tours.

National Council of Senior Citizens (925 15th St. NW, Washington, DC 20005, tel. 202/347–8800) is a nonprofit advocacy group
with some 4,000 local clubs across the country. Annual membership is $10 per person or $14 per couple. Members receive a
monthly newspaper with travel information and an ID card for
reduced-rate hotels and car rentals.

Mature Outlook (Box 1205, Glenview, IL 60025, tel. 800/
336–6330), a subsidiary of Sears, Roebuck & Co., is a travel
club for people over 50, with hotel and motel discounts, and a

bimonthly newsletter. Annual membership is $7.50 per couple. Instant membership is available at participating Holiday Inns.

Travel Tips for Senior Citizens (U.S. Dept. of State Publication 8970, revised Sept. 1987) is available for $1 from the Superintendent of Documents, U.S. Government Printing Office, Washington, D.C. 20402.

The **Inter-Rail senior discount** is the only discount available in Italy of interest to older visitors. Older travelers should be aware that few public buildings, restaurants, and shops in Rome are air-conditioned. Public toilets are few and far between, other than those in bars, restaurants, and hotels. Older travelers may find it difficult to board trains, some city buses, and trams, all of which tend to have high steps and narrow treads.

Further Reading

Literature about Rome exists in abundance. Serious students of the glory that was Rome may like to dip into *The Decline and Fall of the Roman Empire* by English 18th-century historian Edward Gibbon. Those planning doctoral theses should try the six-volume original; others should pick up one of the abridged editions. For a surprisingly accessible portrait of the first days of Rome, read Livy's *The Early History of Rome*, also available in paperback. It contains the first five (of 142) books on Rome Livy penned. For a compelling picture of Imperial Rome, *The Annals of Imperial Rome* by Tacitus is unbeatable; it, too, is available in paperback. Much the same period is covered in Robert Graves's magisterial novels *I, Claudius* and *Claudius the God*. Marguerite Yourcenar's *Memoirs of Hadrian* is an almost equally gripping (and scholarly) fictional portrait of the slightly later Imperial period. Those with a taste for the mysterious Etruscans, who inhabited much of Italy before the rise of Rome, should try D.H. Lawrence's *Etruscan Places*.

An excellent, lavishly illustrated history of Rome, covering the 3,000 years from the Etruscans to Mussolini, is Christopher Hibbert's *Rome—The Biography of a City*. It provides an entertaining and accessible introduction. A highly personal and erudite view of Rome and of eight of its best-known buildings is *Roman Mornings* by architectural historian and raconteur James Lees-Milne. Lovers of the Baroque will find Anthony Blunt's *Guide to Baroque Rome* indispensable, not least for its carefully chosen illustrations. A useful, all-purpose introduction to Italian art and architecture is provided by Peter and Linda Murray's *The Art of the Renaissance*.

Modern novels set in Rome include, among many lesser works, Tennessee Williams's *The Roman Spring of Mrs. Stone*, an elegiac tale of lost love among the piazzas and palaces; Anthony Burgess's rumbustious *Beard's Roman Woman; The Shoes of the Fisherman* by Morris L. West, a thriller that charts the tale of the Russian who became pope; and *The Vatican Rip* by Jonathan Gash.

Getting to Rome

Since the air routes between North America and Rome are heavily traveled, the passenger has many airlines and fares to choose from. But fares change with stunning rapidity, so consult your travel agent on which bargains are currently available.

From North America by Plane

Be certain to distinguish between (1) nonstop flights—no changes, no stops; (2) direct flights—no changes but one or more stops; and (3) connecting flights—two or more planes, two or more stops.

The Airlines The airlines that serve Italy from the United States are **Alitalia,** tel. 800/442–5860; **TWA,** tel. 800/892–4141; and **Pan Am,** tel. 800/221–1111. All fly to Rome and Milan.

Flying Time to Rome From New York: eight and a half hours. From Chicago: 10–11 hours. From Los Angeles: 12–13 hours.

Discount Flights Most of the major airlines offer a range of tickets that can increase the price of any given seat by more than 300%, depending on the day of purchase. As a rule, the further in advance you buy the ticket, the less expensive it is but the greater the penalty (up to 100%) for canceling. Check with airlines for details.

The best buy is not necessarily an APEX (advance purchase) ticket on one of the major airlines. APEX tickets carry certain restrictions: They must be bought in advance (usually 21 days); they restrict your travel, usually with a minimum stay of seven days and a maximum of 90; and they penalize you for changes—voluntary or not—in your travel plans. But if you can work around these drawbacks (and most can), they are among the best-value fares available.

Charter flights offer the lowest fares but often depart only on certain days, and seldom on time. Though you may be able to arrive at one city and return from another, you may lose all or most of your money if you cancel your trip. Travel agents can make bookings, though they won't encourage you, since commissions are lower than on scheduled flights. Checks should, as a rule, be made out to the bank and specific escrow account for your flight. To make sure your payment stays in this account until your departure, don't use credit cards as a method of payment. Don't sign up for a charter flight unless you've checked with a travel agency about the reputation of the packager. It's particularly important to know the packager's policy concerning refunds should a flight be canceled. One of the most popular charter operators is **Council Charter** (tel. 800/223-7402), a division of CIEE (Council on International Educational Exchange). Other companies advertise in Sunday travel sections of newspapers.

Somewhat more expensive—but up to 50% below the cost of APEX fares—are tickets purchased through companies known as consolidators, who buy blocks of tickets on scheduled airlines and sell them at wholesale prices. Here again, you may lose all or most of your money if you change plans, but at least you will be on a regularly scheduled flight with less risk of cancelation than a charter. Once you've made your reservation, call the airline to make sure you're confirmed. Among the best known consolidators are **UniTravel** (tel. 800/325–2222) and **Access International** (250 W. 57th St., Suite 511, New York, NY 10107, tel. 212/333–7280). Others advertise in the Sunday travel section of newspapers as well.

A third option is to join a travel club that offers special discounts to its members. Three such organizations are **Moments Notice** (40 E. 49th St., New York, NY 10017, tel. 212/486 –0503); **Discount Travel International** (114 Forrest Ave., Narberth, PA 19072, tel. 215/668–2182); and **Worldwide Discount Travel Club** (1674 Meridian Ave., Miami Beach, FL 33139, tel. 305/534–2082). These cut-rate tickets should be compared with APEX tickets on the major airlines.

Enjoying the Flight If you're lucky enough to be able to sleep on a plane, it makes sense to fly at night. Many experienced travelers, however, prefer to take a morning flight to Europe and arrive in the evening, just in time for a good night's sleep. The air on a plane is dry, so it helps, while flying, to drink a lot of nonalcoholic liquids; drinking alcohol contributes to jet lag. Feet swell at high altitudes, so it's a good idea to remove your shoes while in flight. Sleepers usually prefer window seats to curl up against; those who like to move about the cabin should ask for aisle seats. Bulkhead seats (adjacent to the Exit signs) have more leg room, but seat trays are attached to the arms of your seat rather than to the back of the seat in front.

Smoking If smoking bothers you, ask for a seat far away from the smoking section. If you are on a U.S. airline and the attendant tells you there are no nonsmoking seats, insist on one: FCC regulations require domestic airlines to find seats for all nonsmokers.

Luggage Regulations Airlines allow each passenger two pieces of check-in luggage and one carry-on piece on international flights from North America. Each piece of check-in luggage cannot exceed 62 inches (length + width + height), or weigh more than 70 pounds. The carry-on luggage cannot exceed 45 inches (length + width + height), and must fit under the seat or in the overhead luggage compartment. On flights within Europe, you are allowed to check a total of 44 pounds, regardless of luggage size. Requirements for carry-on luggage are the same as for transatlantic flights.

Labeling Luggage Put your home address on each piece of luggage, including hand baggage. If your luggage is lost and then found, the airline must deliver it to your home, at no charge to you.

Insurance On international flights, airlines are responsible for lost or damaged property up to $9.07 per pound (or $20 per kilo) for checked baggage, and up to $400 per passenger for unchecked baggage. If you're carrying any valuables, either take them with you on the airplane or purchase additional lost-luggage insurance. Not all airlines sell you this added insurance. Those that do will sell it to you at the counter when you check in, but you have to ask for it. Others will refer you to the privately run insurance booths located throughout airports. These are operated by **Tele-Trip** (tel. 800/228–9792), a subsidiary of Mutual of Omaha. It will insure your luggage for up to 180 days. The insurance is for checked luggage only, and for a minimum of $500 valuation to a maximum of $3,000. Rates vary with number of days. For $500 valuation for 180 days, the rate is $100; for $3,000, $380. **Travelers Insurance Co.** (1 Tower Sq., Hartford,

CT 06183) insures checked or hand baggage for $500 to $2,000 valuation per person, up to 180 days. Rates for one to five days for $500 valuation are $10; for 180 days, $85. Check with your travel agent or the travel section of your newspaper for names of other insurance companies. Itemize the contents of each bag in case you need to file a claim.

From the United Kingdom

By Plane **Alitalia** (tel. 01/602–7111) and **British Airways** (tel. 01/897–4000) operate five direct flights from London (Heathrow) to Rome. Flying time is two and a half hours. There's also one direct flight a day from Manchester to Rome. Standard fares are extremely high. Several less expensive tickets are available. Both airlines offer APEX tickets (usual booking restrictions apply) and PEX tickets (which don't have to be bought in advance). The Eurobudget ticket (no length of stay or advance purchase restrictions) is another option.

Less expensive flights are available: It pays to look around in the classified advertisements of reputable newspapers and magazines such as *Time Out*. But remember to check the *full* price, inclusive of airport taxes, fuel, and surcharges. Some of the bargains are not quite as inexpensive as they seem at first glance.

By Car The distance from London to Rome is 1,124 miles via Calais/Boulogne/Dunkirk, and 1,084 miles via Oostende/Zeebrugge (excluding sea crossings). The drive from the Continental ports takes about 24 hours; the trip in total takes about three days. The shortest and quickest channel crossings are via Dover or Folkestone to one of the French ports (Calais or Boulogne); the ferry takes around 75 minutes and the Hovercraft just 35 minutes. Crossings from Dover to the Belgian ports take about four hours, but Oostende and Zeebrugge have good road connections. The longer crossing from Hull to Zeebrugge is useful for travelers from the north of England. The Sheerness–Vlissingen (Holland) route makes a comfortable overnight crossing; it takes about nine hours.

Fares on the cross-channel ferries vary considerably from season to season. Up until the end of June and from early September onward, savings can be made by traveling midweek. Don't forget to budget for the cost of gas and road tolls, plus a couple of nights' accommodations, especially if crossing in daytime.

Roads from the channel ports to Rome are generally good and are mostly toll-free. The exceptions are the road crossing the Ardennes; the Swiss superhighway network (for which a special tax sticker must be bought at the frontier or in advance); the St. Gotthard Tunnel; and the road between the tunnel and the Italian superhighway system. Remember that the Italian government offers special packages of reduced-price petrol coupons (15%–20% off) and highway toll vouchers. They must be bought in advance from the **AA**, **RAC**, or **CIT** (50 Conduit St., London W1). These are available to personal callers only; the driver must produce his/her passport and vehicle registration document when applying.

If these distances seem too great to drive, there's always the Motorail from the channel ports. However, no car/sleeper expresses run directly to Rome; the closest they come is Milan, 390 miles north of the capital.

By Train Visitors traveling to Rome by train have several options. You can leave London Victoria train station at 11:10 AM for Folkestone and Boulogne; from Boulogne Maritime you pick up the "Napoli Express" for Rome (out of season you change stations at Paris). First- and second-class sleeping cars and second-class couchettes are added at Paris (Gare du Lyon) for the overnight run into Italy. From Paris to Dijon there's a refreshment service, and a buffet car is attached in the morning. The train reaches Rome about 1:30 PM the next day.

Alternatively, the 10 AM train from Victoria meets the Hovercraft in time for a crossing to Paris via Boulogne. It arrives at 4:30 PM, which gives you plenty of time to cross Paris by metro or taxi to catch the 6:47 PM Paris–Rome "Palatino" service. If you don't like the Hovercraft, the 9 AM Victoria service catches the Dover–Calais ferry crossing; arrival time in Paris is 5:20 PM. The "Palatino" leaves Paris at Gare du Lyon and travels via Chambéry and the Mont Cenis tunnel to Turin. Rome is reached by 9:45 AM. The train has first- and second-class sleepers and second-class couchettes, but no ordinary day cars for sitting up overnight. There's a buffet car from Paris to Chambéry and from Genoa to Rome.

The 10:20 AM from Victoria crosses to Basel via Dover and Calais. The "Italia Express" leaves Basel at 1:50 AM, passing through Milan, Bologna, and Florence before reaching Rome at 12:58 PM.

A year-round service leaves Victoria at 4 PM, catching the Jetfoil for Oostende in time to take the 8:53 PM train to Basel, changing at Brussels. The 6:08 AM train from Basel gets you to Rome by 6:05 PM.

By Bus **International Express** (13 Lower Regent St., London SW1Y 4LR, tel. 01/439-9368, or any National Express agent) runs a twice-weekly bus service to Rome that increases to a daily service in July and August. Buses leave Monday and Friday at 9:30 PM (day 1), arriving in Rome at 9:45 AM on day 3. Buses travel via Dover, Calais, Paris, and Lyon. Have a few French francs for spending en route. Fares are quite high, especially when you consider the long and tiring overnight journey and compare the price with that of a charter flight. Further details are available from International Express.

2 Portraits of Rome

Rome at a Glance:
A Chronology

Rome

c. 1000 BC   Etruscans settle in central Italy.

753   Legendary founding of Rome by Romulus.

600   Latin script develops. Rome becomes an urban center.

510   Last of the Etruscan kings—Tarquin the Proud— expelled from Rome; the Republic is founded, headed by two annually elected consuls. The first Temple of Jupiter on the Capitol is built.

471   The first plebeian magistrate is elected.

390   Rome is sacked by the Celts.

380   The Servian wall is built to defend the city.

312   Appius Claudius begins the construction of the Appian Way and the Acqua Appia, Rome's first aqueduct.

280–275   War against Pyrrhus, King of Epirus

260–241   First Punic War: Rome struggles with Carthage in North Africa for control of the central Mediterranean; gains Sicily.

250   Rome completes the conquest of Italy.

220   The Flaminian Way between Rome and Rimini is completed.

219–202   Second Punic War: Hannibal invades Italy and destroys the Roman army in 216; Scipio Africanus carries the war back to Spain and to Carthage; in 206 Rome gains control of Spain; in 203 Hannibal is defeated by Scipio.

168   Rome begins colonization of Greece and defeats Macedonia.

149–146   Third Punic War: Carthage is laid waste for good.

146   Rome completes conquest of Greece.

133   Rome rules the entire Mediterranean basin except for Egypt.

102–101   Gaius Marius defeats Germanic tribes invading from the north.

86   Civil war: Sulla defeats Marius.

82   Sulla becomes dictator of Roman Empire.

71   Slaves revolt under Spartacus.

66–63   Pompey colonizes Syria and Palestine.

49   Gallic War: Julius Caesar defeats Gaul.

47–45   Civil war: Julius Caesar becomes ruler of Rome.

46   Julian calendar introduced.

44   Julius Caesar assassinated.

31   Octavian (later Augustus) defeats Anthony and Cleopatra and becomes sole ruler of Rome.

The World

c. 1000 BC	King David unites tribes of Israel and Judah.
776	First Olympic games in Greece.
c. 750	Beginnings of Mediterranean colonizing by Greek city-states.
720	Assyrian Empire in Persia reaches greatest extent.
550	Foundation of Persian Empire.
479	Death of Confucius.
479–338	Classical Greek culture reaches its peak.
334–323	Alexander the Great destroys Persian Empire and reaches India.
312	Beginning of Seleucid Empire in Persia; introduction of historical dating system.
221	Ch'in dynasty under Shih Huang-ti unites China.
202–AD 9	Han dynasty reunites China.
112	The Silk road across central Asia links China with the West.
50	The first human images of Buddha appear in central India.

Rome

31–AD 14	The Augustan Age: Virgil (70 BC–AD 19); Ovid (43 BC–AD 17); Livy (59 BC–AD 17); Horace (65 BC–AD 27).
27	Octavian becomes the Emperor Augustus (dies AD 14): The Imperial Age begins.

AD 42	Building of harbor at Ostia Antica begins.
43	Emperor Claudius (AD 41–54) invades Britain.
50	Population of Rome reaches one million; the city is the largest in the world.
64	Rome burns; Nero (54–68) begins rebuilding the city.
79	Emperor Titus (79–81) completes the Colosseum.
90–120	The age of Silver Latin: Tacitus (c. 55–120); Juvenal (c. 55–140); Martial (c. 38–102).
98–117	Emperor Trajan builds the Baths of Trajan and Trajan's Market.

100	Roman army reaches its peak, with 300, 000 soldiers.
117	The Roman Empire is at its apex.
116	Conquest of Mesopotamia.

125	Emperor Hadrian (117–138) rebuilds the Pantheon and begins construction of his mausoleum (now Castel Sant' Angelo).
161–180	Rule of Marcus Aurelius, the philosopher–emperor.
165	Smallpox ravages the empire.
211–217	Rule of psychopath Caracalla; he begins the Baths of Caracalla.
284–305	Rule of Diocletian; the empire is divided between West and East.
312–337	Rule of Constantine; he reunites the empire but transfers the capital to Constantinople (later Byzantium, today Istanbul).

313	Edict of Milan recognizes Christianity; Constantine begins the construction of the basilicas of St. Peter's, Santa Maria Maggiore, and San Giovanni in Laterano.
370	Huns appear in Europe.
380	Christianity is made the state religion.
406	Vandals lay waste to Gaul and Spain.
410	Visigoths under Alaric invade Italy and take Rome; the Western Empire collapses.

452	Huns invade northern Italy.
455	Rome sacked by Vandals.

488	Ostrogoths invade Italy; in 493 Theodoric is proclaimed ruler of the Gothic Kingdom of Italy.
536–40	Justinian, the Byzantine emperor, invades Italy

The World

AD 1 Understanding of monsoon winds increases trade between Indian Ocean and Red Sea; Roman artifacts are found in southern India.

30 Jesus is crucified in Jerusalem.

50 The city of Teotihuacán in central Mexico is laid out; the Pyramid of the Sun is constructed.

105 Paper first used in China.

132 Jewish rebellion against Rome leads to the beginning of the diaspora.

150 Buddhism reaches China.

200 Han dynasty in China disintegrates. Cities begin to be built in India's Deccan Plateau.

271 First use of magnetic compass (China).

c. 300 Mayan civilizations of South America begin.

304 Huns invade northern China.

320 Gupta Empire in India begins.

350 Stirrups appear (China).

400 Buddhism becomes principal religion of China.

449 Angles, Saxons, and Jutes begin colonization of Britain.

500 Teotihuacán is now sixth-largest city in the world, with a population of 200,000.

531 Sasanian Empire reaches largest extent.

Rome

553   Italy is reincorporated into the Roman Empire.

570   Lombards gain control of Rome.

590–604   Pope Gregory the Great reinforces the power of the papacy.

609   The Pantheon is consecrated as a church.

610   The Eastern Empire is separated from Rome for good and continues (until 1453) as the Byzantine Empire.

800   Charlemagne is crowned Holy Roman Emperor in Rome.

1073   Gregory VII elected pope; his rule sees the start of a struggle for supremacy between the papacy and the Germanic Holy Roman Empire.

1309   Rome has been sunk in stagnation and ruin for five centuries. The papacy moves to Avignon in southern France.

1347   Cola di Rienzo, adventurer and dreamer, tries to restore the empire; he is hanged six months later.

1377   The popes return to Rome; Gregory XI makes the Vatican the papal residence.

---

c. 1500   The Renaissance spreads to Rome—at this point still little more than a malarial ruin—chiefly in the persons of Bramante (1444–1514); Michelangelo (1475–1564); and Raphael (1483–1520).

1503–1513   Rule of Pope Julius II; he begins rebuilding St. Peter's and commissions Raphael to decorate his apartments (Stanze) and Michelangelo to paint the Sistine.

1527   The Sack of Rome: The confidence of the High Renaissance evaporates as troops of the Holy Roman Empire take the city.

1534   Michelangelo begins the *Last Judgment* in the Sistine Chapel.

1546   Michelangelo commissioned to complete the rebuilding of St. Peter's.

1568   The church of the Gesù is begun.

1595   Annibale Carracci begins painting the *salone* of Palazzo Farnese, ushering in the Baroque Age. Architects Bernini (1598–1680) and Borromini (1599–1667) build churches, palaces, and fountains, largely under ecclesiastical patronage, and transform the face of Rome. Leading painters include Caravaggio (1571–1610); Guido Reni (1575–1642), and Pietro da Cortona (1596–1669).

1626   St. Peter's is completed.

1656–1667   St. Peter's Square is built.

The World

c. 550   Buddhism reaches Japan.

600   Mayan civilization reaches its climax.

624   T'ang dynasty comes to power in China.

632   Death of Mohammed; Islam begins.

658   Chinese Empire reaches its climax.

732   Printing invented in China. Arabs advance through Spain and France to Poitiers.

c. 1000   Vikings reach America (via Greenland).

1096   First European Crusade to the Holy Land.

1161   Chinese use gunpowder in warfare.

1206   Mongols under Genghis Khan begin the conquest of Asia.

1368   Ming dynasty established in China.

1445   Gutenberg prints the first book in Europe.

1492   Columbus discovers America. The Moors are expelled from Spain.

1521   Martin Luther denounced; the Protestant Reformation begins.

1532   Inca Empire destroyed by Pizarro.

1571   The Spanish conquer the Philippines.

1602   Dutch East India Company founded.

1607   First permanent English settlement in America (Jamestown, VA).

1620   The *Mayflower* reaches New England.

1632   The Taj Mahal is built at Agra.

1703   Foundation of St. Petersburg, capital of the Russian Empire.

Rome

1723 The Trevi Fountain is begun.

1735 The Spanish Steps are laid out.

1797 Napoleon captures Rome and proclaims a new republic; Pope Pius VI is expelled from the city.

1808 Pope Pius VII is a prisoner in the Quirinale.

1814 Pius VII is reinstated as ruler of Rome.

1870 Italian nationalists storm Rome and make it the capital of newly reunited Italy; the pope is imprisoned in the Vatican.

1885 The monument to Vittorio Emanuele is begun (completed 1911).

1922 Fascists under Mussolini march on Rome.

1929 The Lateran Treaty establishes formal relations between pope and state: Via dei Fiori Imperiali begun (completed 1933).

1936 Via della Conciliazione begun (completed 1950).

1944 Rome liberated from Germans.

1957 Treaty of Rome establishes the European Economic Community.

1960 Rome hosts Olympic Games.

1978 Pope John Paul II, first Polish pope, is elected. Extremist political activity in Italy reaches climax with kidnapping and assassination of Premier Aldo Moro.

1981 Attempted assassination of Pope John Paul II.

The World

1775–1776	The American Revolution and Declaration of Independence.
1789	French Revolution begins.
1798–1815	Napoleon plunges Europe into war; France is defeated at Waterloo (1815).
1861–1865	The American Civil War.

1898	The Spanish-American War.
1914–1918	World War I; the United States joins the fighting in 1917.
1929	The Great Depression begins.
1937	War begins between Japan and China.
1939–1945	World War II; the United States joins the fighting in 1941; Germany is defeated in 1945 and the atom bomb is droppped on Japan.
1948	The State of Israel is established.

1956	The Suez crisis; Russia stamps out revolt in Hungary.
1962	Cuban Missile Crisis.
1969	The United States lands a man on the moon.
1973	The United States pulls out of Vietnam.

1982	The Falklands War.
1985	Mikhail Gorbachev comes to power in the Soviet Union.

Creative Rome:
Glimpses of Glory

by Roger Jones

After studying classics at Oxford, Roger Jones lived in Rome for two years before taking an art history degree at the Courtauld Institute in London. He co-authored a widely acclaimed study of Raphael.

For the lover of art, Rome remains the richest city in the world, its accumulated treasures proverbially inexhaustible despite centuries of plundering and decay. The epic time span of its art and architecture is immediately apparent to the visitor arriving at the train station/air terminal: While still under the daring modern sweep of its curving forecourt roof (finished in 1950) one can see to the right imposing fragments of the first city walls (of the 4th century BC, but traditionally ascribed to the 6th-century King Servius Tullius) and a walk across the piazza leads to Michelangelo's brilliant adaptation for Christian use in the 1560s of the last of the great imperial Roman baths (finished by Diocletian in AD 306). In fact, the idlest stroll in town still offers a succession of subtle or dramatic pleasures for the eye.

Conservation and export regulations give some protection to the city against property developer and rapacious collector, and the biggest threat to the city's marble monuments since the barbarians and the Barberini now comes from the automobile, whose exhaust fumes cause rain to fall as corrosive sulfuric acid on triumphal arches and ancient columns. Even the Colosseum may have to be given a protective covering until scientists or politicians come up with a solution—or the world's oil runs out. In the meantime, the best way to see what ancient Rome looked like is to study the model of the city in the Museo della Civiltà Romana in EUR, imagining it on the scale of the Vittorio Emanuele monument in Piazza Venezia.

Given Rome's reputation as an artistic center and source of inspiration, it is surprising, but significant, that it has almost never had a native school of art, most of the distinguished works to be seen being either imports, copies, or the work of outsiders in the service of kings, consuls, emperors, or popes. Servius Tullius was the successor of an Etruscan king (and of Romulus, whose legendary foundation of the city is set at 753 BC) and the story of the earliest Roman art is that of domination by the neighboring Etruscans (and, through them, by the colonizing Greeks). The first great temple—that of Jupiter, Juno, and Minerva on the Capitol—was built for Servius's successor, Tarquin the Proud, by "workmen summoned from every part of Etruria," among them the first named artist to work in Rome, the sculptor Vulca from Veii. Only the rough blocks of the temple's base survive, but its lively, colored terra-cotta ornament can be judged from the engagingly grinning faces on antefixes preserved in museums, especially in the Etruscan Museum in Villa Giulia.

From the Etruscans, the Romans adopted the habit of making graven images of their gods and probably also of casting statues in bronze. There are reports of bronzes made at the time of the first kings, but among the earliest and most numinous to survive is the Capitoline Wolf, vigilantly offering her teats to the infants Romulus and Remus, who, perhaps like the legend itself, are of later date. Etruscan, too, is the practice that was to prevail throughout antiquity of setting up commemorative portrait statues in public—of kings and of women but, principally, of military heroes. The victorious Republican, Spurius Carvilius, used the enemy armor he captured in 293 BC to have a giant figure of Jupiter made; and, from the filings left over after the chasing, a statue of himself was cast—as *triumphator* —one of the many precursors of the splendid marble Augustus now in the Vatican. In 158 BC the Forum had become so crowded with portrait statues that the consuls removed those that had not been authorized. Portraits were also commonly made for family reasons. Wax masks of the dead, which could be worn by the living so that a man's ancestors could be present at his funeral, and images, along with triumphal spoils, might be displayed on the lintels of the family house. Portraits were frequent also on the later marble coffins, or sarcophagi, in which even freed slaves might be buried, and although neither sarcophagi nor portraits were invented by the Romans, their eventual mastery (and occasional monotony) of portraiture is legendary; the early bronze bust of "Brutus" on the Capitol is a noble example.

Even the ornament on everyday objects produced in early Rome is Etruscan in style; witness the mirrors and the cylindrical copper toiletry box, known as the *cista Ficoroni*, in Villa Giulia, its elegantly incised figures showing how strongly the Etruscans had been influenced by the Greeks.

Not that elegance was in general a marked feature of early-Roman taste. But the expulsion of the Etruscans and the kings, and the expansion in the last centuries BC of the Republican state that was to dominate Italy, and eventually the whole Mediterranean, brought with them a massive influx into the capital city of foreign booty; not just captured weapons but captured gods and works of art, carried in the triumphal processions of returning generals along with (presumably newly commissioned) paintings of their exploits and set up later as public ornaments. "Prior to this," says Pliny, "Rome knew nothing of these exquisite and refined things . . . rather it was full of barbaric weapons and bloody spoils; and though it was garlanded with memorials and trophies of triumphs there was no sight which was joyful to refined spectators." And as the old-fashioned Cato is reported to have said, "Now I hear far too many people praising and marveling at the ornaments of Corinth and Athens, and laughing at our terra-cotta antefixes of the Roman gods."

Rome was thus exposed to a much more direct contact with Greek art, and the new conquests brought Greek artists and materials as well as booty. Temples retained some traditional Etruscan features in plan but began to look more Greek, such as those in Largo Argentina or the 2nd-century BC Temple of Fortuna Virilis by the Tiber, built of rough local tufa and travertine. The nearby circular Temple of Vesta, dating from the next century, is made of the more "luxurious" material of marble. Not all old-style macho Romans welcomed this, and when Lucius Crassus used foreign marble for his house on the Palatine he was dubbed "the Palatine Venus." The great orator Cicero was not unusual in collecting examples of Greek art for his villa (a practice he called "my voluptuous pleasure"). Similarly, public art galleries were set up. Masterpieces of Greek sculpture were indeed in such demand that war booty did not suffice and many works were mechanically copied by the "pointing" process (invented by the Greeks and now used for the first time on a large scale)—so many in fact that a great proportion of the surviving antique statues in Rome's museums, even the *Belvedere Apollo* in the Vatican, are Roman copies or adaptations of Greek originals.

But we should not think of art in Republican Rome as entirely the consequence of plunder or imported labor. There are some exceptional examples of native artists, principally in the more socially acceptable field of painting, in which a noble, Fabius Pictor, worked as early as the 4th century BC and later emperors such as Nero and Hadrian are reported to have excelled. Mural painting is also a genre in which one can speak of a distinctively Roman contribution. Compared with Pompeii, however, sadly little ancient painting or interior decoration survives in Rome, particularly from the early period. But there are some very fine examples of 1st-century BC painting and stucco—the charming landscape garden of Livia's villa and the "picture gallery" decor of the Farnesina House—in the Terme Museum and on the Palatine.

The transition from a republican to an imperial form of government in the late 1st century BC was achieved gradually, by stealth as well as force. Notably subtle, as well as extensive, use of public art as propaganda was made by Julius Caesar and Augustus to buttress their positions. Famously, this involved big building projects and the claim that Augustus "found Rome brick and left it marble." Marble had of course been introduced earlier, but the forum Augustus built contains a greater variety of foreign colored marbles imported from the subject provinces of the Mediterranean than had been used before. Similarly, he was responsible for the introduction to Rome of the first Egyptian obelisks, which came to play such a distinctive role in the urban fabric (that at Montecitorio was originally used as a giant sundial).

The triple-bayed triumphal arch built for him in the Forum (whose fragments helped to build St. Peter's) also prefigures a characteristically Roman form, but Augustus's patronage was not overwhelmingly self-promoting. He was responsible for, but did not give his name to, the Theater of Marcellus and other buildings, and built a temple in honor of the deified Julius Caesar, but would not allow temples to be dedicated to himself unless they were also dedicated to Rome. His own house was modest, and the most attractive and best-preserved monument from his day is the Ara Pacis (Altar of Augustan Peace), reconstructed near his mausoleum in this century. Its sophisticated carving is interesting as a revival of classical Greek style, though the use of historical imagery, with its portrait scenes, allegories, and episodes from the early history of the city, is characteristically Roman.

Augustus's successors did not need to be so circumspect. While Tiberius followed in his footsteps, and left little personal mark on the city, and Claudius busied himself more with practical matters such as the aqueducts (most imposingly represented by the Porta Maggiore), Caligula and Nero were notorious megalomaniacs—Nero wanted to rename the city Neropolis. Many of Nero's public buildings—the Circus and the first great public baths—and the city planning undertaken after the great fire of AD 64 benefited the city as a whole, but the most extensive project of his reign was the enormous Golden House (the Domus Aurea) he built for himself, an engineering marvel set in park-like surroundings. When it was finished he said he was "at last beginning to live like a human being." The revolving ivory ceilings of the dining rooms are gone, but its dark ruins are still brightened by the paintings of the fastidious Famulus, who always wore a toga at work.

The succeeding Flavian emperors erased the traces of Nero's work. Nero's *Colossus* (a 115-foot gilt statue of him) was converted into an image of the Sun, and an amphitheater was built by Vespasian nearby on the site of the Domus Aurea's ornamental lake. This was the Colosseum, most famous of all Rome's buildings and scene of the grisly spectacles with which all classes of the Roman welfare state, including the slaves, were kept amused. It is also a distinguished piece of engineering, embodying another of the comparatively few architectural forms invented by the Romans—the amphitheater. Not that the Flavians were against self-advertisement. They continued to use the triumphal arch as a billboard to boast of their victories and assert their divinity (a notable survivor is the Arch of Titus, where the emperor is carried to heaven by an eagle) and the style of their sculpture was more robust and confidently ornamental than ever before.

Under the Spaniard Trajan (AD 98–117) the empire reached its largest extent, and, he was the last to add to the series of Imperial Fora (its adjacent market is still fairly intact). His was the biggest forum to date and was financed by the booty from his campaigns against the Dacians in what is modern-day Romania. His exploits are immortalized in the continuous sculpted narrative that spirals round the innovative 120-foot column, which still dominates the area.

Trajan's relative Hadrian (117–138)—the first bearded emperor, a keen hunter, singer, and devotee of the arts, and nicknamed "the little Greek"—was perhaps less concerned with his own fame, but no less active in embellishing the city. To him we owe the rebuilding of the Pantheon, a masterpiece of mathematical proportion and the only surviving building in which we can appreciate the full spectacular impression created by the Romans' increasing use of cladding in colored marbles from the imperial provinces. (Most of the marbles from the other ancient buildings, like the great baths, have long since been stripped off and now adorn the churches and palaces of Christian Rome.) Hadrian was an enthusiastic builder and frequenter of public baths, which, besides offering exercise and hygiene for the body, pleased the eye with their marble and mosaic decorations and their collections of sculpture (the *Farnese Herculese*, now in Naples, was found in the Baths of Caracalla), and nourished the mind with the literature kept in their libraries.

Having made plans for the most elaborate mausoleum in the city (which was later converted into the fortress of Castel Sant' Angelo), Hadrian in fact spent his last years almost exclusively at his sumptuous villa at Tivoli a few miles outside the city. This complex is notable both for the variety and beauty of its experimental architecture, with its references to famous sites in the Hellenistic world that Hadrian knew so well, and for the classical Greek revival sculpture that has been found there, including the Erechtheum caryatids beside the Canopus canal and the

figure of his beautiful Syrian friend Antinoös, now in the Capitoline Museum (one of the many statues of him, sometimes in
the guise of a god, which Hadrian caused to be set up throughout the Empire).

The Greek tradition dominated most Roman art till the time of
Hadrian, but with his successors other ideals become apparent, the change being particularly evident in the differing
styles of the two sculpted panels of the base of the column of
Anoninus Pius (c. 161), now in the Vatican, in the Arch of
Septimius Severus (203), and, later, in the magnificent, if highly eclectic, Arch of Constantine (c. 315). On this arch, reliefs
and statues from earlier monuments of Trajan, Hadrian, and
Marcus Aurelius are juxtaposed, perhaps with a deliberate
programmatic intention, with Constantinian reliefs, which are
striking in their formality, severity, frontality, and, it must be
said, crudity. The first two of these characteristics are often
connected with the increasing absolutism of the Imperial
Court.

T he age of Constantine was a great turning point in the history of Rome and its art. The city was no longer the center
of the empire (Diocletian had spent most of his time in Italy in Milan) and was not safe from external attack (as Aurelian
had judged in 270, when he began building the massive walls
which still ring the city). Constantine himself is famous for
having founded the "New Rome" of Constantinople (later
Byzantium and today Istanbul) in 330, but he did make a notable impact on the old city. Primarily this involved the discreet
promotion, with imperial backing, of his adopted religion,
Christianity, and the building of impressive churches for
Christian worship and the privilege of burial. But this did not
mean immediately abandoning all the old values, and indeed
one of his principal achievements as emperor was the completion of what is now the dominant structure in the Forum, the
Basilica, which had been begun by, and retains the name of, his
rival, Maxentius. In its apse was placed for veneration a gigantic seated figure of the emperor, whose scale can be judged
from the perennially popular fragments of head, hand, and foot
on the Capitol.

For his Christian churches Constantine adopted a form that
had long served a variety of functions in Roman secular life and
which was to remain a standard church design for hundreds of
years: the colonnaded basilica, with a flat roof and semicircular
apse (a barn-like structure with two rows of pillars down its
length and one rounded end). The principal ones, San Giovanni
in Laterano and old St. Peter's, were on a massive scale, but it
is worth noting that Constantine's churches were rather plain
externally and placed on the outskirts of the city on imperial
property. They were not assertively imposed on its civic and religious heart.

The Laterano and St. Peter's have since been remodeled or rebuilt, but a Constantinian interior, though smaller in scale and
circular in plan, may be seen at Santa Costanza, the mausoleum
built for his daughter, who was buried in an awe-inspiring imperial porphyry sarcophagus, now in the Vatican. Here the
artistic continuity between pagan and Christian Rome is neatly
exemplified. The column capitals are not all of the same type
and, like so much of the building material used for subsequent
churches, were clearly taken from earlier buildings, while the

grape-crushing putti in the mosaics (and on the sarcophagus) had long been popular as a Bacchic motif and were now adopted by Christians as an allusion to the Eucharist.

No paintings survive in the early-Christian basilicas, but paintings can be seen in the many catacombs, such as those of Sant'Agnese, near Santa Costanza. (The catacombs had, it's worth pointing out, been used for Christian burials not from fear of persecution or as hiding places but because land for burial was expensive.) In these paintings, too, we see a similar transfer of pagan forms to Christian uses.

After Constantine, no emperor returned to reside permanently in Rome and the next century saw a struggle by the early Church to assert itself in the face of old-established pagan power. Churches were built closer to the center, such as the original San Marco, near the Capitol, and the impressively Roman authority of Christian imagery can be seen in the apse mosaics of Santa Pudenziana (c. 400), where the Apostles wear togas.

By 408 imperial edicts had forbidden the use of pagan temples (or any other place) for pagan worship (though it was not till 609 that the Pantheon became the first pagan temple to be used as a Christian church). The sack of Rome in 410 by the Visigoths (the first major military disaster for the city in 1,000 years) was traumatic, but did not prevent the emergence of the church as the unrivaled heir to the grand cultural dominance exercised previously by the now absent emperor. This is visibly expressed in the large 5th-century churches of Santa Maria Maggiore, where the well-preserved mosaics on the triumphal arch show the Virgin Mary as an empress with a jeweled crown, and Santa Sabina, restored in this century as the most graceful and perfect example of an early-Christian basilica, its 20 Corinthian columns taken from classical buildings.

But the centuries of decline had already begun. The city was sacked again—by the Vandals in 455—and taken over by the Goths. When Gregory the Great became pope in 590, it had been for years a mere outpost of Byzantium, its population shrunk and its urban fabric reduced to a skeleton by decades of war and natural disasters. The Byzantine commander, when cornered in Hadrian's mausoleum, had repelled besieging Goths by having its statues smashed and catapulted at them. The erection of new churches had not entirely stopped: In the 520s the city prefect's audience hall in the Forum was converted into the church of Santi Cosma e Damiano and given mosaics in the more formal and abstract Byzantine style—and, as this example shows, the administration of the city increasingly fell into the hands of the Church. But the future was bleak.

In the eight turbulent centuries that followed, the city's prosperity—and art—depended on the patchy success with which the pope could maintain his claim to temporal and spiritual power in the "western" world, keep the marauding Lombards, Saracens, and Normans at bay and the population of Rome in order. A major revival was signaled in 800, when the German Emperor Charlemagne, who saw himself as a new Constantine, acknowledged the supreme authority of the pope in the West by receiving his crown from Leo III in St. Peter's. Impressive new basilicas such as San Prassede were built and, not surprisingly, given Charlemagne's revivalist ideology, their form and mosaic decoration owed more to the art of Constantine's early church in Rome than to contemporary Byzantium.

But the revival was short-lived, and was not to be matched until the early 12th century, which saw a crop of new churches. In basic form they are almost monotonously traditional basilicas, innocent of developments taking place elsewhere in Europe, but they have attractive extras: tall brick bell towers (Santa Maria in Trastevere); cool colonnaded cloisters (Santi Quattro Coronati) and porticoes (San Lorenzo fuori le Mura); lavish ancient marble fittings and pavements of the kind the Cosmati family were to specialize in and mosaics (San Clemente). At San Clemente in particular, the charming still-life details and lush acanthus scrolls of the mosaics show a renewed interest in the pagan ingredients of early-Christian art. But these ingredients had of course long been absorbed into Christian culture, and the examples of purely pagan art that survived had, if we judge from pilgrim guidebooks, acquired superstitious, magical connotations—like the ancient marble mask installed in the portico of Santa Maria in Cosmedin, reputed to bite the hands of liars.

Further revivals occurred in the 13th century, not so much in architecture—despite Rome's one concession to the Gothic, the now transformed Santa Maria sopra Minerva—as in painting and mosaic. In the 1290s, and especially in Cavallini's mosaics of the *Life of the Virgin* in Santa Maria in Trastevere, methods changed so that pictures of people, buildings, and whole stories became more lifelike than before, changes that later helped Giotto revolutionize pictorial narrative. Giotto himself worked in Rome, painting the triptych for the high altar of the old St. Peter's, now in the Vatican museum. But development in Rome suddenly ground to a halt, as the popes moved to Avignon (1305), and for 100 years the city became a backwater. Petrarch lamented the state of "widowed Rome," cows wandered in the Forum, and the only artistic event of note was the building of the massive stairs up to Aracoeli, part of the populist Cola di Rienzo's fantasy of reviving the ancient Roman republic on the Capitol.

The schism caused by the move of the popes to Avignon ended with the emergence of Martin V, a Roman, as undisputed pope (1417–31). He began the long process of restoration and renewal which, over the next three centuries, eventually resulted in spectacular and successful attempts to rival and surpass the achievements of the ancients.

To begin with, this involved the restoration of civil order and a lot of repair work, but Martin V and his successors lived at a time of artistic resurgence in the rest of Italy, particularly in Florence, and they were able to import distinguished talent from outside. The great Florentine painter Masaccio came to Rome in the 1420s; his colleague Masolino's attractive frescoes survive at San Clemente as the first example of the new, more naturalistic style in painting with its mathematical perspective, while other Florentines—Donatello and Filarete—produced idiosyncratic but impressive sculpture for St. Peter's. All these artists were stimulated by what they could see of ancient Rome, and their patrons by what they could read of its literature. In particular, Nicholas V (1447–55) was a classical scholar and, convinced that the only way of impressing the authority of the Church on the feeble perceptions of the illiterate was by means of "outstanding sights . . . great buildings . . . and divine monuments," he produced an ambitious plan of building and decoration for Rome in general and the Vatican in particular, doubtless with the help of his friend and fellow scholar, the artist Alberti.

His successor Pius II (1458–64) remarked that if the projects "had been completed, they would have yielded to none of the ancient emperors in magnificence," but little progress was in fact made. A rare exception was the decoration in the 1440s by Fra Angelico, with, for him, extraordinarily monumental frescoes. More substantial results were achieved by the Franciscan Sixtus IV (1471–84), who built a new bridge across the Tiber— only two had survived from antiquity, at the island and at Castel Sant'Angelo—and a large up-to-date hospital (Santo Spirito) near the Vatican, both designed to accommodate the pilgrims who flocked to Rome in Jubilee years. Churches, such as Santa Maria del Popolo, and palaces for cardinals, such as the enormous Cancelleria, were begun in new styles that paid increasing if still limited attention to ancient example. Property development was encouraged by new legislation. Although he was something of a philistine in his artistic taste, Sixtus did choose to import such outsiders as Botticelli and Perugino to decorate his large new chapel in the Vatican, and tried to organize painters in Rome by setting up a guild. Although he was not especially interested in classical culture, and, like all the popes of his period, continued to use the ancient ruins as quarries, he performed an important service by setting up on the Capitol the first modern public museum of antique sculpture.

Such at this point was the enthusiasm, and excavation, for antique sculpture that his nephew Julius II (1503–13) was quickly able to stock the sculpture garden that he in turn set up in the Vatican Belvedere with the choicest pieces, such as the *Laocoön* group, dug up in 1506. And it is partly due to the presence in Rome of these rediscovered and revalued treasures that the artists he employed, notably Raphael and Michelangelo, were inspired to evolve their grand styles of painting and sculpture, which we may think of as specifically Roman, even though their art owed so much to Florence.

They must also have been responding to the imperial vision of their employer, the aggressive warrior-pope, who, in his determined efforts to continue his uncle's policy for the city, ordered the demolition of Constantine's St. Peter's, to be replaced by an audacious structure planned by his architect Bramante, nicknamed "the Wrecker," which would, in scale and design, have "placed the dome of the Pantheon on the vaults of the Temple of Peace." For Julius, although he compared himself with previous popes in the dramatic propaganda decoration which Raphael painted in the Stanza of Heliodorus in the Vatican, compared himself with Trajan in murals painted in his castle at Ostia. On his return from an expedition in 1507 a copy of the Arch of Constantine, depicting a history of his own exploits, was erected at the Vatican. Michelangelo's decoration of the Sistine Ceiling, with its grand ensemble of sculptural figures, medallions, and reliefs, is clearly an imaginative exercise in this imperial genre, and his original design for the pope's tomb (which is in San Pietro in Vincoli) "surpassed every an-

cient and imperial tomb ever made . . . in its beauty and magnificence, wealth of ornament and richness" (Vasari).

The luxury-loving Medici pope, Leo X (1513–21), who followed,
asked Raphael to decorate the largest room in the papal apartments with scenes from the life of Constantine, but he also
borrowed jokes from Augustus and is reported to have said,
"Since God has given us the Papacy, let us enjoy it." There is
plenty to enjoy in the long private loggia Raphael and his pupils
decorated next door, where tiny scenes from the Bible are overwhelmed by hundreds of painted and stucco images, mimicking
ancient cameos and the kind of ancient fantasy painting to be
seen in what had become the grottoes of Nero's Golden House
when it was rediscovered in the 1480s. Hence the name "grotesque" for the style of painting that was to become enormously
popular in Roman and, with the spread of engravings, European interior decorations in subsequent years. It was also used in
Raphael's saucy decoration of the nearby (but not visitable)
bathroom of Cardinal Bibbiena and on a grand scale in the imposing unfinished villa that Raphael designed for Leo's cousin,
Villa Madama. This is hard to visit, too, but other attractive villas of the day exist—the Farnesina, also decorated by Raphael,
and the later Villa Giulia.

Villa Madama was a conscious re-creation of the ancient Roman
villa as described by Pliny, and contemporary palaces tried to
re-create the ancient-Roman house with its atrium and courtyards, as described by the Roman architect Vitruvius. Palazzo
Farnese, finished by Michelangelo, is a stunning example,
while Peruzzi's Palazzo Massimo is on a smaller scale but no less
impressive. The courtyards of Palazzo Massimo and Palazzo
Mattei also show how contemporaries displayed their prize antique sculptures—by setting them in the wall as decorations.
Many less wealthy Romans imitated this fashion by having
monochrome sculpture-like frescoes on their facades. A lonely
survivor is Palazzo Ricci in Via di Monserrato.

But in 1527 the fun had to stop when German soldiers sacked
the city, giving a glimpse of Purgatory and causing an exodus of
artists (with further diffusion of their ideas) and, it is often
believed, a change of heart in the city's art. Certainly
Michelangelo's *Last Judgment* in the Sistine Chapel is a tre-
mendous warning to the wicked, but artists such as Salviati
and Perino del Vaga continued to paint in the most exuberant
and deliciously witty styles, for example at Castel Sant'
Angelo.

The Church did attempt to reform itself from inside, however,
and among the churches built for the new religious orders after
the Council of Trent (1545–63) were the Gesù for the Jesuits,
originally rather severe inside, and the Chiesa Nuova for the
Oratorians, one of the many churches to be influenced by the
design of the Gesù, with a broad nave for preaching to large
congregations. Here, St. Philip Neri, the founder of the Oratorians, was frequently found in a state of ecstasy in front of the
painting of the *Visitation* by Barocci, his (and many others') favorite artist.

Spiritual excitement and intensity, theatrically presented,
were to become dominant themes in the next century's art
—most obviously in Bernini's chapel in Santa Maria della
Vittoria, where members of the Cornaro family look out from

their boxes at an ethereal vision of the ecstasy of St. Teresa, bathed in light, the whole executed in the most splendid ancient and modern marbles and materials. Not all artists, though, looked so resolutely to heaven, and the most brilliant and influential painter in the period after Barocci was the passionate criminal Caravaggio, whose dramatically illuminated and controversial work ranged from luscious homosexual pornography for clerics to profound but distinctly earthy religious subjects —notice the obtrusively dirty feet of the adoring peasant in his St. Agostino altarpiece. Other distinguished painters of the day were more traditional—indeed, Annibale Carracci and his relatives pioneered a revival and extension of the styles of Raphael and Michelangelo, notably the opulent Galleria in Palazzo Farnese (c. 1600). Their work can be compared (and contrasted) with that of Caravaggio in Santa Maria del Popolo.

Humble details such as Caravaggio's dirty feet may have moved the lower orders, but art was still effectively commanded by popes and cardinals: If Julius II's artistic propaganda had been grandiose it was almost eclipsed by the whopping stories put out for the 17th-century Church. In painting this means, among others, the extraordinary achievements of Pietro da Cortona, who extended the powerful language of Michelangelo's decorations with a Venetian fluency and sense of color in his exaltation of the Barberini family on the ceiling of their palace's *salone*. But the most spectacularly theatrical effects were created in public architecture, both on a large scale in Bernini's piazza for St. Peter's, for example, where hundreds of huge travertine columns provide encircling porticoes, and in innumerable smaller projects such as Pietro da Cortona's brilliant scenographic setting for Santa Maria della Pace. Perhaps the most gifted and inventive of these architects was Borromini, a difficult (and in the end suicidal) person who did not get the biggest commissions. But his San Carlo and Sant'Ivo show how he could convert a restricted site into a tight ensemble of exhilarating power.

While this architecture was designed to impress, attempts were also made to make the city more comfortable. Bernini's porticoes not only broadcast the fame of Alexander VII but protected pilgrims from rain and sun. From the 16th century on, popes had made major efforts to create straighter, wider streets, making it easier to visit the principal basilicas and speeding the progress of carriages. They also restored some of the ancient-Roman aqueducts. The latter provided increasingly necessary water for the populace and supplied the impressive sculpted fountains which, from Bernini's Four Rivers Fountain in Piazza Navona to Salvi's Trevi Fountain, continue to delight and refresh visitors.

The Trevi Fountain, the Spanish Steps, and Galilei's facade for San Giovanni in Laterano were among the last great spectacles of the late 17th and early 18th centuries. The artistic importance of 18th-century Rome lay not so much in what was done for the city, as in what the city did for its many visitors. These were now the foreign artists studying the history paintings of Raphael and the religious works of Michelangelo in Rome's academies, and the Grand Tourists rather than the pilgrims of old. Piranesi's prints, fighting a magnificent rear-guard action for the grandeur of Rome against the growing popularity of a different, more purely Greek, view of antiquity, provided souvenirs for them; Batoni elegantly painted their portraits; and most of Canova's cool poetic sculptures were produced for export. The most distinguished building commissioned by the Vatican in this period was a museum—the Museo Pio-Clementino.

The power of the popes, and the city's art, continued to decline in importance in the 19th century, as Rome emerged as the secular capital of the modern Italian state. Large but creaking and empty edifices were erected to its ideals—the monument to King Vittorio Emanuele, and the Palace of Justice. The city was besieged by suburbs, and the river embanked to cope with flooding and traffic, but it survived remarkably well even the ambitions of Mussolini. His attempts to re-create something of the glory of the Roman Empire produced monotonous boulevards through the Forum and at St. Peter's, spoiling the effect of Bernini's piazza. But his grandiosity also gave birth to the striking architecture of the suburb of EUR.

Nor, in modern times, has Rome been an international center of the musical and theatrical arts, though ancient theaters and triumphal arches testify to the early Roman love of spectacle—even emperors performed and sang. Nero, who made his operatic debut with a group of sycophants in Naples, put his stage clothes on and sang (not fiddled) to a select audience while Rome burned. Opera-lovers can recapture something of this experience in the ruins of the Baths of Caracalla where Verdi's *Aida* is given in the open air each summer with elephants and gusto.

At the big, summer-long, outdoor, multi-screen movie festival one can see what gives Rome a real claim to modern pre-eminence in the arts—the cinema. Successive generations of filmmakers working in the city and at Cinecittà since the war—Rossellini, Pasolini, and Fellini—have created an enduring art, perceptively chronicling and imaginatively exploring the inside and the outside of modern life, and particularly, and most endearingly, of Roman society.

The City Beneath Rome

by William Weaver

In 1956, the pastor of San Pietro in Vincoli, the Roman church that houses Michelangelo's *Moses*, decided that the basilica needed a new pavement. So he ordered the old floor taken up, to be replaced by the polished travertine marble found there today. Before the digging had gone very far, the workmen came upon some ancient remains; and the simple replacement of the floor turned into a complex project of excavation that went on for several years. Like almost every building in the heart of Rome, San Pietro in Vincoli was built over layers of other constructions. Somewhat to his dismay, the pastor found a cross-section of Roman history beneath his feet.

In their haste to see the *Moses* (and to get back to the bus and on to other sights), tourists scurry past the little iron railing under the portico of the church that marks the entrance to the excavations. Visitors with more time, and more curiosity, seek out a priest (ring the bell in the left nave) and ask to be shown the underground discoveries. The descent is not always comfortable. A certain amount of stooping is involved, and you have to watch out for scraped elbows, but with the priest's guidance, you can discern five layers of Rome: today's church, then traces of the 15th-century church constructed by Sixtus IV; a 5th-century basilica (its columns are embedded in the foundations of the later churches); fragments of a villa from Nero's day (perhaps an adjunct to his Golden House), and fragments of terra-cotta lamps and pots that give evidence of a more primitive settlement. At the Neronian level there is the outline of a Roman pool, but to reach it today you have to crawl on all fours across a stretch of dusty rubble. I took it on faith.

Everywhere in Rome there are patches of the subterranean city, or rather cities: an austere, special world, of which the catacombs and the excavations under St. Peter's are the best-known portions. Rome has its spelunkers who, armed with powerful flashlights, gumboots, and cameras, drop down manholes, essay caverns, or simply dig in open fields. But the sub-Rome is also accessible to less venturesome visitors. For the first glimpse of it, I recommend a visit to San Clemente, a subtly rich little basilica a short walk from the Colosseum.

The present church contains, among other treasures, a superb 12th-century mosaic of the Triumph of the Cross and frescoes by Masolino that include the much-reproduced St. Christopher, a friendly giant carrying the infant Christ. Today's San Clemente was built in the 12th century, over a 4th-century church that, naturally, stood over ancient Roman constructions.

Excavation beneath San Clemente began in the 19th century, under the direction of the Irish Dominicans, who have long governed the church. As you descend the stairs to the lower levels, the first thing you perceive is the silence: It has a different, more intense quality than the hushed atmosphere of the street-level church.

The second level (today's church counts as the first) is the 4th-century church, in use until 1100, with some just legible frescoes, among them a Byzantine-style scene of Christ sitting in judgment. On this level one of the most revered places is the presumed tomb of St. Cyril, who died in Rome in AD 869. With his brother Methodius, he was active among the Slavic nations and invented the Cyrillic alphabet (some modern marble plaques, in that alphabet, here mark the devotion of Eastern European Catholics).

Near this bare, cramped shrine, another staircase leads down to the third, lowest level. The walls of what was probably a large Roman house are now visible; this may have been the titulus of Clement (a titulus, in early Christian Rome, was a private home that served as a place of semiclandestine Christian meeting and worship, and was, in effect, the focus of a parish). A narrow street divides it from what is thought to have been an insula, the Roman equivalent of an apartment house. In its court was a temple to Mithras, a Persian god popular in Rome for the first few centuries after Christ. The temple included a triclinium, where you can still see the stone couches on which devotees of the cult reclined for the ritual feast.

At this level, the unearthly (or under-earthly) silence is broken by a sound of rushing water: a buried stream (you can glimpse it, at one point, through a grille), whose source is one of the mysteries of San Clemente. As I stood in the narrow street, so narrow that I could touch both walls, I was suddenly shocked to hear shrill, childish voices. If they hadn't been crying out in French, they would have seemed the friendly ghosts of children of Trajan's time, playing tag, as some kids of modern Rome were playing in the Via San Giovanni in Laterano, eight or nine yards above my head.

The sense of past life is also strongly felt in the catacombs, strangely, because the catacombs, after all, were cemeteries. But, just as in Italy today (especially in small towns), collective visits to the cemetery were an established practice in the early days of Christianity, religious but also social in nature. Frescoes in many of the catacombs depict the refrigerium, the funeral banquet or commemorative meal at which families gathered at a tomb to break bread together.

In my childhood, the ancient Roman movie was a genre as distinct as the Western; in those pictures the early Christians always seemed pious, boring, and unreal, as, dressed in white, they died, singing hymns or smiling seraphically, while the luckier pagans ate grapes, drank wine, kissed girls and drove fast chariots. But the catacombs give you a different view of the early Christians. Some, indeed, were saints, but many were ordinary people with ordinary pursuits; near their graves (especially in the Sant'Agnese catacomb) you see the incised symbols of their trades—a trowel for a mason, a side of ham for a pig-butcher.

Nobody seems to know how many catacombs there are in Rome: One of my guides said 60, another said more than 100. Besides the Christian catacombs, there are also pagan and Jewish ones. More are being discovered all the time, but many—for reasons of economy—are not regularly open to the public. Cynical travelers say that if you've seen one catacomb, you've seen them all. This is partly true, but the effect of visiting them is cumulative. In any case, asked to recommend one catacomb to stand for all, I would suggest the vast cemetery under the church of San Sebastiano, on the Appian Way. It is not the richest catacomb, but it is certainly the most famous; during the Middle Ages, while the other catacombs were forgotten, pilgrims still came to this spot to pay homage to the early martyrs.

The entrance to the catacombs is through a doorway in the walled forecourt of the little baroque church of San Sebastiano. My latest visit there was on a Monday morning (the catacombs here are open when Roman museums and galleries are closed); I was the only visitor, so I had the guide all to myself. He was an enthusiastic scholar and, I think, a priest; it was hard to tell, because he was wearing a woolly sweater. It was a hot day, but I, too, had brought a sweater along. In the sweltering Roman summer, the catacombs have the added attraction of a temperature reminiscent of the most enthusiastic American air conditioning.

We descended to the first chamber, with the tomb of St. Sebastian himself. The room is plain, except for a simple table altar and a marble bust of the saint, somewhat dubiously attributed to Bernini. Long a place of cult worship, the chapel is still the site of an annual pilgrimage on St. Sebastian's feast day, January 20. From there the real catacombs begin: rows and rows of shelflike niches carved out of the porous tufa rock. Bodies were simply wrapped in shrouds, then sealed in a niche with a slab of marble or, with poorer families, brick. These graves can easily be dated, since Roman tax laws required brick makers to stamp their bricks with a device bearing the emperor's name. The San Sebastiano cemetery was in use from the 1st to the 5th century AD.

As space was needed, the Christians simply dug deeper into the tufa, and the catacombs comprise many miles of passages—needless to say, the visitor is not conducted through all of them. Besides the niches, there are the grander arcosolium tombs, sarcophagi with an arch above them. At the end of the visit there are three impressive brick-faced mausoleums, pedimented like three miniature temples, their elegance in contrast with the more humble Christian graves.

Since the San Sebastiano catacombs were always known, they were subject to vandalism and are relatively bare (though some interesting and beautiful wall decorations do survive, including a charming fresco of an appetizing bowl of fruit with a plump bird pecking at a grape). But the San Callisto catacombs, nearby, were "lost" for more than 1,000 years and rediscovered only in 1849 by the pioneering Italian archaeologist Giovan Battista De Rossi, who found them while visiting a vineyard. Pope Pius IX bought the land at once, and excavations began.

The San Callisto catacombs are a short, pleasant walk from San Sebastiano. After crossing a busy road, you enter the Vatican's property, a flourishing farm, where you proceed between fields of corn and wheat, past a flourishing kitchen garden (I paused for an envious inspection of the fat artichokes and luxuriant tomato plants).

One of De Rossi's early discoveries was the important crypt of the popes, with loculi containing the remains of nine pontiffs from the 3rd century, identified by marble plaques. He went on to bring to light frescoes, mosaics, and carvings, still visible. Among the most striking are the frescoes of six praying figures (in a cell curiously misnamed "The Five Saints") and an early 3rd-century fresco of Christ the Good Shepherd, a favorite theme in several catacombs. The excavation was fresh when Nathaniel Hawthorne visited the catacombs in the late 1850s and used them for a scene in his Roman novel, *The Marble Faun:* "They went joyously down into that vast tomb, and wandered by torchlight through a sort of dream, in which reminiscences of church-aisles and grimy cellars—and chiefly the latter—seemed to be broken into fragments. . . . The intricate passages along which they followed their guide had been hewn, in some forgotten age, out of a dark-red, crumbly stone. On either side were horizontal niches, where, if they held their torches closely, the shape of a human body was discernible in white ashes, into which the entire mortality of a man or woman had resolved itself."

Torchlight has been replaced by electricity, but otherwise today's experience is much like Hawthorne's. His stern puritanism often made him an unsympathetic tourist: The accent on the grimy cellar is indicative. But catacombs are, indeed, not to everyone's taste. In 1788, the more sympathetic Goethe went to San Sebastiano, meaning to visit the catacombs, but he reported: "I had hardly taken a step into that airless place before I began to feel uncomfortable, and I immediately returned to the light of day and the fresh air . . ."

The grottoes of St. Peter's are not catacombs exactly; rather, they are the result of a quarter-century of excavation, begun in 1940 at the command of Pope Pius XII and concluded in 1965, after the discovery not only of the grave of St. Peter but also of most of a skeleton that is generally accepted as the saint's. Visit is by appointment, since groups have necessarily to be kept small.

Our party, about a dozen in all, met in the Piazza dei Protomartiri on the south side of the basilica, once the site of the Circus of Nero, where St. Peter—like countless other Christians—was probably martyred.

In exploring the substrata of Rome, it is often hard, even impossible, to grasp the architectural sense of a complex site. To assist the visitor, in the anteroom of the grottoes there is a scale model, showing the relationship between the first basilica of St. Peter's, erected by Constantine in the 4th century, and the earlier aedicula, the little monument built to protect the remains of St. Peter not long after his death. The aedicula stood within a necropolis bounded by the so-called "red wall" of monumental niches which provided evidence essential to authenticating the site of St. Peter's grave. Visitors are invited to take a long look at this model, which then makes the subsequent progress through the excavations more rewarding.

To build his basilica, Constantine had to level the Vatican hill, covering an ancient graveyard that had occupied the southern slope since the 1st century. The graveyard was not a catacomb; the tombs—like so many little houses—stood in the open air, lined up along narrow streets. The excavations disinterred two of these streets, parallel to each other; and, if in your imagination you can remove the dark ceiling over your head (and the huge basilica above it), you can believe you are walking through a cemetery in the 1st century, when people who had witnessed Peter's martyrdom were still living. The red-brick facades, after a millennium and a half, still have a warm glow, and here again, the sound of voices—those of the party of tourists ahead or behind your own—echoing along the street reinforces the sense of life.

For there is nothing gloomy about these tombs: Some are bright with frescoes of birds and fruit and animals, or with mosaics (one shows Christ as the sun, driving a chariot like Apollo's, against a glowing gold background), or with stucco decoration. The inscriptions tell us that most of the tombs are pagan, but some are Christian and some are both, suggesting that the family owning the little temple was converted.

Finally, you come to the Clementine chapel, built over St. Peter's grave (and directly below the great main altar of today's basilica) by Clement VIII at the end of the 16th century. This is where the excavations ordered by Pius XII began, and it is the heart of St. Peter's. Above the altar is a vertical porphry slab flanked by slabs of plain white marble. This was the rear wall of Constantine's monument over the tomb of St. Peter. From the chapel, one person at a time can go and peer through a grille and see the site of the tomb, the simple, rough wall in which the bones were found and in which they rest today. At this point, the visitor's religious convictions (or lack thereof) are beside the point. You know you are in a holy place.

Then you go back into the chapel. Through other grilles above your head, you can see the floor of the present-day basilica. Not even the sound of shuffling feet, the click of camera shutters, the occasional flare of a flashbulb exploding, can totally erase the profound impression of what you have seen.

The Colosseum

by H.V. Morton

This vivid description of the Colosseum appeared originally in H.V. Morton's 1957 classic, A Traveller in Rome.

The first sight of the Colosseum is highly gratifying. It reassures the most bewildered visitor. No one could mistake it for anything but a large shambles designed with the utmost skill to focus the attention of many thousands of people upon a small field of action, then to disperse them with the greatest possible efficiency.

The amazing thing about the Colosseum is the fact that it is built in a marsh, and that its stupendous weight has been resting for all these centuries upon artificial foundations set in water. This part of Rome is still waterlogged with springs which trickle down from the Esquiline Hill, as you can see today in the underground churches beneath S. Clemente. How the Colosseum was built on such a soil is a wonder of engineering, and I can well imagine that any architect might forsake all else in Rome to study the problems of this triumphant mass. In the year 1864 one of the periodic stories about buried treasure in the Colosseum was revived with success by a certain Signor Testa. He claimed to have a clue to "the Frangipani treasure" believed to have been concealed there in the Middle Ages when that family turned the amphitheatre into a fortress. Pope Pius IX became interested and gave permission for the excavations, which were followed with breathless interest by everyone in Rome. Nothing of intrinsic value was found, though the effort was not wasted as it gave Lanciani his only chance to examine the foundations of the Colosseum. He wrote that he saw "the upper belt of the substructures, arched like those of the ambulacra above ground; and underneath them a bed of concrete which must descend to a considerable depth." So beneath the visible arches of the Colosseum are others, carrying the weight of the building on cores of the indestructible Roman concrete sunk into the water.

It was the Venerable Bede, writing in his monastery at Jarrow somewhere about A.D. 700, who first addressed the building as the Colosseum in the famous proverb that Byron translated as:

While stands the Colosseum, Rome shall stand;
When falls the Colosseum, Rome shall fall;
And when Rome falls—the world.

Bede had never been to Rome, but no doubt he had heard of the Colosseum from Saxon pilgrims and may even have preserved a saying current in Rome in those days.

I climbed all over the mighty monument, thinking that it is the most comprehensible ruin in Rome. It demands little imagination to rebuild it in its splendour and fill it with 80,000 spectators, with Caesar in the royal box, the senators in their privileged seats near the rails, the aristocracy, and the Vestal Virgins; then, ascending, to the mob in the highest seats of all, for the audience in the Colosseum was seated in strict rotation. There was an official called a *designator* who saw to it that people kept in their proper places. There were at various times dress regulations which had to be obeyed. Roman citizens were obliged to attend the games in the toga, and the magistrates and senators came in their official dress. This enormous gathering, rising in tiers and mostly clothed in white, must have presented a mighty spectacle, with the senators in their striped togas and red sandals, the consuls in their purple tunics, the ambassadors and members of the diplomatic corps in the dress of their various countries, the praetorian guard in full dress, and the emperor in his royal robes. High above the gallery protruded stout masts where sailors from the fleet at Misenum, who had been trained in the manipulation of a vast awning, swarmed among the ropes and pulleys as in some gigantic galley. Even with a slight wind the sound of this *velarium* was like thunder, and on gusty days it could not be used at all. One can imagine what it must have been like to walk through the deserted Forum on a day of the games and to hear the flapping of this great awning, then to be pulled up by a savage roar of sound from eighty thousand voices.

Such a gathering of people assembled to enjoy suffering and death must have been a fearful sight, and I remembered the story of St. Augustine's friend, Alypius, who was taken to the games against his will by a number of fellow students. At first Alypius shut his eyes and refused to look, but, hearing a sudden savage shout, he opened his eyes to see a gladiator beaten to his knees. His heart filled with pity for the man, then as the death blow was delivered he "drank down a kind of savageness" and sat there, open-eyed and initiated. With the exception of Seneca, not one of the writers of antiquity, not even the kindly Horace and the gentle Pliny, condemned the degradation of the amphitheater, and the world had to wait for Christianity before men had the courage and the decency to close such places.

As I climbed about the broken tiers and ledges, I thought of the organization which fed this monstrous circle of savagery. All over the empire officials trapped and brought wild animals for the arena, and in the course of centuries the number of noble beasts which died to please the mob is said to have almost exterminated certain species from the Roman world. It is said that the elephant disappeared from North Africa, the hippopotamus from Nubia, and the lion from Mesopotamia. Long before the Colosseum was built this slaughter of animals used to be the popular prelude to the combat of gladiators; one display occupied the morning and the other the afternoon. Sulla once exhibited 100 lions in the arena and this, Cicero says, was the first time these animals were allowed to roam about instead of being tethered to stakes. In 58 BC several crocodiles and the first hippopotamus to be seen in Rome were exhibited in a trench of water in the arena, and during a *venatio* attended by Cicero in 55 B.C., 600 lions were slain and 18 elephants tried to break down the barriers in an attempt to escape. The only animal which roused any compassion in the heartless Roman mob was the elephant. Cicero says that this was due to a notion that it had something in common with Mankind; and the elder Pliny says that these animals, which had been procured by Pompey, "implored the compassion of the multitude by attitudes which surpass all description, and with a kind of lamentation bewailed their unhappy fate," until "the whole assembly rose in tears and showered curses on Pompey." Unfortunately such pity did not go very deep, and for centuries to come the mob continued to watch the slaughter of elephants and every other kind of animal; indeed, as the empire declined these fearful shows became even more extravagant.

There were schools in Rome where men were trained to fight animals and to devise tricks to amuse and thrill the mob. Such men, known as *bestiarii* or *venatores*, were lower in rank than the gladiators. Criminals could be sentenced to join such establishments and to be trained in an arena with the animals. After the Colosseum was built, the animals destined for the amphitheater were kept in a zoo known as the Vivarium, on the neighboring Celian Hill. On the day of the games they were taken under the amphitheater and placed in lifts, worked by pulleys and windlasses, which pulled the cages up to the arena.

The death of animals merely stimulated the palate for the afternoon combat of men. In imperial times there were four state schools in which gladiators lived under strict discipline. They were fed on a special diet and trained in every kind of weapon from the sword and the lance to the net and lassoo. The professional gladiator, like the modern film actor, was the idol of the crowd and, of course, of some women. There is a wall-scribble in Pompeii which describes a certain gladiator as "the maiden's sigh." With good fortune their popularity lasted longer than that of a film star today, for we hear of old warriors, the heroes of a hundred fights, winning the "wooden sword," which was handed to them in the arena as a badge of honorable retirement. There was also a great deal of money to be made.

In addition to the state schools, there were numerous private *Ludi*, where gladiators were maintained at the expense of rich amateurs or businessmen, who hired them out to fulfil engagements all over the country, as the promotors of bullfights today engage *matadores* with their *cuadrilla*. The Colosseum could also be rented. A rich man, or a politician anxious to curry favor, could organize games to take place in the Colosseum, and while they were in progress he occupied a place of honor, the *editoris tribunal*, a special seat which has now disappeared.

The Vestal Virgins were the only women allowed in the official seats, and if the empress attended the games, she sat with them. Women were not encouraged, however, to attend the amphitheater, and could sit only in the upper tiers with the *plebs*. In later times they were allowed to fight and were sometimes pitted against each other as gladiators; but this, like the woman matador of today, was not usual.

How the Vestal Virgins, who were so carefully protected against the harder facts of life, were expected to endure the games, I do not know, and I have read that it was sometimes necessary to move them to the higher parts of the Colosseum where they could not see so much. From the first moment until the last, when a ghastly figure dressed as Charon, or a denizen of the underworld, appeared and tapped with a wooden mallet the heads of those not yet dead, the "entertainment" can hardly have been fit for their eyes, and that these cloistered women were required to be officially present indicates one of the great differences between the pagan and the Christian world.

The gladiators paraded in carriages on a day of the games, just as modern bullfighters do. Arriving at the Colosseum, they lined up and took part in the *paseo* to the sound of music, and marched around the arena, with attendants following, bearing their weapons. When they reached a point opposite the royal box, they would fling up their right hands and give their famous cry: "Hail Caesar, we about to die salute you!"

The weapons were then inspected, and any which had been tampered with were thrown out. Sometimes the duellists were selected by lot; sometimes experts in the use of different weapons would be matched against each other, a swordsman against a man with a net and a trident, and so forth. At a signal from the emperor a series of life and death duels began, while the band of trumpets, horns, flutes, and a hydraulic organ, struck up and added to the noise of excited thousands, and the shouts of the instructors, who urged on the fighters with bloodthirsty incitements and, if they were not really trying, used a whip on them.

The most merciful combats were those in which the beaten gladiator had the right to appeal for his life. If he had fought well, the crowd might save him from death, as they leaned forward with their thumbs up, a sign meaning *Mitte!* ("Let him go"), but if they wished to see him die, the thunbs would be turned down—*Jugula!* ("Kill him!"); and the master of the world, glancing around to interpret the wishes of the multitude, would give the signal of life or death.

No mercy, however, was possible in the combats known as the fight to the death, in which a company of gladiators fought until only one survived; and even more horrible than this were the noon interludes, before the serious contests began, when a crowd of miserable robbers, highwaymen, murderers, and others condemned to death, were driven into the arena and given weapons with which they were compelled to kill each other. The deaths of Christians in the arena in Nero's time, and later, were of this character, but as the Christians could not be expected to slay one another, wild beasts were let loose to do the killing. It is extraordinary to contrast the gravity and dignity of Roman life at its best with the hideous degradation of mind exhibited in the public amusements of Rome.

One of the most vivid impressions of the Colosseum is the account by Dion Cassius of an occasion when the crazy young Emperor Commodus, who wanted to be worshipped as the royal Hercules, appeared as a *bestiarius* in the arena. Dion Cassius was present in his official capacity as a senator, dressed in his robes and wearing a laurel wreath. He describes the young emperor, dressed as Mercury, shooting bears with his bow and arrow as he darted about the galleries of the amphitheater. Then, descending into the arena, Commodius slew a tiger, a sealion, and an elephant. At intervals during these exploits the senators, ashamed to see the son of Marcus Aurelius lowering the imperial dignity, were nevertheless obliged to give certain ritual shouts or acclamations: "You are the master!"; "You are always victorious!" Then, says Dion Cassius, the emperor advanced towards the senatorial benches holding up the head of an animal he had just killed, and, with his dripping sword held aloft, "he shook his head without saying one word, as if by that action he intended to threaten us in the same manner as he had served the beast." Many of the senators were convulsed with laughter, but, as this might have cost them their lives, Dion Cassius says he quietly pulled some of the laurel leaves from his crown and chewed them and "advised those sitting near me to do the same."

Reading these ancient authors I had an idea that many of them disliked the games, but accepted them as a national institution and one that had the blessing of the head of the state. The Emperor Tiberius disliked them and made no secret of it, and so did Marcus Aurelius, who caused great offence by talking and dictating letters while he was seated in the royal box: but it was not until Christian times that opposition could make any real headway and the games gradually fell into disuse. The last games were probably a mere memory of the past, for Cassiodorus says that the wild beasts imported by Theodoric in 519 were a novelty to his contemporaries. The games held by Anicius Maximus in 523 are the last to be recorded. If the bones of horses and bulls discovered by professors in the Colosseum in 1878 belong to this occasion, it would appear that in later times it had become a bullring.

And so it became in the Middle Ages, with occasional plays and pageants. Then, with trees and weeds gaining upon it, robbers and hermits took up residence there, while witches and sorcerers made it the headquarters of the Black Art. It was here on a dark night that Benvenuto Cellini experienced his celebrated encounter with devils. With a Sicilian priest and a young boy from his studio, he went to the Colosseum to hold a seance. A magic circle was drawn, the proper incantations were made, and perfumes burnt; then, visible to the priest and the terrified boy, but not apparently to Cellini, the amphitheater became filled with demons. A million warlike men surrounded them, said the frightened lad, and his terror was shared by the priest, who trembled like a reed. Cellini says he also was afraid, but told them that all they saw was smoke and shadows. The boy shouted "The whole Colosseum is on fire, and the fire is upon us!", and refused to look again. Eventually they left as Matin bells were ringing, and on the way home the boy reported that a couple of the demons were still following them, sometimes frisking ahead or capering on the rooftops.

Centuries later the Georgians and Victorians claimed this same site to be the most romantic ruin in Rome. Upon the ancient stage stained with the blood of innumerable men and beasts our great-grandmothers put up their easels and sketched a shepherd and his goats near a broken marble pedestal. By that time trees and shrubs were growing where senators had once sat in official dignity, and hermits in the upper circles now added a touch of romance.

A botanist wrote a book on the flora of the Colosseum, noting 266 species, which investigators later increased to 420. It became the fashion to see the Colosseum by moonlight. Leaving the candlelight and the card tables, the ices and the after-dinner sweetmeats, satin and velvet would crowd into *carrozze* and go by the light of a full moon to the fallen giant.

"It is not possible to express the solemn grandeur of it," wrote Lady Knight in 1795. "The moon entered the broken part and struck full upon that which is most perfect, and as by that light no small parts were seen, you could almost believe that it was whole and filled with spectators."

Here, later, Byron heard "the owl's long cry." Dickens and Dr. Arnold, and a hundred more, added their tributes to a scene of melancholy that had no equal in the world. Then, as soon as Rome became the capital of Italy, the Colosseum was weeded by archaeologists and the 420 varieties were heartlessly torn from their crevices. So it stands today, still arousing wonder and incredulity: a colossus in stone with a gash in its side from which thousands of tons of travertine crashed in the Middle Ages. If all the stones which once filled that gigantic gap could fly back to their original positions, the Palazzo Venezia, the Palazzo Farnese and the Palazzo della Cancelleria, and many more, would suddenly disintegrate and vanish.

3 Essential Information

Arriving and Departing

By Train **Termini Station** is Rome's main rail terminal for the principal national and international lines. The **Tiburtina** and **Ostiense** stations serve mainly short- and medium-distance commuter lines, and the Ostiense Station, as of December 1989, will be the terminal for the line linking Rome with Leonardo da Vinci Airport at Fiumicino. Some trains for Pisa and Genoa leave Rome from, or pass through, the **Trastevere Station.** For train information, tel. 06/4775 from 7 AM to 10:40 PM. English-speaking staff are available at the Information Office in Termini Station, or request information at travel agencies. Tickets and seat reservations can be booked and purchased either at the main stations or in advance at travel agencies bearing the FS *(Ferrovia dello Stato)* emblem, where you can avoid the lines usually found at the station.

By Bus There is no central bus terminal in Rome. Long-distance and suburban buses terminate either near Termini Station or near metro stops. For ACOTRAL bus information, tel. 06/5915551, Monday–Friday 7 AM–6 PM, Saturday 7 AM–2 PM.

By Car The main access routes from the **north** are the A1 (Autostrada del Sole) from Milan and Florence or the SS1 Aurelia highway from Genoa. The principal route to or from points **south,** including Naples, is the southern leg of the Autostrada del Sole A2. All highways connect with the GRA (Grande Raccordo Anulare), a ring road that encircles Rome and channels traffic into the city. Markings on the GRA are confusing; take time to study the route you need. There are EPT (local) information offices at the Feronia service area on route A1 (tel. 0765/255465)and at the Frascati-Est service area on route A2 (tel. 06/9464341).

From the Airport to Downtown

Rome's principal airport is named after Leonardo da Vinci, but everyone calls it by the name of its location, **Fiumicino.** It's 30 kilometers (18 miles) outside the city. It is by far the better equipped and more efficient of Rome's two airports; the other is **Ciampino,** a military airport used mainly by charter companies.

Leonardo da Vinci, **Fiumicino Airport** Blue ACOTRAL **buses** leave every 15 minutes from 6:30 AM to midnight from outside the arrivals hall of both international and domestic terminals. From midnight to 5 AM they leave on the hour, and from 5 AM to 6:30 AM they leave every 30 minutes. Bus tickets can be bought from the ACOTRAL booths inside the terminals; cost is 5,000 lire. The 50-minute trip ends at the Air Terminal on Via Giolitti, on the side of Termini Station, which is only a short taxi ride to centrally located hotels.

There is a **taxi** stand 30 yards from the bus stop; use only the yellow taxis and beware of rip-offs. A taxi from the airport to the center of Rome costs about 50,000 lire, including supplements. Private limousines can be booked at booths in the arrivals hall; they charge a little more than taxis. Gypsy drivers solicit for fares as you come out of the arrivals hall; they charge exorbitant fees and can be unpleasant if you protest. Yellow taxis wait outside the terminals, but there is a booth inside for taxi information. The ride takes about 30 to 40 minutes depending on the traffic.

By **car,** follow the signs from the airport for Rome and the GRA (the ring road that circles Rome). The direction you take on the GRA depends on where your hotel is located. If it is in the Via Veneto area, for instance, you would take the GRA in the direction of the Via Aurelia, turn off the GRA onto the Via Aurelia and follow it into Rome.

A **train** link between the airport at Fiumicino and the Ostiense Station in Rome is due to open in December 1989. The Ostiense Station connects with the Piramide Station of Metro Line B. Centrally located hotels are a fairly short taxi ride from the Ostiense Station.

Ciampino Airport Ciampino Airport is nearer to the center of the city than Leonardo da Vinci, being only about 15 kilometers (nine miles) out on Via Appia Nuova. An ACOTRAL **bus** connects the airport every hour with the Subaugusta Station of Metro Line A, which takes you into the center of the city. Total cost is about 1,400 lire; have change handy for the ticket machine. A **taxi** from Ciampino to the center of Rome costs about 30,000 lire and the journey time is about 20 minutes. By **car,** take the Via Appia Nuova into downtown Rome.

Important Addresses and Numbers

Tourist Information The main **EPT** (Rome Provincial Tourist Office) is at Via Parigi 5, tel. 06/463748. Open Monday–Saturday 9–1:30, 2–7; closed Sunday. There are also EPT booths at Termini Station and Leonardo da Vinci Airport.

For information on places other than Rome there is a booth at the **ENIT** (National Tourist Board), Via Marghere 2, tel. 06/4971222.

Consulates **U.S. Consulate:** Via Veneto 121, tel. 06/46741. **Canadian Consulate:** Via Zara 30, tel. 06/8441841. **U.K. Consulate:** Via Venti Settembre 80A, tel. 06/4755441.

Emergencies **Police:** tel. 06/4686. **Carabinieri:** tel. 06/112. **Ambulance** (Red Cross): tel. 06/5100. **Doctor:** call your consulate or the private Salvator Mundi Hospital, tel. 06/586041, which has English-speaking staff, for recommendations.

Pharmacies You will find American and British products, or their equivalents, and English-speaking staff at **Farmacia Internazionale Capranica,** Piazza Capranica 96, tel. 056/6794680; **Farmacia Internazionale Barberini,** Piazza Barberini 49, tel. 06/462996; and **Farmacia Doricchi,** Via Venti Settembre 47, tel. 06/4741471, among others. Most are open 8:30–1, 4–8; some are open all night. Sunday opening by rotation.

English Bookstores You'll find English-language paperback books and magazines on newsstands in the center of Rome, especially on Via Veneto. For all types of books in English, go to the **Economy Book and Video Center,** Via Torino 136, tel. 06/4746877; the **Anglo-American Bookstore,** Via della Vite, tel. 06/6795222; or the **Lion Bookshop,** Via del Babuino 181, tel. 06/3605837.

Travel Agencies **American Express,** Piazza di Spagna 35, tel. 06/6796108; **CIT,** Piazza Repubblica 64, tel. 06/4794; **Wagons Lits,** Via Buoncompagni 25, tel. 06/4817545.

Staying in Touch

Telephones
Local Calls
Pay phones take either 200-lire coins, two 100-lire coins, or a token *(gettone)*, 200 lire each. At the airport and Termini Station you will also find new *scheda* phones, which take cards instead of coins. You buy the card at the Telefoni offices, for a value of 3,000, 6,000 or 9,000 lire. To use the card, tear off the perforated corner, insert it, and its value flashes up. After the call, hang up and the card will be returned at the bottom of the phone.

If you happen upon one of the older pay phones that take only tokens and have a little knob at the token slot, insert the token (which doesn't drop right away), dial your number, and wait for an answer. Then complete the connection by pushing the knob. The token drops and the other party can hear you. Buy tokens from the nearest cashier or the token machine near the phone.

For long-distance direct dialing *(teleselezione)* insert at least five coins or tokens and have more handy. Those unused will be returned when you pull the large yellow knob.

International Calls
Since hotels may add exorbitant service charges for long-distance and international calls, it is best to go to the Telefoni offices, where operators will assign you to a booth, help you place your call, and collect payment when you have finished, at no extra charge. There are service offices in several strategic locations:
ASST—Termini Station: main lobby, open 24 hours; lower level, open 8 AM–midnight.
ASST—Fiumicino Airport, International Terminal. Open 24 hours.
SIP—Fiumicino Airport, Domestic Terminal. Open 8 AM–8:45 PM.
ASSI—Central Post Office, Piazza San Silvestro. Open 8 AM–midnight.
ASST—Post Office, Via di Porta Angelica, near St. Peter's. Open Mon.–Fri. 8 AM–9 PM, Sat. 8 AM–2 PM.
SIP—Villa Borghese exit of Piazza di Spagna Metro station. Open Mon.–Fri. 8:30 AM–8:45 PM, Sat.–Sun., 8:30 AM–7:45 PM.

English-Speaking Operators and Information
For general information on telephoning in Europe and the Mediterranean area, dial 06/176. For operator-assisted service in the same areas, dial 15. For operator-assisted service and information regarding intercontinental calls, dial 170.

Mail
Postal Rates
Airmail letters (lightweight stationery) to the United States cost 1,050 lire for the first 19 grams, 1,650 lire from 20 to 50 grams; airmail postcards cost 850 lire if the message is limited to a few words and signature, otherwise they cost letter rate. Airmail letters to the United Kingdom cost 650 lire, postcards 550 lire.

Outgoing mail will arrive much faster if mailed from the Vatican; the Vatican post office is open Monday to Friday from 8:30 AM to 7:15 PM, Saturday from 8:30 AM to 6 PM. (It is closed Wednesday AM during papal audiences.) There are mailboxes near the post office. During peak tourist season a blue-and-white Vatican post office van branch office parks in St. Peter's Square.

Receiving Mail   You can have mail sent to you c/o **American Express,** Piazza di
Spagna 38, tel. 06/67641; the mail service desk is open for cli-
ents Monday–Friday 9–5:30, Saturday 9–1. Or you can have
mail addressed to you c/o **Palazzo delle Poste,** Piazza San
Silvestro, 00186 Roma, and marked "Fermo Posta." To collect
your mail you must show your passport or other photo-bearing
ID, and pay a small fee. Open 8:15 AM–9 PM.

Getting Around

Rome is not large in comparison to London, say, or even Paris,
but it is still too large for you to be able to rely mainly on getting
around on foot. Having said which, most of the central areas
are reasonably compact; plus there's no question but that they
reveal themselves most rewardingly to those who take the trouble to seek them out on foot (quite aside from the obvious fact
that their twisting alleys and hidden byways are mostly too
small for cars or buses). So, even if you take the metro or a bus
to whatever area you plan to visit, expect to do a considerable
amount of walking once you're there. Wear a pair of comfortable, sturdy shoes, preferably with rubber or crepe soles to
cushion the impact of the cobblestones. Heed our advice on security and get away from the noise and polluted air of heavily
trafficked streets, taking parallel streets wherever possible.
You can buy transportation route maps at newsstands and at
ATAC information and ticket booths. The free city map distributed by the Rome EPT offices at Via Parigi 5, Termini Station,
Leonardo da Vinci Airport, and Autostrada service areas is
good; it also shows metro and bus routes, the latter not always
clearly.

By Metro   This is the easiest and fastest way to get around Rome. The
metro opens at 5:30 AM and the last trains leave the central terminals at 11:30 PM. The newer Line A runs from the eastern
part of the city, with a stop at San Giovanni Laterano on the
way, to Termini Station and past Piazza di Spagna and Piazzale
Flaminio to Ottaviano, near St. Peter's and the Vatican Museums. The fare is 700 lire. There are change booths at major
stations, elsewhere there are complicated ticket machines; it's
best to buy single tickets or books of five or 10 (latter only 6,000
lire) at newsstands and tobacconists. The *BIG* daily tourist
ticket, good on buses as well, costs 2,800 lire, and is sold at
metro and ATAC ticket booths.

By Bus   Orange ATAC city buses (and two tram lines) run from about 6
AM to midnight, with skeleton *(notturno)* services on main
lines through the night. Remember to board at the rear and to
exit at the middle. The fare is 700 lire; you must buy your ticket
before boarding. Tickets are sold singly or in books of five or 10
(latter only 6,000 lire) at tobacconists and newsstands. A
Biglietto Orario, valid on all lines for a half-day, either 6 AM to 2
PM or 2 PM to midnight, costs 1,000 lire. A weekly tourist ticket
costs 10,000 lire and is sold at ATAC booths. The *BIG* tourist
ticket is also valid on the metro *(see* above).

By Taxi   Taxis wait at stands but can also be called by phone, in which
case you're charged a small supplement. The meter starts at
2,800 lire; there are supplements for service after 10 PM and on
Sundays and holidays, and for each piece of baggage. Use me-
tered yellow cabs only. To call a cab, dial 3875, 3570, 4994, or
8433. **Radio Taxi** (tel. 06/3875) accepts American Express and

Rome Metro

S. Maria del Soccorso — B LINE
Monti Tiburtini
Pietralata
Staz. Tiburtina
Pza. Bologna
Policlinico
Castro Pretorio
Villa Borghese
Flaminio
A LINE
Lepanto
Ottaviano
Spagna
Barberini
Repubblica
Termini
Vittorio Emanuele
Manzoni
S. Giovanni
Re di Roma
Ponte Lungo
Furio Camillo
Calli Albani
Arco di Travertino
Porta Furba
Numidio Quadrato
Lucio Sestio
Giulio Agricola
Sabaugusta
Cinecittà
Anagnina
A LINE
Cavour
Colosseo
Circo Massimo
Piramide C.C.
Garbatella
S. Paolo
St. Peter's / Vatican City
Tiber
TO E. U. R.
B LINE
Magliana

Diner's Club credit cards. Specify when calling that payment will be made by credit card.

By Bicycle This is a pleasant way to get around when traffic is light. But remember: Rome was built on seven hills, and has since incorporated several more. There are bike rental shops at Via Del Pellegrino 82, tel. 06/6541084; near Campo dei Fiori; and at Piazza Navona 69, next to Bar Navona. Rental concessions are at the metro stops at Piazza di Spagna, Piazza del Popolo, Largo San Silvestro, and Largo Argentina. There are also two concessions in Villa Borghese; at Viale della Pineta, and at Viale del Bambino on the Pincio.

By Scooter You can rent a moped or scooter and mandatory helmet at **Scoot-a-Long,** Via Cavour 302, tel. 06/6780206 or **Scooters For Rent,** Via della Purificazione 66, tel. 06/465485.

Guided Tours

Orientation Tours **American Express** (tel. 06/67641), **CIT** (tel. 06/4794372), **Appian Line** (tel. 06/464151), and other operators offer three-hour tours in air-conditioned 60-passenger buses with English-speaking guides. There are four itineraries: "Ancient Rome" (including the Roman Forum and Colosseum); "Classic Rome" (including St. Peter's Basilica, Trevi Fountain, and the Janiculum Hill); "Christian Rome" (including some major churches and the catacombs); and "The Vatican Museums and Sistine Chapel." Most cost about 25,000 lire, but the Vatican Museums tour costs about 33,000 lire. American Express tours depart from Piazza di Spagna; CIT from Piazza della Repubblica; Appian Line picks you up at your hotel.

American Express and other operators can provide a luxury car for up to three people, a limousine for up to seven, a minibus for up to nine, all with English-speaking driver, but guide service is extra. A minibus costs about 250,000 lire for three hours. Almost all operators offer "Rome by Night" tours, with or without pizza or dinner and entertainment. You can book tours through travel agents.

One of the least expensive organized sightseeing tours of Rome is that run by **ATAC**, the municipal bus company. Tours leave from Piazza dei Cinquecento, in front of Termini Station, last about two hours, and cost about 6,000 lire. There's no running commentary, but you're given an illustrated guide with which you can easily identify the sights. Buy tickets at the ATAC information booth in front of Termini Station.

The least expensive of all sightseeing tours are the routes followed by bus 56, from Via Veneto to Trastevere, or the long, leisurely circle route of the 30 tram. These routes take you past sights and give you a look at both the upscale and the workingman's neighborhoods on the way from Piazza Risorgimento, near St. Peter's, to Piazza San Giovanni di Dio, beyond Trastevere. For both, the cost is the 700-lire one-way fare.

Special-Interest Tours You can attend a public papal audience in the Vatican or at the pope's summer residence at Castelgandolfo through **CIT** (tel. 06/4794372), **Appian Line** (tel. 06/464151), or **Carrani** (tel. 06/460510). A bus tour of the sights which includes a stop at the Vatican and entrance to a papal audience, with return to or near your hotel, costs about 25,000 lire. An excursion to Castelgandolfo costs about 30,000 lire.

Tourvisa Italia (Via Marghere 32, tel. 06/4950284) organizes boat trips on the Tiber, leaving from Ripa Grande, at Ponte Sublicio. There are spring and September excursions to Ostia Antica, with a guided visit of the excavations and return by bus. During the summer, boats equipped with telescopes head upstream on stargazing expeditions in the late evenings; astronomers are on hand to point out the planets.

Walking Tours If you have a reasonable knowledge of Italian, you can take advantage of the free guided visits and walking tours organized by Rome's cultural associations and the city council for museums and monuments. These usually take place on Sunday mornings. Programs are announced in the daily papers.

Excursions Most operators offer half-day excursions to Tivoli to see the fountains and gardens of Villa D'Este. **Appian Line's** (tel. 06/464151) morning tour to Tivoli also includes a visit to Hadrian's Villa, with its impressive ancient ruins. Again, most operators have full-day excursions to Assisi, to Pompeii and/or Capri, and to Florence. **CIT** (tel. 06/4794372) also offers excursions to Anzio and Nettuno; its "Etruscan Tour" takes you to some interesting old towns in the beautiful countryside northwest of Rome.

Personal Guides You can arrange for a personal guide through **American Express** (tel. 06/67641), **CIT** (tel. 06/4794372), or the main **EPT Tourist Information Office** (tel. 06/463748).

Opening and Closing Times

Banks Banks are open weekdays from 8:30 to 1:30 and 3 or 3:30 to 4 or 4:30.

Museums and Churches Museum hours vary and may also change with the seasons. Always check with the EPT Tourist Information Office (tel. 06/463748). The list in the *Trovaroma* Saturday supplement of the Italian newspaper *La Repubblica* is usually up to date. Churches are usually open from early morning to noon or 12:30 PM, when they close for two hours or more; they open again in the afternoon, closing about 7 or even later, although hours may vary. St. Peter's is open all day.

Shops Shops are open, with individual variations, from about 9:30 to 1 and from 3:30 or 4 to 7 or 7:30. Food shops open earlier in the morning and later in the afternoon. All shops are closed on Sunday and a half-day during the week; for example, most shops close Monday morning, or Saturday afternoon in July and August. Food shops close on Thursday afternoon, or Saturday afternoon in July and August. Some tourist-oriented shops are open all day, as are some large department stores and supermarkets.

Post Offices Post offices are open from 8 to 2; the main post office and main district post offices stay open until 8 or 9 PM for some operations. Remember that you can buy stamps at tobacconists.

Tipping

Although restaurants include a 15% service charge (usually entered as a separate item on your check) it's customary to leave an additional 5% tip for the waiter. Tip 100 lire for whatever you drink standing up at a café, 500 lire or more for table service at a smart café, less in neighborhood bars. At a hotel bar tip 1,000 lire for cocktails.

In **hotels** tip bellboys 1,000 to 2,000 lire for carrying your bags. Give doormen 500 lire for calling a cab; tip a minimum of 1,000 lire for valet or room service. Give the concierge about 15% of the bill for services, or from 5,000 to 15,000 lire depending on how helpful he or she was. For two people in a double room, leave the chambermaid about 1,000 lire per day, about 4,000 to 5,000 lire a week. These are average figures: In deluxe hotels and restaurants you should increase these amounts by up to half, in accordance with service given.

Checkroom attendants expect 500 lire per person. Washroom attendants get from 200 lire in public rest rooms, much more in posh hotels and restaurants.

Taxi drivers are usually happy with 10% of the meter amount. Railway and airport porters charge a fixed rate per suitcase. Tip an additional 500 lire per person; more if the porter has been particularly helpful.

Theater ushers expect 500 lire per person. Give a **barber** 1,000 to 2,000 lire, a hairdresser's assistant 2,000 to 5,000 lire for a cut or tint, depending on the type of establishment.

On **sightseeing tours,** tip guides about 1,000 lire per person for a half-day group tour, more if the service is very good. In some museums and places of interest admission is free, but a tip is expected; anything from 500 to 1,000 lire is usually welcome.

Service station attendants are tipped only if they are particularly helpful.

Participant Sports

Biking Pedaling through Villa Borghese, along the Tiber, and through the center of the city when traffic is light is a pleasant way to see the sights, and is good exercise as well. For bicycle rentals, *see* Getting Around.

Tennis Increasingly popular with Italians, tennis is played in private clubs and many public courts that can be rented by the hour. Your hotel *portiere* can direct you to the nearest courts and can book them for you. One of Rome's most prestigious private clubs is the **Tennis Club Parioli** (Largo de Morpurgo 2, Via Salaria, tel. 06/8390392).

Golf The oldest and most prestigious golf club in Rome is the **Circolo del Golf Roma** (Via Acqua Santa 3, tel. 06/783407). The newest is the **Country Club Castelgandolfo** (Via Santo Spirito 13, Castelgandolfo, tel. 06/9313084) with a course designed by Robert Trent Jones and a 17th-century villa as a clubhouse. The **Golf Club Fioranello** (Viale della Repubblica, tel. 06/608291) is at Santa Maria delle Mole, off the Via Appia Antica. There is an 18-hole course at the **Olgiata Golf Club** (Largo Olgiata 15, on the Via Cassia, tel. 06/3789141). Non-members are welcome in these clubs but must show membership cards of their home golf or country clubs.

Swimming The large Olympic swimming pool at the **Foro Italico** (Lungotevere Maresciallo Cadorna, tel. 06/3608591) is open to the public from June to September. The outdoor pools of the **Hilton Hotel** (Via Cadlolo 101, tel. 06/31511), and the **Hotel Aldovrandi** (Via Ulisse Aldovrandi 15, tel. 06/841091) are lush summer oases open to nonresidents. Open throughout the year is the **Roman Sport Center** (Via del Galoppatoio 33, tel. 06/3601667), a full-fledged sports center occupying the premises next to the underground parking lot in Villa Borghese. It has two Olympic swimming pools, a gym, aerobic workout areas, squash courts, and saunas, and is affiliated with the **American Health Club** (Largo Somalia 60, tel. 06/8394488), where there's another pool.

Bowling There's a large American-style bowling center, **Bowling Brunswick** (Lungotevere Acqua Acetosa, tel. 06/3966697), and a smaller one, **Bowling Roma** (Viale Regina Margherita 181, tel. 06/861184).

Riding There are several riding clubs in Rome. The most central of all is the **Associazione Sportiva Villa Borghese** (Via del Galoppatoio 23, tel. 06/3606797). You can also ride at the **Società Ippica Romana** (Via Monti della Farnesina 18, tel. 06/3966214) and at the **Circolo Ippico Olgiata** (Largo Olgiata 15, tel. 06/3788792), located outside the city on the Via Cassia.

Hotel Fitness Facilities Although many hotels advertise all kinds of sports "nearby," investigation reveals that travel to and permission to use these facilities can be difficult. Few hotels provide health club facilities on the premises; three do: **The Cavalieri Hilton** (Via Cadlolo 101, Monte Mario, tel. 06/3151) offers a 600-meter jogging path on the hotel grounds in the elegant Monte Mario area, an outdoor pool, two clay tennis courts, exercise area, plus sauna and steam room. **The Sheraton Roma** (Viale del Pattinaggio, tel.

06/14223) has a heated outdoor pool, a tennis court, two squash courts, and sauna; no gym, however. **The St. Peter's Holiday Inn** (Via Aurelia Antica 415, tel. 06/5872) has two tennis courts on the hotel grounds, plus two more nearby, which also belong to the hotel. They have an outdoor 25-meter pool.

Jogging Rome offers lots of history, but not much room for jogging. Best bet in the inner city is at **Villa Borghese.** A circuit of the Pincio, among the marble statuary, measures one-half mile. A longer run in the park of Villa Borghese itself might include a loop around **Piazza di Siena,** a grass horse track measuring one-quarter mile. Although most traffic is barred from Villa Borghese, official government and police cars sometimes speed through. Be careful and stick to the sides of the roads. For a long run away from all traffic, try **Villa Ada** and **Villa Doria Pamphili** on the Janiculum. On the other hand, if you really love history, you can jog at the old **Circus Maximus,** now reduced to a large traffic island surrounded by honking vehicles. A loud, dusty, shadeless loop measures just over a half mile. A trail is cleared away near the inside of the Circus, where footing is easiest.

Spectator Sports

Soccer Italy's favorite spectator sport stirs rabid enthusiasm among partisans. Games are usually held on Sunday afternoons throughout the fall–spring season. Two teams—Roma and Lazio—play their home games in the Olympic Stadium at **Foro Italico,** currently being enlarged to handle the crowds expected for the World Cup Soccer Championships in 1990. Tickets are on sale at the box office before the games; your hotel portiere may be able to help you get tickets in advance. The Olympic Stadium is on Viale dei Gladiatori, in the extensive Foro Italico sports complex built by Mussolini on the banks of the Tiber (tel. 06/3964661).

Tennis A top-level international tournament is held at the Tennis Stadium at **Foro Italico** in May. For information, call the **Italian Tennis Federation** (Viale Tiziano 70, tel. 06/36858213).

Riding The **International Riding Show,** held the last few days of April and the first week in May, draws a stylish crowd to the amphitheater of Piazza di Siena in Villa Borghese. The competition is stiff and the program features a cavalry charge staged by the dashing mounted corps of the Carabinieri. For information call the **Italian Federation of Equestrian Sports** (Viale Tiziano 70, tel. 06/36858202).

Racing There's flat racing at the lovely century-old **Capanelle** track (Via Appia Nuova 1255, tel. 06/7990551), frequented by a chic crowd on big race days. The trotters meet at the **Tor di Valle** track (Via del Mare, tel. 06/5924205).

Beaches

The beaches nearest Rome are at **Ostia,** which is a busy urban center in its own right; **Castelfusano,** nearby; **Fregene,** a villa colony; and **Castelporziano,** a public beach area maintained by the city. At Ostia and Fregene the beach is pretty well monopolized by beach establishments, where you pay for changing cabins, cabanas, umbrellas, and such, and for the fact that the sand is kept clean and combed. Some establishments, such as **Kursaal** (Lungomare Catullo 36 at Castelfusano, tel. 06/5621303), have swimming pools, strongly recommended as alternatives to the murky waters of the Mediterranean, which are notoriously polluted. You can reach Ostia by metro from Termini or Ostiense Station; Castelfusano and Castelporziano are reached by bus from Ostia; Fregene can be reached from Rome by ACOTRAL bus from the Via Lepanto stop of Metro Line A. All beaches are crowded during July and August.

For cleaner water and more of a resort atmosphere you have to go farther afield. To the north of Rome, **Santa Marinella** and **Santa Severa** offer shoals, sand, and attractive surroundings. To the south, **Sabaudia** is known for miles of sandy beaches, **San Felice Circeo** is a classy resort, and **Sperlonga** is a picturesque old town flanked by beaches and pretty coves.

4 Exploring Rome

Introduction

From ancient times, Romans have been piling the present on top of the past, blithely building, layering, and overlapping their more than 2,500 years of history to create the haphazard fabric of modern Rome. The result is a city where antiquity is taken for granted, where a simple bus ride takes you past some of Western civilization's greatest monuments, where you can have coffee in a square designed by Bernini and go home to a Renaissance palace. Normal life in Rome is carried on in the most extraordinary setting.

Don't be self-conscious in your wanderings about the city. Poke and pry under the surface of things. Walk boldly through gates that are just ajar to peek into the hidden world of Roman court-yards. But do it with a smile, to show the people you meet that you are truly interested in them. Warm and straightforward, the Romans are pleased to show you the nooks and crannies of their hometown, of which they are inordinately proud. Or they are just as happy to leave to you the joy of discovering them for yourself. No one is going to *tell* you of the splendor of ocher-colored palaces under the blue sky, drenched with the sublime light of a Roman afternoon. You'll simply have to find it on your own.

The vital, good-humored Romans have their problems, of course. The city is noisy, polluted, afflicted with hellish traffic, and exasperatingly inefficient. But at least the traffic problem is being tackled. Sizable areas of the city center have been designated for pedestrians only, so you can sightsee without feeling as if you are a combatant in World War III. The pollution is less easy to cure, and far too many of the monuments you will want to see are shielded in fine green netting, while work proceeds on cleaning and repairing them.

Keep your sightseeing flexible. You'll have to plan your day to take into account the wide diversity of opening times, which will mean mixing classical sites with Baroque, museums with parks, the center with the environs. However you do it, be sure to take plenty of time off for simply sitting and drinking in this kaleidoscopic city and the passing pageant of its teeming streets.

Numbers in the margin correspond with points of interest on the maps.

Ancient Rome

Rome, as everyone knows, was built on seven hills. It is the monuments and ruins on and around the two most historic of these hills—the Capitoline and the Palatine—that this tour explores. Together they formed the hub of ancient Rome, the center of the civilized world. The Capitoline was the site of the Capitol, the "head of the world," as a 12th-century writer put it, and a name commemorated in every "capital" city in the world as well as in buildings such as Washington's Capitol. The Palatinate was the home of the earliest recorded inhabitants of Rome; later, it was the site of the emperors' vast and luxurious palace. Between them are the expansive marketplace that was the Forum—the civic heart of ancient Rome—and the Imperial Fora, built by a succession of emperors to augment the original overcrowded Forum (and to glorify themselves).

If you stand on the Capitoline and gaze out over the ruins of the Forum to the Palatinate, with the Colosseum looming in the background, you can picture how the area looked when Rome was the center of the civilized world. Imagine the Forum filled with immense temples. Picture the faint glow from the little temple of Vesta, where the Vestal Virgins tended their sacred fire, and the glistening marble complex, its roofs studded with statues, where the emperors and their retinues lived in almost unimaginable luxury. Then think how the area looked in the Dark Ages, when Rome had sunk into almost unimaginable squalor; at one point the city had not a single inhabitant for 40 days. There were few improvements in the following centuries. "How lamentable is the state of Rome," wrote a 14th-century English traveler. "Once it was full of great lords and palaces, now it is full of huts, thieves, wolves, and vermin."

The Campidoglio

The logical place to start your walking tour is the place where Rome itself began: the **Campidoglio,** the Capitol itself, located at the summit of the Capitoline Hill, just behind Piazza Venezia. Though most of the buildings you'll see here today date from the Renaissance, this was once the epicenter of the Roman Empire, where the Senate met to promulgate laws that governed practically all the then-known world.

Originally, the Capitoline Hill consisted of two peaks: the Capitolium and the Arx. The hollow between them was known as the Asylum; it was here, in the days before the Republic was founded in 510 BC, that prospective settlers came to acknowledge the protection of Romulus, legendary first king of Rome, and to be granted "asylum." Later, during the Republic, the austere, public-spirited period in which the Roman Empire was established, Roman temples occupied both peaks, and, later still, in 78 BC, the Tabularium, or Record Office, was built to house the city archives. It stood just about where the medieval **Palazzo Senatorio,** still the city hall, now stands.

Throughout the Middle Ages, the Campidoglio was little more than a rubble-strewn hill, used mainly as a goat pasture. Nonetheless, its fame lingered on in men's minds—Petrarch, the 14th-century Italian poet, was just one of many to extol its original splendor though its sumptuous marble palaces and temples had long since crumbled.

The Campidoglio began to assume its present shape in 1537. The Romans of the Renaissance had by then achieved a fairly sophisticated understanding of ancient Rome and, even if their attempts at restoration mostly took the form of carrying away what remained of the original buildings to use as materials for their own building projects or buying newly unearthed statues and other works of art to display in their new sculpture galleries and their palaces, they were conscious of the glory of the ancient city and of the decline it had endured for so long.

In 1537 Pope Paul III called in Michelangelo and charged him with restoring the Campidoglio. The aim was not just to re-create its former glory, but to provide a fitting setting for the imminent visit of Charles V, the Holy Roman Emperor, ruler of Spain and much of central Europe. The purpose of his visit was to receive the plaudits of a grateful pope for a notable victory over the Moors in North Africa. It was decided—very much in emulation of ancient Roman triumphal processions—that

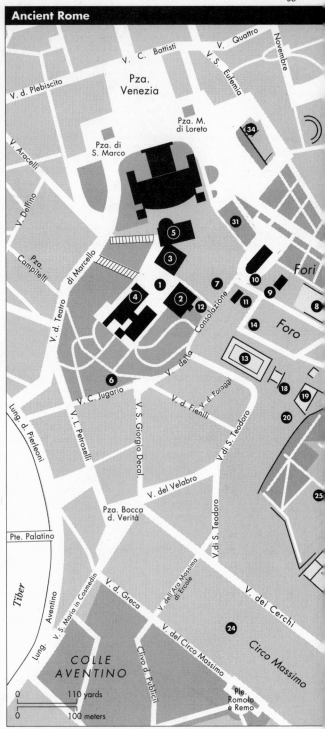

Ancient Rome

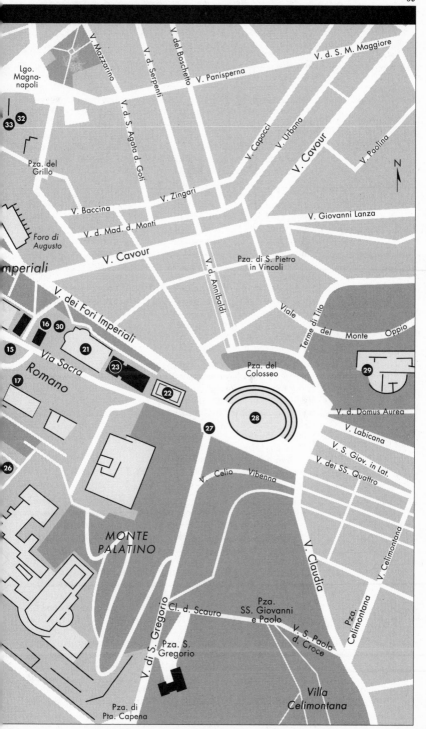

Charles V should proceed through the city to the Campidoglio, following what was believed to have been the route used by the ancient emperors after their triumphs.

In any event, much of Michelangelo's plan was not finished for almost a century, but almost everything you'll see today follows his original designs. You approach the Campidoglio up a gently sloping ramp, the *cordonata*. As you climb it, the buildings of the Campidoglio gradually reveal themselves. Until very recently, a magnificent equestrian statue of the Emperor **Marcus Aurelius** stood in the center of the piazza, placed here by Michelangelo so that the Renaissance emperor, Charles V, climbing the cordonata himself, would have his status as a modern emperor echoed, and the link between him and the ancient emperor reinforced, as he reached the piazza. There are plans to place a replica of the statue here while restoration on the original takes place; whether they will come to anything is unconfirmed at our press time. The statue itself is one of the finest ancient Roman works to have survived, though it's likely that it owes its survival principally to the fact that it was mistakenly believed to have been of the Christian Emperor Constantine rather than of the pagan Marcus Aurelius. It's claimed that Michelangelo was so struck by the statue's vivid naturalism that, having placed it in the piazza, he commanded it to walk. Another legend claims that if the statue's original gold patina returns, the end of the world will be imminent. To give destiny a hand, the city fathers are trying to save not only what's left of the gold, but also the bronze, until now seriously menaced by air pollution, of which the statue is made. Work will continue at least through 1990.

Today, the buildings flanking the piazza and Palazzo Senatorio, both with facades designed by Michelangelo, are museums (they have the advantage of being practically the only two in Rome open in the late afternoon). Their collections are based on those assembled in the 15th century by Pope Sixtus IV, one of the earliest of the great papal art lovers. To your right, as you face Palazzo Senatorio, is the Museo Conservatori; to your left is the Museo Capitolino. Your ticket—buy it at either museum—is good for both. *Piazza del Campidoglio, tel. 06/ 6782862. Admission: 4,000 lire. Open Tues. and Sat. 9–1:30 and 5–8, Wed.–Fri. 9–1:30, Sun. 9–1.*

Those with a taste for Roman and Greek sculpture will appreciate both museums; others may find the collections dull. Though the museums contain some of the finest and most celebrated sculptures of the ancient world, seeing them in serried ranks in dark galleries is hardly an ideal introduction to works that inspired generations of artists from the 15th century onward. It's also worth remembering that many of these statues have been restored by overconscientious 18th- and 19th-century collectors, who added limbs and heads with considerable abandon, and that originally almost all these works would have been brilliantly colored and gilded. Remember, too, that many of the works here are Roman copies of Greek originals. For hundreds of years, family businesses in ancient Rome prospered by copying Greek statues—they used a process called "pointing," by which exact copies could be made—but, though faithful, their copies are often strangely lifeless. Portraiture was one area in which the Romans outstripped the Greeks. The hundreds of Roman portrait busts in the Museo Capitolino are probably the highlight of a visit here.

❸ Begin your visit at the **Museo Capitolino.** As you enter the **courtyard** you'll find the reclining figure of Marforio, to which anonymous political protests and satirical poems were fixed in ancient times. The collection begins with a few Egyptian sculptures and some colossal statues, but the most interesting pieces are upstairs, where the first room contains the poignant sculpture of the *Dying Gaul* and the delicate *Marble Faun* that inspired 19th-century novelist Nathaniel Hawthorne's novel of the same name. The **Sala del Fauno** next door displays the delightful red-marble *Drunken Faun*, and the *Child with a Goose*, both Roman copies of Greek bronzes. In the large room there's a basalt statue of an obese *Hercules as a Boy*, as well as two much finer pieces: an old and a young centaur in gray marble. The *Wounded Amazon*, in the same room, is a famous Roman copy of a 5th-century BC Greek original.

Next, the fascinating **Sala dei Filosofi** and **Sala degli Imperatori** present you with row upon row of portrait busts, a kind of ancient *Who's Who*, though they are unfortunately rather haphazardly labeled. In the Sala degli Imperatori, look for the handsomely austere Augustus, on a pedestal in front of the window; for cruel Caracalla and vicious Nero; for the haughty Marcus Aurelius; and for the dissolute, eerily modern Heliogabalus. And, in front of the other window, don't miss the extraordinary bust of an unidentified Roman matron.

❹ **Palazzo dei Conservatori,** on the opposite side of the piazza, contains similar treasures. In the courtyard stand a huge head and hand, fragments of a colossal statue of the Emperor Constantine, and amusing props for a souvenir photograph. You ascend a monumental staircase to the resplendent **Salon of the Orazi and Curiazi,** used by city authorities for official ceremonies, with a magnificent gilt ceiling and carved wooden doors providing the setting for some glorious 16th-century frescoes by Cavalier d'Arpino. At either end of the salon reign statues of the Baroque period's most important popes: Bernini's marble sculpture of his patron, Urban VIII, and Algardi's portrait in bronze of Innocent X. In the rooms that follow you'll find more frescoes depicting scenes of ancient Roman history; a colorful geometric mosaic unearthed during the construction of the Via Nazionale in the 19th century; and the *Capitoline Wolf*, an Etruscan bronze of the 6th century BC. (the figures of the twins Romulus and Remus were added later in 1509). Romulus and Remus were, legend claims, the founders of Rome. They were found, as infants, on the banks of the Tiber by a she-wolf, who suckled them (hence, of course, this statue). They had been dispossessed by a wicked uncle, but were really the sons of the god Mars and a Latin princess. A shepherd adopted the twins, and they grew to become strong and ambitious young men. The gods favored them and encouraged them to build a city. The spot they chose in 735 BC was the place where they met the she-wolf, close by the Palatine. During the building of the city the brothers quarreled and, in a fit of anger, Romulus killed Remus—which is how the city became Roma, not Rema. In the corner room, the lovely *Boy with a Thorn* attracts the most attention, but don't miss the impressive bust in bronze of an austere and intense *Brutus*, last of the great Republicans and the man who stabbed Julius Caesar, the warrior-turned-statesman-turned-emperor who ushered in the Imperial age of ancient Rome.

The **Galleria degli Orti Lamiani** contains sculptures found on the Esquiline Hill (today the site of the church of Santa Maria

Maggiore), including the *Esquiline Venus*. At the end of the corridor you can get a glimpse of the **Passaggio del Muro Romano,** and see the great gray stone blocks that formed the base of the **Temple of Jupiter,** most sacred spot in ancient Rome and center of Roman religious life. These blocks, dating from 509 BC, are believed to be the oldest fragments of any building in the city. In its heyday, the temple was lavishly decorated with gold, precious jewels, and numerous tablets, banners, and medallions. It was here that Roman military triumphs were celebrated. The conquering general, dressed in a purple toga and painted a brilliant red like the statue of Jupiter in the temple, would offer up his sacrifice. Simultaneously, his vanquished enemies were done to death in the Mamertine prison below the Capitol. (Much later, Julius Caesar and Augustus were granted the right to wear these godlike robes whenever they chose, thereby becoming gods themselves.) The splendors of the temple were plundered by successive waves of invading Goths and Vandals when the empire fell. Gradually, what remained of the building was carried away for use in other structures around the city until all that was left were these simple stone slabs.

Upstairs, you'll want to visit the **Pinacoteca Capitolina** to see its splendid paintings: a Tintoretto *Magdalene*, Rubens's *Romulus and Remus*, a portrait of Bernini by Velázquez, Caravaggio's *Young St. John* and, in another room, one of his versions of *The Fortune Teller*.

Off to one side of the Campidoglio, at the head of a formidable flight of steep steps—122 in all—stands the stark, red-brick **church of the Aracoeli.** To get there, cross Michelangelo's piazza and climb the steps on the far side of the Museo Capitolino. This side of the hill has served as a religious site since the dawn of Rome. The ancient Romans came up here to worship at the Temple of Juno Moneta, which also housed the Roman mint (hence the origin of the word money). Legend recounts that here the Sybil predicted to Augustus the coming of a Redeemer. The emperor responded by erecting an altar, the Ara Coeli —the Altar of Heaven—on the spot. The site subsequently saw the building of one of the first Christian churches in Rome, Santa Maria d'Aracoeli. The church passed to the Benedictines in the 10th century and to the Franciscans in 1250, who restored and enlarged it in Romanesque-Gothic style. In the Middle Ages, before the present Campidoglio was built, the city elders used to meet here to discuss affairs of state, just as the ancient Romans had met in the temple of Jupiter.

Inside the church you'll find evidence of the successive eras of Rome's past. There are classical columns and marble fragments from pagan buildings, a 13th-century Cosmatesque pavement —so called because, like so many other brilliantly colored mosaics of the period, this was the work of the prolific Cosmati family—and a rich Renaissance gilded ceiling that commemorates the naval victory of Lepanto in 1571 over the Turks. Among these artistic treasures, the first chapel on the right is noteworthy for Pinturicchio's calm 16th-century frescoes of the life of *San Bernardino of Siena*. There's a Byzantine **madonna** over the altar, where the Emperor Augustus and the Sybil are depicted in the apse amid saints and angels, a most unusual position for a pagan emperor, to put it mildly. In the third chapel on the left you can admire Gozzoli's 15th-century fresco of *St. Anthony of Padua;* on the right of the main portal there's a handsome polychrome monument to Cardinal D'Albret by

Bregno, and next to it a tombstone by Donatello, worn by the passage of time and the faithful, now finally moved to an upright position.

But the most famous object in the Aracoeli is the figure of the **Santo Bambino,** the Holy Child, said to have been carved out of olive wood from the Garden of Gethsemane. From Christmas Eve to Epiphany, January 6, the Santo Bambino is moved from his glass case in a small chapel in the sacristy to a place of honor in the *presepio,* or Christmas crèche, in the second chapel in the left nave. During this period, Roman children come to honor him and delight their proud parents by reciting appropriate verses from the small pulpit opposite.

The Campidoglio gardens offer the best general views of the sprawling Forum (covered in more detail below). **Caesar's Forum** lies below the garden to the left of Palazzo Senatorio. It's the oldest of the Imperial (as opposed to Republican) Fora, built when the original Forum became too small for the burgeoning city's needs. Half-hidden by the trees, across Via dei Fori Imperiali, the broad avenue created by Mussolini, are **Trajan's Forum** on the left, with its huge semicircular market building, and **Trajan's Column,** under which the Emperor Trajan was buried. On the right of **Trajan's Market** are the ruins of the **Forum of Augustus.**

Take Via del Campidoglio on the right of Palazzo Senatorio and then Via del Tempio di Giove for a look at the Roman Forum from the vantage point of the **Belvedere Tarpeia,** the infamous Tarpeian Rock from which traitors were dashed to the ground below. Here, in the 7th century BC, Tarpeia betrayed the Roman citadel to the besieging Sabines, sworn enemies of the early Romans, asking, in return, for what they wore on their left arms, thinking of their heavy gold bracelets. The scornful Sabines did indeed shower her with their gold as they passed, but added the crushing weight of their heavy shields, also carried on their left arms. Use your imagination to reconstruct what the area below looked like when most of these magnificent ruins were covered over by marshy pastureland, and cows grazed beside half-buried columns and trod 2,000-year-old marble paving slabs. It was a sight that held a particular fascination for the city's Grand Tourists in the 18th and 19th centuries, who had come themselves to contemplate the glory of the ancient city.

Returning to the gardens above Caesar's Forum, you can take Via San Pietro in Carcere, actually a ramp of stairs that lead down to the **Mamertine Prison,** two gloomy cells where Rome's vanquished enemies, most famously the Goth Jugurtha and the indomitable Gaul, Vercingetorix, were imprisoned and died of starvation or strangulation. In the lower cell, St. Peter himself is believed to have been held prisoner and to have miraculously brought forth a spring of water in order to baptize his jailers. *Donations requested. Open daily 9–12:30 and 2–7:30.*

The Roman Forum

From the main entrance on Via dei Fori Imperiali, you descend into the labyrinthine archaeological complex that is the **Roman Forum.** Don't confuse it with the later, Imperial Forums (or, more properly, Fora) located just on this side of Via dei Fori Imperiali. This was the original Forum, the civic heart of Republican Rome, the austere, stern Rome that existed before the emperors and the pleasure-loving, ever-more-corrupt imperial Romans of the 1st to the 4th centuries AD.

Today, despite massive archaeological programs, the Forum seems little more than a baffling series of ruins, with roofless buildings, isolated columns, occasional paving stones, and grass everywhere, growing up, around, and between what's left. Centuries of plunder and the unstoppable urge of later Romans to carry off what was left of the better building materials reduced the Forum to this desolate state. It is almost impossible to imagine this enormous area as the pulsating heart of a Rome that ruled over a vast empire, filled with stately and extravagant buildings—temples, palaces, and shops—and crowded with people from all corners of the empire. Adding to the confusion is the fact that the Forum developed over many hundreds of years; what you see today are not the ruins from just one period but from almost 900 years, from about 500 BC to AD 400. As the original buildings became too small or were thought too old fashioned for a Rome that grew ever more powerful, they were pulled down and replaced by more lavish and larger structures. But as often as not, the foundations of these older buildings remained and many have survived to the present, pitted and scarred with age, alongside their later cousins. Making sense of these gaunt and craggy ruins is no easy business, and many may find them no more than heaps of old stones that reveal little or nothing of their glorious past. If ever there were a site that cried out for imagination in picturing it in its days of pomp, this is it.

8 Walk past the **Basilica Emilia** on the right; this was a meeting place for merchants and a kind of community center of the 2nd century BC, later rebuilt in the 1st century AD by Augustus. The term "basilica" refers not to a church as such, but to a particular architectural form developed by the Romans. This was a great colonnaded hall that served as a court of law or a center for business and commerce. Some of these Roman basilicas were later converted into churches, and these early models proved remarkably enduring in the design of later Roman churches; there are 13th-century churches in the city that are fundamentally no different from many built in the 5th and 6th centuries AD.

The Roman Forum lies in what was once a marshy valley between the Capitoline and Palatine hills, a valley crossed by a mud track and used as a cemetery by the Iron-Age settlers on the Palatine. Over the years, a marketplace and some huts were established here, leading eventually to what would become the civic heart of Rome—the Forum—after the land was drained in the 6th century BC. *Entrances on Via dei Fori Imperiali, Piazza Santa Maria Nova, and Via di San Gregorio, tel. 06/ 6790333. Admission: 5,000 lire. Open Apr.–Sept. 9–6; Oct.–Mar. 9–3; closed Tues.*

9 Beyond the Basilica Emilia, as you look toward the Campidoglio, you'll see the large brick **Curia,** which survives as it was in the era of Diocletian in the late 3rd century AD. By that time the Senate had lost practically all of the power and prestige that it had possessed during the Republican era, when it had met in an earlier Curia building. The open space in front of **10** the Curia is the **Comitium,** political center of ancient Rome. Here were the **Rostra,** podiums from which orators spoke to the people (hence the term "rostrum"), and here, under protective roofing, is the black pavement that supposedly marks the burial place of Romulus, first king of Rome, in that primitive cemetery near the mud track. Legend is supported by the fact that the funeral monuments underlying the black pavement bear the earliest-known Latin inscription in characters somewhat resembling Greek.

Julius Caesar rearranged the Comitium, moving the Curia to its present site and transferring the Imperial Rostra (decorated originally with the prows of captured ships, or *rostra)* to a spot on the left of the Arch of Septimius Severus. It was from this platform that Mark Antony delivered his funeral address in Caesar's honor.

⑪ The **Arch of Septimius Severus** was built in AD 203 to celebrate the Emperor Severus's victory over the Parthians. It was the most richly decorated arch yet seen, and was topped by a bronze equestrian statuary group with no fewer than six horses. The sculptured stone reliefs on the arch were probably based on huge painted panels that the emperor had sent to Rome to publicize his achievements.

Across the space that separates the Forum from the Campidoglio, next to the ruined platform that was the **Temple of Concord,** stand three graceful Corinthian columns, all that ⑫ remains of the **Temple of Vespasian.** They marked the site of the Forum through the centuries when the rest was hidden under overgrown rubble. On the left of the Rostra rises the **Temple of Saturn,** where ancient Rome's state treasury was kept.

Turn back now to the open space between the Basilica Emilia ⑬ and the **Basilica Julia** (named for Julius Caesar) on your right. This was the heart of the Forum proper, prototype of Italy's famous piazzas, and center of civic and social activity in ancient ⑭ Rome. The **Column of Phocas** was the last monument to be added to the Forum; it was erected in AD 608 in honor of a Byzantine emperor who had donated the Pantheon to Pope Boniface IV. At the end of the Forum, nearest the entrance to ⑮ the excavations, stands the **Temple of Caesar,** built by Augustus, Caesar's successor, over the spot where Julius Caesar's body was cremated on a pyre improvised by distraught and grief-crazed citizens who fed the flames with their own posses⑯ sions. From here, the Via Sacra leads past the **Temple of Antoninus and Faustina,** best-preserved of the Forum's monuments.

⑰ The small circular temple in front of it is the **Temple of Vesta,** where the haughty and highly privileged Vestal Virgins kept the sacred flame alive. Next to the temple, the ruins of their **House of the Vestals** give no hint of the splendor in which they lived out their 30-year vows of chastity. Inside was the garden courtyard of their palace, surrounded by airy colonnades, behind which lay at least 50 rooms. The Vestals lived on the second floor of the palace, though there may have been a third floor as well. The six Vestal Virgins dedicated their lives for 30 years to keeping the sacred fire, a tradition that dated back to the very earliest days of Rome, when guarding the community's precious fire was essential to its well-being. Their standing in Rome was considerable, indeed they were second in rank only to the empress. Their intercession could save a condemned man, and they did, in fact, rescue Julius Caesar from the lethal vengeance of his enemy, Sulla. The virgins were handsomely maintained by the state, but if they broke their vows they were buried alive, and if they allowed the sacred fire to go out they were scourged by the high priest. The Vestal Virgins were one of the last of ancient Rome's institutions to die out, enduring to as late as the end of the 4th century AD, even after Rome's emperors had become Christian. They were finally suppressed by Theodosius.

18 Off to the side is the **Temple of Castor and Pollux,** dedicated in 484 BC to the twin brothers of Helen of Troy. Legend says that they carried the news of a great victory to Rome and paused to **19** water their horses at the **Fountain of Juturna,** the rectangular, marble-lined pool near the temple. Behind the temple at the **20** foot of the Palatine Hill stands the church of **Santa Maria Antiqua,** an imperial construction that was converted into a Christian church some time in the 5th or 6th centuries. It contains some exceptional frescoes of Eastern saints, similar to those in the rock churches of Cappadocia in Turkey.

Now go back past the House of the Vestals and follow Via Sacra again. You'll pass some smaller temples and the great arched **21** vaults of the **Basilica of Maxentius** on the left. Begun under the Emperor Maxentius about AD 306, it was a center of judicial and commercial activity, the last of its kind to be built in Rome. What remains is only one third of the original. Like so many other Roman monuments, it served as a quarry for building materials and was stripped of its lavish marble and stucco decorations. Note its coffered vaults, later copied by so many Renaissance artists and architects.

After the basilica, you will come at last to the **Arch of Titus,** which stands in a slightly elevated position on a spur of the Palatine Hill. The view from the arch is superb. Now cleaned and restored, the Arch of Titus was erected in AD 81 to celebrate the recapture of Jerusalem 10 years earlier, after the great Jewish revolt. It's famous for a relief representing the seven-branched candlestick—a Jewish menorah—that was part of the **22** spoils of war. Beyond it stands the **Temple of Venus and Rome,** begun by Hadrian in AD 121, its truncated columns framing the Colosseum beyond. The church next to the Basilica of **23** Maxentius is **Santa Francesca Romana,** a 10th-century edifice with a Renaissance facade. It's dedicated to the patron saint of motorists; on her feast day, March 9, cars and taxis crowd the space below the church for a special blessing. Its incomparable setting also makes it a favorite for society weddings.

The Palatine

The **Palatine Hill,** located to the south of the Forum and overlooking it, is the oldest inhabited site in Rome. Archaeologists have uncovered remains of an Iron-Age settlement here dating as far back as the 9th century BC. In fact, the ancient Romans always believed that Romulus, founder of Rome, lived on the Palatine. During the Republican era it was an exclusive residential area for wealthy families such as the Flacci and the Crassi and, in the Imperial age, the emperors took it over as a suitable site for their huge and splendid palaces. Tactful and shrewd Augustus, the first emperor to live on the Palatine, had simple tastes and was content to keep the modest rooms he had had as a private citizen. Not so his successors. Tiberius was the first to build a palace here; others followed. But in the 1st century AD the Emperor Domitian outdid them all. He ordered his architects to put up two separate palaces: the **Palazzo dei Flavi,** which was to serve for official functions and ceremonies, and the **Domus Augustana,** private apartments for himself and his family. His architects began the task of adapting the Palatine to the emperor's wishes. Older dwellings were razed, hollows were filled in, and terraces were extended out toward the Circus Maximus to increase the surface area. Next to his palace, Domitian created a vast open space, the **Stadium.** This may simply have been an immense sunken garden; alternatively, it may have been used to stage games and other amusements for the benefit of the emperor.

There are few more atmospheric places to wander in Rome than the Palatine, discovering hidden corners and restful, shady lanes, glimpsing sudden views of the modern city past centuries-old ruins, and allowing yourself to enjoy a sense of the far-off majesty that was Rome. Though picnicking is frowned on, you might well bring along a circumspect snack and enjoy it in this unique setting.

The path at the northern end of Domitian's Stadium offers excellent views as it leads you to the **Belvedere,** where you have a panorama of the Circus Maximus, the green slopes of the Aventine and Celian hills, the bell tower of Santa Maria in Cosmedin on the right, and the obelisk of Axum on the left near the immense white marble block of the UN's Food and Agriculture Organization headquarters. Like the emperors, whose Imperial box still looks out from the Palatine, you can look

24 straight down on the elongated oval of the **Circus Maximus,** ancient Rome's oldest and largest racecourse, situated in the natural hollow of the Mursia valley between the Palatine and Aventine hills. In its heyday it could hold more than 300,000 spectators. On certain occasions there were as many as 24 races a day and meetings could last for 15 days. The noise, the color, and the excitement of the crowd must have been astounding. Later, when Rome was ruled by the popes, another kind of spectacle drew crowds to this site: the execution of criminals and other transgressors of papal laws.

Now retrace your steps past the remains of the **Baths of Septimius Severus** and return to the top of the Palatine. Look

25 for a shed that shelters the **House of Livia,** one of the only remaining examples of a well-to-do Republican family's dwelling. Its delicate, delightful frescoes give you an idea of the sophisticated taste of wealthy Romans, whose love of beauty and theatrical conception of nature was inherited, much later, by their descendants, Alessandro Farnese among them. He was a nephew of Pope Paul III and he commissioned the 16th-century architect Vignola to lay out the archetypal Italian gar-

26 den, the **Orti Farnesiani,** over the ruins of the Palace of Tiberius, up just a few steps from the House of Livia. This pleasure garden was originally much larger than it is now, and the existing aviary had a twin. From here you can return to the Arch of Titus in the Forum by way of the path known as the clivus Palatinus, whose worn, original paving stones were trod by both slaves and emperors. (The Roman word "clivus" means a slope, hence our word declivity and, of course, decline and incline.)

The Arch of Constantine and the Colosseum

27 The majestic **Arch of Constantine,** studded with rich marble decorations, stands near the Colosseum. It is one of Rome's most imposing monuments, erected in AD 315 to commemorate Constantine's victory over Maxentius at the Milvian Bridge. It was just before this battle, in AD 312, that Constantine—the emperor who converted Rome to Christianity—had a vision of a cross in the heavens and heard the words "In this sign thou shalt conquer." The economy-minded Senate ordered that many of the decorations for the arch be taken from earlier monuments; perhaps this was a tacit recognition of the greater artistic value of these earlier sculptures in comparison with the slipshod reliefs commissioned for the arch. It doesn't take much imagination to picture Roman legionnaires marching under the arch's great barrel vault. Excavations under way between the arch and the Temple of Venus and Rome have revealed the remains of the **Meta Sudans**, a conical fountain built by Titus and blithely buried by Mussolini's engineers in 1936.

Looking at the Arch of Constantine, the most ornate and splendid of all the remaining triumphal arches in Rome, it's worth considering just how the Romans came to build these remarkable structures at all. What was their purpose? Why were the Romans so fond of them? It's known there were upwards of 50 such arches in Rome alone, while hundreds, large and small, were built in other parts of the empire. Curiously, though the Romans were nothing if not pragmatic and materialistic, it's now known that their triumphal arches had no practical purpose at all. Why should these hardheaded people have lavished so much time and energy on building these imposing but ultimately useless ceremonial constructions?

The reason seems simply to have been that the Roman emperors put up "these monstrous toys," as one writer has called them, to celebrate their own prowess: as symbols of their power and achievements. It is no accident that the triumphal arch developed as *the* symbol of Rome during the Imperial era. While in the austere Republican period conquests and triumphs were made in the name of Rome, in the later Imperial period similar conquests were celebrated in the name of the general or emperor responsible for them. It rapidly became the convention for the current conquering hero to put up a new—and preferably more ostentatious—arch, under which he and his victorious troops would march on their return (about the only practical use the arches ever had). A modern expert has called Rome's triumphal arches "idle contrivances of grand but nonsensical irrelevance"—and no arch in Rome deserves these epithets more than Constantine's.

28 Now turn to the **Colosseum,** the most stupendous extant monument of ancient Rome. It was begun by the Flavian Emperor Vespasian in AD 72 and was inaugurated by Titus eight years later with a program of games and shows lasting 100 days. On the opening day alone, 5,000 wild beasts perished in the arena. Its construction was a remarkable feat of engineering, for it stands on marshy ground reclaimed by draining a lake in the grounds of Nero's Domus Aurea (the "golden house"); Vespasian thus intended to make amends to the Roman people for Nero's confiscation of the land. Originally known as the Flavian amphitheater, it came to be called the Colosseum by later Romans who identified it with the site of the famous Colossus of Nero, a 115-foot-tall statue of gilded bronze that stood at the entrance to what's now Via dei Fori Imperiali. Twelve pairs of elephants were needed to transport the statue here from its original site at the entrance to the Domus Aurea; it was still standing in AD 334, only to be destroyed by Pope Gregory the Great at the end of the 6th century.

The Colosseum was designed to hold more than 50,000 spectators for gory entertainments such as combats between wild beasts and gladiators. It has a circumference of 573 yards and was faced with stone from Tivoli. An ingenious system of awnings could be opened out to shade the arena's occupants from the hot Roman sun. Look at the way the three tiers of columns on the outside become progressively more ostentatious. Those on the lowest level are quite plain, with no more than simple slabs forming the capital (the uppermost part). On the second level the capitals are given graceful curves. On the top level they are carved with ornate leaves, a typical classical motif derived from the acanthus plant. This simple progression is one of the key elements of classical architecture, one that fascinated architects of the 16th, 17th, and 18th centuries, as well as the ancient Romans. The idea behind this use of the "orders," as the three basic forms of capital are known, was that one should naturally use the stoutest and thus strongest at the lowest level as this was the one with the greatest load to carry. As you progressed upward and the load lessened, so you could use more decorative forms. The names of these columns are, from the bottom up, Doric, Ionic, and Corinthian.

For an entrance fee you can explore the upper levels, where behind glass you can see a scale model of the Colosseum as it was. The upper tiers provide a good view of the excavations of the subterranean levels. Look for the traces of ancient-Roman stucco decoration that remain in the entrance arch on the metro station side.

Legend has it that as long as the Colosseum stands, Rome will stand; and when Rome falls, so will the world. This threat didn't deter Renaissance princes from using the Colosseum as a quarry for building materials for such noble dwellings as Palazzo Barberini and Palazzo Farnese. Earlier, the Colosseum had been seriously damaged by earthquakes and, during the Middle Ages, had been transformed into a fortress. Some experts maintain that it was in Rome's circuses, and not here, that thousands of early Christians were martyred. Still, tradition has reserved a special place for the Colosseum in the story of Christianity, and it was Pope Benedict XIV who stopped the use of the building as a quarry when, in 1749, he declared it sanctified by the blood of the martyrs. A tiny chapel built in the 6th century under one of the Colosseum's arches was restored and reconsecrated for the 1983 Holy Year. *Piazza del Colosseo, tel. 06/735227. Admission free, admission to upper levels: 3,000 lire. Open daily 9–one hour before sunset.*

㉙ Behind the Colosseum at the Colle Oppio on the **Esquiline Hill,** you can see what's left of Nero's fabulous **Domus Aurea.** To build this palace, the capricious emperor confiscated a vast tract of land right in the center of Rome, earning the animosity of most of his subjects. The palace was a sumptuous residence, with a facade of pure gold, sea water piped into the baths, decorations of mother-of-pearl and other precious materials, and vast gardens. Not much has survived of all this; a good portion of the buildings and grounds disappeared under the public works with which subsequent emperors sought to make reparation to the Roman people for Nero's phenomenal greed.

The largest of the buildings put up by later emperors over the Domus Aurea was the great complex of baths built by Trajan. As a result, the site of the Domus Aurea itself remained unknown for many centuries; indeed, when a few of Nero's original halls were discovered at the end of the 15th century, no one realized that they actually were part of the palace. Raphael was one of the artists who had themselves lowered into the rubble-filled rooms, which resembled grottoes. The artists copied the original painted Roman decorations, barely visible by torchlight, and, like modern, ill-mannered tourists, scratched their names on the ceilings. Raphael later used these models—known as *grotesques* because they were found in grottoes—in his decorative motifs for the Vatican Loggia. Today you can enjoy the pleasant park laid out around the ruins of Trajan's Baths.

Time Out Facing the Colosseum is the appropriately named **Il Gladiatore,** a handy place for a moderately priced lunch. *Piazza del Colosseo 15. Closed Wed.*

The Imperial Fora

Leave the park by way of Viale del Monte Oppio and follow it back down to the Colosseum taking Via dei Fori Imperiali toward Piazza Venezia. On the walls on your left, you'll see plaques in marble and bronze that show the extension of the Empire in various areas, then—on the same side of the street —the soaring arches and coffered vaults of the Basilica of
㉚ Maxentius. The church of **Santi Cosma e Damiano** next door was adapted in the 6th century, probably from the audience hall of the city prefect. It was restored in the 17th century by the Barberini Pope Urban VIII, who couldn't resist adding a few bees from his family's coat of arms to the lower left-hand side of the 6th-century mosaic in the apse. There's a Neapolitan *presepio*, or Christmas crèche, on permanent display in a chapel. Part of the church was built over the Temple of Romulus.

㉛ Continuing along past the entrance to the Roman Forum, you'll come to the **Forum of Caesar** on the left. When the broad Via dei Fori was laid out over the ruins of the Imperial Forums to provide a suitable setting for what Mussolini expected would be his own imperial triumphs, a statue of every emperor who had built a forum was set up in front of his particular forum. Without fail, on the Ides of March, an unknown hand lays a bouquet at the foot of Caesar's statue.

㉜
㉝ Across the avenue are the **Fora of Nerva** and **Augustus's** and **Trajan's Markets,** which are best visited from the entrance on Via Quattro Novembre. A street separates the well-preserved remains of Trajan's Market from the rather desolate expanse of his forum. This was once the most imposing of the Imperial Fora, laid out by Apollodorus of Damascus in a magnificent succession of temples, basilicas, and libraries. One important
㉞ monument has survived since AD 113: **Trajan's Column,** with a remarkable series of reliefs spiraling up it, celebrating the emperor's victories over the Dacians in what today is Yugoslavia. Despite the copious written records of Roman military campaigns, the scenes on the column represent just about the best primary source material on the Roman army. The column has been under restoration for years, but it's due to be unveiled by 1989. A statue of St. Peter replaced that of Trajan at the summit in 1587. An inscription on the base declares that the column was erected in Trajan's honor to mark the height of the hill that his architect Apollodorus razed to make way for his project.

The emperor's ashes were kept in a golden urn in a chamber at the column's base.

The smaller of the two charming churches here is **Santa Maria di Loreto,** built by Sangallo the Younger in the 15th century on handsome Renaissance lines. The lantern above its dome was created by Michelangelo's disciple, Jacopo del Duca. The larger church, **Santissimo Nome di Maria,** is 18th century. One of Trajan's libraries stood on this site.

The Vatican

Though it's not a large city as capitals go, Rome nonetheless has three separate centers. This triple focus is a testimony to the city's great age. As the city developed in different periods, so it grew around different centers. Ancient Rome grew up around the Forum. In the Middle Ages, the center shifted north to what's now called Old Rome, the spur of land locked inside the loop of the river Tiber as it flows first west and then east through the city. The third great center is the one covered in this chapter: the Vatican, the heart and spiritual focus of the Roman Catholic Church.

There are two principal reasons for seeing it. One is to visit the church of St. Peter's, the largest church in the world, built over the tomb of St. Peter, and the most imposing and breathtaking architectural achievement of the Renaissance. The other is to visit the Vatican Museums, which contain collections of staggering richness and diversity, including, of course, the Sistine Chapel. There's little point trying to take it all in on just one visit, however. See St. Peter's on your first visit and come back later to see the Vatican Museums. Or, if your interests are chiefly to do with art rather than architecture, do it the other way round.

Castel Sant'Angelo

Since St. Peter's is open all day, start your walk at Castel Sant'Angelo—which is closed in the afternoons—the fortress that for many hundreds of years guarded the Vatican. You **❶** should approach the castle across **Ponte Sant'Angelo**—the Sant'Angelo Bridge—lined with Baroque angels. These were designed by Bernini, Baroque Rome's most prolific architect and sculptor. In fact, he carved only two of the angels, both of which were moved to the church of Sant' Andrea delle Fratte shortly afterward for safekeeping. Though copies, the angels on the bridge today convey forcefully the grace and characteristic sense of movement—a key element of Baroque sculpture —of Bernini's best work.

❷ Facing you as you cross the bridge is **Castel Sant'Angelo** itself, a great circular building with one of the most distinctive silhouettes of any structure in Rome. Anyone still harboring doubts as to the power and almost unimaginable wealth of ancient Rome's emperors will have them dashed here: Though it may look like a fortress, Castel Sant'Angelo was in fact built as a mausoleum, or tomb, for the Emperor Hadrian. Work began in AD 135, and was completed, by the emperor's son, Antoninus Pius, about five years later. When first finished, it consisted of a great square base topped by a marble-clad circular structure on which were planted a ring of cypress trees. Above them tow-

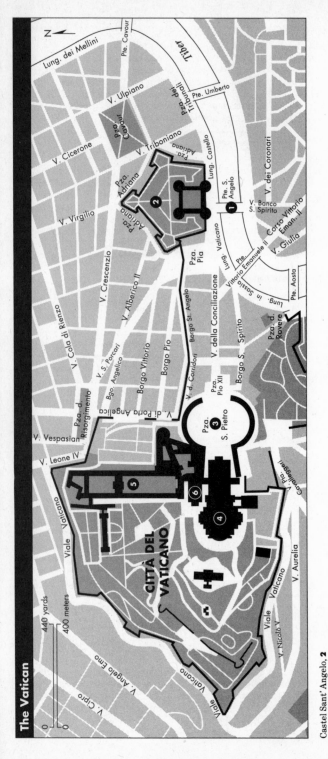

Castel Sant' Angelo, **2**
Piazza di San Pietro, **3**
Ponte Sant' Angelo, **1**
St. Peter's, **4**
Sistine Chapel, **6**
Vatican Museums, **5**

ered a gigantic statue of Hadrian. As with so many Roman buildings, later generations saw no reason why it should not be converted to their purposes; there was no sense letting such an immense and potentially useful building go to waste. Thus from about the middle of the 6th century AD the building became a fortress, the military key to Rome for almost 1,000 years and place of refuge for numerous popes during wars and sieges. Its name—Sant'Angelo means "holy angel"—dates from 590. Then, Pope Gregory the Great, returning to the Vatican during a terrible plague, saw an angel standing on the summit of the castle in the act of sheathing its sword. Taking this as a heavenly sign that the plague was at an end, the pope built a chapel on the spot where he had seen the angel. Next to it he had a statue of the angel placed. Henceforth, it became known as Castel Sant'Angelo.

Enter the building through the original Roman door of Hadrian's tomb. From here you pass through a courtyard that was enclosed in the base of the classical monument. You descend into a vaulted brick corridor that hints at grim punishments in dank cells. On the right, a spiral ramp leads up to the chamber in which Hadrian's ashes were kept. Where the ramp ends, the Borgian Pope Alexander VI's staircase begins. Part of it consisted of a wooden drawbridge, which could isolate the upper part of the castle completely. The staircase ends at the Cortile, or courtyard, dell'Angelo, which has become the resting place of the marble angel that stood above the castle. (It was replaced by a bronze sculpture in 1753.) The stone cannon balls you'll see piled in the courtyard look like oversize marble snowballs. In the rooms on the right of the Cortile dell'Angelo, there's a small collection of arms and armor; on the left, some frescoed halls, which are used for temporary exhibitions, and the chapel of Pope Leo X, with a facade by Michelangelo.

You'll emerge into the courtyard named after Pope Alexander VI, where there's a well head bearing the Borgia coat of arms. The courtyard is surrounded by gloomy cells and huge storerooms that could hold great quantities of oil and grain in case of siege. Benvenuto Cellini, the rowdy 16th-century Florentine goldsmith, sculptor, and boastful autobiographer, spent some time in Castel Sant'Angelo's foul prisons; so did Giordano Bruno, a heretical monk, who was later burned at the stake in Campo dei Fiori, and Beatrice Cenci, accused of patricide and incest, and executed just across Ponte Sant'Angelo. Her story forms the lurid plot of Shelley's verse drama, *The Cenci.*

Take the stairs at the far end of the courtyard to the open terrace. From here, you have some wonderful views of the city's rooftops and of the lower portions of the castle. You can also see the **Passetto,** the fortified corridor connecting Castel Sant'Angelo with the Vatican. Pope Clement VII used it to make his way safely to the castle during the Sack of Rome in 1527. Opening off the terrace are more rooms containing arms and military uniforms. There's also a bar where you can pause for refreshments.

Continue your walk along the perimeter of the tower and climb the few stairs to the **papal apartments.** Though used by the popes mainly in times of crisis, these splendid rooms are far from spartan. The sumptuous **Pauline Room,** the first you enter, was decorated in the 16th century by Pierino del Vaga and his assistants with lavish frescoes of scenes from the Old Testament and the lives of St. Paul and Alexander the Great. Look for the trompe l'oeil door with a figure climbing the stairs. From another false door, a black-clad figure peers into the room. He's believed to be a portrait of an illegitimate son of the powerful Orsini family. The **Perseus Room,** next door, is named after a frieze in which del Vaga represents Perseus with damsels and unicorns. The classical theme is continued in the next room, the **Amor and Psyche Room,** used by the popes as a bedroom. From the Pauline Room a curving corridor covered with grotesques—a form of decoration much favored in the Renaissance, and based on ancient Roman and Greek wall paintings, many of them originally found in grottoes, hence the name for these otherwise far from grotesque decorative motifs—leads to the **library,** some smaller rooms, and the **treasury.** Here the immense wealth of the Vatican was brought for safekeeping during times of strife; it was stored in the large 16th-century strongboxes you see today. You can continue on to the upper terrace at the feet of the bronze angel for a magnificent view and a more than passing thought for Tosca, Puccini's poignant heroine in the opera of the same name, who threw herself off the ramparts. *Lungotevere Castello 50, tel. 06/6875036. Admission: 3,000 lire. Open Apr.–Sept., Mon. 3–8, Tues., Wed. and Fri. 9–2, Thurs. and Sat. 9–7, Sun. 9–1; Oct.–Mar., Tues. –Sat. 9–1, Sun. 9–12, closed Mon.*

Piazza di San Pietro

Leaving Castel Sant'Angelo, turn right on to **Via della Conciliazione.** This broad, rather soulless avenue was begun by Mussolini in 1936 to celebrate the "conciliation" between the Vatican and the Italian government, a conciliation brought about by the Lateran Pact of 1929 which thereafter regulated the relationship between church and state. The road links the Vatican with the rest of Rome, and, when built, it was a physical expression of the newfound accord between the secular and the spiritual powers. To make way for it, two old streets and a row of houses were razed. In doing this the picturesque old approach to St. Peter's was changed entirely. Formerly, there was the sudden thrill of emerging from narrow, shadowy byways into the immense space and light of Piazza di San Pietro, St. Peter's Square, a similar but much greater effect than that which you feel when you turn a corner and see the Trevi Fountain. This was the stuff that Baroque art was made of. Still, even if this original and intensely dramatic explosion of grandeur has been lost, the approach to St. Peter's along Via della Conciliazione does at least give you time to become accustomed to the enormous dimensions of the square and the huge church beyond it.

❸ St. Peter's Square, or **Piazza di San Pietro,** the great open space in front of St. Peter's, was designed by Bernini. The work began in 1656 and was completed just 11 years later. Though it is called a square, it isn't actually square at all; in fact, though it appears to be circular, it isn't even that, either. It's an ellipse, the sides of which are formed by two immense colonnades, each consisting of four rows of giant columns. If you stand on the two stone discs set into the ground in front of each of the two colonnades (they're located about midway between the obelisk in the dead center of the square and the two fountains to either side of it), the colonnades seem to consist of a single row of columns.

The 85-foot-high Egyptian **obelisk** was brought to Rome by Caligula in AD 38 and was probably placed in his circus, believed to have been near here. It was moved to its present site in 1586 by Pope Sixtus V. The monumental task of raising it almost ended in disaster when the ropes started to give way. In the absolute silence—the spectators had been threatened with death if they made a sound—a voice called "Water on the ropes!" Thus a Genoese sailor saved the day, and was rewarded with the papal promise that thereafter the palms used in St. Peter's on Palm Sunday should come from Bordighera, his hometown.

The emblem at the top of the obelisk is the Chigi star, placed here in honor of Alexander VII, the Chigi pope under whom the piazza was built. Alexander had been categorical in dictating to Bernini his requirements for the design of the piazza. It had to make the pope visible to as many people as possible from the Benediction Loggia and from his Vatican apartments; it had to provide a covered passageway for papal processions; and it had to skirt the various existing buildings of the Vatican, while incorporating the obelisk and the fountain already there. (This fountain was moved to its present position and a twin fountain was installed to balance it.)

On the left of the square are the **Vatican Information Office** (open Monday–Saturday 8 AM–7 PM) and **Vatican Bookshop** (open Monday–Friday 8–2 and 3–6, Saturday 8–2). There are Vatican post offices (known for fast handling of outgoing mail) on either side of St. Peter's, and, in peak tourist season, a blue-and-white post office van is parked in the square. You can buy Vatican stamps and coins at the shop near the information office. Public toilets are located near the Information Office, under the colonnade opposite, and outside the exit of the crypt.

St. Peter's

❹ The story of **St. Peter's** goes back to the year AD 319, when the Emperor Constantine built a basilica over the site of the tomb of St. Peter. The original church stood for more than 1,000 years, undergoing a number of restorations and alterations, until it threatened to collapse toward the middle of the 15th century. In 1452 a reconstruction job was begun; it was quickly abandoned for lack of cash. In 1506 Pope Julius II instructed the architect Bramante to raze all the existing buildings and to rebuild a new basilica, one that would surpass even Constantine's for grandeur. But it wasn't until 1626 that the basilica was completed and dedicated. Five of Italy's greatest Renaissance artists died while working on the new and greater St. Peter's—Bramante, Raphael, Peruzzi, Antonio Sangallo the Younger, and Michelangelo.

Though Bramante made only little progress in rebuilding St. Peter's, he succeeded nonetheless in outlining a basic plan for the church, and, crucially, built the piers of the crossings—the massive pillars supporting the dome. After Bramante's death in 1514, Raphael, the Sangallos, and Peruzzi all proposed variations on the original plan at one time or another. Again, however, lack of finance, rivalries between the competing architects, and, above all, the turmoil caused by the Sack of Rome in 1527 and the mounting crisis of the Reformation conspired to ensure that little serious progress was made. In 1546, however, Pope Paul III turned to Michelangelo, and more or less forced the aging artist to complete the building. Michelangelo, in turn, insisted on having carte blanche to do as he thought best. He returned to Bramante's first idea of having a centralized Greek-cross plan—that is, with the "arms" of the church all the

St. Peter's

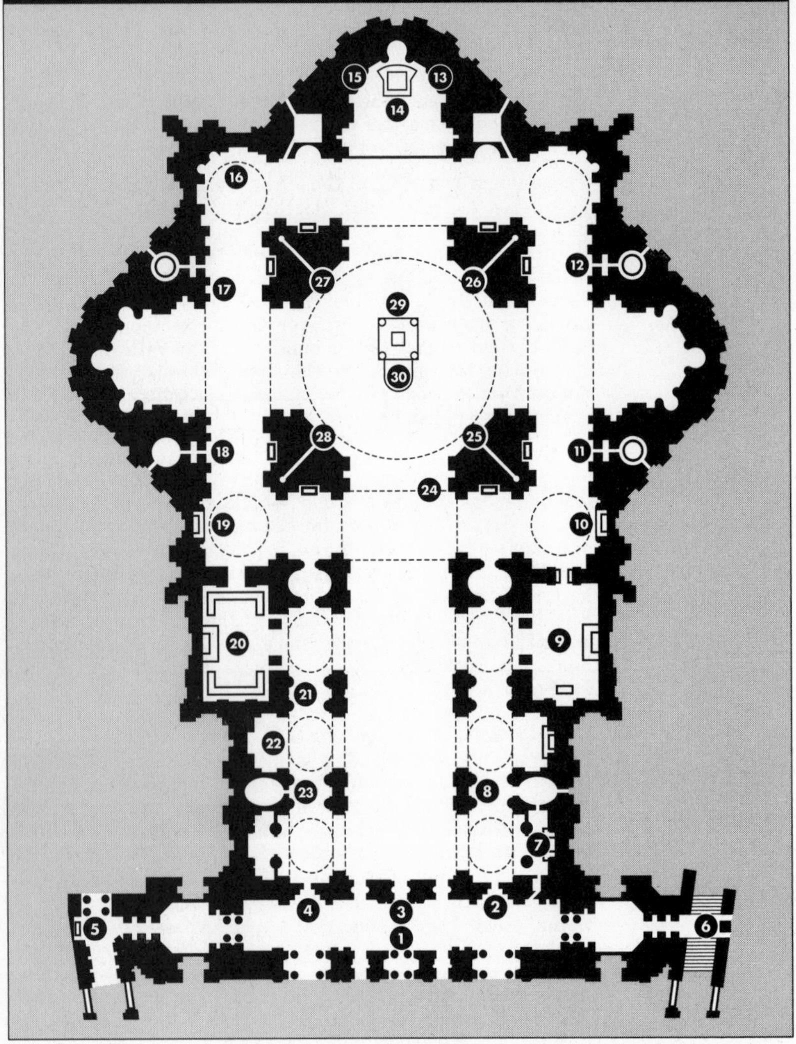

Vestibule: The Ship, Giotto mosaics, **1**

Holy Door, **2**

Central Door, **3**

Bronze Door, **4**

Charlemagne, **5**

Emperor Constantine, **6**

Chapel of the Pietà; Pietà (Michelangelo), **7**

Christina of Sweden monument, **8**

Chapel of the Holy Sacrament, **9**

Gregorian Chapel, **10**

Entrance to Cupola, **11**

Clement XIII monument, **12**

Urban VIII monument, **13**

Gloria, with St. Peter's Chair, **14**

Paul III monument, **15**

Chapel of the Column; altar and tomb of St. Leo the Great, **16**

Alexander VII monument, **17**

Pius V monument (below: entrance to sacristy), **18**

Clementine Chapel; (under altar: St. Gregory the Great tomb), **19**

Chapel of the Choir, **20**

Innocent VIII monument, **21**

Chapel of the Presentation; John XXIII monument, **22**

Clementina Sobieski monument, opp. Pillar of the last Stuarts; exit from Cupola, **23**

St. Peter, **24**

St. Longinus; entrance to Crypt, **25**

St. Helen, **26**

The Veronica, **27**

St. Andrew, **28**

Bronze Baldachino, **29**

Confession, **30**

same length—and completed most of the exterior architecture except for the dome and the facade. To see the best examples of his work you have to go behind the church (at the left), or survey them from the roof. His design for the dome, however, was modified after his death by Giacomo della Porta. The nave, too, was altered after Michelangelo's death. Pope Paul V wanted a Latin-cross church (a church with one "arm" longer than the rest), so Carlo Maderno lengthened one of the arms to create a nave. He was also responsible for the facade. This was much criticized at the time because it hides the dome from observers below. It is also wider than it is high.

As you climb the shallow steps up to the great church, flanked by the statues of Sts. Peter and Paul, you'll see the Benediction Loggia over the central portal. This is the balcony where newly elected popes are proclaimed and where they stand to give their apostolic blessing on solemn feast days. Look at the vault above you, encrusted with rich stucco work, and at the mosaic above the central entrance to the portico, a much-restored work by the 14th-century painter Giotto that was in the original basilica. The bronze doors of the main entrance also were salvaged from the old basilica. The sculptor Filarete worked on them for 12 years; they show scenes from the *Council of Florence* and the *Life of Pope Eugene IV*, his patron (1431–47). The large central figures are Sts. Peter and Paul. Once inside the basilica, look at the inside of these doors for the amusing "signature" at the bottom in which Filarete shows himself and his assistant dancing with joy, tools in hand, at having completed their task. To the left are two modern bronze doors, the so-called *Doors of Death*, in both of which you'll see Pope John XXIII. On the right of the main entrance are the *Door of the Sacraments* and the *Holy Door*, opened only during Holy Years.

Once inside the great building, pause a moment to judge its size. Observe the people near the main altar, dwarfed by the incredible dimensions of this immense temple. Look at the statues, the size of the pillars, and the holy-water stoups borne by colossal cherubs. Look also at the brass inscriptions in the marble pavement down the center of the nave, indicating the approximate length of the world's principal Christian churches, all of which fall far short of the apse of St. Peter's.

Immediately to your right is Michelangelo's **Pietà**, one of the world's most famous statues. Now it is safely screened behind shatterproof glass after having been damaged by a maniac in 1972 and masterfully restored in the Vatican's workshops.

Exquisite bronze grilles and doors by Borromini open into the third chapel in the right aisle, the **Chapel of the Most Holy Sacrament,** with a Baroque fresco of the *Trinity* by Pietro da Cortona and carved angels by Bernini. At the last pillar on the right (the pier of St. Longinus) is a bronze statue of **St. Peter,** whose big toe is kissed by the faithful. It is attributed to the 13th-century sculptor Arnolfo da Cambio. In the right transept, over the door to the **Chapel of St. Michael,** usually closed, Canova created a brooding neo-Classical monument to Pope Clement XIII.

In the central crossing, Bernini's great bronze *baldacchino*—a huge, twisty-columned canopy—rises high over the papal altar. Bernini's Barberini patron, Pope Urban VIII, had no qualms about stripping the bronze from the Pantheon in order to provide Bernini with the material to construct this curious structure. The Romans reacted with the famous quip, "Quod non fecerunt barbari, fecerunt Barberini" ("What the barbarians didn't do, the Barberini did."). A curious legend connected with the baldacchino, which swarms with Barberini bees (the bee was the Barberini family symbol), relates that the pope commissioned it in thanks for the recovery of a favorite niece who had almost died in childbirth. The story is borne out by the marble reliefs on the bases of the columns: The Barberini coat of arms is surmounted by a series of heads, all but two of which seem to represent a woman in what might be the pain of labor, while a smiling baby's face appears on the base at the right front.

Beautiful bronze vigil lights flicker around the **confessio** (see below) under the papal altar. The antique casket in the niche contains the *pallia*, bands of white wool which are conferred by the pope on archbishops as a sign of authority. These pallia are made by nuns from the wool of two lambs blessed every year in the church of St. Agnes on her feast day, January 21. When completed, they are blessed by the pope during the rites of the feast of St. Peter on June 29 and are stored in the casket that you see. The confessio is the ceremonial entrance to the crypt; this more or less corresponds with the site of St. Peter's burial place, deep in the foundations of the basilica.

The splendid gilt-bronze **throne** above the main altar in the apse was designed by Bernini to contain a wooden and ivory chair that St. Peter himself is said to have used, though in fact it doesn't date back further than medieval times. (You can see a copy of the chair in the treasury.) Above it, Bernini placed a window of thin alabaster sheets that diffuses a golden light around the dove, symbol of the Holy Spirit, in the center.

Two of the major papal tombs in St. Peter's are located to either side of the apse. To the right is that of **Pope Urban VIII;** to the left is that of **Pope Paul III.** Paul's tomb is the earlier, and was designed between 1551 and 1575, by della Porta, the architect who completed the dome of St. Peter's after Michelangelo's death. It was very much in emulation of this splendid late-Renaissance tomb that Urban VIII ordered that Bernini should design his tomb. The lavish use of marble, bronze, and gilding on Urban VIII's tomb is typical of the Baroque love of opulent and extravagant materials. Notice the skeleton figure of Death writing the pope's name on a marble slab. The hardly less ostentatious tomb that della Porta designed for Paul III caused a considerable stir when unveiled, and indeed continued to do so down the years. The nude figure of Justice was widely believed to be a portrait of the pope's beautiful sister, Giulia. The charms of this alluring figure were such that in the 19th century it was thought that she should no longer be allowed to distract worshipers from their prayers and she was swathed in marble drapery. Those with a taste for Baroque funerary monuments should search out the **tomb of Pope Alexander VII,** also designed by Bernini; it stands to the left of the altar as you look up the nave, behind the farthermost pier of the crossing.

Under the Pope Pius V monument, the entrance to the **sacristy** leads also to a small collection of Vatican treasures. They range from the massive and beautifully sculptured 15th-century tomb of Pope Sixtus IV by Pollaiuolo, which you can view from above, to a jeweled cross dating from the 6th century; a famous *dalmatic*, or liturgical cloak, that was believed to have been donated by Charlemagne—first Holy Roman Emperor, and ruler of what are now France and Germany—but probably dates to the 14th century; and a marble tabernacle by the mid-15th-century Florentine sculptor Donatello. (There's a small-scale copy of Michelangelo's *Pietà* here, too.) Among the other priceless objects are a platinum chalice presented to Pope Pius VI by Charles III of Spain in the middle of the 18th century, and an array of sacred vessels in gold, silver, and precious stones. *Admission: 2,000 lire. Open Apr.–Sept., daily, 9–6:30; Oct.–Mar., daily, 9–2:30.*

Continue on down the left nave past Algardi's monument to Pope Leo XI. The handsome bronze grilles in the **Chapel of the Choir** here were designed by Borromini to complement those opposite in the Holy Sacrament Chapel. The next pillar holds a rearrangement of the Pollaiuolo brothers' austere monument to Pope Innocent VIII, the only major tomb to have been transferred from the old basilica. The next chapel contains the handsome bronze monument to Pope John XXIII by contemporary sculptor Emilio Greco. On the last pier in this nave stands a monument by the late-18th-century Venetian sculptor Canova marking the spot in the crypt below where the last of the ill-fated Stuarts, the 18th-century Roman Catholic claimants to the British throne, and long exiled in Rome, were buried. Among them are Bonnie Prince Charlie, who in 1745 came close to seizing the throne, and who passed his declining years in poverty and drunkenness in Rome, still dreaming of the glory that so nearly was his.

Take the elevator, near the right crossing, or climb the long flights of shallow stairs to the **roof** of the church, the vast sloping terraces of which are punctuated by the skylights over the various chapels, and from where you have remarkable views of the dome and the piazza. The terrace is equipped with the inevitable souvenir shop, and with toilets. Climb the stairs at the top of the drum—the base of the dome—where, appropriately enough, there's a bust of Michelangelo, principal designer of the dome. Within the drum, a short ramp and staircase lead to the gallery that encircles the base of the dome and gives you a dove's-eye view of the interior of the church. It's well worth the effort to make your way up here, though not if you suffer from vertigo. If you're stout of heart and sound of wind you should then make the taxing climb from the drum of the dome up to the lantern at the very apex of the dome. A narrow, seemingly interminable staircase follows the curve of the dome between inner and outer shells, finally releasing you into the cramped space of the lantern balcony for an absolutely gorgeous panorama of Rome and the countryside. There's also a nearly complete view of the palaces, courtyards, and gardens of the Vatican. We can't emphasize too strongly, however, that it's a tiring, slightly claustrophobic, and one-way-only climb—which means that you can't turn back if you change your mind! *Entrance to roof and dome between Gregorian Chapel and right crossing. Admission: 3,000 lire, including use of elevator to roof, 2,000 lire if you use spiral ramp of stairs. Open Apr.–Sept., daily, 8–7; Oct.–Mar., daily, 8–6.*

Finally, plunge from the heights to the depths and visit the **crypt** (Tombs of the Popes). The entrance is at the base of the pier dedicated to St. Longinus. As the only exit from the crypt leads outside St. Peter's, it is best to leave this visit for last. The crypt is lined with marble-faced chapels and simple tombs occupying the area of Constantine's basilica and standing over the cemetery in which recent excavations have brought to light what is believed to be the tomb of St. Peter himself. *Entrance* at St. Longinus Pier, but alternatively at one of the others. Admission free. Open Apr.–Sept., daily, 7–6; Oct.–Mar., daily, 7–5.

With advance notice you can tour the **excavations** under the basilica, which give a fascinating glimpse of early-Christian Rome. Guides are available, or you can use a taped guide. *Apply several days in advance to the Ufficio Scavi (Excavations Office), on the right beyond the Arco delle Campane entrance to the Vatican, left of the basilica. Tell the Swiss guard you want the Ufficio Scavi and he will let you enter the confines of Vatican City. Tel. 06/6985318. Cost: 5,000 lire for guide, 3,000 lire with taped guide.*

The Vatican City

The Vatican City is an independent, sovereign state, established by the Lateran Treaty of 1929, which was signed by the Holy See—the pope—and the Italian government. It covers 108 acres on a hill west of the Tiber, separated from the city on all sides by high walls, except at Piazza di San Pietro. Inside the walls, about 1,000 people live as residents. The Vatican newspaper, *L'Osservatore Romano*, is consulted throughout the world. The Vatican issues its own stamps, strikes commemorative coins, and has its own postal system. Within its territory are administrative and foreign offices, a pharmacy, banks, an astronomical observatory, a print shop, a mosaic school and art restoration institute, a tiny train station, a supermarket, a small department store, and several gas stations. Radio Vaticano, a powerful transmitting station, broadcasts in 14 languages to six different continents. At the Vatican Information Office you can book tours of the Vatican gardens; all must be booked a day or two in advance. *Garden Tour costs 9,000 lire. Available Oct.–Mar., Tues., Fri., and Sat.; Nov.–Feb., Tues., Thurs., Sat. Garden and Sistine Chapel Tour costs 18,000 lire. Available Oct.–Mar., Mon. and Thurs. All tours begin at 10 AM.*

The sovereign of this little state is Pope John Paul II who, until his election on October 16, 1978, was Cardinal Karol Wojtyla, Archbishop of Cracow. He is the 264th pope of the Roman Catholic Church, the first non-Italian for 456 years, and the first-ever Pole to hold the office. He has full legislative, judicial, and executive powers, with complete freedom under the Lateran Treaty to organize armed forces within his state (the Swiss Guards and the Vatican police) and to live in or move through Italian territory whenever he so desires. The pope reigns over 700 million Roman Catholics throughout the world and is assisted in his task by the College of Cardinals and, increasingly in recent years, by Synods of Bishops. The intricate rules of etiquette that were once characteristic of the Vatican have been greatly relaxed by recent popes, and much of the Apostolic Palace has been redecorated in severely simple style. But the colorful dress uniforms of the Swiss Guards are a reminder of past ostentation and worldly power.

For many, a papal audience is a highlight of a trip to Rome. The pope holds mass audiences on Wednesday mornings at about 11, and at 10 in the hottest months. During the winter they take place in a modern audience hall, which has a capacity of about 7,000. From March to October, they are held in St. Peter's Square, and sometimes at the papal residence at Castel Gandolfo. You must apply for tickets in advance; you may find it easier to arrange for them through a travel agency. *For tickets, apply in writing well in advance, or go to the Papal Prefecture (Prefettura) which you reach through the Bronze Door in the right-hand colonnade, tel. 06/6982. Open Mon.–Tues. 9–1, Wed. 9 to shortly before audience commences (but last-minute tickets may not be available). You can arrange for tickets and transportation to and from the audience through a travel agent: Carrani Tours, Via V.E. Orlando 95, tel. 06/460510; Appian Line, Via Barberini 109, tel. 06/464151. Cost is about 25,000 lire if booked through an agent or hotel portiere.*

Of course, you can avoid any formalities by seeing the pope when he makes his weekly appearance at the window of the Vatican Palace every Sunday at noon when he is in Rome. He addresses the crowd and blesses all present.

Around the Vatican

The Vatican Palace has been the residence of the popes since 1377. It consists of a number of individual buildings containing an estimated 1,400 rooms, chapels, and galleries. The pope and his household occupy only a small part of the palace, most of the rest of which is given over to the Vatican Library and Museums. The Vatican runs a bus service from the Information Office in Piazza di San Pietro through the Vatican gardens, to a secondary entrance of the Vatican Museums. (Fare: 1,000 lire. Service daily, except Sun. and Wed., 9–12:30, on the half hour.)

Time Out The street of Borgo Pio, a block or two from St. Peter's Square, has several trattorias offering tourist menus for about 13,000 lire. For about 15,000 lire you can have a simple à la carte meal at **La Casareccia.** *Borgo Pio 40. Closed Thurs.*

❺ The collections of the **Vatican Museums** are immense, covering about four and a half miles of displays. Special posters at the entrance and throughout the museum plot out a choice of four color-coded itineraries, the shortest taking approximately 90 minutes and the longest five hours, depending on your rate of progress. You can rent a taped commentary in English explaining the Sistine Chapel and the Raphael Rooms. You're free to photograph what you like, barring use of flash, tripod, or other special equipment, for which permission must be obtained. The main entrance is on Viale Vaticano and it can be reached by the #49 bus from Piazza Cavour, which stops right in front; or on foot from the #81 bus or #30 tram which stops at Piazza Risorgimento; or from the Ottaviano Metro Line A stop. *Viale Vaticano, tel. 06/6983333. Admission: 8,000 lire; free on last Sun. of month. Open Easter and July–Sept., Mon.–Sat. 9–5 (no admission after 4); Oct.–June (except Easter) 9–2 (no admission after 1). Closed Sun. year-round except last Sun. of month, and on religious holidays: Jan. 1, Jan. 6, Feb. 11, Mar. 19, Easter Sun. and Mon., May 1, Ascension Thurs., Corpus Christi, June 29, Aug. 14–15, Nov. 1, Dec. 8, Dec. 25–26.*

Among the incredible riches contained in the small area of Vatican City, probably the single most important is the Sistine Chapel. However, unless you're following one of the two abbreviated itineraries, you'll begin your visit at the **Egyptian Museum** (in which Room II reproduces an underground chamber tomb of the Valley of Kings).

The **Chiaramonti Museum,** next on the itinerary, was organized by the neo-Classical sculptor Canova, and contains almost

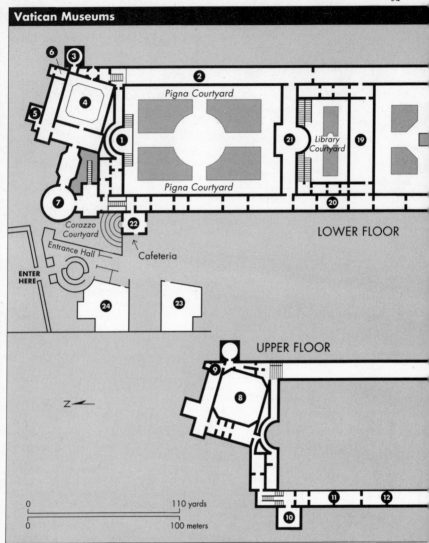

Vatican Museums

Pigna Courtyard

Pigna Courtyard

Library Courtyard

LOWER FLOOR

Corazzo Courtyard

Entrance Hall

Cafeteria

ENTER HERE

UPPER FLOOR

0   110 yards
0   100 meters

Antiquarium, **9**
Borgia Rooms, **18**
Candelabra Gallery, **11**
Chiaramonti Museum, **2**
Egyptian Museum, **1**
Etruscan Museum, **8**
Gallery of Busts, **5**
Hall of the Immaculate Conception, **16**

Map Gallery, **13**
Mask Room, **6**
New Wing, **21**
Octagonal Courtyard, **4**
Pagan, Christian Antiquities, and Ethnological Museums, **24**
Pinacoteca Gallery, **23**
Pio-Clementino Museum, **3**

Pius V Rooms, **14**
Quattro Cancelli, **22**
Raphael Rooms, **17**
Room of the Rotunda, **7**
Sala della Biga, **10**
Sistine Chapel, **19**
Sobieski Room, **15**
Tapestry Gallery, **12**
Vatican Library, **20**

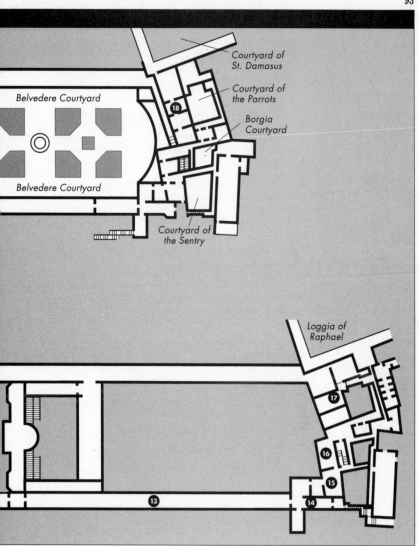

Courtyard of
St. Damasus

Courtyard of
the Parrots

Borgia
Courtyard

Belvedere Courtyard

Belvedere Courtyard

Courtyard of
the Sentry

Loggia of
Raphael

1,000 copies of classical sculpture. The gems of the Vatican's sculpture collection are in the **Pio-Clementino Museum,** however. Just off the hall in Room X, you'll find the *Apoxyomenos* (The Scraper), a beautiful 1st-century AD copy of a bronze statue of an athlete. There are other even more famous pieces in the **Octagonal Courtyard,** where Pope Julius II had them moved in 1503 from his private collection. In the left-hand corner stands the celebrated *Apollo Belvedere*. In the far corner, on the same side of the courtyard, is the *Laocoön* group, found on Rome's Esquiline Hill in 1506, held to be almost the single most important antique sculpture group in terms of its influence on Renaissance artists. These days interest in ancient Roman and Greek sculpture is at an all-time low, but from the Renaissance right up to about 1900 one of the prime measures of one's taste and education was how much one knew about works just like this. Indeed, in the Renaissance, interest in antique sculpture knew no bounds, and the discovery of a group like the *Laocoön* was one of the most talked-about and exciting events for many years.

The next hall is dedicated to animals and is filled with sculpture and mosaics done in colored marble, some very charming. Then, there's a gallery of classical statues and a **room of busts;** the smallish **Mask Room** boasts a lively mosaic pavement from the Emperor Hadrian's Villa at Tivoli just outside Rome, and a copy of Praxiteles' *Cnidian Venus*. (Praxiteles was the Michelangelo of his day, in 4th-century BC Greece.) In the next hall, that of the Muses, the *Belvedere Torso* occupies center stage. This is a fragment of a 1st-century BC statue, probably of Hercules, all rippling muscles and classical dignity; it was much admired by Michelangelo. The lovely neo-Classical **room of the Rotonda** has an ancient mosaic pavement and a huge porphyry basin from Nero's palace, as well as several colossal statues. The room on the Greek-cross plan contains two fine porphyry sarcophagi (great marble burial caskets), one of Costantia (you may already have seen a copy in the church of Santa Costanza), and one of St. Helena, mother of the Emperor Constantine.

If your itinerary includes the **Etruscan Museum** you'll be able to see the extraordinarily rich objects from the Regolini-Galassi find near Cerveteri, and a wealth of other material as well. There follow three sections of limited interest: the **Antiquarium,** with Roman originals; three small rooms of Greek originals (followed by a broad staircase lined with Assyrian reliefs); and a vase collection. The domed **Sala della Biga** comes next. The *Biga* (chariot) group at the center was extensively reconstructed in 1780. The chariot itself is original and was used in the church of San Marco as an episcopal throne.

All itineraries merge in the **Candelabra Gallery,** where the tall candelabra—immense candlesticks—under the arches are, like the sarcophagi and vases, of ancient origin. In the **Tapestry Gallery** that follows, the walls facing the windows are hung with magnificient tapestries executed in Brussels in the 16th century from designs by Raphael. On the window walls are tapestries illustrating the life of Pope Urban VIII. They were done in a workshop that the Barberini family set up in Rome in the 17th century expressly for this purpose.

Now you'll enter the long, intriguing **Gallery of Maps,** frescoed with 40 topographical maps of Italy and the papal territories, commissioned by Pope Gregory XIII in 1580. On each map there's a detailed plan of the region's principal city. The ceiling is decorated with episodes from the history of the regions. The flow of visitors through this corridor can speed up a bit, but it is worth taking your time to go through, especially if you are interested in history and geography seen through the eyes of former generations.

The Gallery of Maps leads to the **Apartment of Pius V,** where you'll find a small hall hung with tapestries. Facing the windows are some precious 15th-century works from Tournai, in Belgium, with scenes of the *Passion* and *Baptism of Christ.* Now go through the chapel and, if you're following the longer itineraries, turn left into the **Sobieski Room,** which gets its name from the huge painting by the Polish artist Lalejko. It shows the *Victory of Vienna*, a decisive defeat of the invading Ottoman forces in the late 17th century; the Turks were poised to take Vienna, and had they succeeded there seems little doubt but that they would rapidly have overrun much of central Europe. A massive display case in the **Hall of the Immaculate Conception** shows some preciously bound volumes containing the text of the papal bull promulgating that particular dogma.

Now you'll enter the **Raphael Rooms,** which are directly over the Borgia apartments. Pope Julius II moved into this suite of rooms in 1507, four years after his election, reluctant to continue living in the Borgia apartments with their memories of his ill-famed predecessor, Alexander VI. He called in Raphael and his assistants to decorate the rooms. The first room you enter was the last to be painted in Raphael's lifetime, and was executed mainly by Giulio Romano, who worked from Raphael's drawings for the new pope, Leo X. Known as the **Incendio Room,** it served as the pope's dining room. The frescoes depict stories of previous popes called Leo, the best of them showing the great fire in the Borgo (the neighborhood between the Vatican and Castel Sant'Angelo) that threatened to destroy the original St. Peter's in the year AD 847. Miraculously, Pope Leo IV extinguished it with the sign of the cross. The other frescoes show the *Coronation of Charlemagne* by Leo III in St. Peter's, the *Oath of Leo III*, and a naval battle with the Saracens at Ostia in AD 849, after which Pope Leo IV showed clemency to the defeated.

The **Segnatura Room,** which you come to next, was the first to be frescoed and was painted almost entirely by Raphael himself. The theme of the room—which may broadly be said to be "learning"—reflects the fact that this was Julius's private library. Theology triumphs in the fresco known as the *Disputa*, or *Debate on the Holy Sacrament*, on the wall behind you as you enter. Opposite, the *School of Athens* glorifies philosophy in its greatest exponents. Plato is on the right (perhaps a portrait of Leonardo da Vinci) debating a point with Aristotle. The pensive figure on the stairs is sometimes thought to be Raphael's rival, Michelangelo, who was painting the Sistine Chapel at the same time that Raphael was working here. In the foreground on the right is Euclid, a portrait of the architect Bramante, and, on the far right, the handsome youth just behind the white-clad older man is Raphael himself. Over the window on the left, Parnassus represents poetry, with Apollo, the Muses, and famous poets, many of whom are likenesses of Raphael's contemporaries. In the lunette over the window opposite,

Raphael painted figures representing and alluding to the Cardinal and Theological Virtues, and subjects showing the establishment of written codes of law. Beautiful personifications of the four subject areas, Theology, Poetry, Philosophy, and Jurisprudence, are painted in circular pictures on the ceiling above.

Third in the series of rooms is the **Eliodoro Room,** a private antechamber. Working on the theme of Divine Providence's miraculous intervention in defense of endangered faith, Raphael depicted *Leo the Great's Encounter with Attila;* it's on the wall as you enter. The *Expulsion of Heliodorus from the Temple of Jerusalem*, opposite the entrance, refers to Pope Julius II's insistence on the Church's right to temporal possessions. He appears on the left, watching the scene. On the left window wall, the *Liberation of St. Peter* is one of Raphael's best-known and most effective works.

It's hard to overstate the importance of these calm and noble frescoes, and hard not to feel awed that they were painted by a man not yet 30. When people talk about the High Renaissance, it's these frescoes they're probably thinking about. All the principal characteristics of Italian Renaissance painting are here: naturalism (the figures are complete and whole, and lack any sense of the strain or awkwardness that pictures painted only a few years earlier still contained); humanism (the idea that man is the most noble and admirable of God's creatures); and a profound interest in the antique world (evident in the handsome and spacious classical architecture of the backgrounds and in the choice of philosophers and men of letters from the ancient world as the principal subject matter).

There's a tendency to go into something of a stupor when confronted with "great art" of this kind, with all the overtones of "improving" qualities it implies. In fact, part of the reason why Raphael is so superb an artist is that his work, much like Mozart's, is supremely accessible. It's true, of course, that it contains many classical and religious allusions that are largely lost on modern audiences, but even so his paintings have a clarity and a sort of understated boldness that make them remarkably easy to appreciate. It can also be instructive to compare these stately and ordered frescoes with those Michelangelo was painting on the Sistine chapel ceiling at the same time. Where Raphael's work is a hymn to reason and logic, Michelangelo's is tortured and intense. Both celebrate man; but where Raphael celebrates man's ability to order his universe, Michelangelo sees him largely as owing his existence to a God who can be vengeful as well as loving.

Next door to the Raphael Rooms, you come to the **Hall of Constantine,** decorated by Giulio Romano and other assistants of Raphael after his untimely death in 1520. The frescoes represent various scenes from the life of the Emperor Constantine. A door in the corner leads to the *loggia*, the terrace, designed and frescoed by Raphael with Old Testament subjects and with the grotesques, the small decorative patterns, he had copied from the walls of Nero's Domus Aurea after the discovery of its ruins in the early 16th century. Now you pass through the richly decorated **Chiaroscuri room**—it contains Michelangelo's model for the dome of St. Peter's—to enter the tiny **chapel of Nicholas V,** aglow with Fra Angelico frescoes of episodes from the life of St. Stephen (above) and St. Lawrence (below).

If your itinerary takes you to the **Borgia apartments,** you'll see its elaborately painted ceilings, designed but only partially executed by Pinturicchio at the end of the 15th century and greatly retouched in later centuries. In the **Room of the Sybil,** it's generally believed that Cesare Borgia murdered his sister Lucrezia's husband, Alphonse of Aragon. In the **Room of the Saints,** Pinturicchio painted his self-portrait in the figure to the left of the possible portrait of the architect Antonio da Sangallo(his profession is made clear by the fact that he holds a T-square). The lovely picture of St. Catherine of Alexandria is said to be Lucrezia Borgia herself. The *Resurrection* scene in the next room, the **Room of the Mysteries,** offers excellent portraits of the kneeling Borgia pope, of Cesare Borgia (the soldier with a lance at the center), and of the young Francesco Borgia (the Roman at the soldier's side), who was also probably assassinated by Cesare. These and the other rooms of the Borgia apartments have been given over to exhibits of the Vatican's collection of **Modern Religious Art,** which continues on lower levels of the building. This interminable series of works—the artistic equivalent of unwanted wedding gifts—constitutes what *Time* Magazine has called "something between a pork barrel and a junk pile." Once you've seen the Borgia rooms, you can skip the rest in good conscience and get on to the Sistine Chapel. Just retrace your steps through the Borgia apartments and follow the signs.

❻ The Sistine Chapel

In 1508, the redoubtable Pope Julius II commissioned Michelangelo to fresco the more than 10,000 square feet of the Sistine Chapel's ceiling. The task took four years, and it's said that for many years afterward Michelangelo couldn't read anything without holding it up over his head! The result, however, was the masterpiece that you see. A pair of binoculars, incidentally, helps greatly. As the crowds here can be like those at a popular ballgame, try to get in early, before the pressure builds up.

Before its consecration in 1483, the lower walls of the chapel had been decorated by a group of artists, including Botticelli, Ghirlandaio, Perugino, and Signorelli, all of them working under the direction of Pinturicchio. They had painted scenes from the life of Moses on one wall and episodes from the life of Christ on the other. Later, Julius II, dissatisfied with the simple vault decoration—it consisted of no more than stars painted on the ceiling—decided to call in Michelangelo. It was not a commission Michelangelo could refuse, which is not to say he wouldn't have liked to. At the time, Michelangelo was carving Julius II's gargantuan tomb—a project that never came near completion—and, considering himself a sculptor first and a painter second, had no desire to give the project up in order to paint a ceiling (painting was in any case a task he considered to be below him). Julius was not, however, a man to be trifled with and Michelangelo reluctantly began work. The project proceeded fitfully until Michelangelo decided that he would paint the ceiling himself and dismissed his assistants (by contrast, substantial sections of Raphael's *Stanze* were the work of assistants; probably only the principal figures are actually by Raphael himself).

Michelangelo's subject was the story of humanity before the coming of Christ. It is told principally by means of the scenes depicted in nine main panels. These show, working from the altar: the *Separation of Light from Darkness*, the *Creation of the Heavenly Bodies*, the *Separation of Land and Sea*, the *Creation of Adam*, the *Creation of Eve*, the *Fall of Man and the Expulsion from Paradise*, the *Sacrifice of Noah*, the *Flood*, and the *Drunkenness of Noah*. These focal scenes appear in an architectural framework, further embellished with Old Testament figures, prophets, sybils, and 20 *ignudi*, or nude youths. In the lunettes below, the spaces between the windows, he painted the ancestors of Christ.

The ceiling is approaching the end of an ambitious program of restoration, scheduled to end in late 1988. It is a process that has caused great controversy. The restored ceiling is brilliantly colored, a startling contrast to the dark and veiled coloring known for so many years. Was Michelangelo a master of vibrant color? Many experts believe so. Or is the "new" Sistine a travesty of Michelangelo's intentions? Opinions are divided and it seems safe to assume they will remain so for years yet. What of course remains unchanged, however, is the quite remarkable power and imagination of the ceiling. Notice the way that the later scenes—the *Creation of Adam* is a good example—are larger and more simply painted than the relatively more detailed early scenes. As the work advanced, so Michelangelo became progressively bolder in his treatment, using larger forms and simpler colors.

More than 20 years later, Michelangelo was called on again, this time by the Farnese Pope Paul III, to add to the chapel's decoration by painting the *Last Judgment* on the wall over the altar. The subject was well suited to the aging and embittered artist, who had been deeply moved by the horrendous Sack of Rome in 1527 and the confusions and disturbances of the Reformation. The painting stirred up controversy even before it was unveiled in 1541, shocking many Vatican officials, especially one Biagio di Cesena, who criticized its "indecent" nudes. Michelangelo retaliated by painting Biagio's face on the figure with donkey's ears in Hades, in the lower right-hand corner of the work. Biagio pleaded with Pope Paul to have Michelangelo erase his portrait, but the pontiff replied that he could intercede for those in Purgatory but had no power over Hell. In 1564, a later pope, Pius IV, went so far as to commission one Daniele da Volterra to paint draperies (which would disappear in the new campaign of cleaning) over the more obvious nudes. Michelangelo painted his own face on the wrinkled human skin in the hand of St. Bartholomew.

If Michelangelo's Sistine ceiling may be taken as an expression of the confidence of the High Renaissance, a period when there seemed no limit to mankind's potential or of the excitement at the rediscovery of the ancient world, the *Last Judgment*, by contrast, is a profoundly depressing and personal view of the human state. Needless to say, the subject matter has much to do with this—the end of the world is hardly a frivolous affair—but whereas other artists tackling the subject concentrated on the theme of redemption by an all-loving God, here Michelangelo pulls no punches in making clear that punishment by a vengeful God is the keynote. Many people have pointed out the quality the Italians call *terribilità* in the work, a sort of fearsome intensity, typical of late Michelangelo. Even as a young man, Michelangelo had been described as "frightening" by Pope Julius II. How much more "frightening" had he become by the time he painted this dark and swirling mass of figures?

After seeing this stunning masterpiece—and assuming you've managed to survive the astonishing overcrowding—you'll pass through the exhibition halls of the **Vatican library,** one of the finest in the world. We highly recommend that you look in at Room X, the **Room of the Aldobrandini Marriage,** for its beautiful ancient frescoes of a Roman nuptial rite, named for their subsequent owner, Cardinal Aldobrandini.

From the Alexandrine Room of the library you can visit the **New Wing** (Braccio Nuovo). You'll find more ancient Greek and Roman statues here, the most famous of which is the *Augustus of Prima Porta;* it's in the fourth niche from the end on the left. It's considered a faithful likeness of the Emperor Augustus, 40 years old at the time. Note the workmanship in the reliefs on his armor. The two gilt bronze peacocks in the gallery were in the courtyard of the original basilica of St. Peter's. Before that it's likely that they stood in the Emperor Hadrian's mausoleum, today Castel Sant'Angelo. To the ancient Romans the peacock was a symbol of immortality.

At the Quattro Cancelli you'll find the cafeteria for a well-earned break and then, if you're doing the complete itinerary, you'll enter the **Pinacoteca,** or Picture Gallery. The paintings are almost exclusively of religious subjects and are arranged in chronological order, beginning with what in the 19th century were called the "primitives" of the 11th and 12th century. **Room II** has a marvelous Giotto triptych, painted on both sides, which stood on the high altar in the old St. Peter's. In **Room III** you'll see Madonnas by the 15th-century Florentine painters, Fra Angelico and Filippo Lippi. The **Raphael Room** contains the exceptional *Transfiguration,* the *Coronation of the Virgin,* and the *Foligno Madonna* as well as the tapestries that Raphael designed to hang in the Sistine Chapel. The next room contains Leonardo's *St. Jerome* and a Bellini *Pietà.*

Outside the Pinacoteca turn left to admire the reliefs from the base of the Column of Antoninus Pius displayed in the courtyard. Now head for the **Museum of Pagan Antiquities** (Museo Gregoriano Profano), which contains classical statues and other objects found in the Papal States. Up-to-date display techniques here heighten interest in this extensive collection of Roman and Greek sculptures.

Next come the **Museum of Christian Antiquities** (Museo Pio Cristiano), where the most famous piece is the 3rd-century AD statue of the *Good Shepherd,* and the **Ethnological-Missionary Museum** (Museo Missionario-Etnologico). Both these museums are bursting with art and artifacts from exotic places all over the world. There are some precious Oriental statuettes and vases, scale models of temples, and full-scale Melanesian spirit huts. At the very end of the complete itinerary is the recently opened **Historical Museum** (Museo Storico), with a collection of state carriages—including an early version of the Popemobile, an ordinary car adapted to take an armchair in the back—uniforms, arms, and banners.

All these last collections are full of fascinating items, but, coming at the end of a long and exhausting journey through the rest of the vast complex of the Vatican, they do not always get the attention they deserve. It might be an idea to return and do the last sections—say from the cafeteria onward—on another day.

Time Out On Via Leone IV, the avenue on the left at the bottom of Viale Vaticano, there are two good neighborhood trattorias which are far less touristy than those opposite the Vatican Museum entrance. At **Trattoria Reali** (Via Leone IV 91, closed Wed.) and **Hostaria Tonino** (Via Leone IV 60, closed Sun.) you can dine on typical Roman fare, fresh from the nearby outdoor market of Trionfale. Both are moderately priced, even inexpensive for a light lunch.

Old Rome

A district of narrow streets with curious names, airy Baroque piazzas, and picturesque courtyards, Old Rome (Vecchia Roma) occupies the horn of land that pushes the Tiber westward toward the Vatican. During the Renaissance, when the popes ruled both from the Vatican and from the Lateran, the area in between became the commercial hub of the city. Artisans and shopkeepers toiled in the shadow of the huge palaces built to consolidate the power and prestige of the leading personages of the Papal Court. Writers and artists, such as the satirist Aretino and the goldsmith-sculptor Cellini, made sarcastic comments on the alternate fortunes of the courtiers and courtesans who inhabited the area. Artisans and artists still live in Old Rome, though their numbers are diminishing as the district becomes ever more desirable and expensive. It's an area to be seen on foot, both on weekdays, when the little shops are open and it hums with activity, and on Sundays, when there's much traffic and noise to distract you.

The Gesù to Piazza Navona

❶ Start from **Piazza Venezia,** and take Via del Plebiscito on the
❷ left to the huge church of the **Gesù**, mother church of the Jesuits and grandmother of all Baroque churches. It was designed in 1568 by the Florentine architect Vignola, but wasn't decorated inside for 100 years or more. It had been intended originally that the interior be left plain to the point of austerity —but, when it was finally embellished, no expense was spared. For sheer, unadulterated grandeur, no church in Rome, save perhaps St. Peter's, compares. The most striking element is the ceiling frescoes, swirling down from on high and merging with the painted stucco figures at their base. Baciccia, their painter, achieved extraordinary effects in these frescoes, especially that in the nave celebrating *The Triumph of the Holy Name of Jesus.* Here, the heretics cast out of heaven seem to be hurtling down onto the observer. Further grandeur is supplied by the altar in the **chapel of St. Ignatius** in the left-hand transept, the "arm" of the church to your left as you face the main altar. This is surely the most sumptuous Baroque altar in Rome; though you may blanch at the glittering clump of lapis lazuli that crowns it, keep in mind that its only a shell of lapis over a stucco base. The heavy bronze altar rail by architect Carlo Fontana maintains the tone of magnificence.

The architectural significance of the Gesù extends way beyond the splendid interior. The church was the first of the great Counter-Reformation churches; that is, the first important church put up after the Council of Trent (1545–63) had signaled the determination of the Roman Catholic Church to fight back against the Reformed "Protestant" heretics of northern Europe. It's role in this respect is underlined by the fact that it was built for the Jesuits, a new religious order, founded in 1540, whose purpose as "soldiers of Christ" for the new militant church was expressly to reinforce the absolute authority of the Catholic Church. Thus, the building was given a wide nave, ideal for preaching to large numbers; the choir—the area immediately before the altar—was clearly separated from the nave to emphasize the distinction between laity and clergy; there were side chapels for the worship of individual saints (which had the additional benefit of being easy to sell to rich individuals, a convenient source of always-needed ready cash); and the great length of the church focused worshipers' attentions firmly on the altar. The Gesù spawned imitations throughout Italy and the other Catholic countries of Europe, an unmistakable measure of its success.

After seeing the Gesù, head for **Piazza della Minerva,** where a new luxury hotel is about to open. In the center of the piazza there's a charming elephant, by Bernini, carrying an Egyptian obelisk on its back, and with an inscription on the base stating something to the effect that it takes a strong mind to sustain solid wisdom. This curious little monument stands in front of **❸** the church of **Santa Maria sopra Minerva,** whose name tells that it was built over *(sopra)* the ruins of a temple of Minerva. Erected in 1280 by the Dominicans on severe Italian Gothic lines, it has undergone a number of more or less happy restorations to the interior. Certainly, as the city's only Gothic church, it provides a refreshing contrast to Baroque flamboyance. Have some coins handy to illuminate the **Carafa Chapel** in the right transept, where Filippino Lippi's beautiful 15th-century frescoes are well worth the small investment. Under the main altar is the tomb of Italy's patron saint, Catherine of Siena. Left of the altar you'll find Michelangelo's statue of the *Risen Christ* and the tomb of the gentle artist, Fra Angelico; it's behind a modern sculptured bronze screen. As you return to the entrance, note the unusual and little-known Bernini monument to the Blessed Maria Raggi on the fifth pier from the door.

❹ Outside, the huge building in front of you is the **Pantheon.** Turn down Via della Minerva to reach its entrance on **Piazza della Rotonda.** This majestic circular building is the best-preserved monument of Imperial Rome. Built on the site of an earlier pantheon erected in 27 BC by Augustus's general, Agrippa, it was entirely rebuilt by the Emperor Hadrian around AD 120. It was actually designed *by* Hadrian, much as were the temples, palaces, and lakes of his enormous villa outside the city at Tivoli. Curiously, however, Hadrian retained the inscription over the entrance from the original building that gave Agrippa as the builder, in the process causing enormous confusion among historians until, in 1892, archaeologists discovered that all the bricks used in the Pantheon were stamped AD 120.

The most striking thing about the Pantheon is not its size, immense though this is (until 1960 the dome was the largest ever

Old Rome

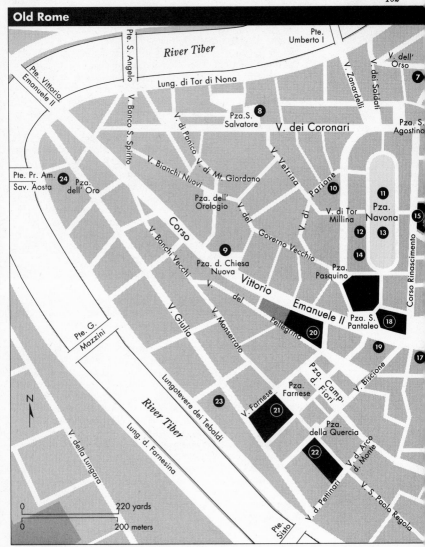

River Tiber

Pte. Umberto I

Pte. S. Angelo

Pte. Vittorio Emanuele II

Lung. di Tor di Nona

V. dell' Orso

V. Zanardelli

V. dei Soldati

Pza.S. Salvatore

V. dei Coronari

Pza. S. Agostina

V. di Panico

V. di Mt. Giordano

V. Vetrina

V. Banco S. Spirito

V. Bianchi Nuovi

V. di Parione

Pte. Pr. Am. Sav. Aosta

Pza. dell' Oro

Pza. dell' Orologio

V. del Governo Vecchio

V. di Tor Millina

Pza. Navona

Corso

V. Banchi Vecchi

Pza. d. Chiesa Nuova

V. del

Vittorio

Emanuele II

Pza. Pasquino

Pza. S. Pantaleo

Corso Rinascimento

V. Giulia

V. Monserrato

Pellegrino

Pza. Camp. d. Fiori

V. Biscione

Pte. G. Mazzini

Pza. Farnese

Pza. della Quercia

V. Farnese

V. d. Arco d' Monte

River Tiber

Lungotevere dei Tebaldi

Lung. d. Farnesina

V. della Lungara

V. d. Pettinari

V. S. Paolo Regola

N

0 — 220 yards
0 — 200 meters

Pte. Sisto

Chiesa Nuova, **9**
Fountain of the Four Rivers, **13**
Il Gesù, **2**
Monkey Tower, **7**
Palazzo della Cancelleria, **20**
Palazzo Farnese, **21**
Palazzo Madama, **15**
Palazzo Massimo, **18**

Palazzo Pamphili, **14**
Palazzo Spada, **22**
Pantheon, **4**
Piazza Navona, **11**
Piazza San Luigi dei Francesi, **5**
Piazza Venezia, **1**
Piccola Farnesina, **19**
San Giovanni dei Fiorentini, **24**
San Salvatore, **8**
Sant' Agnese in Agone, **12**

Sant' Agostino, **6**
Sant' Andrea della Valle, **17**
Sant' Ivo alla Sapienza, **16**
Santa Maria dell' Orazione e Morte, **23**
Santa Maria della Pace, **10**
Santa Maria sopra Minerva, **3**

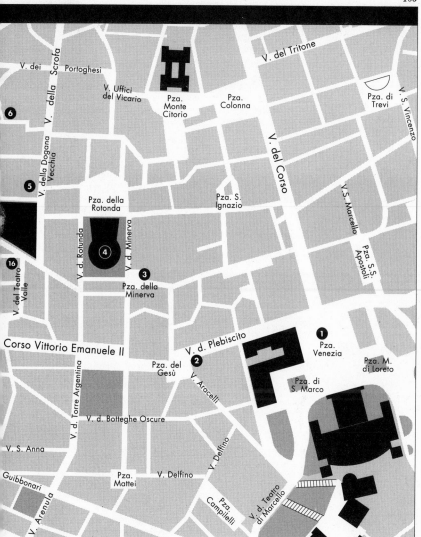

built), nor even the phenomenal technical difficulties posed by so vast a construction; rather, it is the remarkable unity of the building, "the calm and majestic sense of the classical world," as one writer put it, that it exudes. You don't have to look far to find the reason for this harmony: The diameter of the dome is exactly equal the height of the walls. It is the use of such simple mathematical balance that gives classical architecture its characteristic sense of proportion and its nobility and timeless appeal. When produced on such an enormous scale, of course, the results are simply astonishing.

Why, alone among the monuments of Imperial Rome, did the Pantheon survive intact? The answer is that it became a church, in AD 608 to be exact. Needless to say, no building, church or not, was going to escape some degree of plundering through the turbulent centuries of Rome's history after the fall of the empire. In 655, for example, the gilded bronze covering the dome was stripped. Similarly, in the early 17th century, Pope Urban VIII removed the bronze that covered the wooden beams of the portico, using the metal to produce the *baldacchino* that covers the high altar at St. Peter's. Nonetheless, the exterior of the Pantheon is substantially the same as it was when built. Inside, however, it's a different story, principally as a result of the many tombs that have been placed here over the years. The most famous is Raphael's (it's between the second and third chapels on the left as you enter). The inscription reads "Here lies Raphael; while he lived the great mother of all things [Nature] feared to be outdone; and when he died she, too, feared to die." Two of Italy's 19th-century kings are buried here, too: Vittorio Emanuele II and Umberto I. The tomb of the former was partly made from bronze taken from the Pantheon by Urban VIII, cast as cannons by him, and then symbolically remelted and returned here. The great opening at the apex of the dome is not a later addition; nor is it evidence that even Hadrian couldn't complete the dome. It was always here, and was intended as a symbol of the "all-seeing eye of heaven." *Piazza della Rotonda. Admission free. Open Tues.– Sat. 9–2, Sun. 9–1.*

Time Out The café scene in the square in front of the Pantheon rivals that of Piazza Navona. This area is ice-cream heaven, with some of Rome's best *gelaterie* within a few steps of each other. Romans consider **Giolitti** superlative; the scene at the counter often looks like the storming of the Bastille! Remember to pay the cashier first, and hand the stub to the counterperson when you order your cone. Giolitti has a good snack counter, also. *Via Uffizi del Vicario 40. Closed Mon.*

---

❺ Take Via della Dogana Vecchia to **Piazza San Luigi dei Francesi**, which takes its name from the French colony's church in Rome (Luigi is the Italian for Louis). The church is famous for its three magnificent Caravaggios, painted at the beginning of the 17th century, in the **Chapel of St. Matthew** (the last on the left as you face the altar). The coin machine will light up these canvases, and Caravaggio's mastery of light effects takes it from there. They are, from the left, *The Calling of St. Matthew, Matthew and the Angel,* and *Matthew's Martyrdom.* When painted, they caused considerable consternation to the clergy of San Luigi, who thought the artist's dramatically realistic approach was scandalously disrespectful. A first version of the altarpiece was rejected; the priests were not particularly happy with the other two either. Time has fully vindicated Caravaggio's patron, Cardinal Francesco del Monte, who commissioned these works and stoutly defended them. They're recognized to be among the artist's greatest paintings. *Open Fri.–Wed. 7:30–12:30 and 3:30–7, Thurs. 7:30–12:30.*

❻ Turn left outside San Luigi and take the second street on the left into little Piazza di Sant'Agostino, dominated by the 15th-century facade of **Sant'Agostino.** Entering the richly marbled church, you can see immediately on your left Jacopo Sansovino's marble *Madonna* (1521), one of the most popular statues in Rome, which is almost overwhelmed by the candles and votive offerings heaped up around it. On the first altar on the left is Caravaggio's somber but moving altarpiece the *Madonna of Loreto* (1605). In the nave, Andrea Sansovino's marble *Holy Family* has now been returned to its original site, below the figure of *Isaiah* that Raphael, at his most Michelangelesque, frescoed on one of the piers (1512).

❼ Turn left outside Sant'Agostino and, retracing your steps, saunter along Via della Scrofa (the Street of the Sow), which cuts through this interesting neighborhood of artisan workshops and unusual little shops and eating places. Make a few detours in and out of the side streets here: They're typical of Old Rome. Continuing on, turn left into **Via dei Portoghesi** and pause a moment for a look up at the building that divides the street in two. On top of it is the **"Monkey Tower,"** pride of neighborhood lore. In the building, so the story goes, a pet monkey ran amok one day, seizing a baby and carrying it to the top of the tower. Here the crazed animal seemed about to dash the child to the street below. A crowd of neighbors and bystanders invoked the Madonna's intercession and the monkey carefully descended with the baby, carrying it to safety. In gratitude, the father placed a statue of the Madonna on the tower, along with a vigil light, both of them still neighborhood landmarks. (One version of the story relates that the monkey was sold to pay for the statue.) Via dell'Orso, to the right of the tower, is a street of artisans, cabinetmakers, and antique-restorers. It ends at Vicolo dei Soldati, where the famous **Hostaria dell'Orso** has been serving guests since the 15th century.

❽ Follow Vicolo dei Soldati into Piazza Zanardelli. There's another detour here down the street of the Rosary-Makers, Via dei Coronari, which is now lined with antique shops. At Piazza San Salvatore in Lauro, look for a small door to the left of the church. It opens into a charming little 15th-century cloister, one of Rome's hidden delights. The delicate church of **San Salvatore** seems strangely reminiscent of a Venetian church, both inside and out.

Continue down Via dei Coronari—which, if you're keen on antiques, is a mecca—and Vicolo del Curato to Via del Banco di Santo Spirito. The little piazza, standing at the end of Ponte Sant'Angelo, was the scene in 1599 of the execution of Beatrice Cenci and others of her family involved in the tragic affair that later inspired Shelley's play. Turn left into Via del Banco di Santo Spirito. A marble inscription on the left pillar of Arco dei Banchi, which led to Renaissance financier Agostino Chigi's counting-rooms, testifies that this street was often flooded by the Tiber. The fine old palaces here include the one on the corner of Via dei Banchi Nuovi, in which Rome's oldest bank, the Banco di Santo Spirito (Bank of the Holy Spirit), has operated since the early 1600s.

Go down Via dei Banchi Nuovi, a dark little street that leads into Piazza dell'Orologio. This was named after Borromini's frivolous clock tower on the **Oratory of the Filippini**, in turn named not for the islands but for Rome's favorite saint, Philip Neri, founder in 1551 of the Congregation of the Oratorians. Like the Jesuits, the Oratorians—or Filippini, as they were known—were one of the new religious orders established in the mid-16th century as part of the Counter-Reformation, the great regrouping of the Catholic Church in the face of the split of the Protestants of northern Europe from Rome. But where the Jesuits were stern and uncompromising in their determination to spread abroad the message of the newly aggressive church, the Oratorians, under the benign leadership of Philip Neri, acted under a code of humility and good works. Neri, a man of rare charm and wit, insisted that the members of the order—most of them young noblemen whom he had recruited personally—not only renounce their worldly goods and declare their good intentions by acts such as parading the streets dressed in rags, but work as common laborers in the building of Neri's great church here, **Santa Maria in Vallicella,** or the **Chiesa Nuova,** the new church, as it's generally known. The church was built toward the end of the 16th century and boasts a sturdy Baroque interior, all white and gold, with ceiling frescoes by Pietro da Cortona and three magnificent altarpieces by Rubens. An enormous statue of Neri is in the sacristy. Next to the church is the **Oratory** itself, headquarters of the order and built by Borromini between 1637 and 1662. Its gently curving facade is typical of Borromini's near obsession with introducing movement into his buildings.

Turn left, skirting the side of the Chiesa Nuova, go left again on Via del Governo Vecchio, and immediately right to Palazzo di Monte Giordano, known as **Palazzo Taverna.** Once part of the Orsini family's Rome stronghold, it is now divided into highly sought-after apartments. Look past the doorway to the pretty fountain in the courtyard, one of those picturesque corners that reward your search for Old Rome's secrets.

Return to Via del Governo Vecchio (street of the Old Government) and turn left. The street takes its name from the 15th-century **Palazzo Nardini,** at #39, once seat of Rome's papal governors and later a law court. There are lots of good pizzerias and restaurants in this area.

Turn left onto Via di Parione and follow it into Piazza della Pace, where a semi-circular portico stands in front of the 15th-century church of **Santa Maria della Pace.** Pietro da Cortona, who was commissioned in 1656 to restore the church and design its facade, demolished a few buildings here and there to create the spacious approach to the church. Then he added arches to give architectural unity to the piazza. The church is usually closed, but if it happens to be open when you pass by stop in to see Raphael's fresco of the Sybils above the first altar on your right, and the fine decorations of the Cesi Chapel, designed in the mid-16th century by Sangallo, second on the right.

Piazza Navona to Via Giulia

From here, Via Tor Millina leads into **Piazza Navona,** the beautiful Baroque piazza that stands over the ruins of Domitian's stadium. It still has the carefree air of the days when it was the scene of Roman circus games, medieval jousts, and 17th-century carnivals. Even now it's the site of a lively Epiphany fair in January and many other entertainments throughout the year.

Piazza Navona still looks much as it did during the 17th and 18th centuries, after the Pamphili Pope Innocent X decided to make it a monument to the Pamphili family that would rival the Barberinis' palace at the Quattro Fontane. The low houses, some of them with enviable terrace gardens, overlook Borrominis' graceful Baroque facade of **Sant' Agnese in Agone** (from "Agona," the source of the word "Navona" and a corruption of "agonalis," the Roman name of Domitian's circus). The marvelous **Fountain of the Four Rivers,** the piazza's most famous work of art planted right in the center, was created for Pope Innocent X by Bernini in 1651, before work on the church's facade was begun. The obelisk rising out of the fountain, a Roman copy, had stood in the Circus of Maxentius on Via Appia Antica. Bernini's powerful figures of the four rivers represent the four corners of the world: the Nile, with its face covered in allusion to its unknown source; the Ganges; the Danube; and the Plate, with its hand raised. The piazza dozes in the morning, when small groups of pensioners sun themselves on stone benches and children pedal tricycles around the big fountain. In the late afternoon, the sidewalk cafés fill up for the aperitif hour. In the evening, especially in good weather, Piazza Navona comes to life with a colorful throng of vendors, street artists, tourists, and Romans out for their evening *passeggiata* (promenade). Sometimes in the evening you can get a tantalizing glimpse of Pietro da Cortona's magnificent frescoes through the great illuminated windows of **Palazza Pamphili,** next to Sant'Agnese. The palace is now the Brazilian Embassy.

Time Out The sidewalk tables of the **Tre Scalini** café offer a grandstand view of the piazza and the action. This is the place that invented the *tartufo,* a luscious chocolate ice cream specialty. The annex restaurant has the same view. *Piazza Navona 30. Closed Wed.*

At the end of the piazza, little Via della Cuccagna (street of the Grease Pole, a favorite game in Piazza Navona) leads to **Palazzo Braschi** on the right. This is the Rome city museum, although it's now undergoing renovations and is closed for an indefinite period.

If you leave Piazza Navona at the center, through Corsia Agonale, you'll see the handsome 17th-century **Palazzo Madama** in front of you on Corso Rinascimento. It's a onetime Medici palace, now seat of the Italian Senate. To the right along Corso Rinascimento, the austere building at #40 once housed Rome's university. If you can, look in at the beautiful courtyard and the entrance to Borromini's Baroque church of **Sant'Ivo alla Sapienza.** Here is what must surely be one of the most delightful domes in all Rome—a golden spiral said to have been inspired by a bee's sting. Needless to say, Borromini built the church on commission from the Barberini Pope Urban VIII. It is now guarded by an armed soldier, since it is part of Senate offices. However, the church is open once a week for mass on Sunday at 10 AM. If you're in the vicinity, it's worth a look, especially if you share a taste for Borromini's complex mathematical architectural idiosyncrasies.

On **Corso Vittorio Emanuele II,** the huge 17th-century church of **Sant'Andrea della Valle** looms over its piazza and fountain. Its dome, by Maderno, is the highest in Rome after St. Peter's. Imposing though its dimensions are, the church is remarkably balanced in design. Inside, where Puccini set the first act of *Tosca*, note the early-17th-century frescoes in the choir vault by Domenichino and those by Lanfranco in the dome, one of the earliest ceilings in full Baroque style. Richly marbled and decorated chapels flank the nave. The last two piers of the nave at the transept hold the Renaissance tombs of the two Piccolimini popes, which were moved here from St. Peter's.

(18) Almost opposite Sant'Andrea della Valle is **Palazzo Massimo alle Colonne,** which the architect Baldassare Peruzzi adapted in the 1530s to take the place of an earlier palace belonging to the Massimo family. If you're here on March 16, you'll be able to go upstairs in the palace, getting a look at the courtyard and loggias on your way to the family chapel. On this day there are commemorations of a prodigious miracle performed here in 1583 by Philip Neri, who is said to have recalled a young member of the family, one Paolo Massimo, from the dead.

The smallish Renaissance building on the left-hand side of the **(19)** Corso Vittorio Emanuele is known as the **Piccola Farnesina.** Built for a French prelate, as the lilies—symbols of France—in the frieze testify, it houses the small but select **Baracco Museum,** and a collection of ancient sculpture. Both will probably remain closed for renovations through 1989. Go on to the next corner and turn left into Piazza della Cancelleria. On the right is **(20)** the massive and beautiful **Palazzo della Cancelleria,** built for a nephew of the Riario Pope Sixtus IV toward the end of the 15th century, and reputedly paid for by the winnings of a single night's gambling by another nephew. The Riario family symbol of the rose appears on the windows of the main floor and in the pillars and pavement of the courtyard. The palace houses the offices of the Papal Chancery and is part of the Vatican's extraterritorial possessions. It is not open to the public.

Built into a corner of the palace, the church of **San Lorenzo in Damaso** is one of the oldest churches of Rome. Founded in the 4th century, it was then rebuilt, probably by Bramante, during the construction of the Cancelleria at the beginning of the 16th century.

A few steps away is the bustle and color of **Campo dei Fiori's** morning market, one of Rome's most appealing sights. Brooding over the piazza is a hooded statue of the philosopher Giordano Bruno, who was burned at the stake here in 1600 for heresy. His was the first of the executions that drew Roman crowds to Campo dei Fiori in the 17th century, much as similar executions had drawn the ancient Romans to the Colosseum and the circuses.

Vicolo del Gallo leads to Piazza Farnese, site of the magnificent **(21)** **Palazzo Farnese,** built for Alessandro Farnese by Sangallo, Michelangelo, and Giacomo della Porta in the mid-16th century. Of all of Rome's Renaissance palaces, this is the most beautiful. Unfortunately, you can't visit it as it's now the French Embassy. You can, on the other hand, if you write a month or so in advance, visit the **Galleria,** the palace's most celebrated interior. (Visits take place only on Wednesday afternoons; write to The Ambassador, French Embassy, Piazza Farnese 64, 00186 Rome.) The reason for seeing the room—and for putting up with the considerable inconvenience of arranging the visit—is the magnificent ceiling fresco, painted between 1597 and 1604 by Annibale Caracci. The ceiling is usually considered a mark of the end of the sterile period that overtook Italian painting toward the end of the 16th century—sterile only when measured against what came before and afterward—and the beginning of the Baroque. The subject of the fresco is the loves of the gods, a supremely pagan theme that Caracci embraced with gusto. The ceiling is a riot of voluptuous reveling, painted in colors that still glow vividly. It's said that Caracci, having completed his gigantic task, was so dismayed at the miserly fee he received—the Farnese family was extravagantly rich even by the standards of 15th- and 16th-century Rome's extravagantly rich—that he took to drink and died shortly thereafter. Those who sympathize with the poor man's fate will be further dismayed to learn that the French government pays one lira every 99 years as rent for their sumptuous embassy.

Left of Palazzo Farnese, take Vicolo dei Venti into tiny Piazza **㉒** della Quercia to see **Palazzo Spada,** covered with stuccoes and statues especially attractive in the courtyard. Whether you share a taste for the excesses of the Baroque or not, be sure to see the remarkable little gallery in the garden. It's a delightful example of the sort of architectural games rich Romans of the 17th century found irresistible. Standing at the end of the gallery you appear to be looking down an imposing colonnaded loggia stretching to a distant statue. In fact, the loggia is all of about 30 feet long and the statue is tiny, no more than about two feet high. What's happening, of course, is that the gallery gets progressively narrower and the columns progressively smaller as they near the statue, hence the illusion of depth. Step into the far end and you practically have to bend double. It was long thought that Borromini was responsible for this ruse; in fact it's now known that it was designed by an Augustinian priest, Giovanni Maria da Bitonto. The picture gallery in the palace has some outstanding works. Among them are Breughel's *Landscape with Windmills,* Titian's *Musician,* and Andrea del Sarto's *Visitation. Piazzo Capo di Ferro 13, tel. 06/6561158. Admission: 2,000 lire. Open Mon. and Tues. 9–2, Wed.–Sat. 9–2 and 3–7, Sun. 9–1.*

Outside Palazzo Spada, turn left, left again, and then right along Via Giulia, named after Pope Julius II. He had it built early in the 16th century as part of a scheme to open up a grandiose approach to St. Peter's. Though the plan was never completed, the street became an important thoroughfare in Renaissance Rome, lined with elegant churches and palaces. Until the 1950s, Via Giulia was run-down and tacky, but in recent decades it has attracted an elite of antique dealers and international residents who have turned its decrepit rooftops into fabulous penthouses overlooking the Tiber. As you walk **㉓** along, you'll recognize the church of **Santa Maria dell'Orazione e Morte** by the stone skulls on its door. These are a symbol of a confraternity that was charged with burying the bodies of the unknown dead found in the city streets. There are several other curious old churches along this route, but most of them are closed except on special occasions. On the left you'll see a forbidding brick building that housed the **Carceri Nuove,** Rome's prison for more than two centuries. Now it contains justice department offices.

At the end of Via Giulia is the pretty Piazza dell'Oro, which was the heart of the Florentine colony in Old Rome and center for **㉔** the goldsmiths. Here rises the stately church of **San Giovanni**

dei Fiorentini, in which Borromini executed a splendid altar for the Falconieri family chapel in the choir.

Toward the Spanish Steps and the Trevi Fountain

This tour covers one of the most varied and historic areas of Rome. It begins at Piazza Venezia, the square in front of the frothy marble confection that is the monument to Vittorio Emanuele, and heads up the Corso, one of the busiest shopping streets in the city. Major attractions include a series of imposing Renaissance and Baroque palaces—among them Palazzo Borghese, the luxurious home of one of 17th-century Rome's most famous families—and a number of striking churches. Those with a taste for the sumptuous theatricality of Roman ecclesiastical architecture, and in particular for heroic illusionistic ceiling painting, will find this a rewarding area. But for most, the highlights of this area are the Spanish Steps, 18th-century Rome's most famous example of city planning, and the Trevi Fountain, the most ornate and thrilling of the city's great fountains.

Piazza Venezia and the Corso

No visitor to Rome will fail to see the huge white mass of the **Vittorio Emanuele Monument** at some point. It's an inescapable and handy landmark. Some have likened it to a huge wedding cake; others to an immense Victorian typewriter in white marble. However modern eyes may look at it, it was a splendid focus of civic pride to turn-of-the-century Romans. Built to honor the reunification of Italy and the nation's first king, Vittorio Emanuele II, it also shelters the tomb of Italy's **Unknown Soldier,** the **Institute of the History of the Risorgimento**—the reunification of Italy in the 19th century—and the more prosaic water tanks that supply its fountains. Though it has been closed to the public for many years, a movement is afoot to open it again. The views from the top of its gleaming white staircases are among Rome's best.

In order to create this elaborate marble monster and the vast piazza in which it stands, its architects blithely destroyed many ancient remains and altered the slope of the Capitoline Hill which abuts it. Fragments on the left of the monument mark the site of a 1st-century AD tomb that was known to have stood at the beginning of Via Flaminia, the road that leads east out of Rome across Italy to Fano on the Adriatic Sea. The initial tract of Via Flaminia, from Piazza Venezia to Piazza del Popolo, is now known as the **Corso,** after the horse races *(corse)* run here during the wild Roman carnivals of the 17th and 18th centuries. Look at the enclosed wooden veranda on the palace on the corner of Via del Plebiscito and the Corso. For the many years that she lived in Rome, Napoleon's mother had a fine view from here of the goings-on below.

To the left of the monument on the piazza looms Palazzo Venezia, built in the 15th century for the Venetian Cardinal Pietro Barbo, who became Pope Paul II. To the left of the palace is the ancient church of **San Marco,** used by Paul II for official ceremonies. Tradition relates that St. Mark wrote his gospel in Rome, and the church is dedicated to the evangelist, as well as

Piazza Venezia to the Spanish Steps

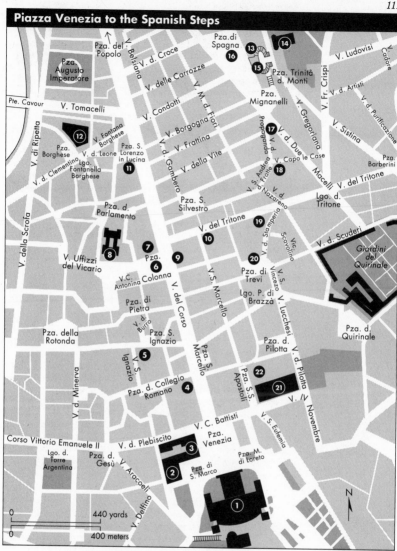

Barcaccia Fountain, **16**

Basilica of Santi
Apostoli, **22**

Column of Marcus
Aurelius, **6**

Galleria, **9**

Keats and Shelley
Memorial House, **15**

Montecitorio, **8**

Palazzo Borghese, **12**

Palazzo Chigi, **7**

Palazzo Colonna, **21**

Palazzo Doria
Pamphili, **4**

Palazzo Poli, **19**

Palazzo Propaganda
Fide, **17**

Palazzo Venezia, **3**

San Lorenzo, **11**

San Marco, **2**

Sant'Andrea delle
Fratte, **18**

Sant'Ignazio, **5**

Santa Maria in Via, **10**

Spanish Steps, **13**

Trevi Fountain, **20**

Trinità dei Monti, **14**

Vittorio Emanuele
Monument, **1**

to the 4th-century Pope Mark, whose relics are under the main
altar. One of many Roman churches built as a basilica, the original edifice was destroyed by fire and replaced in the 6th
century. The third church, the one you see today, was built in
the 9th century by Pope Gregory IV, as the dedication in the
Byzantine apse mosaics testifies. The church is a perfect example of Rome's layering of history, of periods and styles built up
one upon another, from the early-Christian architectural
motifs to the Romanesque bell tower; from the Byzantine mosaics to the windows in the nave, obvious transitions from
convoluted Gothic to spacious early Renaissance. Then there's
the full flowering of Renaissance style in the magnificent gilt
ceiling and the ample portico that Pope Paul II built to provide
shelter for himself and his retinue during outdoor rites in bad
weather. On the right wall of the portico is the tomb of
Vannozza Cattanei. She was the mistress of the Borgia pope,
Alexander VI; she bore him three children, including Lucrezia
and Cesare. Originally located in the church of Santa Maria del
Popolo, the tomb was moved here under mysterious circumstances. No one has ever been able to discover why, when, or by
whom.

A massive female bust in the corner of the piazza is known to
the Romans as Madama Lucrezia; it was one of the "talking
statues" on which anonymous poets hung verses pungent with
political satire. If the courtyard under the arch beside San
Marco is open, take a peek at its 17th-century fountain and
statue of a Venetian doge.

❸ The main entrance to **Palazzo Venezia** is on Piazza Venezia, under the balcony from which Mussolini harangued crowds
massed in the square. The palace is a mixture of Renaissance
grace and heavy medieval lines, and offers a unique chance to
see what a Renaissance palace really looked like inside. It
houses a fine collection of paintings, sculptures, and objets
d'art in handsome salons, some of which Mussolini used as his
offices. (A light burned permanently in one window during
Mussolini's reign, a typically bombastic attempt by the Italian
dictator to prove he never slept.) *Via del Plebiscito 118, tel. 06/
6798865. Admission: 4,000 lire. Open Mon.–Sat. 9–2, Sun.
9–1.*

As you start your walk up the Corso, on your left you'll see the
❹ graceful 18th-century facade of **Palazzo Doria Pamphili.** The
foundations of this immense complex of buildings probably date
back to classical times. But the present building dates from the
15th century, with the exception of the facade. It passed
through several hands before it became the property of the famous seafaring Doria family of Genoa, who had married into
the Roman Pamphili clan. As in most of Rome's older patrician
residences, the family still lives in part of the palace but rents
out much of its 1,000 rooms, five courtyards, and four monumental staircases to various public and private enterprises to
help pay the taxes. You shouldn't miss seeing the incredibly
rich family art collection, open to the public a few mornings a
week. Pride of place is given to the famous Velázquez portrait
and to the Bernini bust of the Pamphili pope, Innocent X. Of
the three Caravaggios in the collection, the *Rest on the Flight
to Egypt* is the finest. You'll also find a Titian and some splendid
17th-century landscapes by Claude Lorrain and Gaspar
Dughet. It was landscapes like these, evoking a lost classical
idyll, with glimpses of temples, lakes, and forests, that lead

more or less directly to the development of the classical 18th-century English park—those noble, rolling acres that the English aristocracy, dreaming of creating their own pastoral idylls, built to surround their stately Palladian mansions. Don't miss the guided tour of the state apartments, which include a Baroque chapel, a ballroom, and three authentically furnished 18th-century salons. In the private apartments are an *Annunciation* by Filippo Lippi, a family portrait by Lotto, and a stately portrait of Andrea Doria by Sebastiano del Piombo. But it's the glimpse of an aristocratic lifestyle that makes this tour special. *Piazza del Collegio Romano 1/a, tel. 06/6794365. Admission to picture gallery: 2,000 lire, to private apartments: 2,000 lire. Open Tues., Fri., Sat., and Sun. 10–1. Guided visits to the state apartments offered at regular intervals during opening hours.*

From Piazza del Collegio Romano, where Rome's most famous Jesuit school was conducted for three centuries until 1870, take Via di Sant'Ignazio to the enchanting piazza and late-17th-century church of **Sant'Ignazio.** To get the full effect of the marvelous illusionistic ceiling by Andrea del Pozzo, stand on the small disk set into the floor of the nave. The heavenly vision above you, seemingly extending upward almost indefinitely, represents the *Glory of St. Ignatius Loyola* and is part of del Pozzo's cycle of works in this church exalting the early history of the Jesuit Order, whose founder was the mystic Ignatius Loyola. The artist repeated this illusionist technique, so popular in the late 17th century, in the false dome, which is actually a flat canvas. The overall effect of the frescoes is dazzling (be sure to have coins handy for the machine that switches on the lights) and was fully intended to rival that produced by Baciccio in the nearby church of the Gesù. As you emerge from the church you'll have an even better view of Raguzzini's 18th-century Rococo piazza, where the buildings are arranged almost as in a stage set. But then, of course, theatricality was a key element of almost all the best Baroque and Rococo art.

Follow Via del Burro to Piazza di Pietra, where the Rome **Stock Exchange** occupies the site of an ancient temple, whose columns were incorporated into the side of the building. From here it's just a few steps down Via dei Bergamaschi to Piazza Colonna, named for the famous **Column of Marcus Aurelius.** The 2nd-century AD column, for a time mistakenly believed to celebrate Antoninus Pius, is composed of 28 blocks of marble covered with a series of reliefs that spiral up to a statue of St. Paul, who dispossessed the effigy of Marcus Aurelius in the 16th century.

Time Out **Alfio,** on the corner of Via dei Bergamaschi, is popular with Romans for a stand-up lunch of sandwiches at the counter or a more relaxing meal upstairs in the dining room. *Via della Colonna Antonina 33. Closed Sun.*

As you enter Piazza Colonna from Via dei Bergamaschi, the 16th- to 17th-century **Palazzo Chigi,** where the Italian government has its cabinet offices, stands in front of you. On the left of Palazzo Chigi is **Montecitorio,** where the Chamber of Deputies meets. Montecitorio has its own large piazza, adorned with a 6th-century BC Egyptian obelisk that once served as a sundial; it was placed here by the Emperor Augustus in the 1st century AD. The obelisk was later moved and was restored in the 18th century and returned to the site it had occupied in antiquity.

The facade of Montecitorio was designed by Bernini, though the huge palace extends through to another monumental facade, on Piazza del Parlamento, two blocks farther down the Corso.

❾ Romans like to meet at the large **Galleria** mall in front of Piazza Colonna. It is similar to those in Milan and Naples and shelters shops, a famous bar, and a pastry shop—Bernardo's—and a bookstore where you can find all kinds of guides, maps, and English-language books. Stroll to the left through the gallery **❿** to the exit in front of the small 16th-century church of **Santa Maria in Via** on the corner of Via del Tritone. This is definitely something of a collector's item: It is the only church in Rome with a spa inside it. In a small room on the right, an attendant at a zinc-topped counter dispenses curative water from a spring that bubbles up on this site, having once brought up with it, it's claimed, the icon of the Madonna that's now over the altar. Across Via del Tritone is Piazza San Silvestro, hub of public transportation in Rome and location of the main post office and international telephone bureau.

From Piazza Colonna down to Piazza del Popolo the Corso leads past a concentration of shops and boutiques. Opposite the end of the Via Frattina, turn left off the Corso into Piazza San Lo-
⓫ renzo in Lucina. The ancient church of **San Lorenzo** here was probably founded on the site of an early-Christian meeting place under the aegis of a Roman matron named Lucina. Behind its 12th-century portico and campanile (the bell tower), the interior is mostly disappointing. There's one exception, however: **Fonseca Chapel,** the fourth on the right, designed by Bernini. His bust of Fonseca, Innocent X's physician, represents the donor in moving contemplation. On the chapel's right wall, a 17th-century painting shows Elisha pouring salt into the waters of Jericho in order to purify them; it's a clear reference to Fonseca's concern with purifying the malarial waters of Rome and its *campagna*, the area surrounding the city. The 17th-century *Crucifixion* over the main altar is by Guido Reni. The church guards relics of the grill on which the early Christian martyr St. Lawrence was roasted alive. Cynics treasure his reported words to his torturers, "Turn me over, I'm done on this side."

From San Lorenzo take Via del Leone into Piazza Borghese to take a look at another of the princely palaces of Rome's aristo-
⓬ cratic families. **Palazzo Borghese** is a huge, rambling, Renaissance building, begun in 1590 for a Spanish cardinal by architect Martino Longhi who designed the sturdy facade facing Largo Fontanella Borghese. In 1605 Cardinal Borghese celebrated his election as Pope Paul V by purchasing the palace; it later passed to his nephew, Cardinal Scipione Borghese, who assembled his magnificent art collection here. Still used by the Borghese family, though part of it is rented out, the palace is closed to the public. Nevertheless you can usually enter the main portal to take a look at the irregularly shaped courtyard with its porticoes, loggias, and Rococo fountains. From the inner courtyard, or the entrance on Via Ripetta, you can sometimes enter an auction gallery that occupies rented quarters in the palace. If the gallery is open, go in to take a look at the frescoed salons. Imagine how the palace looked when beautiful and capricious Pauline Borghese, Napoleon's favorite sister, lived here as bride of Prince Camillo Borghese, flaunting her infidelities in the face of Rome's gossips and setting

tongues wagging with her nonchalance at posing nude for Canova's famous statue of her. At Piazza della Fontanella Borghese there's a little market selling old books and prints; you may even find some attractive souvenirs. You're expected to bargain, of course.

The Spanish Steps and Trevi Fountain

From Largo Goldoni on Via del Corso you start up Via Condotti **13** and get a head-on view of the **Spanish Steps** and the church of **14** **Trinità dei Monti.** Via Condotti is Rome's most elegant and expensive shopping street, bar none. You can carom from Bulgari to Gucci to Valentino to Ferragamo with no effort at all.

Time Out You may prefer to limit your shopping here to the window variety, but there's one thing on Via Condotti that everybody can afford, and that's a coffee at the bar at the **Antico Caffè Greco,** a 200-year-old institution, the haunt of artists and literati. With its tiny, marble-topped tables and velour settees, it's a nostalgic old place. Goethe, Byron, and Liszt were habitués; Buffalo Bill stopped in when his road show hit Rome. It's still very much a haven for writers and artists, and for ladies carrying Gucci shopping bags. *Via Condotti 86. Closed Sun.*

Piazza di Spagna and the famous Spanish Steps take their name from the Spanish Embassy to the Holy See—the Vatican—which has occupied the historic palace facing the American Express office since the 17th century. However, the idea for a monumental staircase connecting the piazza with the French church of Trinità dei Monti at the top of the hill originated with the French minister, Mazarin. Its construction in 1723 was partially financed by French funds. Perfect for sitting and lounging, and for photographing from all angles, the steps have always attracted a picturesque crowd, from 19th-century artists' models in folk costumes to present-day visitors. On weekend and holiday afternoons the square, along with Via del Corso and neighboring streets, is packed with teenagers out for a mass stroll. The Spanish Steps are glorious in mid-April and early May, when they're blanketed with huge azaleas in bloom. The area around the steps was the colorful bohemian quarter of 18th- and 19th-century Rome, especially favored by the English. Many Italian and foreign artists still live here or have studios nearby, particularly on Via Margutta.

Time Out On the left at the foot of the steps, **Babington's Tea Room** has catered to the refined cravings of Anglo-Saxon travelers since its establishment by two genteel English ladies in 1896.

15 On the right of Babington's, at #26, is the **Keats and Shelley Memorial House,** in which the English Romantic poet Keats lived. You can visit his rooms, which have been preserved as they were when he died here in 1821. They contain a rather quaint collection of memorabilia of English literary figures of the period—Byron, Shelley, Severn, and Leigh Hunt as well as Keats—and an exhaustive library of works on the Romantics. *Piazza di Spagna 26, tel. 06/6784235. Admission: 3,000 lire. Open Apr.–Sept., Mon.–Fri. 9–1 and 3:30–6:30; Oct.–Mar., Mon.–Fri. 9–1 and 2:30–5:30.*

16 At the center of the piazza is the curious **Barcaccia Fountain,** representing a half-sunken boat. The water spills out of the fountain rather than cascading dramatically as in most other Roman fountains, the result of the area's low water pressure. It was thanks to the Barberini Pope Urban VIII, who commissioned the fountain, that there was any water at all in this area, which was becoming increasingly built-up during the 17th century. He restored one of the ancient Roman aqueducts that once fed water here. The bees and suns on the boat constitute the Barberini trademark. Some insist that Bernini intended the fountain to be a reminder that this part of town was often flooded by the Tiber; others that it represents the Ship of the Church; and still others that it marks the presumed site of the Emperor Domitian's water stadium where sea battles were re-enacted in the glory days of the Roman Empire. On August dog days, when there's no one around, tourists use it as a refreshing footbath.

Time Out   **La Rampa,** in a corner of Piazza Mignanelli behind the American Express office, is an attractively picturesque place for lunch, with an extensive menu of moderately priced dishes. *Piazza Mignanelli 18. Closed Sun.*

In the narrow part of the piazza, an ancient column supports a statue dedicated to the Immaculate Conception. On December 8, a crack unit of the Rome Fire Department sends one of its best men up a ladder to replace the garland crowning the Madonna, and the pope usually stops by in the afternoon to pay his **⑰** respects. At the far end of this part of the piazza stands **Palazzo di Propaganda Fide,** brain center of the far-flung missionary activities of the Jesuits. Bernini created the simpler facade on the piazza in 1644, while his arch-rival Borromini designed the more elaborate one on Via di Propaganda not long before his death in 1667.

⑱ At the end of Via di Propaganda is the church of **Sant'Andrea delle Fratte,** the interior of which is entirely decorated with painted marbling, and where the two angels that Bernini himself carved for the Ponte Sant'Angelo stand on either side of the choir. Step through the side door into one of Rome's hidden gardens, where orange trees bloom in the cloister. Borromini's contributions—the dome and a curious bell tower—are best seen from Via Capo le Case, across Via Due Macelli.

From Via Sant'Andrea delle Fratte, turn left onto Via del Nazareno and cross busy Via del Tritone to Via della Stamperia. On your right is the 16th-century **Palazzo Poli,** which is **⑲** being renovated to house a National Graphics Institute. Some of its salons have been used for years by the Calcografia di Stato, which preserves an invaluable collection of antique presses and copper engraving plates, most notably by the 18th-century Roman artist, Piranesi.

Across the street, Palazzo Carpegna is the home of the **Galleria di San Luca,** a private academy of the arts. Its gallery is open to the public and contains some fine Renaissance paintings. *Piazza di San Luca 77, tel. 06/6789243. Admission: 2,000 lire. Open Mon., Wed., Fri., and last Sun. of month, 10–1.*

⑳ By now you can probably hear the rushing waters of the **Trevi Fountain,** just around the corner behind Palazzo Poli. This aquatic marvel, all the more effective for its cramped setting in the tiny piazza, is one of the city's most exciting sights. One wall of Palazzo Poli is alive with rushing waters and marble sea creatures, commanded by an imperious Oceanus. The work of

Nicola Salvi—though it's thought that Bernini may have been responsible for parts of the design—it was completed in 1762 and is a perfect example of the Roroco taste for dramatic theatrical effects. The water comes from the Acqua Vergine aqueduct, built by the ancient Romans, and is so called because of the legend that it was a young girl, a *vergine*, who showed its source to thirsty Roman soldiers. The story is pictured in the relief on the right of the figure of Oceanus.

Time Out **Enzo** is a small, simple trattoria where you can fill up inexpensively on hearty Roman fare. *Vicolo dello Scavolino. Closed Sun.*

From the Trevi Fountain, Via Lucchesi leads you to Piazza della Pilotta and picturesque Via della Pilotta, where bridges
㉑ overhead connect **Palazzo Colonna** with the gardens of **Villa Colonna** on the Quirinal Hill. The immense Palazzo Colonna on your right is home to one of Rome's oldest and most patrician families, whose picture gallery is open to the public one day a week. In it you'll find works by Poussin, Tintoretto, and Veronese, and a number of portraits of illustrious members of the family such as Vittoria Colonna, Michelangelo's muse and long-time friend, and Marcantonio Colonna, who had a hand in the great naval victory at Lepanto in 1577. *Via della Pilotta 17, tel. 06/6794362. Admission: 3,500 lire. Open Sat. 9–1.*

㉒ The **Basilica of Santi Apostoli,** around the corner on the piazza of the same name, is a mixture of architectural styles, the result of successive restorations of an ancient church. One of its best features is the lovely double portico on the facade, dating from the 15th century. The piazza often serves as a gathering place for heated political rallies and demonstrations.

Time Out A few steps away is the **Birreria Tempera,** one of Rome's oldest, most atmospheric little restaurants. You can have a good light lunch or supper here in congenial surroundings. *Via San Marcello 19. Closed Sun.*

Trajan's Market to San Giovanni in Laterano

This tour starts at one of ancient Rome's most famous monuments—Trajan's Market. It then visits one of the ancient city's most populous neighborhoods—the Suburra, a dark warren of many-storied dwellings and cramped home to a substantial portion of ancient Rome's teeming citizens. But it is churches that form the basis of the tour: San Pietro in Vincoli, containing Michelangelo's statue of Moses; majestic Santa Maria Maggiore, its interior gleaming with gold; and the echoing vastness of San Giovanni in Laterano. All are among the oldest of the city's churches, though all have been restored and remodeled down through the centuries. If you want just to see the highlights of this walk, visit these three churches.

Trajan's Market and San Pietro in Vincoli

❶ Make **Piazza Venezia** your starting point and walk up **Via Quattro Novembre.** As you bear right, following Via Quattro Novembre, the red-brick walls of the upper levels of

2 **Trajan's Market** rear up in front of you. Though certainly much better preserved than most of the buildings that stood in the neighboring Forum and the Imperial Fora, the market gives only a hint of its original splendor. When at the instigation of the Emperor Trajan—the same Trajan whose military exploits are celebrated on the reliefs spiraling up Trajan's Column in the Forum below—the market was built in the early 2nd century AD it was immediately considered one of the wonders of the classical world. The architect of both Forum and market was Apollodorus of Damascus, by far the most successful architect of the day. In addition to the market buildings, discussed below, the Forum contained temples and libraries, statues and fountains, all decked out in the most luxurious materials that could be found.

The market stands on the site of what was originally a low hill running between the Quirinale Hill to the northeast and the Capitoline Hill to the west. It speaks volumes for the confidence of Apollodorus and his patron—not to mention the almost unlimited slave labor at their disposal—that they could so blithely remove this great quantity of earth just to build a market, even one as splendid as this. In fact the architectural centerpiece of the market is the enormous curved wall—technically known as an exedra, a form of apse—that shores up the side of the Quirinale Hill which had been exposed by Apollodorus's gangs of laborers. Here the Romans would come to meet and to gossip, sitting on the seats Apollodorus thoughtfully provided and that extended the length of the exedra.

Enter the large vaulted hall in front of you. Two stories of shops rise up on either side. It's thought that they were probably a bazaar or a similar sort of specialty market. Head for the flight of steps at the far end. These lead down to Via Biberatica, Pepper Street (in fact *biberatica* is a medieval corruption of the Latin *piper* meaning pepper). Here the super-rich came to buy this much sought-after luxury and other spices. From here head back to the three tiers of shops that line the upper levels of the great exedra and look out over the remains of the Forum. Though empty and largely ruined today, they were once ancient Rome's most glamorous shopping mall, a sort of Roman Bloomingdale's. Wine, oils, flowers, perfumes, shoes, clothing, and household goods were all sold in this thriving market—everything a burgeoning and sophisticated population desired. *Via Quattro Novembre 94, tel. 06/67103613. Admission: 1,500 lire. Open Apr.–Sept., 9–1:30, Sun. 9–1, Tues., Thurs., and Sat. also open 4–7, closed Mon.; Oct.–Mar., 9–1:30, Sun. 9–1, closed Mon.*

Leave the market and walk to the church of San Pietro in Vincoli. You take Via dei Fori Imperiali toward the Colosseum and turn left onto **Via Cavour,** a busy, rather drab thoroughfare that leads to Termini train station. Turn right onto Via San Francesco da Paola, otherwise known as the Salita dei Borgia, a dark staircase that passes under what was once Palazzo Borgia, hotbed of Renaissance intrigue. Here, it's said, at the close of a banquet given by his mother Vannozza Cattanei, the younger brother of Lucrezia and Cesare Borgia was assassinated by his fiendish siblings, an affair that their father, Pope Alexander VI, quickly hushed up.

3 As you emerge into the piazza, you'll see **San Pietro in Vincoli** on your left. In high season it's a madhouse of guided tours and souvenir vendors; if you're lucky—go early in the morning—you'll find it fairly empty and you'll be able to take a good look

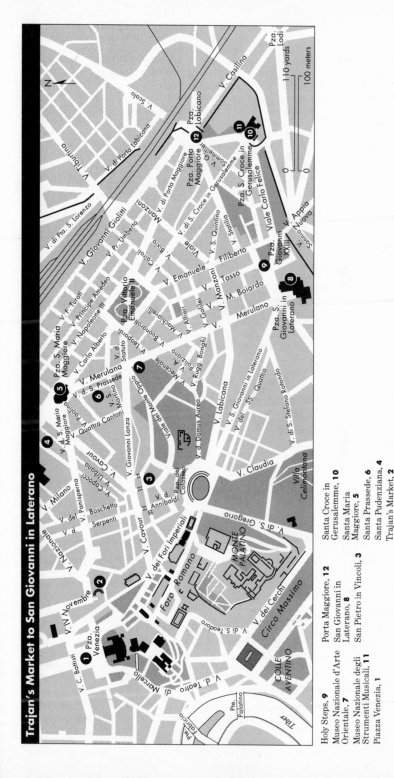

Trajan's Market to San Giovanni in Laterano

Holy Steps, **9**
Museo Nazionale d'Arte Orientale, **7**
Museo Nazionale degli Strumenti Musicali, **11**
Piazza Venezia, **1**

Porta Maggiore, **12**
San Giovanni in Laterano, **8**
San Pietro in Vincoli, **3**

Santa Croce in Gerusalemme, **10**
Santa Maria Maggiore, **5**
Santa Prassede, **6**
Santa Pudenziana, **4**
Trajan's Market, **2**

at what has put this church on the tourist maps: the monumental statue of *Moses*, carved by Michelangelo in the early 16th century for the tomb of his patron, Pope Julius II. The fierce power of this remarkable sculpture dominates its setting, a reduced version of Michelangelo's original design for the enormous tomb. People say that you can see the sculptor's profile in the lock of Moses's beard right under his lip, and that the pope's profile is also there somewhere. But don't let the search distract you from the overall effect of this marvelously energetic work. Of the rest of the design for the tomb, only the flanking statues of *Leah* and *Rachel* were completed. (The unfinished *Prisoners*, now in Florence's Accademia gallery, were also part of Michelangelo's ambitious project.) Behind the *Moses*, a large souvenir shop obtrudes a crassly commercial air. As for the rest of the church, St. Peter, after whom the church is, after all, named, takes second billing to Moses. What are reputed to be the chains that bound St. Peter during his imprisonment by the Romans in Jerusalem—"in vincoli" means chained—are in a bronze and crystal reliquary (an urn or casket in which a saint's earthly remains, or some item associated with him, were placed) under the main altar. Other treasures in the church include a 7th-century mosaic of St. Sebastian in front of the second altar on the left of the main altar, and, by the door, the tomb of the Pollaiuolo brothers, two lesser Florentine 15th-century artists.

Santa Maria Maggiore

If you choose to go on to Santa Maria Maggiore, continue along Via Cavour. Turn left onto Via delle Vasche and right into Via Urbana, where you'll come upon the early-Christian, though ❹ much-restored, church of **Santa Pudenziana**. It's well worth a visit for its strikingly colored 5th-century apse mosaic representing Christ and the Apostles, in which Sts. Praxides and Pudenziana hold wreaths over the heads of Sts. Peter and Paul.

❺ Although the facade of **Santa Maria Maggiore**—literally, St. Mary Major—that you see from Via Cavour seems to be the front of the church, it is in fact the rear of the building. More than that, it also gives a completely misleading impression of the interior. What you see is a gracefully curving 18th-century building, the very model of a classical building of the period. In fact, Santa Maria Maggiore is one of the oldest churches in Rome, built around 440 by Pope Sixtus III. Not only is it one of the seven great pilgrimage churches of Rome, it is also by far the most complete example of an early-Christian basilica in the city—one of the immense, hall-like buildings derived from ancient-Roman civic buildings and divided into three by two great rows of columns marching up the nave. Of the other six— San Giovanni in Laterano and St. Peter's are the most famous —all have been entirely transformed, or even rebuilt. Paradoxically, however, the major reason why the church is such a striking example of early-Christian design is that the same man who built the incongruous exteriors in around 1740— Ferdinando Fuga—also conscientiously restored the interior, throwing out later additions and, crucially, replacing a number of the great forest of columns.

It was long believed that the church came to be built when the Virgin Mary appeared in a dream to Pope Sixtus III and ordered him to build a church in her honor. It was to stand on the spot where snow would fall on the night of August 5, an event

Santa Maria Maggiore

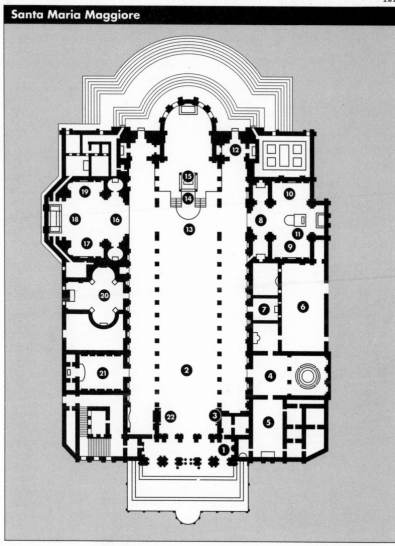

Baptistery, **4**
Below in crypt: 13th-century altar front, **11**
Byzantine Virgin, **18**
Ceiling (da Sangallo), **2**
Cesi-Massimi Chapel, **21**
Clement IX monument, **3**

Clement VIII tomb, **19**
Henry IV of France column, **6**
High Altar, **15**
Holy Relics Chapel, **7**
In floor: family tomb of the Berninis, **12**
Nicholas IV monument, **22**
Overhead: Triumphal Arch, 5th-century mosaics, **13**

Paul V tomb, **17**
Pauline Chapel, **16**
Philip IV of Spain, **1**
Pius V tomb, **10**
Pius IX statue, **14**
Sacristy, **5**
Sistine Chapel, **8**
Sixtus V tomb, **9**
Sforza Chapel, **20**

about as likely in a Roman August as snow in the Sahara. True or false, the legend is commemorated every August 5, the feast of the Madonna of the Snows, with a special mass in the Sistine chapel at which a shower of white rose petals falls from the ceiling.

Precious 5th-century mosaics lining the nave walls and on the triumphal arch in front of the main altar are splendid testimony to the basilica's venerable age. Those along the nave show 36 scenes from the Old Testament (unfortunately, they are hard to see clearly without binoculars), while those on the arch illustrate the *Annunciation* and the *Youth of Christ*. The majestic mosaic in the apse was created by a Franciscan monk named Torriti in 1275. The resplendent carved wood ceiling dates from the early 16th century; it's supposed to have been gilded with the first gold brought from the New World. The Cosmatesque pavement in the central nave is even older, dating from the 12th century.

The **Sistine Chapel,** which opens onto the right-hand nave, was created by architect Domenico Fontana for Pope Sixtus V in 1585. (Sistine, by the way, is simply the adjective from Sixtus.) Elaborately and heavily decorated with precious marbles "liberated" from the monuments of ancient Rome, the chapel includes a lower level in which some 13th-century sculptures by Arnolfo da Cambio are all that's left of what was once the incredibly richly endowed chapel of the *presepio*, the Christmas crèche, looted during the Sack of Rome in 1527. Directly across from it stands the **Pauline Chapel,** a rich Baroque setting for the tombs of the Borghese popes Paul V—who commissioned the chapel in 1611, with the declared intention of outdoing Sixtus's chapel across the nave—and Clement VIII. The *Madonna* above its altar is a precious Byzantine image, painted perhaps as early as the 8th century. Take a peek at the **Sforza Chapel** next door; it was designed by Michelangelo, though completed by della Porta (the same partnership that was responsible for the dome of St. Peter's).

❻ Opposite the basilica, off Piazza Santa Maria Maggiore, on Via di Santa Prassede, is the 9th-century church of **Santa Prassede,** known above all for the exquisite little chapel of **San Zenone.** It's just to the left of the entrance, and gleams with vivid mosaics that reflect their Byzantine inspiration. Though much less classical and naturalistic than those in the earlier mosaics of Santa Pudenziana, they are no less splendid. Note the square halo over the head of Theodora, mother of St. Pasquale I, the pope who built this church. It indicates that she was still alive when she was depicted by the artist. The chapel also contains one curious relic: a miniature pillar, supposedly part of the column at which Christ was flogged during the Passion. It was brought to Rome in the 13th century. Just by the entrance to the chapel is an early work of Bernini, a bust of Bishop Santoni, executed when the sculptor was in his mid-teens. Over the main altar, the magnificent mosaics on the arch and apse are also in rigid Byzantine style. Pope Pasquale I wears the square halo of the living and holds a model of his church.

San Giovanni in Laterano

Via Merulana runs straight as an arrow from Santa Maria Maggiore to the immense Cathedral of Rome, San Giovanni in

San Giovanni in Laterano

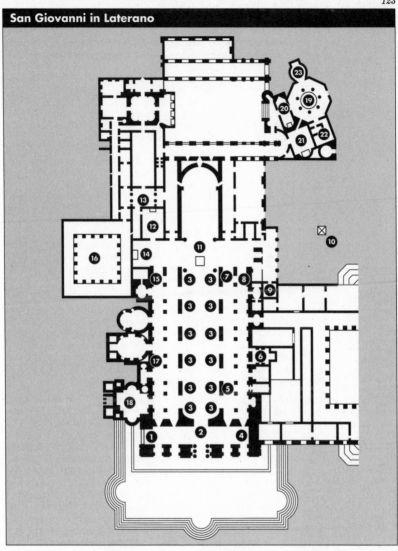

Altar of the Holy
Sacrament (4 Roman
Columns), **14**

Ancient statue of
Constantine, **1**

Caracciolo
monument, **17**

Chapel of Ss. Seconda
and Rufina, **20**

Cloisters, **16**

Colonna Chapel, **12**

Constantine
Baptistery, **19**

Corsini Chapel, **18**

Entrance to the
Cloisters, **15**

Farnese tomb, **7**

Giotto fresco, **5**

Henry IV of France, **9**

Holy Door, **4**

Martinez de Chiaves
tomb, **8**

Massimo Chapel, **6**

Obelisk, **10**

Papal Altar, **11**

Roman bronze doors, **2**

Sacristy, **13**

St. John
the Baptist Chapel
(ancient doors), **23**

St. John the Evangelist
Chapel, **22**

St. Venanzio Chapel, **21**

The 12 Apostles, **3**

Laterano. If you're interested in Oriental art, stop off en route
7 to see the collection of Middle and Far Eastern art at the **Museo
Nazionale d'Arte Orientale;** it's being continually enriched by
the finds of Italian archaeological expeditions in those areas.
*Via Merulana 248, tel. 06/737891. Admission: 3,000 lire. Open
Mon., Tues., and Wed. 9–2; Thurs. 9–2 and 3:30–7; Fri. and
Sat. 9–2; Sun. 9–1.*

Time Out For a good lunch in a typical Roman trattoria, stop at **Da Michele,** where the *fettuccine* are homemade. *Via Merulana 236.
Closed Tues.*

8 The basilica of **San Giovanni in Laterano** is one of Rome's most
imposing churches. It is also, historically speaking, the most
important church in the city, more so even than St. Peter's. As
the official seat of the Bishop of Rome—otherwise known as
the pope—it is here that he officiates in all ceremonies concerned specifically with Rome as opposed to those concerned
with the papacy in general. The towering facade dates from
1736 and was modeled on that of St. Peter's. On it are 15 colossal statues; Christ, John the Baptist, John the Evangelist, and
12 doctors of the church look out on the sea of dreary suburbs
that have spread out from Porta San Giovanni to the lower
slopes of the Alban Hills.

San Giovanni was founded in the 4th century on land donated by the Emperor Constantine, who had obtained it
from the wealthy patrician family of the Laterani. Vandals,
earthquakes, and fire damaged the original and successive
constructions. Finally, in 1646 Pope Innocent X commissioned
Borromini to rebuild the church, and it's Borromini's rather
cool, tense Baroque interior that you see today.

Under the portico on the left stands an ancient statue of Constantine. Another link with Rome's past is the ancient central
bronze doors, brought here from the Curia building in the Forum. Inside, little is left of the early decorations. A famous
fragment of a fresco, supposedly by the 14th-century Florentine painter Giotto, on the first pillar in the double aisle on the
right, depicts Pope Boniface VIII proclaiming the first Holy
Year in 1300. The mosaic in the apse was reconstructed from a
12th-century original by Torriti, the same Franciscan friar
who executed the apse mosaic in Santa Maria Maggiore. The
papal altar at the center of the church contains a wooden table
believed to have been used by St. Peter to celebrate the Eucharist. The altar's rich Gothic tabernacle dates from 1367 and,
somewhat gruesomely, contains what are believed to be the
heads of Sts. Peter and Paul.

San Giovanni is surrounded by monuments that in some ways
are more interesting than the church itself. You shouldn't miss
the **cloisters,** with their little twin columns and frieze encrusted with 13th-century Cosmatesque mosaics by the
Vassallettos, a father-and-son team. The columns are crowned
by richly carved capitals. Enter the cloister from the last chapel at the end of the left aisle.

You won't be able to see the interior of the adjoining **Lateran
Palace,** which was the popes' official residence until their exile
to Avignon in the south of France in the 14th century and which
is still technically part of the Vatican. Now it houses the offices
of the Rome Diocese. The present palace is fairly modern by

Roman standards; it was built by Domenico Fontana in 1586. Across the street, in front of the palace, a 16th-century building encloses the famous **Holy Steps** (Scala Santa), which tradition holds to be the staircase from Pilate's palace in Jerusalem, brought to Rome by St. Helena, mother of the Emperor Constantine. Wood protects the 28 marble steps worn smooth by the knees of pilgrims through the centuries. There are two other staircases that you can ascend to see the **Sancta Sanctorum,** the private chapel of the popes in the old Lateran Palace. Visible only through a window grate, it's a masterpiece of Cosmatesque mosaics. *Open daily 8–12 and 3:30–7.*

To get to the **baptistry of San Giovanni,** you circle round to the back of the basilica, skirting **Piazza San Giovanni,** with Rome's oldest and tallest obelisk. This originally stood in front of the Temple of Ammon in Thebes, Egypt, in the 15th century BC. It was brought to Rome by Constantine in AD 357 to stand in the Circus Maximus, and finally set up here in 1588. Across the square is the big, rambling city hospital of San Giovanni, which was founded in the Middle Ages as a kind of infirmary of the Lateran Palace. The baptistry of San Giovanni, though much altered through the centuries, is the forerunner of all such buildings: simply, buildings where baptisms take place. It was built by Constantine in the 4th century AD, and enlarged by Pope Sixtus III about 100 years later. It stands on the site of the baths attached to the home of Constantine's second wife, Fausta, who, emperor's wife or not, was suffocated in the hot room of the baths after having falsely accused Constantine's son by his first wife of having tried to rape her. This exceedingly unpleasant death was one of the accepted Roman methods of dealing with members of the ruling classes who were implicated in scandals of this type. Of the four chapels ranged around the walls of the baptistry, the most interesting is the first on the right (as you enter). It has a set of ancient bronze doors whose hinges send out a musical sound when the doors are opened and closed. They probably came from the Baths of Caracalla. The first chapel on the left has a 5th-century mosaic on the vault. But notice also the splendid porphyry columns that support the entire structure, typical of the Romans' love of luxurious and exotic materials.

Those who prefer present-day luxury should make for the shops along Via Appia Nuova. On the corner of the big square is **Coin,** one of Rome's handful of upscale department stores. In contrast, on Via Sannio, to the left, there's a bustling morning street market with new and used clothing.

While you're in this part of town, continue on to yet another of Rome's earliest churches: **Santa Croce in Gerusalemme.** From the outside, much like Santa Maria Maggiore and San Giovanni in Laterano, the church certainly doesn't look too old. There's a Romanesque bell tower off to one side, put up in the 12th century, while the facade was rebuilt in the 18th century. But the church, despite extensive 17th- and 18th-century remodeling of the interior, dates from the 4th century AD. It stands on the site of what was probably part of St. Helena's 4th-century AD palace. St. Helena, mother of the Emperor Constantine, was an indefatigable collector of holy relics. Her most precious discovery was fragments of the Holy Cross—the cross on which Christ was crucified—which she had unearthed during one of many forays through the Holy Land. The relics of the cross—if indeed these are what they are—are in the modern chapel at the end of the left aisle. There are otherwise few indications of the church's venerable age. To all intents and purposes you seem to be in a Baroque building. Even the chapel dedicated to St. Helena, located in the lower level of the building, was redecorated in the 15th century with brilliant gold and blue mosaics.

If you're at all interested in musical instruments, stop in at the **⓫ Museo Nazionale degli Strumenti Musicali;** it's just behind Santa Croce. Among its sizable collection of instruments from prehistory to the present are a 16th-century clavichord and the Barberini Harp. *Piazza Santa Croce in Gerusalemme 9/a, tel. 06/7575936. Admission: 2,000 lire. Open 9–1; closed Sun.*

From here you can either return to the metro station at San **⓬** Giovanni or go on to the bus stops at the **Porta Maggiore.** Take a look at this massive 1st-century monument, not really a city gate but part of the Acqua Claudia aqueduct. On the Piazzale Labicano side of the portal, be sure to see the delightful **Baker's Tomb,** erected in the 1st century BC by the grieving wife of a prosperous baker. She saw to it that the tomb was decorated with stone ovens and charming friezes illustrating her deceased husband's trade.

The Quirinale to Piazza della Repubblica

This tour takes in some of the key Baroque buildings of Rome, notably the two churches of San Andrea del Quirinale and San Carlo alle Quattro Fontane, and the imposing Palazzo Barberini, grandest of 17th-century Rome's stately palaces. It begins on the Quirinale Hill and ends at Piazza della Repubblica, the busy and noisy square overlooked by the daring modern sweep of Termini Station and the gaunt ruins of the Baths of Diocletian. A side trip out to the early-Christian shrines of Sant' Agnese and Santa Constanza is also suggested.

It is, however, the Baroque that dominates this exploration. Those who find the excesses of 16th-century Roman architecture and painting to their taste will find much to enjoy. Others should consider visiting only the early-Christian churches, or perhaps going straight to the Piazza della Repubblica, where they can pay further homage to Michelangelo or visit the extraordinary ruins of the Baths of Diocletian.

The Quirinale and Quattro Fontane

❶ Begin your tour at **Piazza del Quirinale,** the substantial square at the summit of the Quirinal Hill, highest of the seven hills of Rome. In the 7th century BC this was the home of the Sabines, deadly enemies of the Romans, who lived on the Capitoline and Palatinate Hills (all of a half a mile away). Three sides of the piazza are surrounded by palaces; the fourth is open and gives one of the most striking views in the city, all the way to the dome of St. Peter's. In the center of the piazza stands a huge Roman statue, copied from a Greek original, of **Castor and Pollux**—they're also known as the Horse Tamers—struggling to control two massive marble steeds. Unlike just about every other ancient statue in Rome, this group survived the Dark Ages intact, and accordingly became one of the great sights of Rome, especially during the Middle Ages. Next to them are an

The Quirinale to Piazza della Repubblica

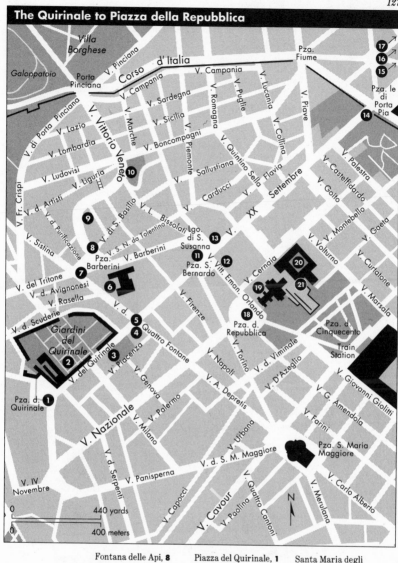

obelisk, put here by Pope Pius VI at the end of the 18th century, and an ancient-Roman **fountain,** put here by Pope Pius VII at the beginning of the 19th century.

Most famous and important of the palaces on Piazza del Quirinale is the **Quirinal Palace** itself, located at the west end of the square. It was begun in 1574 by Pope Gregory XIII, who intended it as no more than a summer residence, choosing the site mainly for the superb view. However, as early as 1592 Pope Clement VIII decided to make the palace the permanent home of the papacy, largely to escape the malarial conditions of the low-lying Vatican. It remained the official papal residence right up until 1870, in the process undergoing a series of extensions and alterations by a succession of architects. When Italian troops under Garibaldi stormed the city in 1870, making it the capital of the newly united Italy, the popes moved back to the Vatican and the Quirinal became the official residence of the kings of Italy. Today, it is the home of the president of the country.

The palace isn't open to the public, but you get a fair idea of its splendor from the size of the building, especially the vast facade lining Via del Quirinale. At 4 PM daily you can see the changing of the president's guards, the *corazzieri*. They are a stirring sight in their magnificent crimson and blue uniforms, their knee-length boots glistening and their steel helmets adorned with tossing plumes.

Just a few steps along Via del Quirinale on the right is the church of **Sant'Andrea,** a small but oddly imposing Baroque

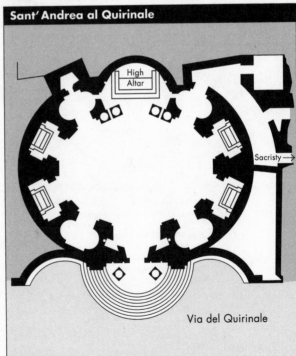

Sant' Andrea al Quirinale

church designed by Bernini. His son wrote that Bernini considered this one of his best works and that he used to come here occasionally just to sit and enjoy it. Here, and in the little church of San Carlo down the street (see below), the two greatest architects of the Baroque period had a chance to create as they pleased, unhindered by the need to adapt existing structures. Bernini chose a simple oval plan, then gave it drama and movement in the decorations, which carry the story of St. Andrew's martyrdom and ascension into heaven, starting with the painting over the high altar, up past the figure of the saint over the chancel door, to the angels at the base of the lantern and the dove of the Holy Spirit that awaits on high.

Where Bernini appears, you can be sure that Borromini will not be far behind. In fact, his church of **San Carlo** is at the Quattro Fontane crossroads. San Carlo (or San Carlino, as it is sometimes called) is one of Borromini's masterpieces. In a space no larger than the base of one of the piers of St. Peter's, he created a church that is an intricate exercise in geometric perfection, with a coffered dome that seems to float above the curves of the walls. Borromini's work is often bizarre, definitely intellectual, and intensely concerned with pure form. In San Carlo, he invented an original treatment of space that creates an effect of rippling movement, especially evident in the double-S curves of the facade. Characteristically, the interior decoration is subdued, in white stucco with no more than a few touches of gilding, so as not to distract from the form. Don't miss the **cloisters,** an understated Baroque jewel. The graceful portico and the loggia above echo the lines of the church.

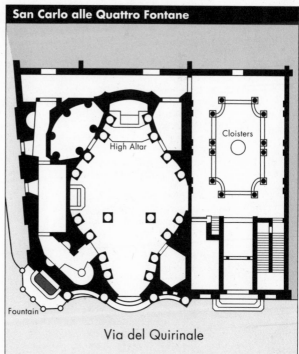

San Carlo alle Quattro Fontane

Cloisters

High Altar

Fountain

Via del Quirinale

❺ At the **Quattro Fontane** intersection, four Baroque fountains—representing the Tiber (on the San Carlo corner), the Nile, Juno, and Diana—frame views in four directions: to the obelisk in Piazza del Quirinale, along Via Venti Settembre to the Porta Pia, to the left across Piazza Barberini to the obelisk of Trinità dei Monti, and to the right as far as the obelisk and apse of Santa Maria Maggiore.

Palazzo Barberini and Via Veneto

❻ Turn left down Via delle Quattro Fontane to Rome's most splendid 17th-century palace, **Palazzo Barberini.** Both Bernini and Borromini worked on this massive building, but the overall plan was produced by Carlo Maderno in the early 17th century. Pope Urban VIII had acquired the property and given it to a nephew who set out to build an edifice worthy of his generous uncle and the ever-more powerful Barberini clan. You'll get an idea of the grandeur of the place as you visit the **Galleria Nazionale di Arte Antica,** which occupies part of the palace. Unfortunately, a good part of the rest of the building has been occupied for years by an army club, forcing the Galleria to split its collection between here and Palazzo Corsini on the other side of the Tiber. The grounds are disappointingly unkempt.

You enter the palace on the left, climbing the broad marble staircase designed by Bernini. On the main floor (keep your ticket handy as you'll have to show it again upstairs) you'll find several magnificent paintings, including Raphael's *Fornarina*, a luminous portrait of one of the handsome artist's lady-loves, identified by later legend as a baker's daughter. A dramatic Caravaggio depicts a lovely young Judith regarding with some horror the neatly severed head of Holofernes. There's a Holbein portrait of *Henry VIII* in the finery he donned for his wedding with Anne of Cleves in 1540, and two small but striking El Grecos. The palace's large main salon is part of the gallery. It was decorated in the 1630s by Pietro da Cortona and is a glorious and surprisingly early example of the Baroque practice of glorifying patrons by depicting them on the ceiling as part of the heavenly host. In this case, Pope Urban VIII appears as the agent of *Divine Providence*. Also featured in this glowing vault are some huge, mutantlike Barberini bees, the heraldic symbol of the family. Note how the real space of the room is extended into the illusionistic space of the painting, where a series of brilliantly colored and heroic figures swirl and swoop in the sky. Pietro da Cortona has been called the Italian Rubens, and this magnificent ceiling, in many ways his masterpiece, shows clearly the fluency and imaginative power of this underrated painter. Upstairs you'll find an array of 17th- and 18th-century paintings, including some pretty little views of Rome by Vanvitelli, and four handsome Canalettos. Don't miss the stunning suite of rooms redecorated in 1728 for the marriage of a Barberini heiress to a scion of the Colonna family. *Via delle Quattro Fontane 13, tel. 06/4754591. Admission: 3,000 lire. Open Sun.–Tues. 9–1, Wed.–Sat. 9–7.*

Downhill from the palace (turn right when you leave) you'll come upon **Piazza Barberini,** a handy starting point for exploring the Ludovisi district and Via Veneto. One of Rome's more modern quarters, it was built at the end of the 19th century on the site of the beautiful Villa Ludovisi, which had in turn been built over the famous ancient-Roman gardens of Sallust. The piazza, a picturesque marketplace in the 17th and 18th centuries, has lost its original charm in the rush of progress. A big hotel, a movie theater, and the metro station distract you from

7 its centerpiece, Bernini's lovely Baroque **Tritone Fountain,** created in 1637 for Pope Urban VIII, whose Barberini coat of arms is at the base of the large shell.

Time Out Along Via degli Avignonesi and Via Rasella (both narrow streets off Via delle Quattro Fontane, opposite Palazzo Barberini) there are some good, moderately priced trattorias. One of the most popular with Romans is **Gioia Mia.** *Via degli Avignonesi 34. Closed Wed.*

At the beginning of **Via Vittorio Veneto,** there's another foun-

8 tain that Bernini designed for Urban VIII: the **Fontana delli Api,** or fountain of the bees. Today, only the upper shell and the inscription are original. This inscription was the cause of a considerable scandal when the fountain was first put up in 1644. It stated that the fountain had been erected in the 22nd year of the pontiff's reign, while in fact the 21st anniversary of Urban's election to the papacy was still some weeks away! The last numeral was hurriedly erased, but to no avail—Urban died eight days before the beginning of his 22nd year as pope. The superstitious Romans, who had immediately recognized the inscription as an almost foolhardy tempting of fate, were vindicated.

9 Just a few steps beyond is the 17th-century **Santa Maria della Concezione,** built for the Capuchin monks and famous for its crypt. Here, the ghoulish can see skeletons and scattered bones of 4,000 dead monks, arranged in four subterranean chapels (Via Veneto 27, tel. 06/462850. Voluntary admission charge. Open daily 9–12 and 3–6). Upstairs in the church, the first chapel on the right contains Guido Reni's mid-17th-century painting of *St. Michael Trampling the Devil.* This caused great scandal after an acute contemporary observer remarked that the face of the devil bore a surprising resemblance to the Pamphili Pope Innocent X, archenemy of Reni's Barberini patrons. Compare the devil with the bust of the pope that you saw in the Galleria Doria Pamphili and judge for yourself!

From here you move to the lower reaches of Via Veneto, very much its quietest and most sedate stretch. The broad avenue curves up the hill past travel agencies and hotels, with a sidewalk café or two, where the only clients seem to be tired tourists and expensive call girls. Then, at the intersection with Via Bissolati, Rome's "Airline Row," Via Veneto comes to life.

10 The big white palace on the right is **Palazzo Margherita,** built in 1890 as the residence of Italy's Queen Margherita. It's now the U.S. Embassy; security is inconspicuous but tight, and you couldn't get inside if you wanted to. American citizens on routine business (and that includes losing your passport) are directed to the big reddish consulate building next door. Embassy and consulate are part of a carefully guarded complex that includes United States Information Service offices and the American Library. The ambassador's residence is in another walled compound close by in the Parioli section.

The flower vendors and big newsstands at the corner of Via Ludovisi hint that this is where the passing parade intensifies. Sure enough, just a few steps up on the left is the famous **Café**

de Paris, erstwhile hub of La Dolce Vita. In fact, Via Veneto's atmosphere has sobered down considerably since the halcyon days of press agents and *paparazzi* in the early '60s, and today its cafés cater more to tourists than to barefoot cinema *contessas.*

On the right is the huge white palace of the **Excelsior Hotel,** one of the city's most luxurious. Its recessed entrance is always busy with the comings and goings of shiny limousines. Right next door is **Doney's,** the café that was a longtime favorite with Americans, who preferred it to the more clubby **Café de Paris.** Doney's has always had the advantage of getting the sun earlier than its rival, which makes it a better spot for daytime sidewalk-sitting three seasons of the year.

Past the big cafés, Via Veneto continues in a succession of more newsstands, boutiques, expensive shops, and a snack bar or two. If you intend to picnic in the Villa Borghese grounds (they're just at the top of the street), this is your chance to pick up some foodstuffs, whether ready-to-go from the snack bars or do-it-yourself from the *alimentari* stores on the side streets. (You won't find anything near the Galleria.) The avenue ends in glory at Porta Pinciana with the solid old **Flora Hotel** (another American favorite), and **Harry's Bar** opposite. Harry's, which has nothing but its name in common with its more famous counterparts in Venice and Florence, is popular with businessmen and journalists for a quiet drink.

Santa Susanna and Santa Maria Vittoria

From Via Veneto backtrack to Palazzo Margherita and the U.S. Embassy, and from there head up Via Bissolati to **Piazza San Bernardo.** If you haven't stopped in before, this is your chance to pick up brochures and booklets on Rome at the **EPT Information Office** at Via Parigi 11, behind the Grand Hotel, a historic and *very* grand hostelry.

Piazza San Bernardo, intersection of several important avenues, hums and roars with traffic. Over on one side of the piazza is the Baroque church of **Santa Susanna** (Rome's American Catholic church). Its foundations incorporate parts of a Roman house where Susanna was martyred, but the frescoes, carved ceiling, and stucco decorations all date from the late 16th century. Across the way, on the corner of Via Vittorio Emanuele Orlando, there's a huge fountain, the **Fontanone dell'Acqua Felice** (which translates like something from *Hiawatha* as "The Big Fountain of the Happy Water"). It was built by Domenico Fontana toward the end of the 16th century when Pope Sixtus V completed the restoration of the ancient Roman Acque Felice aqueduct. As the story goes, a sculptor named Prospero da Brescia had the unhappy task of executing the central figure, which was to represent Moses (like Moses, Sixtus liked to think of himself as having provided water for his thirsting population). The comparison with Michelangelo's magnificent *Moses* in the church of San Pietro in Vincoli was inevitable, and the critical comments elicited by Prospero's work are said to have driven him to his grave. Perhaps the most charming aspect of the fountain are the smug little lions spewing water in the foreground.

From the fountain, cross **Via Venti Settembre** to the church of **Santa Maria della Vittoria.** Like Santa Susanna across the way, this church was designed by Carlo Maderno, but it's best known for the sumptuous Baroque decoration of the **Cornaro Chapel,** located on the left when you face the altar. Here, Bernini produced an extraordinary fusion of architecture, painting, and sculpture, most notably *The Ecstasy of St. Theresa,* focal point of the chapel. Your eye is drawn effortlessly from the frescoes on the ceiling down to the marble figures of the angel and the swooning saint, to the earthly figures of the Cornaros (the family that commissioned the chapel) both living and dead to the two inlaid marble skeletons in the pavement, representing the hope and despair of souls in Purgatory. As has been repeatedly pointed out, the out-and-out theatricality of the chapel—the members of the Cornaro family witnessing the scene are placed in what are, in effect, theater boxes, and twist to see the great moment of divine love being played out before them as though they were indeed actually at the theater —allied to a masterly fusion of the elements used by Bernini to make the Cornaro Chapel one of the key examples of the mature Roman High Baroque. Notice the way the sculptor has carved the swooning saint's robes as though they are almost on fire, quivering with life. See, too, how the white marble group seems suspended in the heavens as golden rays illuminate the scene. An angel assists at the mystical moment of Theresa's vision as the saint abandons herself to the joys of divine love. In all, Bernini represented this mystical experience in what, to modern eyes, can seem very earthly terms. No matter what your reaction may be, you'll have to admit that it's great theater.

Via Nomentana

There's an intriguing side trip from **Piazza San Bernardo** out to the early-Christian churches of Sant'Agnese and Santa Costanza, located a mile or more out beyond the old city walls. You can either walk—head straight up Via Venti Settembre, past Porta Pia—or take the bus: 36, 37, 60, 136, and 137 all run straight to the two churches.

14 The first landmark you come to as you head toward the churches is the **Porta Pia,** one of the principal city gates and, interestingly, also Michelangelo's last piece of architecture, completed in 1564. Nearby, a monument marks the breach in the walls created by Italian troops when they stormed into Rome in 1870 to claim the city from the pope for the new Italian state. Past the Porta Pia, as you ride along Via Nomentana in the direction of some of Rome's older residential suburbs, you'll **15** pass the **Villa Torlonia** on your right. This was Mussolini's private residence; now it's a public park.

16 A few stops farther on, get off the bus at **Sant'Agnese.** The saint, who was probably martyred about AD 304 on the site marked by the church of the same name in Piazza Navona, was laid to rest here in a Christian cemetery on the city's outskirts. Her cult spread quickly, and it was probably a member of Constantine's family who built a church over her tomb, sometime before AD 349. To reach the basilica, you go around the corner onto Via di Sant'Agnese. The present church, dating from the 7th century, was built to replace the original basilica. The antique columns and 7th-century mosaics, representing the saint in Byzantine dress, are more in keeping with the surroundings than the 19th-century frescoes. On January 21 each year, two flower-bedecked lambs are blessed before Agnes's altar. They are then carried to the pope, who blesses them again before they're sent to the nuns of Saint Cecilia in Trastevere. Here, they use the wool to weave the episcopal *pallia* kept in the casket in the niche of the *Confessio* in St. Peter's. The catacomb is worth a visit; its entrance is on the left of the church. *Via di Sant'Agnese, tel. 06/8320743. Admission: 2,000 lire. Open Mon.–Sat. 9–12 and 4–6, Sun. 4–6.*

Ask the custodian of the catacomb to accompany you up the hill to open the small round church of **Santa Costanza.** (Admission is free; if you have not purchased a ticket to the catacomb, a tip is in order.) This was originally the tomb of Costantia, daughter of the Emperor Constantine. It was probably she who built the first church over the tomb of St. Agnes, and her tomb in turn is one of the most important examples of early-Christian architecture in Rome. It was circular, like the great tombs of Augustus and Cecilia Metella. Transformed into a baptistry, it was then consecrated as a church in 1254 and dedicated to St. Constantia. The 4th-century mosaics on the vault of the circular nave that surrounds the domed central space are among the oldest in Rome—and are perhaps also the most beautiful. The grapevine motif, executed on a white ground, seems more Bacchic than Christian. It's a shame that the similarly beautiful mosaics on the dome were destroyed in the 16th century to make way for the frescoes you see there now. The figures on either side of the entrance probably represent Constantia and her husband. Opposite the entrance is a copy of the original heavy porphyry sarcophagus that is in the Vatican Museums. Its carved decorations are an adaptation of pagan symbols to Christian use, as in the peacock and the sheep, whose flesh was held to be incorruptible. Later mosaics in the niches date from the 6th and 7th centuries.

Around Piazza della Repubblica

Piazza della Repubblica is a characteristic 19th-century addition to Rome, a bustling hub of activity even at dawn, when buses stand with idling motors, waiting for passengers bound for Siena, Sorrento, or even Sicily. On summer evenings the band at the Caffè Italia plays golden oldies for tourists ensconced at the tables and for a milling crowd of eavesdroppers.

Cross over to the **fountain** in the middle of the piazza to get a better look at the voluptuous bronze ladies wrestling happily with marine monsters. The pope, when he unveiled the fountain in 1870, was spared any embarrassment as the figures were not added until 1901. Predictably, they caused a great scandal, for it's said that the sculptor, Rutelli, modeled them on the ample figures of two musical comedy stars of the day.

The ancient-Roman red-brick facade on one side of the square marks the entrance to the church of **Santa Maria degli Angeli.** Behind it, in the same building, is the **Museo Nazionale Romano,** or the Museo delle Terme, the museum of the baths. The building is, in fact, all that remains of the colossal Baths of Diocletian, erected about AD 300, and the largest and most impressive of the ancient baths. In 1561 Michelangelo was commissioned to convert the vast *tepidarium,* the central chamber of the baths, into a church. His work was altered by Vanvitelli in the 18th century, but the huge transept, one of the "arms" of the church, which formed the nave in Michelangelo's plan, has remained as he adapted it. The eight enormous monolithic columns of red granite that support the great beams are the original columns of the *tepidarium*, 45 feet high and more than five feet in diameter. The great hall is 92 feet high. Though the interior of the church is small in comparison to the vast baths Diocletian built here, they give a better impression of the quite remarkable grandeur of ancient Rome's most imposing public buildings than any other building in the city.

Leaving the church, turn left for the entrance to the Museo Nazionale Romano, which occupies the halls and gardens of other sections of the baths, themselves adapted in the 16th century to house a Carthusian monastery adjoining the basilica. For years, much of the museum has been closed to the public because of the deterioration of the building. Though not yet complete, restorations have enabled the curators to open the section containing the famous **Ludovisi Throne,** with a 5th-century BC relief of Venus rising from the waves. In an upstairs gallery are the stuccos and wall paintings found in the area of the Farnesina Palace and the frescoes from Empress Livia's villa at Prima Porta, delightful depictions of a garden in bloom and an orchard alive with birds. Their colors are remarkably well preserved. These delicate decorations covered the walls of cool, sunken rooms in Livia's summer house outside the city. Other sections of the museum are due to open, perhaps even in **㉑** 1989, in **Palazzo Massimo** across the square on the other side of the gardens. It will, however, be some time before the entire collection is on view. *Via delle Terme di Diocleziano, tel. 06/ 4750181. Admission: 4,000 lire. Open Tues.–Sat. 9–2, Sun. 9–1.*

Villa Borghese to the Ara Pacis

There are a number of highlights on this tour. Given its length, you may find it sensible to go straight to one (or more) of them. In the order we cover them they are: Villa Borghese itself, the 17th-century pleasure gardens laid out by Cardinal Scipio Borghese and site of one of the finest museums in the city; Villa Giulia, a late-Renaissance papal summer house now containing a stunning collection of Etruscan art; the Museo Nazionale d'Arte Moderna, which will appeal to those sated on the art of past ages; the Pincian Hill, from where, many say, the finest view in Rome is to be had; the small church of Santa Maria del Popolo, which contains two stunning Caravaggios and architecture by Bramante and Raphael; and the Augusteum and the Ara Pacis, two monuments celebrating the golden age of the Emperor Augustus.

Villa Borghese

❶ Begin your tour at the **Porta Pinciana,** the Pincian gate, one of the historic city gates in the Aurelian Walls surrounding Rome. These walls were built by the Emperor Aurelius around AD 270 against the threat of Barbarian invasion. The Porta Pinciana itself, framed by two squat, circular towers, was constructed in the 6th century. Take care crossing the road to the gate: The traffic here comes hurtling in from all directions. Pass through the gate and into Villa Borghese.

Although the name **Villa Borghese** might suggest some stately Roman palazzo, it is in fact the name of a park, originally part of

Villa Borghese to the Ara Pacis

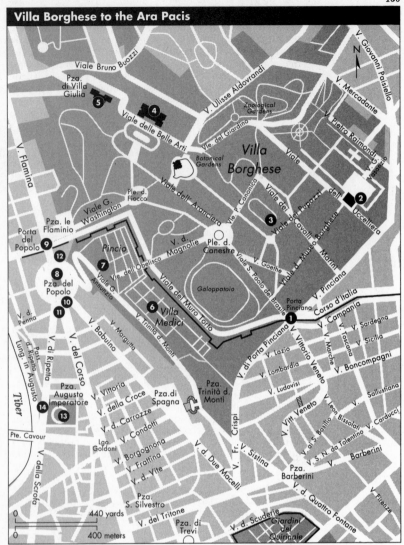

the pleasure gardens laid out in the early 17th century by Cardinal Scipione Borghese, a worldly and cultivated cleric and nephew of Pope Paul V. Today's gardens bear little resemblance to the originals. Not only do they cover a much smaller area—by 1630, the perimeter wall was almost three miles long—they have also been almost entirely remodeled. This occurred at the end of the 18th century, when a Scottish painter, Jacob More, was employed to transform them into the style of the "cunningly natural" park so popular in 18th-century England. Hitherto, the park was probably the finest example of an Italian-style garden in the entire country, a style that was largely derived from the gardens of the Emperor Hadrian's villa at Tivoli outside Rome. In contrast to the formal and rigidly symmetrical gardens of 17th-century France—that at Versailles is the best example—these Italian gardens had no overall symmetrical plan. Rather, they consisted of a series of small, interlinked formal gardens attached by paths and divided by meticulously trimmed hedges. Flowers—the Romans were particularly fond of tulips—statues, ponds, and small enclosures for animals (the more exotic the better; lions and peacocks were favorites) were scattered artfully around. Here, the cardinal and his friends strolled and discussed poetry, music, painting, and philosophy. Today the area immediately in front of the casino (see below) and the sunken open-air "dining room" are all that remain from the cardinal's original gorgeous creation.

2 Once into the park, turn right and make for the **Galleria Borghese,** the art collections housed in the casino, or summer house. You'll pass the open-air dining room on your right. The casino itself was built (from 1613) partly to house the cardinal's rich collections of painting and sculpture, partly as an elegant venue for summer parties and musical evenings. Despite its considerable size, it was never lived in. The building has been undergoing substantial renovations for some years, and the work will continue through the end of 1989 at least. As a result the second floor, site of the picture collection, has been closed. The sculpture galleries of the first floor are still open, however. During construction, the entrance to the building is from Via Raimondi, reached from Via Pinciana. *Piazzale Museo Borghese, tel. 06/858577. Admission free for the duration of renovations. Open Mon. 9–2, Tues.–Sat. 9–7, Sun. 9–1.*

Like the gardens, the casino and its collections have undergone many changes since the 17th century. It was Camillo Borghese, the husband of Napoleon's sister Pauline, who was responsible for most of them. He sold off a substantial number of the paintings to Napoleon and swapped 200 of the classical sculptures for an estate in Piedmont, in northern Italy, also courtesy of Napoleon. These paintings and sculptures are all still in the Louvre in Paris. At the end of the 19th century a later member of the family, Francesco Borghese, replaced some of the gaps in the collections, and also transferred to the casino the remaining works of art housed in Palazzo Borghese. In 1902 the casino, its contents, and the park were sold to the Italian government.

The most famous work in the collection is Canova's sculpture of Pauline Borghese. It's technically known as *Venus Vincitrix,* but there has never been any doubt as to its real subject. Pauline reclines on a Roman sofa, covered only in a seemingly transparent gown, the very model of haughty detachment and sly come hither. Surprisingly, Camillo Borghese seems to have been remarkably unconcerned that his wife had posed for this erotic masterpiece. Pauline, on the other hand, is known to have been shocked that her husband took such evident pleasure in showing off the work to guests. This coyness seems all the more curious given the reply Pauline is supposed to have made to a lady who asked her how she could have posed for the sculpture: "Oh, but the studio was heated." But then it was exactly the combination of aristocratic disdain and naivete that is said to have made her so irresistible in the first place. At all events, and much to the dismay of Canova, following Camillo and Pauline's divorce, the statue was locked away for many years, though the artist was occasionally allowed to show it to a hand-picked few. This he would do at night by the light of a single candle.

The next two rooms hold two key early Baroque sculptures: Bernini's *David* and *Apollo and Daphne*. Both illustrate the extraordinary technical facility of Bernini. As important, both also demonstrate the Baroque desire to invest sculpture with a living quality, to transform inert marble into living flesh. Where Renaissance sculptors wanted to capture the idealized beauty of the human form that they had discovered in ancient Greek and Roman sculptures, Baroque sculptors like Bernini wanted to make their work dramatic, too. They wanted movement and they wanted drama. The *Apollo and Daphne* shows the moment when, to escape the pursuing Apollo, Daphne turns herself into a laurel tree. Leaves and twigs sprout from her fingertips as she stretches agonizingly away from Apollo, who instinctively recoils in terror and amazement. This is the stuff that really makes the Baroque exciting. There are more Berninis to see in the collection, notably a very uncharacteristic work, a large unfinished figure of *Verità*, or Truth. Bernini had started work on this brooding figure after the death of his principal patron, Pope Urban VIII. His successor as pope, Innocent X, had little love for the ebullient Urban, and, as was the way in Rome, this meant that Bernini, too, was excluded from the new pope's favors. Bernini's towering genius was such, however, as to gain him the patronage of the new pope with almost indecent haste. The *Verità* was accordingly left incomplete.

Once you've torn yourself away from Cardinal Scipione's collections, you can enjoy the vast park to your heart's content. On the right, as you leave the casino, you can continue along to the rather dreary Rome **zoo,** where there's a simple but good restaurant. Alternatively, turn left onto Viale dei Pupazzi and head to Piazza dei Cavalli Marini, with its sea-horse fountain.

❸ Continue on or turn right: Either way you'll come upon the **Piazza di Siena,** a grassy hippodrome shaded by tall pines. Turn left as you leave this peaceful spot by way of the broad Viale Acqua Felix and you'll come to the entrance of the delightful botanical garden. Here there's a pretty little lake with the neo-Classical **Temple of Aesculapius,** and a café under the trees.

❹ From the temple head up to the **Galleria Nazionale d'Arte Moderna** (the National Gallery of Modern Art), a massive white building boasting the leading collection of 20th-century works in the country. A large new wing was opened in 1988. *Via delle Belle Arti 131, tel. 06/802751. Admission: 4,000 lire. Open Tues.–Sat. 9–2, Sun. 9–1.*

⑤ Near the museum is the **Museo di Villa Giulia**, a massive villa built around 1551 for Pope Julius III (and originally surrounded by a park planted with no less than 36,000 trees). Among the team called in by the pleasure-loving pope to build the villa were Michelangelo and his fellow Florentine, Vasari. Most of the actual work, however, was done by Vignola and Ammanati. Never intended to be a dwelling, the villa was used by the pope for a day's distraction from the cares and intrigues of the Vatican. The villa was designed in and around a garden, and its **nymphaeum**—or sunken sculpture garden—is a superb example of a late-Renaissance princely pleasure ground.

Today, the Villa Giulia houses one of the world's most important collections of Etruscan art. Be warned that though it's well arranged and displayed, it's overwhelming in size. Unless you're an Etruscan buff, you probably won't be enthralled by hundreds of look-alike statuettes and vases, so concentrate on the highlights. Most of the exhibits come from sites in Etruria, the area north of Rome between the Tiber and the Arno that was once the Etruscan heartland. However, you'll also see fascinating objects from other parts of central Italy that were dominated by the Etruscans before the rise of Rome.

No one knows precisely where the Etruscans originated. Many scholars maintain that they came from Asia Minor, appearing in Italy about 1000 BC. Like the Egyptians, they buried their dead with everything that might be needed in the afterlife, and painted their tombs with happy scenes of everyday activities. Thus, in death they have provided the present day with precious information about their life. There are countless artistic treasures in the Villa Giulia, and you'll find that even the tiniest gold earrings and brooches and the humblest bronze household implements display marvelous workmanship and joyful inventiveness. The most striking works are the terra-cotta statues. Some, like the *Apollo of Veio*, still retain traces of their original multicolored decoration; others, like the serenely beautiful *Sarcophagus of the Sposi*, are worn to a warm, glowing golden patina. There are rooms full of vases (most of them Greek); the Etruscans prided themselves on their refined taste for these handsome objects. Off the large central gallery displaying the vases of the Castellani collection (directly above the main entrance) there's a treasure trove in a small, locked room on the far left. The museum guard will admit you on request (leave your passport or other ID with him) to the breathtaking Castellani collection of ancient and antique jewelry. Some are original, some are copies crafted in precious materials. *Piazza di Villa Giulia 9, tel. 06/3601951. Admission: 4,000 lire. Open Tues.–Sat. 9–7, Sun. 9–1.*

From the Pincio to the Ara Pacis

The southwestern corner of the Villa Borghese is taken up by the Pincio, or Pincian Hill, one of the seven hills of ancient Rome. It is also the site of the upscale Casino Caladier, where you can enjoy the view from the terrace café, and of the beautiful **Villa Medici** over the trees. Purchased by Napoleon and today the home of the French Academy, the Villa Medici, otherwise closed to the public, stages prestige art exhibits. Check with the tourist office to see if anything is being shown during your stay.

7 The **Pincio Gardens** are laid out in the rather formal style of the early 19th century on the site of what must have been the far more elaborate terraced gardens of Lucullus, the famous Roman gourmet whose banquets were legendary. A favorite spot for strolling couples and students on recess from nearby schools, the Pincio's pathways are lined with white marble busts of Italian heroes. Along with the similar busts on the Janiculum, these pose a constant problem. Since the busts first went up, a preferred sport of young Roman vandals has been a game that might be called "knock-nose," that is, knock the nose off the statue. Depending on the date of the last nose-knocking wave, you'll see the Pincio's busts forlornly noseless or in the throes of obvious plastic surgery.

The view from the Pincio terrace is one of Rome's most celebrated. Below you is Piazza del Popolo, as it was laid out around 1820 by the architect Giuseppe Valadier, who also planned the Pincio's gardens. Across the Tiber, Via Cola di Rienzo cuts across the Prati district toward the heights of Monte Mario. That low, brownish building on top of the hill is the Rome Hilton. Off to the left are Castel Sant'Angelo and the dome of St. Peter's. In the foreground is the curve of the Tiber, embracing Old Rome, where the dark dome of the Pantheon emerges from a sea of russet-tiled rooftops and graceful cupolas. A Roman sunset seen from the Pincio, when the clouds are afire with glorious shades of gold and pink and purple and you can see the rays of the sun through the windows below the dome of St. Peter's, is a spectacular sight.

8 Decorative and immense, **Piazza del Popolo,** located just below the Pincio, is a fitting introduction to the city for visitors entering from the roads to the north, all of which converge here. The desire to make this entrance to Rome something special inspired popes and their architects over three centuries. The piazza takes its name from the 15th-century church of Santa **9** Maria del Popolo, huddled on the right side of the **Porta del Popolo.** The medieval gate in the Aurelian Walls was replaced in 1561 by the present one, which was further embellished by Bernini in 1655 for the much-heralded arrival of Queen Christina of Sweden, who had abdicated her throne to become a Roman Catholic. Not many years later, the twin churches of **10** **Santa Maria in Montesanto** (on the left as you face them) and **11** **Santa Maria del Miracoli** (on the right) were added to the piazza at the point where Via del Babuino, Via del Corso, and Via di Ripetta converge. The piazza has always served as something of a society meeting place, crowded with fashionable carriages and carnival revelers in the past, today a magnet for youngsters on flashy motorcycles and their blasé elders at café tables. At election time, it's the scene of huge political rallies.

Time Out A café that has never gone out of style, **Rosati** is a rendezvous of literati, artists, and actors. There's a sidewalk cafè, a tearoom, and an upstairs dining room for a more upscale lunch. *Piazza del Popolo 4. Closed Tues.*

---

12 The church of **Santa Maria del Popolo** goes almost unnoticed in the vast piazza, but it has one of the richest collections of art of any church in Rome. Bramante enlarged the apse of the church, which had been rebuilt in the 15th century on the site of a much older place of worship. Around 1513, the banker Agostino Chigi commissioned Raphael to build him a chapel—the Chigi

Chapel, as it is now, unsurprisingly, known—and in the mid-17th century another Chigi, Pope Alexander VII, commissioned Bernini to restore and decorate the building. Inside, in the first chapel on the right, you'll see some frescoes by Pinturicchio; the adjacent Cybo Chapel is a 17th-century exercise in marble decoration. The organ case of Bernini in the right transept bears the Della Rovere oak tree, part of the Chigi family's coat of arms. The choir, with vault frescoes by Pinturicchio, contains the handsome tombs of Ascanio Sforza and Girolamo delle Rovere, both designed by Andrea Sansovino. The Cerasi Chapel, to the left of the high altar on the side walls, boasts two stunning Caravaggios, both key early-Baroque works. Compare their earthly realism and harshly dramatic lighting effects with the much more restrained and classically "pure" *Assumption of the Virgin* by Caravaggio's contemporary and rival, Annibale Carracci; it hangs over the altar of the chapel. Raphael's Chigi Chapel is the second on the left. Raphael also provided the cartoons for the vault mosaic and the designs for the statues of *Jonah* and *Elijah*. More than a century later, Bernini added the oval medallions on the tombs and the statues of *Daniel* and *Habakkuk*.

Time Out Starting down Via di Ripetta you'll find several places where you can stop for sustenance. **Cose Fritte** means "Fried Things," and those include rice croquettes, batter-fried vegetables, and other tasty snacks to take out. *Via di Ripetta 3. Open 11–3 and 5–midnight; closed Sun.*

On the left you pass the San Giacomo Hospital and on the right the horseshoe-shaped, neo-Classical building of the Academy of Fine Arts, from which chattering students spill out onto the adjacent streets and up to the Pincio.

⑬ From Via di Ripetta you step out into the vast piazza surrounding the **Augusteum**, the mausoleum built by Augustus for himself and his family (and unfortunately closed to the public for an indefinite period). Its Etruscan inspiration is evident; it's quite similar to the marble-girded tumulus tombs at Cerveteri. Transformed into a fortress during the Middle Ages and later into a garden, it was used for rousing public spectacles such as bullfights and fireworks displays until as late as the 1800s, and was to be restored to its original form in 1936. Inside, a series of concentric corridors leads to the central crypt, where the funerary urns were kept.

⑭ On the side of the Augusteum nearest the Tiber stands the **Ara Pacis,** a harmonious classical altar covered by a basic modern protective shell. The Ara Pacis, or Altar of Augustan Peace, was erected in 13 BC by order of the Senate to celebrate the epoch of peace heralded by Augustus's victories in Gaul and Spain. It was reconstructed here in 1938 after many years of painstaking assembly (some of the fragments were scattered as far away as the Louvre). The simple marble altar is enclosed by a marble screen decorated entirely with magnificent reliefs. Most notable is that of *Aeneas's Sacrifice*, on the right of the main entrance, and the procession of historical figures on the sides. *Via di Ripetta, tel. 06/6710271. Admission: 1,500 lire. Open Tues.–Sat. 9–1:30, Sun. 9–1.*

For a pleasant walk back to Piazza del Popolo, follow Passeggiata di Ripetta along to Via della Penna, a street of popular trattorias and shops.

Toward Trastevere

For the authentic atmosphere of old Rome, the areas covered in this tour are unbeatable. It takes you through three separate communities, each staunchly resisting the tides of change. You begin in the old ghetto, on the banks of the Tiber, a neighborhood that has proudly retained its Jewish heritage. Right up to the end of the 19th century, this really was a ghetto, its dark buildings clinging to the sides of ancient ruins for support. From it, you cross to Tiberina Island, and from there to Trastevere itself. Despite creeping gentrification, Trastevere remains about the most tightly knit community in Rome, its inhabitants proudly proclaiming descent—whether real or imagined—from the ancient Romans. From Trastevere you climb the Janiculum Hill, which offers views spanning the whole city, and is beloved of all Romans.

The Ghetto and Isola Tiberina

1 **Piazza Venezia** is the starting point for touring this ancient quarter of the city. From the piazza below the Campidoglio take **Via del Teatro Marcello** and turn right at Via Montanara into Piazza Campitelli, with its Baroque church and fountain. Take Via dei Funari at the end of the piazza and follow it into Piazza Mattei, where one of Rome's loveliest fountains, the **2** 16th-century **Fontana delle Tartarughe** (Fountain of the Turtles) is tucked away. A few steps down Via Caetani you'll find a doorway into the public part of the old **Palazzo Mattei,** worth a peek at the sculpture-rich courtyard and staircase.

From the fountain, take Via delle Reginella into **Via Portico d'Ottavia,** heart of the Jewish ghetto. Look closely at the buildings, where medieval inscriptions, ancient friezes, and half-buried classical columns attest to the venerable history of this neighborhood, a lively commercial quarter of old palaces and good restaurants. Here, warm weather brings family life out onto the streets: Tables and ill-assorted chairs appear in the piazzas toward evening, while steaming casseroles are carried down from cramped kitchens and the young and old of the clan prepare to enjoy an alfresco supper and a game of *briscola* with the neighbors.

Time Out **Meeting Meal** serves excellent kosher fast food. Try the *tortiglioni,* spicy chopped veal baked in pastry. *Via Portico d'Ottavia 7/b. Closed Sat.*

Until the 13th century the Jews were esteemed citizens of Rome. Among them were the bankers and physicians to the popes, who had themselves given permission for the construction of the synagogue. But later popes of the Renaissance and Counter-Reformation revoked this tolerance, confining the Jews to the ghetto and imposing a series of restrictions, some of which were enforced as late as 1870.

3 The old church of **Sant'Angelo in Peschiera** was built right into the ruins of the Portico d'Ottavia which serves as a kind of foyer for the long-gone Temples of Jupiter and Juno. A stone plaque on a pillar, a relic of the time when there was an important fish market here, admonishes in Latin that the head of any fish surpassing the length of the plaque was to be cut off "up to the first

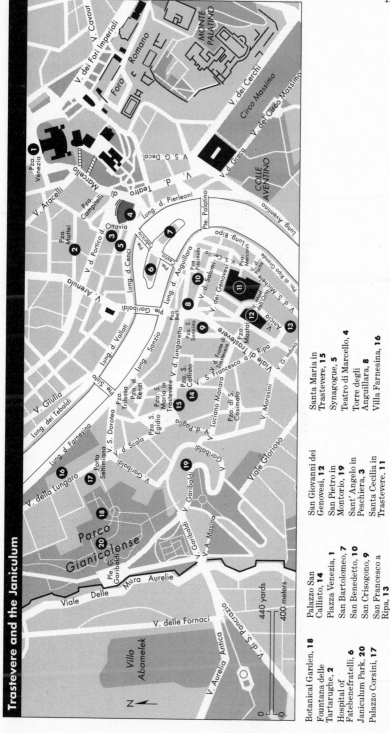

Trastevere and the Janiculum

Botanical Garden, **18**
Fountana delle Tartarughe, **2**
Hospital of Fatebenefratelli, **6**
Janiculum Park, **20**
Palazzo Corsini, **17**

Palazzo San Callisto, **14**
Piazza Venezia, **1**
San Bartolomeo, **7**
San Benedetto, **10**
San Crisogono, **9**
San Francesco a Ripa, **13**

San Giovanni dei Genovesi, **12**
San Pietro in Montorio, **19**
Sant' Angelo in Peschiera, **3**
Santa Cecilia in Trastevere, **11**

Santa Maria in Trastevere, **15**
Synagogue, **5**
Teatro di Marcello, **4**
Torre degli Anguillara, **8**
Villa Farnesina, **16**

fin" and given to the city fathers or else the catcher was to pay
a fine of 10 gold florins. The heads were used to make fish soup
and were considered a great delicacy.

❹ The nearby **Teatro di Marcello** is hardly recognizable as a theater today, but originally it was a huge place, designed to hold
20,000 spectators. It was begun by Julius Caesar and completed by the Emperor Augustus in AD 13. Like other Roman
monuments, it was transformed into a fortress in the Middle
Ages. During the Renaissance, it was converted into a palace
for the Savelli family. To your right, on Lungotevere Cenci, is
❺ the big, bronze-roofed **synagogue.** It contains an interesting
permanent exhibit documenting the history of the Jewish
community in Rome. *Lungotevere Cenci, tel. 06/6564648.
Admission free. Open Mon.–Fri. 10–2, Sun. 10–12.*

Now cross **Ponte Fabricio,** built in 62 BC and the oldest bridge in
the city. It spans the river Tiber to the Isola Tiberina, the little
❻ island in the river and a charming backwater, where the **hospital of Fatebenefratelli** (literally, "Do good, brothers") continues
a tradition that began in 291 BC when a temple to Aesculapius,
with annexed infirmary, was erected here. Aesculapius—
Asclepius to the Greeks—was the ancient god of healing, and
the son of the god Apollo. His symbol was the snake. The Romans adopted him as their god of healing in 293 BC during a
terrible plague. A ship was sent to Epidaurus in Greece—
heart of the cult of Asclepius and a sort of Greek Lourdes—to
obtain a statue of the god. As the ship sailed back up the Tiber,
a great serpent was seen escaping from it and swimming to the
island. This was taken as a sign that a temple to Aesculapius
should be built there. Here the sick would come to bathe in the
island's spring waters and to sleep in the temple, hoping that
Aesculapius would visit them in their dreams to cure them.
There's no trace of the temple now, but the island has been
associated with medicine ever since—hence of course the
presence of the hospital (it stands on the site of a medieval hospital).

❼ Next to it is the church of **San Bartolomeo,** built at the end of
the 10th century by the Holy Roman Emperor Otto III. Restorations and rebuilding down through the years have resulted in
the sad fact that almost nothing remains of Otto's original
church. It's thought, however, that the little wellhead on the
chancel steps—the steps leading to the choir—is original, and
that it stands on the site of the spring in the temple. The tradition of healing is continued in the belief that Rahere, an English
Augustinian monk in the 12th century, visited the church and
had a vision that led to his founding the hospital of St.
Bartholomew—the English for Batolomeo—in London, still
going strong 800 years later.

Into Trastevere

From the Isola Tiberina, cross Ponte Cestio into Trastevere.
Literally translated, Trastevere means "across the Tiber," and
indeed the *Trasteverini* have always been proud and combat-
ive, a breed apart. In the Middle Ages, Trastevere wasn't even
considered part of Rome, and the "foreigners" who populated
its maze of alleys and piazzas fought bitterly to obtain recognition for the neighborhood as a *rione*, or official district of the
city. In the 14th century the Trasteverini won out and became

full-fledged Romans. Since then they have stoutly maintained
their separate identity, though in recent years popular tradition has been distorted into false folklore for the benefit of the
tourists in the most-frequented locales. The real Trasteverini
are still there, however, hearty and uninhibited, greatly an-
noyed at the name their quarter has justifiably acquired for
purse-snatching and petty thievery and for the creeping
gentrification of the area.

Start your walk around Trastevere at **Piazza Belli,** dedicated to
the top-hatted, 19th-century dialect poet whose bronze effigy
watches over the square. On the left is the 13th-century **Torre
degli Anguillara**—"torre" means tower—with a faithfully restored medieval house at its base. The church on the right at
the far end of the piazza is that of **San Crisogono,** founded in the
6th century and rebuilt 600 years later, when the pretty campanile, or bell tower, was added. Step inside to see the beautiful
Cosmatesque pavement and the 13th-century mosaic in the
apse.

Time Out As its name suggests, the **Casa del Tramezzino** (House of Sandwiches) specializes in the earl of Sandwich's invention, offering
a tantalizing variety over the counter. *Viale Trastevere 81.
Closed Thurs.*

Next, cross Viale Trastevere and take Via della Lungaretta
past some intriguing alleys into **Piazza in Piscinula** (from "pis-
cina" meaning pool), which takes its name from some ancient
Roman baths on the site. The tiny church of **San Benedetto,** the
smallest church in the city, on the piazza is much older than its
18th-century facade would lead you to believe. It was probably
built in the 4th century AD. Opposite is the medieval **Casa dei
Mattei.** Rich and powerful, the Mattei family lived here until
the 16th century, when, after a series of murders on the premises, they decided to move out of the district entirely, crossing
the river to build their magnificent palace in the ghetto.

Take Via in Piscinula at the side of the church, crossing Via dei
Salumi, where the sausage-makers stored their goods, into
tiny Vicolo dell'Atela. It was in this minuscule byway, in 1849,
that excavators discovered the famous statue of the *Apoxyomenos*, the athlete holding a strigil, or scraper, that is
now in the Vatican Museum. Turn left into Via dei Genovesi and
then right to the piazza in front of the church of **Santa Cecilia in
Trastevere.** It commemorates one of ancient Rome's most celebrated early Christian martyrs, the aristocratic St. Cecilia,
done to death by the Emperor Diocletian around the year AD
300. After an abortive attempt to suffocate her in the baths of
her own house (a favorite means of quietly disposing of aristo-
crats in Roman days), she was brought before the executioner.
But not even three blows of the executioner's sword could dis-
patch the young girl. She lingered for several days, converting
others to the Christian cause, before finally dying. Trastevere
mothers and their children love to wander in the delightful little garden in front of the church, and there's no reason why you
shouldn't join them for a bit. A beautiful white marble figure of
the saint lies below the main altar. If you've timed your visit to
the church for Tuesday or Thursday morning, between 10 and
noon, or Sunday, from 11 to noon, you can enter the cloistered
convent to see what remains of Pietro Cavallini's powerful and
rich fresco of the *Last Judgment.* It is the only major fresco in

existence known to have been painted by Cavallini, a forerunner of Giotto. The fresco dates from 1293.

Explore the little streets and piazzas around the church. **Ripa Grande** on the Tiber—the road running beside the river—was the site of Trastevere's port, the largest in Rome until it was destroyed to make way for the modern embankments earlier this century. **Via del Porto** gives you a fine view of the Aventine Hill across the Tiber. **Piazza dei Mercanti** is especially noted for its colorful, if touristy, restaurants. Take **Via di San Michele**, which skirts what was once a huge Renaissance convent and is now destined to house ministry offices and cultural institutes. Turn right into **Via Madonna dell'Orto**, where there's a church decorated with obelisks. Take a detour to the right on **Via Anicia** as far as #12. Here you should ring for the guardian, **⑫** who'll show you the extraordinary 15th-century cloister of **San Giovanni dei Genovesi**, with its secluded garden. Return down **⑬** Via Anicia to **San Francesco a Ripa**, a Baroque church attached to a 13th-century Franciscan monastery. The church is noted for one of Bernini's last works, a dramatically lighted statue of Blessed Ludovica Albertoni. It seems to take the ecstasy of Bernini's St. Theresa a step further into a realm of mysticism, in which it is hard to distinguish spiritual from bodily ecstasy.

Take Via San Francesco a Ripa across Viale Trastevere and then make the next left into **Piazza San Cosimato**, scene of a busy market on weekday mornings, and known for its fine fish restaurants. On the right is the 10th-century porch of the church of **San Cosimato;** the church is closed to the public. Follow Via di San Cosimato into Piazza San Callisto, where the big **⑭** palace on your right is the 17th-century **Palazzo San Callisto**. Today it belongs to the Vatican.

Here you'll enter the very heart of the *rione*, or district, of Trastevere, the lovely **Piazza di Santa Maria in Trastevere**, with its elegant raised fountain and sidewalk cafés. This piazza has seen the passing of innumerable generations of tourists and travelers, who come to lounge on the steps of the church or to drink an espresso. As far back as the Middle Ages, Trastevere had a large foreign colony, composed mainly of Orientals. Before they moved over to the ghetto on the other side of the river, the Eastern Jews who came to Rome also settled here. Raphael's model and mistress, the dark-eyed Fornarina (literally, "the baker's daughter"), is believed to have been a *Trasteverina*. And for Romans and foreigners alike, Piazza Santa Maria is the meeting place of Trastevere, a sort of outdoor living room, open to all comers.

⑮ **Santa Maria in Trastevere** is supposedly the first church in Rome to have been dedicated to the Virgin Mary. It's known, however, to have been built by the 4th century, making it at least one of the oldest churches in the city. The present church was built in the 12th century, and the portico, the entrance, was added in the 19th century. The mosaics on the facade, which add light and color to the piazza, date from the 12th and 13th centuries. There are more mosaics of the same periods inside the church. In that representing the *Life of the Virgin*, note the little building labeled "Taberna Meritoria" just under the figure of the Virgin in the Nativity scene, with a stream of oil flowing from it. It recalls the legend that on the day Christ was born, a spring of pure oil flowed from the earth on the site of the piazza, signifying the coming of the grace of God. At one corner of the piazza, there's a little street called Via delle Fonte dell'Olio in honor of this miracle. It leads to **Piazza dei Renzi,** where you bear right into Via della Pelliccia or Vicolo dei Renzi to Via del Moro and thence to **Piazza Trilussa.**

The Villa Farnesina and the Janiculum

Piazza Trilussa is on the edge of Trastevere, at the end of **Ponte Sisto,** built in the 15th century by Pope Sixtus IV to expedite commercial traffic in view of the upcoming Holy Year of 1475. The bridge is open only to pedestrian traffic.

Off to the side of Piazza Trilussa stands a monument to the racy dialect poet **Trilussa,** beloved of *Trasteverini*. A neighborhood baglady or two and occasional homeless brethren have elected him their protector. They doze in the little garden behind his statue and make their sketchy ablutions in the fountain. Take the street off the right of the piazza onto **Via Santa Dorotea,** where at #20 you'll pass the house where it is said that Raphael's mistress, the Fornarina, lived.

16 Passing through Porta Settimiana and taking Via della Lungara, you'll come to the beautiful **Villa Farnesina** on the right, with its green, tree-shaded gardens. The villa was built by Baldassare Peruzzi for wealthy banker Agostino Chigi about 1511. Raphael designed some of the decorations in the airy loggias, now glassed in to protect their artistic treasures. When he could steal a little time from his work on the Vatican Stanze, and from his wooing of the Fornarina, he came over to execute some of the frescoes himself, notably a luminous *Galatea*. Stroll through the salons, where popes and princes of 16th-century Rome were entertained by extravagant host Agostino. He delighted in impressing his guests by ordering his servants to clear the table by casting into the river the precious silver and gold dinnerware used at open-air suppers. His extravagance was not quite so boundless as he wished to make it appear, however: He strung nets under the water to catch the precious plates as they were flung into the muddy waters.

Your visit starts in the **Loggia of Psyche** on the ground floor, where Giulio Romano and others worked from Raphael's designs. The *Galatea* is in the adjacent room. On the floor above you can see the trompe l'oeil effects in the aptly named Hall of Perspectives by Peruzzi. Agostino Chigi's bedroom, next door, was frescoed by Il Sodoma with scenes from the life of Alexander the Great, notably the *Wedding of Alexander and Roxanne*, which is considered to be the artist's best work. The palace is now home of the prestigious Accademia dei Lincei, and it also houses the Gabinetto Nazionale delle Stampe, a treasure house of old prints and drawings. When the Tiber embankments were built in 1879, the remains of a classical villa were discovered under the Farnesina gardens, and their decorations were transferred to the Museo delle Terme. *Via della Lungara 230, tel. 06/6540565. Admission free. Open Mon.–Sat. 9–1.*

17 Cross Via della Lungara to **Palazzo Corsini,** which currently is housing the 17th- and 18th-century sections of the collection of the Galleria Nazionale d'Arte Antica until they can be moved to Palazzo Barberini. Among the most famous paintings in the collection is Guido Reni's *Beatrice Cenci*. (Via della Lungara 10, tel. 06/6542323. Admission: 3,000 lire. Open Tues.–Sat. **18** 9–7, Sun. and Mon. 9–1.) Behind Palazzo Corsini is Rome's **Botanical Garden,** an attractive oasis of greenery that was once part of the extensive Corsini estate. (Largo Cristina di Svezia, at the end of Via Corsini, tel. 06/6564193. Admission free. Open Mon.–Sat. 9–5.)

Retrace your steps back to Porta Settimiana and turn right into Via Garibaldi, which climbs to the Janiculum. Continue up Via Garibaldi to the terrace in front of the church of **San Pietro in Montorio;** it offers a stirring view of the Palatine and Aventine hills across the river. The church was built by order of Ferdinand and Isabella of Spain in 1481 over the spot where, tradition says, St. Peter was crucified. A handsome and dignified edifice, the church contains a number of well-known works, including the *Flagellation* in the first chapel on the right, painted by the Venetian Sebastiano del Piombo from a design by Michelangelo, and the *St. Francis in Ecstasy,* in the next-to-last chapel on the left, in which Bernini made one of his earliest experiments with concealed lighting effects. However, perhaps the most famous work here is the circular **Tempietto,** the little temple, in the cloister. This sober little building—though tiny, holding only 10 people, it is actually a church in its own right—is one of the key Renaissance buildings in Rome. It was designed by Bramante, the original architect of the new St. Peter's, in 1502, and represents one of the earliest and most successful attempts to produce an entirely classical building; one in which the lessons of ancient Greek and Roman architecture are fully evident. The basic design was derived from a circular temple on the grounds of the Emperor Hadrian's great villa at Tivoli outside Rome. However, Bramante altered this by extending the inner cylinder—in plan, the building is essentially no more than two interlocking cylinders—upward. On it he built a hemispherical dome. As ever with the most rigorously classical buildings, the proportions of the constituent parts are extremely carefully worked out. Thus the diameter of the inner cylinder is exactly half that of the outer cylinder, and the height of the building is exactly double its width. Bramante's original plan called for a new cloister to be built around the Tempietto. This, too, was to be circular and its proportions would echo that of the Tempietto.

As you head up the Janiculum, you come upon the huge **Acqua Paola** fountain, an early 17th-century creation with a vast pool that can be tempting on a hot day. The fountain marks the entrance to the **Janiculum Park,** famous for its splendid view of Rome, its noontime cannon, its statues of Giuseppe and Anita Garibaldi (Garibaldi was the guiding spirit behind the unification of Italy in the 19th century; Anita was his long-suffering wife), and, like the Pincio, its nose-less and bedaubed busts. If you're tired or pressed for time, the #41 bus in the direction you're following will take you to St. Peter's or to the other side of the Tiber at Corso Vittorio. If you prefer to walk, follow the road as it curves lazily downward past a curious lighthouse, a gift of the Argentines in recognition of Garibaldi's efforts on behalf of *their* independence.

The Aventine to St. Paul's

This tour takes you around one of Rome's quietest and greenest neighborhoods, the Aventine Hill, one of the seven hills of Rome, that rises serenely above the streams of heavy traffic pouring around it. Stroll up it and you come to a number of Rome's oldest and least-visited churches as well as to one of the city's most surprising delights: the keyhole in the gate to the garden of the Knights of Malta. Beyond lies Testaccio, mecca for those who value traditional inexpensive Roman food, and the pyramid, one of Rome's most distinctive and idiosyncratic landmarks: it's a tomb, built by an ancient Roman with more than half an eye on posterity. The tour ends at one of the greatest pilgrimage churches in Italy, the medieval basilica of San Paolo fuori le Mura, St. Paul's outside the Walls.

① Start your walk at the southern end of **Via del Teatro Marcello** by the little church of **San Nicola in Carcere.** The interior of the church is unexceptional, but the exterior illustrates to perfection the Roman habit of building and rebuilding ancient sites, incorporating parts of existing buildings in new buildings, adding to them, and then adding to them again. The church stands on the site of a temple built around 250 BC, some of the columns of which can be seen to the right of the church as you face it, beside what remains of the medieval campanile, or bell tower. The facade dates from the mid-16th century and is thought to have been designed by Giacomo della Porta, the architect who completed the dome of St. Peter's after Michelangelo's death.

② ③ The ruins of two small temples now face you: the rectangular **Temple of Fortuna Virilis** and the circular **Temple of Hercules,** both built around 100 BC. The steps of the Temple of Fortuna Virilis give an excellent view over the Tiber to Trastevere. Opposite them is **Casa di Crescenzio,** one of only a handful of medieval houses in Rome to have survived. The inscription on its facade announces that the house was built by Nicolò, son of Crescenzio, and that in building it he wished—and you must at least admire his ambition—to re-create the glory of ancient Rome. To this end he incorporated various classical fragments in the facade. However, the Colosseum it is not.

④ Walk around the corner to **Piazza del Bocca della Verità**—the Square of the Mouth of Truth. It's on the site of the Forum Boarium, ancient Rome's cattle market, later used for public executions. Its sinister name is derived from the gaping marble mouth—actually part of an ancient drain cover, found in the Middle Ages half-buried—set into the facade of the church of **⑤** **Santa Maria in Cosmedin.** Those suspected of lying—especially women accused of adultery—would be brought here and made to put their right hand into the mouth. If they continued to lie, the statue's jaws would slam shut, severing their fingers. Or so it was believed. In fact, the ordeal of this public humiliation was such as to make most, innocent or not, admit their guilt. The church itself is one of the oldest in Rome, built in the 6th century for the city's burgeoning Greek population, hence its original name: Santa Maria de Schola Graecia, "schola" meaning group, and "Graecia" meaning Greek. At the end of the 19th century the church was restored to its original basilica, or hall-like, form.

Turn onto Via della Greca and head up the Aventine Hill, taking the first road on the right, Clivo del Publici. This skirts **Valle Margia,** the city's rose garden; it's glorious in May and June. You pass next by a little park, **Parco Savello,** known for its orange trees.

⑥ Next door is the majestic church of **Santa Sabina,** an early-Christian basilica that has been extensively restored to its original simplicity. Its beautifully carved and preserved wooden doors are the oldest of their kind in existence. Like the church, they date from the 5th century. Just a few steps from Santa Sabina you'll come upon the entrance to the courtyard of another ancient church, **Sant'Alessio,** founded in the 4th century. What you see is the result of reconstructions and restorations over the centuries. In addition to the Romanesque bell tower and crypt and the 15th-century cloister, you should look for the curious marble sculpture at the head of the left nave. It commemorates the death of St. Alexis, son of a wealthy patrician family of early Christian times. St. Alexis disdained the luxury to which he had been born and endured years of penitence and prayer before returning home so emaciated that no one recognized him. Ever humble and self-effacing, he elected to live as a servant in his family's household, sleeping under the stairs for 17 years until his death.

Via di Santa Sabina leads to **Piazza Cavalieri di Malta,** the Square of the Knights of Malta. The knights are members of the world's oldest and most exclusive order of chivalry, founded in the Holy Land in 1080. Though nominally tenders of the sick in those early days, a role that has since become the order's raison d'etre, the knights amassed huge tracts of land in the Middle East and established themselves as a fearsome mercenary force. From 1530 they were based on the Mediterranean island of Malta, having been expelled from another Mediterranean stronghold, Rhodes, by the Turks in 1522. In 1798 Napoleon expelled them from Malta, and in 1834 they established themselves in Rome. The buildings belonging to the knights in this square, however, are not part of this headquarters. Rather, they are the headquarters of the Italian branch of the order, designed around 1765 by Piranesi, 18th-century Rome's foremost engraver (and not a bad architect, either). To one side of the square is the monumental entrance to the knights' (private) garden. Look through the keyhole in the door in the center for one of the most memorable and surprising views in Rome: an avenue of trees exactly framing the distant dome of St. Peter's.

Follow Via di Sant'Anselmo through the district's quiet residential streets. You'll cross busy Viale Aventino at Piazza Albania and climb the so-called Piccolo Aventino on Via di San Saba to the peaceful little garden that holds the 13th-century church of **San Saba,** built probably in the 10th century for Oriental monks (the Orient to the Romans of the Middle Ages meant Arabia, not China and Japan). Go to the aisle on the left-hand side of the church to see its unusual frescoes, painted by an unknown 13th-century artist. The most famous scene shows three young girls lying naked on a bed. Taken at face value, this apparently lewd scene seems unsuitable for a church; it, however, illustrates the good works of St. Nicholas, the prototype, as it were, for Santa Claus. The girls are the daughters of a high-born but impoverished father; that's him standing on the right of the bed, looking very unhappy. They are naked because the only future for them is prostitution, or so their despairing father thinks. Outside the window, however, is St. Nicholas, about to toss a bag of gold coins into the room to rescue the poor maidens from their lives of shame.

From the church, cut across the little park to Via Marmorata and Piazza Testaccio, hub of one of Rome's most authentic

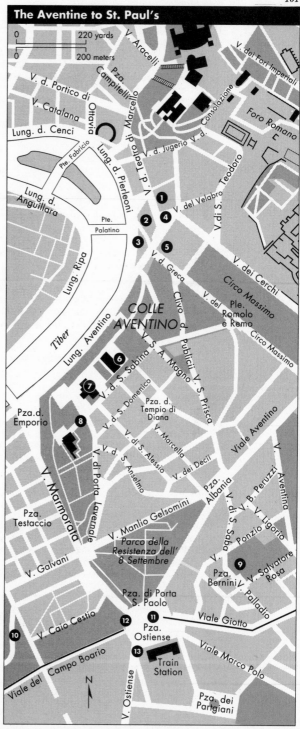

The Aventine to St. Paul's

working-class neighborhoods. Testaccio is known for two quite
⑩ different attractions. One is **Monte Testaccio,** a green hill about
150 feet high. What makes this otherwise unremarkable
looking hill special is the fact that it's made from fragments of pottery—pieces of amphorae, pitchers used in ancient times to transport oil, wheat, wine, and other goods.
What began as a dump for the broken pitchers seemed in time
to have taken on a life of its own, until, by the Middle Ages, the
hill, growing even larger, had become a place of pilgrimage.
Testaccio's other claim to fame is its excellent local restaurants. You won't find much in the way of haute cuisine—the
food here is traditional Italian working-class, with the emphasis on innards and other inexpensive cuts—but those with a
taste for this kind of simple but hearty fare will find much to
enjoy.

Time Out Among the many down-to-earth eating places in Testaccio, try
Il Cantinone, a favorite among locals as it offers reasonably
priced dishes. *Piazza Testaccio 31. Closed Wed.*

The Pyramid and San Paolo

⑪ From Testaccio make your way to **Porta San Paolo,** one of the
ancient city gates built by the Emperor Aurelian in the 3rd century AD. The dominant feature here is not the gate, however,
⑫ but the immense **pyramid of Gaius Cestius,** reaching 120 feet
into the sky. Gaius, an immensely wealthy praetor, or magistrate, in Imperial Rome had this monumental tomb built for
himself in 12 BC. Though an otherwise unremarkable figure, his
desire for something approaching immortality found concrete
expression in this megalomaniac structure.

⑬ Your goal now is the church of **San Paolo fuori le Mura;** literally,
St. Paul's outside the Walls. Take the metro, or bus 23, 318, or
673 for the ride to the church. San Paolo, for all the dreariness
of its suburban location—and, indeed, for all of its exterior's
dullness (19th-century British writer Augustus Hare said the
church looked like "a very ugly railway station")—is one of the
most historic and important churches in Rome, second in size
only to St. Peter's. This is as it should be: As St. Peter's is built
over the site where St. Peter was buried, so St. Paul's is built
over the site where St. Paul was buried. The building has had a
distinctly checkered past. It was built by the Emperor Constantine in the 4th century AD, then rebuilt and considerably
enlarged about a century later. It was then the largest church
in Europe, larger by far than Constantine's St. Peter's. The
church's location away from the city meant that it was especially vulnerable to attack, and indeed it was sacked by the
rampaging Saracens in 846. The then pope, John VIII, took the
precaution of fortifying it. Nevertheless, over the next 200
years, the church gradually declined in importance, especially
once the marshes surrounding it became infected with malarial
mosquitoes. Sheep wandered around the basilica, undisturbed
by the few remaining monks, themselves largely sunk in a stupor of drunkenness and lethargy. This sorry state of affairs
came to a sudden end in the middle of the 11th century with the
arrival of a new abbot, Hildebrandt. He restored the building,
recruited new monks, and made St. Paul's a revered center of
pilgrimage once more. And such it remained until July 1823.
Then, in a catastrophic fire, the church burned to the ground.
It's said that the pope, Pius VII, who had himself been a monk

at St. Paul's, had been troubled by dreams of a disaster. (It was this same pope who had been arrested and carted off to France by Napoleon during the French Revolution, a humiliation from which he had never really recovered.) Furthermore, it had been pointed out by many that when Pius died and his portrait was placed in the basilica alongside those of his predecessors, there would be no room for further papal portraits. The omens were more than vindicated when the fire swept through the church. All that remained, apart from a few mosaics and other decorations, were the cloisters. Although the rebuilt St. Paul's has a sort of monumental grandeur, its columns stretching up the dusky nave, its 19th-century mosaics glinting dully, it's only in the cloisters that you get a real sense of what must have been the magnificence of the original building. The columns supporting the arcades of the cloisters are remarkable for their variety and richness. Some are slim and straight, others cork-screw violently; some are carved in creamy marble, others are encrusted with mosaics. Look for the little animals carved in the spaces between the columns. The entrance to the cloisters is from the right transept, the right "arm" of the church as you face the altar.

The Celian Hill and the Baths of Caracalla

This tour concentrates on some of the oldest and most venerable churches in Rome. It ends, however, at one of the most spectacular classical sites in the city, the Baths of Caracalla. Those who have had their fill of Rome's churches can make straight for the baths. Nonetheless, particularly if you have already explored many of the busier and noisier districts of the city, the charms of many of these churches are considerable, not least because they are all on or around the Celian Hill, one of the quietest and most relaxing areas of Rome.

The Celian Hill

❶ Start your walk at the **Arch of Constantine**—it's right by the Colosseum—and walk down Via di San Gregorio. To your right, on the slopes of the Palatine Hill, are all that remains of the great aqueduct built by the Consul Appius Claudius around 300 BC. At the end of Via di San Gregorio, a shallow ❷ flight of stairs leads to the little church of **San Gregorio Magno,** the church of St. Gregory the Great. It was built around 750 by Pope Gregory II to commemorate his predecessor and namesake, Pope Gregory the Great (590–604). It was from the monastery on this site that Gregory the Great dispatched St. Augustine to Britain in 596 to convert the heathens there, a mission that led to the foundation of Canterbury Cathedral, still Britain's premier cathedral and the seat of the primate of all England, the Archbishop of Canterbury. The church of San Gregorio itself appears to all intents and purposes to be a typical Baroque structure, the result of remodeling in the 17th and 18th centuries. But you can still see what's said to be the stone slab on which the pious Gregory the Great slept; it's in the far right-hand chapel. Outside, among a grove of cypress trees, are three chapels. The one on the left contains the simple table at which Gregory fed 12 poor men every day. A 13th appeared one day—an angel. The chapel in the center, dedicated to St.

Andrew, contains two monumental frescoes showing scenes from the life of St. Andrew. They were painted at the beginning of the 17th century by Domenichino (*The Flagellation of St. Andrew*) and Guido Reni (*The Execution of St. Andrew*). Serious students of early Baroque painting will appreciate the opportunity to compare the sturdy, if sometimes stiff, classicism of Domenichino with the more flamboyant and heroic Baroque manner of Guido Reni.

❸ From the church, head up the hill to the ancient church of **Santi Giovanni e Paolo.** The square in which it stands has been described as "one of the few spots in Rome [which] a medieval pilgrim would have little difficulty recognizing." The church itself has a fascinating history. It was built on the site of two ancient-Roman houses around the year 370 by a Roman senator called Pammachius (who, following the death of his wife, gave away his money and saw out his days in monastic seclusion, dying in 410). Despite later rebuilding and remodeling, the church you see today is fundamentally that built by Pammachius. The houses over which it was built belonged to Sts. John and Paul, not the Apostles of those names but a pair of aristocratic early Christian martyrs who had served as officers at the court of the Christian Emperor Constantine. Constantine's successor, Julian the Apostate, was the emperor who tried vainly to stem the rising tide of Christianity and to restore to Rome her pagan gods. John and Paul were early victims of his paganizing fervor; they were beheaded after having refused to serve as officers in Julian's court. A steep staircase in the far right-hand corner of the church leads down to the remains of their houses and their burial place. Frescoes, almost certainly dating from the same period, depict the beheading of two men and a woman; they are thought to have been early worshipers at the graves of John and Paul who, for their pains, received the same treatment at the hands of Julian.

Opposite the church, a gate marks one of the entrances to **Villa Celimontana,** not a house but a city park, still largely unknown to most visitors to the city. The gate is sometimes locked; if so, there's another entrance on Via San Paolo della Croce just around the corner. Keep to the left as you wander through the park to reach the main entrance on Piazza della Navicella, the site of a fountain shaped like a little boat. It's actually a Renaissance copy of a classical work, installed here by Pope Leo X early in the 16th century. Facing the fountain is the church of **❹** **Santa Maria in Domnica,** another early Christian structure built over the house of a Roman martyr, St. Cyriaca, about whom little seems to be known other than that she was wealthy. The vibrantly colored 9th-century mosaics in the apse behind the altar are worth seeing. Notice the handkerchief carried by the Virgin: It is a *mappa,* a fashionable accoutrement in 9th-century Byzantium.

Turn into Piazza Celimontana, passing the entrance to the military hospital, and continue straight ahead into Via Celimontana. This leads to Via San Giovanni in Laterano. Here **❺** turn right to the church of **San Clemente,** Rome's Irish church —it belongs to Irish Dominican monks—and one of the most extraordinary archaeological sites in Rome. If you think exploring another ancient church built on the site of ancient-Roman buildings is something that ranks low on your scale of priorities, you may be tempted to miss San Clemente. If, on the

The Celian Hill and the Baths of Caracalla

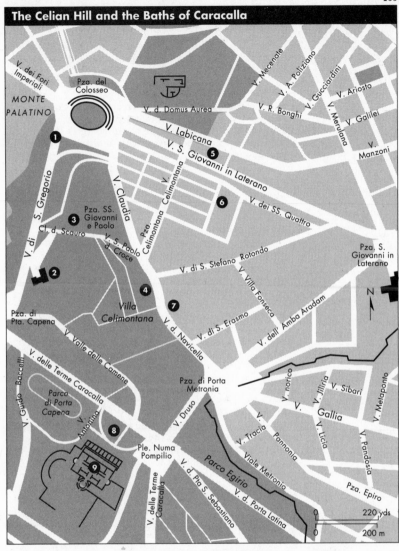

MONTE PALATINO

V. dei Fori Imperiali

Pza. del Colosseo

V. d. Domus Aurea

V. Mecenate

V. A. Poliziano

V. Gucciardini

V. Ariosto

V. R. Bonghi

V. Galilei

V. Merulana

V. Labicana

V. Manzoni

V. S. Giovanni in Laterano

V. di S. Gregorio

V. Claudia

Pza. SS. Giovanni e Paolo

Cl. d. Scauro

V. S. Paolo d. Croce

V. Celimontana

Pza. Celimontana

V. dei SS. Quattro

Pza. S. Giovanni in Laterano

V. di S. Stefano Rotondo

V. Villa Fonseca

N

Villa Celimontana

V. d. Navicella

V. di S. Erasmo

V. dell' Amba Aradam

Pza. di Pta. Capena

V. Valle delle Camene

V. delle Terme Caracalla

Pza. di Porta Metronia

V. norico

V. Ilitria

V. Sibari

V. Metaponto

V. Guido Baccelli

Parco di Porta Capena

Gallia

V. Tracia

V. Pannonia

V. Licia

V. Pandosia

V. Druso

V. Antonina

Ple. Numa Pompilio

Parco Egirio

Viale Metronio

Pza. Epiro

V. delle Terme Caracalla

V. d. Pta S. Sebastiano

V. d. Porta Latina

220 yds

200 m

Arch of Constantine, **1**

Baths of Caracalla, **9**

San Clemente, **5**

San Gregorio Magno, **2**

Santa Maria in Domnica, **4**

Santi Giovanni e Paolo, **3**

Santi Nereo e Achilleo, **8**

Santi Quattro Coronati, **6**

Santo Stefano Rotondo, **7**

other hand, the opportunity to see more remarkable archaeological remains appeals, this is the place for you.

San Clemente as it stands today is the third church built on this site. The first, a private home which was used as a place of Christian worship, was built in the 1st century AD. Little remains of it, but the second church, built in the 4th century, and over which today's church stands, has survived almost intact, perhaps because it was rediscovered only in the 19th century. Alongside these Christian churches you can also visit the remains of a 2nd-century AD temple to the god Mithras; it's buried deep under the second church. Allow at least 45 minutes if you want to see everything here.

San Clemente has one of the few complete medieval interiors in Rome. The most interesting features are by the altar. Look at the marble panels in the choir, the area leading to the altar. These were originally in the 4th-century church, and were moved here when the present church was built. They are decorated with early Christian symbols: doves, vines, fish. In front of the altar is a sunken tomb containing the relics of St. Clement himself. The 16th-century canopy over the tomb is decorated with a large anchor, a reference to the martyrdom of St. Clement, or, at any rate, to the legend of his martyrdom. St. Clement was the fourth pope and was reputedly banished to the Crimea in Russia by the Emperor Trajan around the year 100. Here, chiefly as a result of his success in converting his fellow exiles, he was tied to an anchor and thrown into the sea. When, miraculously, the waters receded, his body was found in a tomb built by angels. At the beginning of the left nave, be sure to see the frescoes illustrating the life of St. Catherine of Alexandria, another early Christian martyr. Her story is memorable even by the standards of early Christian martyrs. She was born—no one seems to know when—in Alexandria in present-day Egypt. Having publicly protested the worship of idols, she ensured the death of 50 pagan philosophers whose arguments against Christianity she had emphatically demolished; their punishment for failure was to be burned at the stake. Having then refused to marry the local governor, she was tied to a spiked wheel—hence the catherine wheel—which immediately disintegrated. This so impressed 200 watching Roman soldiers they converted to Christianity on the spot. Eventually, however, she was beheaded, whereupon angels carried her soul to Mount Sinai in the Holy Land. The frescoes were painted around 1400 by the Florentine artist Masolino, a key figure in the development of Italian painting from the two-dimensional decorative styles of the 14th century to the naturalism of the Renaissance.

Now you should descend into the remains of the 4th-century church. The entrance is in the right nave. A series of walls built along the nave of the 4th-century structure to support the newer church above make it hard to form a coherent picture of the layout. But though the gloomy interior is confusing, there are a number of areas that bring the building vividly to life. The most notable—not to mention bizarre—are the frescoes on the left wall of the nave illustrating scenes from the life of St. Clement, probably painted in the 11th century. Here, in two panels, one above the other, Clement is shown getting the better of a wealthy Roman called Sisinnus. In the top panel, Sisinnus is struck deaf and dumb after having followed his wife Theodora, a Christian, to Clement's church. In the lower panel Clement cures Sisinnus, but the enraged Roman orders his servants to tie up the holy man and to carry him away. Due to the intervention of Divine Providence, the slaves and Sisinnus mistake some columns lying on the ground for Clement and his companions, and struggle furiously with ropes to strap them up. Perhaps the most unusual element of this farcical scene is the inscription under the lower panel in which Sisinnus bellows at his hapless slaves, "Go on, you sons of harlots, pull!"

Now walk to the apse at the end of the church. From here, steps lead to the remains of the 1st-century AD Roman house over which the 4th-century church stands. Only a few weighty stone blocks are left. Far more interesting are the remains of the Temple of Mithras. "Temple" is actually a misleading word here: What you see was once the first floor of a 2nd-century AD Roman apartment building (almost all ancient Romans, except the super rich, much like modern New Yorkers, lived in apartments or *insulae*), which was used for religious purposes, in this case the worship of the god Mithras. The cult of Mithras, which spread from Persia and gained a hold in Rome at about the time of the collapse of the Roman Republic around 50 BC, is interesting mainly because it was the only pagan religion that offered the possibility of life after death. It was thus the only serious rival to Christianity at the time when Christianity was spreading across the Roman Empire. Moreover, it was the only pagan cult to continue to be practiced widely after the official "disestablishment" of paganism in favor of Christianity by the Romans in AD 382. The religion was confined to men only (it was extremely common among Roman soldiers, which is perhaps not surprising also in view of the fact that it valued loyalty above all other virtues). Its rituals were always held in secret, generally in cavelike grottoes. Interestingly, the most complete part of the shrine left is the *triclinium*, a room used for religious banquets, the roof of which is studded with small rocks in imitation of a cave. Your visit is made all the more eerie by the sound of running water. The temple stands over an underground stream, and its gurgling and splashing provide a sinister accompaniment. *Via San Giovanni in Laterano, tel. 06/7315723. Voluntary admission charge. Open Mon.–Sat. 9–12 and 3:30–6, Sun. 10–12.*

Outside San Clemente take Via Santi Quattro Coronati and **❻** climb the hill to the 12th-century church of **Santi Quattro Coronati,** part of a fortified abbey that provided refuge to early popes and emperors. It's one of the most unusual and unexpected corners of Rome, a quiet island that has resisted the tide of time and traffic flowing below its ramparts. The original 9th-century church, which was half as large as the present one, was reconstructed in 1116 after the abbey was partially destroyed during the Normans' sack of Rome 30 years earlier. This explains the inordinate size of the apse in relation to the small nave. The apse frescoes are clearly Baroque, but the rest of the church is redolent of the Middle Ages. Don't miss the cloister, with its well-tended gardens and 12th-century fountain. The entrance is the door in the left nave; ring if it's not open.

There's another medieval gem hidden away off the courtyard at the church entrance: the chapel of **San Silvestro.** (Enter the door marked "Monache Agostiniane" and ring the bell at the left for the nun; she will pass the key to the chapel through the wheel beside the grille.) The chapel has remained, for the most part, as it was when consecrated in 1246, decorated with marbles and frescoes. These tell the story of the Christian Emperor Constantine's recovery from leprosy thanks to Pope Sylvester I. Note, too, the delightful fresco of the *Last Judgment* above the door, in which the angel on the left neatly rolls up sky and stars like a backdrop, signaling the end of the world. When you leave, lock the door and return the key to the nun, with a voluntary admission fee if you like.

Turn right outside the church and continue down Via Santi Quattro Coronati to the old hospital of St. John. Here, turn right onto Via Santo Stefano Rotondo to another church, **Santo Stefano Rotondo.** This church dates from the 5th century and was inspired perhaps by the design of the church of the Holy Sepulcher in Jerusalem. Unfortunately, however, it has been closed for restoration for as long as many Rome residents can remember. From it, you are little more than a step from Piazza della Navicella, where you turn left down Via della Navicella and right onto Via Druso. Cross huge Piazza Numa Pompilio toward the Baths of Caracalla. The little church of **Santi Nereo e Achilleo** on the right is worth seeing if you're lucky enough to find it open. One of Rome's oldest churches, probably dating from the 4th century, it has accumulated treasures such as 8th-century mosaics, a medieval pulpit on a multicolored marble base from the Baths of Caracalla, a 13th-century mosaic choir, and a fine episcopal, or bishop's throne.

The Baths of Caracalla

Your tour ends with a visit to one of ancient Rome's most celebrated monuments, the **Baths of Caracalla,** begun in AD 206 by the Emperor Septimius Severus and completed by his son, Caracalla. These baths were not the largest in Rome—Diocletian's baths, built around AD 320, and with a capacity for 3,000 people had that honor (Caracalla's baths, by contrast, could hold only 1,600 bathers)—but they seem to have been by far the most opulent. It was long believed that the ancient Romans' passion for baths was one of the prime reasons for the fall of their empire, that instead of conquering new lands and repulsing the barbarian hordes of the north the Romans lounged around in these magnificent public baths, pampering themselves and idling away the time with aimless chat. In fact, modern historians have come to recognize the Romans' baths as a remarkable social invention, one that encouraged a sense of common purpose rather than one that dissolved it, and one moreover that introduced notions of hygiene that might almost be thought acceptable today. The important point is that the Romans saw their baths as much more than places to wash. It's true that bathing was the basic purpose of these establishments, but there were shops, art galleries, and libraries to improve the mind, and exercise rooms and sports grounds to improve the body, in addition to gardens and areas just to sit in and talk, too. Even the smallest public baths had at least some of these amenities. In Rome itself, they were provided on a lavish scale. Imagine a combined shopping mall and health center, decked out with precious marbles rather than with steel and plastics, and one that, in place of a diesel-fired central-heating system, had gangs of slaves toiling in a warren of tiny rooms and passages under the stately halls above.

Taking a bath was a long and complex process, though eminent-
ly understandable if you see it as a social activity first and
foremost (and remember, too, that for all their sophistication
the Romans didn't have soap). You began in the *sudatoria*, a series of small rooms resembling saunas. Here you sat and
sweated. From these you moved to the *calidarium*, a large circular room that was humid rather than simply hot. This was
where the actual business of washing went on. You used a *strigil*, or scraper, to get the dirt off; if you were rich your slave did
this for you. Next you moved to the *trepidarium*, a warmish
room, the purpose of which was to allow you to begin gradually
to cool down. Finally, you splashed around in the *frigidarium*,
the only actual "bath" in the place; in essence a shallow swimming pool filled with cold water. The rich might like to complete the process with a brisk rubdown with a scented towel.
It was not unusual for a member of the opposite sex to perform
this favor for you (the baths were open to men and women,
though the times when they could use them were different).

The Baths of Caracalla are probably most famous these days as
the setting for spectacular outdoor opera performances, with
Verdi's *Aida*, a work that's always at its most impressive with a
mammoth cast, especially when augmented with elephants,
camels, and horse-drawn carriages, a perennial favorite. If you
get tickets, be sure to take along a warm wrap or jacket; the
nights here can be cool and damp, even in summer. You may
find that the cheaper seats at the back of the auditorium are a
false economy, especially when the wind is in the wrong direction. *Via delle Terme di Caracalla. Admission: 3,000 lire.
Open Apr.–Sept., Tues.–Sat. 9–6, Sun. and Mon. 9–1; Oct.–
Mar., Tues.–Sat. 9–3, Sun. and Mon. 9–1.*

The Catacombs and the Appian Way

This tour is intended to give you a respite from museum-going,
though be warned that it's no easier on the feet! Do it on a fine
day and either take along a picnic or plan to have lunch at one of
the pleasant restaurants near the catacombs. You take the #118
bus from San Giovanni in Laterano to Via Appia Antica, "The
Queen of Roads," which was completed in 312 BC by Appius
Claudius, who also built Rome's first aqueduct. He intended it
to connect Rome with the south of the country. Not far beyond

1 Porta San Sebastiano, you'll pass the little church of **Domine
Quo Vadis,** built on the spot where tradition says Christ appeared to St. Peter as the Apostle was fleeing Rome, and
persuaded him to return and face martyrdom. Get off the bus at

2 the **Catacomb of San Callisto.** This is one of the most important
and best-preserved underground cemeteries, the burial place
of many popes of the 3rd century. One of the friars who act as
custodians of the catacomb will guide you through its crypts
and galleries. *Via Appia Antica 110, tel. 06/5136725. Admission: 2,000 lire. Open Apr.–Sept., Thurs.–Tues. 8:30–12 and
2:30–6; Oct.–Mar., Thurs.–Tues. 8:30–12, 2:30–5.*

3 Just beyond is the 4th-century church of **San Sebastiano,** named
after the saint who was buried in the catacomb. It burrows underground on four different levels. This was the only ancient
Christian cemetery to remain accessible during the Middle

Ages. It was this cemetery from which the term "catacombs" is derived. It's located in a spot where the road dips into a hollow, known to the Romans as *catacumbas* (Greek for "near the hollow"). The Romans used the name to refer to the cemetery that had existed there since the 2nd century BC. The term came to be applied to all the underground cemeteries discovered in Rome in later centuries. *Via Appia Antica 136, tel. 06/7808847. Admission: 2,000 lire. Open Apr.–Sept., Fri.–Wed. 8:30–12 and 2:30–5:30; Oct.–Mar., Fri.–Wed. 8:30–12 and 2:30–5.*

The catacombs aren't Rome's oldest cemeteries. Even before Christianity reached Rome, those citizens who couldn't afford a fine funeral monument along one of thè consular roads were either cremated or buried in *necropolises* (cemeteries) outside the city gates. An imperial law prohibited burial within the city—except for deified emperors. During the 1st and 2nd centuries AD, Rome's Christians were buried together with their pagan brothers in these common burial grounds. Since the Christians had adopted the Hebrew tradition of burying their dead rather than cremating them, they soon required more space. They began to build cemeteries of their own, where they might also perform their religious rites. With the approval of the city fathers, they dug their cemeteries in the hilly slopes that lined the consular roads, usually on private land that the owner—often a Christian himself—granted for this purpose. As the need for space became more pressing, the cemeteries were extended in a series of galleries, often on two or more levels.

The general belief that the catacombs served as secret hiding places for the Christians during the persecutions that broke out during early Christian times is romantic but unrealistic. Rome's early Christians may have been a little odd in their ways, but they weren't stupid. The last place in the world they would have sought refuge would have been in the blind tunnels of the catacombs, whose location was common knowledge in Rome.

Between persecutions, the bodies of the martyrs who had fallen under the sword or had met death by fire, water, or wild beasts were interred in the catacombs. Their remains were given a place of honor, and their presence conferred great prestige on the underground cemetery in which they lay, attracting a stream of devout pilgrims. When this happened, the catacomb was embellished with frescoes, and existing staircases and galleries were enlarged to accommodate the faithful. Sometimes older parts of the cemetery were dug out to make room for underground basilicas. Here services in honor of the patron martyr were held, as at Sant'Agnese on Via Nomentana.

You'll see a great variety of tombs and decorations in the catacombs. They range from a simple rectangular niche in the wall which was closed by bricks or marble slabs, to a sarcophagus carved out of the wall and surmounted by a niche, or a freestanding sarcophagus in terra-cotta, marble, or lead. Off some of the galleries you'll see rooms lined with niches, where members of the same family or community were buried. Later, when space became scarce, tombs were dug in the pavement. Each tomb was distinguished by a particular mark or sign so that the deceased's relatives could recognize it among the rows of niches. Sometimes this was an object, such as a coin or oil lamp; sometimes it was an inscription. The wealthier fami-

Catacomb of San Callisto, **2**

Domine Quo Vadis, **1**

San Sebastiano, **3**

Tomb of Cecilia Metella, **4**

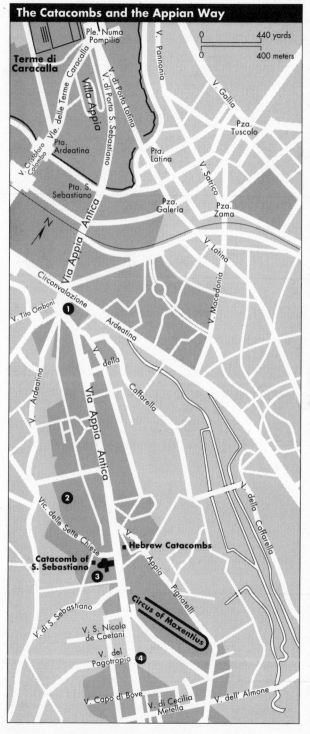

The Catacombs and the Appian Way

lies called in painters to decorate their tombs with frescoes and ordered sculptured sarcophagi from artisans' workshops.

After AD 313 when Constantine's edict put an end to the persecutions and granted full privileges to the Christians, the construction of the catacombs flourished; they were increasingly frequented by those who wished to honor their own dead and to venerate the tombs of the early martyrs. During the Dark Ages, invading armies made a habit of showing up at the gates of the city, devastating the countryside, and plundering from the living and the dead. When this part of the Campagna Romana became a malaria-infested wasteland, the popes prudently decreed that the remains of the martyrs be removed from the catacombs and laid to rest in the relative security of Rome's churches. With the loss of these holy relics and the appearance of the first cemeteries within the city walls, the catacombs fell into disuse and were abandoned and forgotten, with the sole exception of the catacomb of San Sebastiano.

On the other side of Via Appia, opposite San Sebastiano, are some Hebrew catacombs, not open to the public. Just beyond lie the ruins of the Circus of Maxentius, built in AD 309. You can see the ruins of the *spina*, the wall that divided it down the center. The obelisk in the Piazza Navona was found here. Farther

❹ along Via Appia is the **Tomb of Cecilia Metella,** a Roman noblewoman of the Republican era and a contemporary of Julius Caesar. There's a frieze of bull's skulls near the top, and the turreted crown is a reminder that the tomb was turned into a fortress in the 14th century.

Time Out There are several trattorias along Via Appia Antica, most of which are moderately priced (*see* Dining). For a sandwich or a snack, the bar on the corner of Via Appia Antica and Via Cecilia Metella, just beyond the tomb, can provide sustenance and a relaxing pause in the annexed garden.

The Tomb of Cecilia Metella marks the beginning of the most interesting and evocative stretch of Via Appia, lined with tombs and fragments of statuary. Cypresses and umbrella pines stand guard over the ruined sepulchers, and the occasional tracts of ancient paving stones are the same ones trod by Roman legions returning in triumph from southern conquests. The area is destined to become an archaeological park. This should save it from the tide of modern apartment buildings that is sweeping dangerously close. Stroll along as far as you wish, but remember that you'll have to get back to the Tomb of Cecilia Metella to catch your bus back to the city.

Sightseeing Checklists

Historical Buildings and Sites

Ara Pacis. This is the altar of Augustan Peace, erected by decree of the Senate in 13 BC to commemorate the Emperor Augustus's military victories and the era of peace they were expected to usher in. (*See* Villa Borghese to the Ara Pacis.)

Baths of Caracalla. Inaugurated by the Emperor Caracalla in the 2nd century AD, these were the most luxurious public baths in the Roman world. Today, operas are performed here in summer. (*See* The Celian Hill and the Baths of Caracalla.)

Castel Sant'Angelo. Built by the Emperor Hadrian in the 2nd century AD as his family tomb, this immense structure was later converted into a fortress and place of refuge for the popes. Children love this fairy-tale castle. (*See* The Vatican.)

Catacombs. Of the 40 catacombs in or near Rome only a few are open to the public. These places of early Christian burial, mile upon mile of underground passages, remain one of the most evocative and moving sights in Rome. (*See* The Catacombs and the Appian Way.)

Colosseum. Ancient Rome's best-known monument, the emblem of the city, dates from the 1st century AD. It has been renovated countless times, but never fails to recall the gore and violence of its heyday. (*See* Ancient Rome.)

Forum. The Roman Forum and adjoining Imperial Fora were the humming center of ancient Rome, the city's civic and commercial heart. Today, they form probably the most important archaelogical complex in Europe. (*See* Ancient Rome.)

Mamertine Prison. This was the state prison of ancient Rome, today the site of the church of San Pietro in Carcere, built to commemorate the incarceration here of St. Peter and the miraculous spring of water he brought forth to baptize his jailers. (*See* Ancient Rome.)

Monument to Vittorio Emanuele. An enormous and startling white marble confection built in the later 19th century to celebrate the unification of Italy. It contains the Tomb of the Unknown Soldier. (*See* Toward the Spanish Steps and the Trevi Fountain.)

Palazzo Barberini. The highlight of this sumptuous home of Rome's leading 17th-century family is the heroic ceiling in the main hall by Pietro da Cortona. (*See* The Quirinale to Piazza della Repubblica.)

Palazzo Farnese. This late-Renaissance palace was built by a succession of architects, notably Michelangelo. Today it's the French Embassy. (*See* Old Rome.)

Pantheon. This noble circular "home of the gods" was built by the Emperor Hadrian in the 2nd century AD, and converted into a church in the 6th century. Until 1960 its dome was the largest in the world. (*See* Old Rome.)

Piazza Navona. Rome's most celebrated 17th-century piazza is a striking example of Baroque city planning. Two major architects vie for honors here: Bernini, designer of the heroic Four Rivers Fountain in the center, and Borromini, architect of the church of Sant'Agnese that dominates one side. (*See* Old Rome.)

Piazza del Popolo. All roads to Rome from the north meet at this spacious square below the Pincio, framed by the twin churches of Santa Maria del Miracoli and Santa Maria di Montesanto. At the far end of the square is another church, Santa Maria del Popolo. (*See* Villa Borghese to the Ara Pacis.)

Piazza del Quirinale. One of the best-known sights in Rome, with a view over to the Vatican, this is the site of the Presidential Palace—until 1870 the papal residence—and a colossal equestrian statue of Castor and Pollux. (*See* The Quirinale to Piazza della Repubblica.)

Piazza di San Pietro. Bernini's heroic elliptical square in front of St. Peter's is Baroque Rome's single greatest achievement, a triumph of the marriage of symbolism and architectural grandeur. (*See* The Vatican.)

Ponte Sant' Angelo. This bridge linking Old Rome, on the east bank of the Tiber, with the Castel Sant' Angelo and the Vatican was built in the 2nd century AD and is decorated with copies of angels originally designed by Bernini. (*See* The Vatican.)

Porta Pia. Though later remodeled, this gateway still shows the hand of Michelangelo, who designed it in 1561. (*See* The Quirinale to Piazza della Repubblica.)

Pyramid. This curious white marble pyramid, 120 feet high, is the tomb of Roman magistrate Gaius Cestius, who died in 12 BC. (*See* The Aventine to St. Paul's.)

Temple of Vesta. The holiest shrine in ancient Rome, where the sacred fire of Vesta burned, tended by the Vestal Virgins. The present circular building dates from the 2nd century AD, though its origins are thought to be much older. (*See* Ancient Rome.)

Tomb of Cecilia Metella. This cylindrical tomb on Via Appia Antica was built for a Roman noblewoman of the Republican era. It was turned into a fortress in the 14th century. (*See* The Catacombs and the Appian Way.)

Trajan's Column. One of the most famous and influential monuments of ancient Rome, put up to commemorate the Emperor Trajan's victorious campaign in Yugoslavia in the 2nd century AD. The scenes that spiral up it are a mine of information on Roman military matters. (*See* Ancient Rome.)

Trajan's Market. A multistoried commercial building that housed all manner of shops. Here slaves selected fish for their masters from fresh- or salt-water tanks. (*See* Trajan's Market to San Giovanni in Laterano.)

Villa della Farnesina. This exquisite 16th-century villa was decorated by Raphael. You can see his *Galatea* in the loggia, and rooms, frescoed by other artists, are upstairs. (*See* Toward Trastevere.)

Museums and Galleries

Galleria Aurora Pallavincini. Visit the pavilion—the Casino Aurora—to see Guido Reni's magnificent ceiling fresco of the *Aurora*, a Baroque masterpiece, painted in 1615. *Via XXIV Maggio 43, tel. 06/4744019. Admission free. Open the first day of every month only, 10–12 and 3–5.*

Galleria Colonna. The sumptuous salons of the once-powerful Colonna family's palace almost overshadow the collections here. (*See* Toward the Spanish Steps and the Trevi Fountain.)

Galleria Doria-Pamphili. One of the finest small collections in the city, with works by Velásquez, Titian, and Caravaggio; the opulent setting makes this a museum to treasure. (*See* Toward the Spanish Steps and the Trevi Fountain.)

Galleria Nazionale d'Arte Antica. This is Italy's principal collection of art from the 13th to the 18th centuries. It's housed in two locations, Palazzo Barberini and Palazzo Corsini. (*See* The Quirinale to Piazza della Repubblica, and, Toward Trastevere.)

Galleria Nazionale d'Arte Moderna. A large neo-Classical palace on the fringes of Villa Borghese is home to Italy's premier collection of modern art. (*See* Villa Borghese to the Ara Pacis.)

Keats and Shelley Memorial House. The Rome home of the English 19th-century poets Keats and Shelley. It's located at the foot of the Spanish Steps. (*See* Toward the Spanish Steps and Trevi Fountain.)

Museo Capitolino. Two elegant late-Renaissance palaces, designed by Michelangelo, house a superb collection of ancient-Greek and Roman works. This is one of the great collections of classical art. (*See* Ancient Rome.)

Museo della Civiltà Romana. Visit this museum for the excellent model of ancient Rome; it gives probably the single best overview of how classical Rome looked. *Piazza Giovanni Agnelli 10, tel. 06/5926135. Admission: 4,000 lire. Open Tues., Wed., Fri., and Sat. 9–1:30, Thurs. 9–1:30 and 5–8, Sun. 9–1.*

Museo delle Mura. Located at Porta San Sebastiano, one of the original city gates in the Aurelian Walls, the museum charts the construction and expansion of the city's walls down the centuries. You can walk along sections of the walls from here, too. *Porta San Sebastiano 18, tel. 06/7575384. Admission: 1,500 lire. Open Tues.–Sat. 9–1:30, Sun. 9–1.*

Museo Napoleonico. This small museum contains a specialized and rich collection of Napoleonic memorabilia. The highlight for some is a plaster cast of Pauline Borghese's left breast (she was Napoleon's sister). *Via Zanardelli 1, tel. 06/6540286. Admission: 1,500 lire. Open Tues.–Sat. 9–1:30, Sun. 9–1.*

Museo di Palazzo Venezia. Pope Paul II's 15th-century apartments, authentically restored to give a fascinating flavor of aristocratic life in Renaissance Rome. (*See* Toward the Spanish Steps and the Trevi Fountain.)

Museo Nazionale d'Arte Orientale. This museum contains Italy's leading collection of art and artifacts from the Mid and Far East. (*See* Trajan's Market to San Giovanni in Laterano.)

Museo Nazionale delle Arti e Tradizioni Popolari. Here is a collection of Italian folk costumes and folklore. Some sections may be closed, but temporary exhibits are frequently staged. Children love it. *Piazza Marconi 10, tel. 06/5926148. Admission free. Open Thurs.–Tues. 9–1, Wed. 9–1 and 4–6.*

Museo Nazionale di Villa Giulia. Summer villa of Pope Julius III, now home to a stunning collection of Etruscan art. (*See* Villa Borghese to the Ara Pacis.)

Museo Nazionale Romano. Those with a taste for archaeological remains will appreciate this substantial museum, housed in a former monastery, itself adapted from a portion of the immense Baths of Diocletian. (*See* The Quirinale to Piazza della Repubblica.)

Museo Nazionale Pigorini. This museum has an extensive collection of prehistoric remains documenting early man's development in the areas around Rome. There's also a prestigious ethnographic collection. *Piazza Marconi 14, tel. 06/5910702. Admission: 3,000 lire. Open Mon.–Sat. 9–2, Sun. 9–1.*

Churches

Rome's churches have erratic and unpredictable opening times; they are *not* open all the time. Most are open from about 7 AM to noon and 3 PM to 7 PM, but don't be surprised if the church you are especially keen to see is closed even during these times. Many churches that are shut during the week can, however, often be visited on Sundays. Appropriate dress—no shorts—is required to see any church.

Sant'Agnese. Standing opposite Bernini's sensational Four Rivers Fountain in Piazza Navona, this is one of the most monumental and dynamic churches in Rome. The facade was designed by the idiosyncratic Borromini in 1655; its high dome and twin flanking towers dominate the square. (*See* Old Rome.)

Sant'Andrea al Quirinale. Though this is one of Rome's smaller Baroque churches, it lacks nothing in gravity or, almost, monumentality. Bernini was the architect, and he considered it one of his finest creations. (*See* The Quirinale to Piazza della Repubblica.)

Sant'Andrea della Valle. The church is interesting for the vibrant and powerful early Baroque frescoes in the dome by Lanfranco and in the apse by his arch-rival Domenichino. The dome is second only to that at St. Peter's in size. (*See* Old Rome.)

San Carlo alle Quattro Fontane. This is perhaps the most exciting and unusual Baroque church in Rome—as well as one of the smallest: It could fit inside one of the piers of St. Peter's. It was designed by Borromini. (*See* The Quirinale to Piazza della Repubblica.)

Santa Cecilia in Trastevere. This small and important early Christian church, notable for the powerful 13th-century frescoes in the cloisters and the attractive little garden in front of it, has an appeal that owes much to the picturesque streets and squares of surrounding Trastevere. (*See* Toward Trastevere.)

San Clemente. The real interest here is not the existing 14th-century church but the underlying remains of a 4th-century church, and, below it, the vestiges of a 1st–3rd century AD Roman house in which a shrine to Mithras had been installed. (*See* The Celian Hill and the Baths of Caracalla.)

Santa Croce in Gerusalemme. The body of this church formed part of an Imperial palace in ancient Rome. It was almost entirely rebuilt in the 18th century providing Rome with one of its few Rococo churches. (*See* Trajan's Market to San Giovanni in Laterano.)

Il Gesù. The Gesù, designed by Vignola in about 1560, exerted an enormous influence on subsequent church architecture. It was built for the Jesuits, and remodeled in the mid-16th century; the spiraling ceiling fresco above the nave is almost the most extreme example of high-Baroque illusionism. (*See* Old Rome.)

San Giovanni in Laterano. The principal church in Rome from the time of Constantine in the 4th century to the Renaissance and still the Cathedral of Rome. Despite extensive remodeling, especially on the exterior, it remains one of the most striking early Christian basilicas in the city. (*See* Trajan's Market to San Giovanni in Laterano.)

San Gregorio Magno. This plain but captivating late-Baroque building is famous for the adjoining chapels containing frescoes illustrating scenes from the life of St. Peter. (*See* The Celian Hill and the Baths of Caracalla.)

Sant' Ignazio. This is another of the Jesuits' Roman churches, built in the mid-17th century by architects Grassi and Algardi. The chief delights are the startling ceiling frescoes. The one above the nave is the most giddy example of its type. The dome fresco is a marvelous trick: There is no dome at all but the artist (Pozzo) created a wonderful illusionistic substitute. (*See* Old Rome.)

Sant'Ivo alla Sapienza. This is another of Borromini's remarkable and highly personal masterpieces. Cramped on an awkward site, it combines movement, variety, and symbolism on a unique star-shaped plan. The dome is a triumph of idiosyncratic architecture. (*See* Old Rome.)

San Luigi dei Francesi. An artistic treasure house: the principal attractions are Caravaggio's three powerful paintings showing scenes from the life of St. Matthew. Among the other splendors is a series of serene frescoes by Domenichino. (*See* Old Rome.)

Santa Maria degli Angeli. This was not a church at all originally, but the Baths of Diocletian, the largest baths in Imperial Rome. They were transformed by Michelangelo and the grandeur of his design survives 18th-century remodeling. (*See* The Quirinale to Piazza della Repubblica.)

Santa Maria in Cosmedin. Built in the 6th century near the site of the Forum Boarium—ancient Rome's livestock market—the church was used by the city's Greek colony. It retains much of its medieval atmosphere. (*See* The Aventine to St. Paul's.)

Santa Maria Maggiore. This is one of the original seven pilgrimage churches of Rome, 18th-century on the outside, early Christian inside. It contains a series of remarkable treasures, including the reputed remains of the crèche in which Jesus was born. (*See* Trajan's Market to San Giovanni in Laterano.)

Santa Maria sopra Minerva. Santa Maria sopra Minerva is the only Gothic church in the city, restored to its original form in the last century. It contains Michelangelo's *Risen Christ*. Outside is a marble elephant supporting a small obelisk, one of Bernini's more eccentric creations. (*See* Old Rome.)

Santa Maria della Pace. Santa Maria della Pace, tucked behind Piazza Navona, is one of the most charming Baroque churches in Rome, designed by Pietro da Cortona in the early 17th century. The sober cloisters were designed by Bramante. (*See* Old Rome.)

Santa Maria del Popolo. Come here to see Caravaggio's disturbing *Crucifixion of St. Peter* and *The Conversion of St. Paul* and compare them with Carracci's stately *Assumption of the Virgin*. Parts of the church were designed by Bramante and Raphael. (*See* Villa Borghese to the Ara Pacis.)

Santa Maria della Vittoria. You'll want to visit here to see Bernini's Cornaro Chapel, containing the most famous sculptural group in Rome, *The Ecstasy of St. Theresa*. It's a genuinely dramatic work, right down to the theater "boxes" on either side. Don't miss it. (*See* The Quirinale to Piazza della Repubblica.)

Santa Maria in Trastevere. This is one of Rome's oldest churches, founded in the 3rd century. The bell tower and mosaics on the facade date from the 12th century. (*See* Toward Trastevere.)

Santa Maria in Vallicella (Chiesa Nuova). Unremarkable by itself, this church contains many treasures, foremost among them the ceiling frescoes by Pietro da Cortona. There is a giant statue of the church's founder, St. Philip Neri, in the sacristy. (*See* Old Rome.)

Santa Maria in Via Lata. The most interesting feature of this early Christian church is Pietro da Cortona's facade, designed in 1650. It's a typical example of the High Baroque fascination with movement in architecture—notice how the close-set columns appear to jostle one another—and grandeur, especially the use of rich and costly marbles. *Via Lata.*

Santi Martina e Luca. Two churches in one: St. Martin is in the crypt; St. Luke is the main church above. It was remodeled by Pietro da Cortona in the mid-17th century. *Via dei Fori Imperiali.*

Oratory of St. Philip Neri. This is the headquarters of the Oratorians, next door to Santa Maria in Vallicella, and interesting mainly for Borromini's elegantly curving facade, built between 1637 and 1662. (*See* Old Rome.)

San Paolo fuori le Mura. St. Paul's—fuori le mura (beyond the walls) means that it was built outside the ancient-Roman city walls—is one of the seven great pilgrimage churches of Rome, built in the 4th century over the grave of St. Paul. It was rebuilt in the last century after a fire. The cloisters are the only part of the original building to have survived. No one should miss them. (*See* The Aventine to St. Paul's.)

San Pietro. Even the most casual visitor to the city is unlikely to miss St. Peter's, mother church of the Catholic Church, the largest church in the world, and the supreme architectural achievement of the Renaissance and Baroque. (*See* The Vatican.)

San Pietro in Vincoli. This is one of Rome's oldest churches, built to house the chains with which, it's claimed, St. Peter was bound after he was arrested in Jerusalem. Most visitors are drawn by Michelangelo's powerfully disturbing statue of Moses. (*See* Trajan's Market to San Giovanni in Laterano.)

Santi Quattro Coronati. One of Rome's least-known delights, the church of Quattro Coronati is an 11th-century building standing on the site of a 9th-century church. It's located in a quiet corner of the little-visited Celian Hill. (*See* The Celian Hill to the Baths of Caracalla.)

Tempietto di San Pietro in Montorio. Built by Bramante in 1502, this is generally considered to be the first building of the High Renaissance in Rome. It is a small, austere circular "temple" of rigorously classical design. (*See* Toward Trastevere.)

Trinità dei Monti. Rising high above the Spanish Steps, the church is beautiful not so much in itself but for its dramatic location and magnificent views. (*See* Toward the Spanish Steps and the Trevi Fountain.)

Santi Vincenzo ed Anastasio. Martino Longhi was the architect of this vigorous Baroque church, built toward the end of the 17th century. His use of tightly grouped columns and pilasters on the facade gives a characteristic sense of movement and life. *Via del Lavatore and Via di San Vincenzo.*

Fountains

One of the most distinctive features of Rome is its many fountains. Although one might expect so Mediterranean a city to be parched, Rome is served by an abundant and pure freshwater supply. The ancient Romans capitalized on this happy fact by building enormous aqueducts, in themselves considerable feats of engineering and organization, that brought water to the heart of the city. From the Renaissance onward, it was these same aqueducts, rebuilt and restored, that provided the city's water and fueled its fountains. There are no ancient-Roman fountains left, but there are large numbers of Renaissance and Baroque fountains. Those built toward the beginning of the 16th century are restrained. Water trickles rather than gushes from them. But as the Baroque period unfolded, so the city's fountains became ever more lavish, spectacular, and theatrical, culminating in the most dramatic of them all: the Trevi Fountain.

Acqua Felice. The Acqua Felice was the first of the great Renaissance fountains, built by Pope Sixtus V as the terminal point of the restored aqueduct of Severus. The central figure is of Moses; Sixtus, not a man to miss an opportunity for self-advertisement, wished to imply that like Moses he had brought water to a thirsting population. (*See* The Quirinale to Piazza della Repubblica.)

Acqua Paolo. The end of Trajan's aqueduct, restored in the early 17th century by Pope Paul V, is marked by the Acqua Paolo. *Via Garibaldi.*

Barcaccia. For many years it was thought that the Barcaccia was the work of Bernini's father; in fact it's now known to be by Bernini himself. It represents a shallow barge over which water plays slowly. (*See* Toward the Spanish Steps and the Trevi Fountain.)

Fontana dei Fiumi. This is the Four Rivers Fountain, the most dramatic of all Bernini's Roman fountains. (*See* Old Rome.)

Fontana delli Api. Bernini's Barberini patron, Pope Urban VIII, is commemorated in this small fountain—"api" means bees, the Barberini family emblem. (*See* The Quirinale to Piazza della Repubblica.)

Fontana del Moro. Giacomo della Porta was responsible for this fountain. Later, Bernini added the central figure of the Moor. (*See* Old Rome.)

Fontana del Tritone. Inevitably perhaps, this, too, was designed by Bernini. Virile Triton sits high on a shell, blowing a stream of water into the air. (*See* The Quirinale to Piazza della Repubblica.)

Fontana di Trevi. The Trevi Fountain is the best known of the city's Baroque waterworks. It dominates the little square in which it's located, occupying the whole of one side. (*See* Toward the Spanish Steps and the Trevi Fountain.)

Le Quattro Fontane. In comparison to many of the later Roman fountains, these four late-16th-century fountains seem tame. But many find their restraint welcome after the majestic excesses of so many of the city's other fountains. (*See* The Quirinale to Piazza della Repubblica.)

Tartarughe. Four graceful boys support bronze dolphins, from whose mouths water gushes forth into marble shells. In their other hands, they hold bronze tortoises who drink from the fountain above. Is this the most charming fountain in the city? It was designed by Giacomo della Porta in 1585. *Piazza Mattei.*

Parks and Gardens

Rome's public gardens are remnants of the vast parks created by Renaissance princes and popes in imitation of ancient-Roman "villas," or country estates. They provide a pleasant diversion from more formal sightseeing. In good weather they're perfect for picnics.

Colle Oppio. This was the land confiscated by Nero for the site of his extravagant palace, the Domus Aurea. Later, Trajan and Titus built public baths here, the ruins of which can be visited. (*See* Ancient Rome.)

Janiculum. Known to the Romans as the Gianicolo, this park was laid out in 1870 in honor of those who fought here in a desperate attempt to oust the French troops guarding the Vatican. Visit it for the view of the city and to see the lighthouse, a gift from Argentina. (*See* Toward Trastevere.)

Valle Murcia. Few people associate Rome with roses, but this small park on the Aventine contains a superb rose garden. (*See* The Aventine to St. Paul's.)

Villa Borghese. The Villa Borghese is the most famous park in Rome, laid out as a private garden in the 17th century and purchased by the Italian government in 1902. (*See* Villa Borghese to the Ara Pacis.)

Villa Celimontana. This lush, walled park covers the western slopes of the Celian Hill. The main entrance is at Piazza della Navicella. (*See* The Celian Hill and the Baths of Caracalla.)

What to See and Do
With Children

Traveling with children can be enjoyable and rewarding, but there often comes a point when the kids refuse point blank to do any more sightseeing and start to throw tantrums at the thought of entering yet another church or museum. Fortunately, there's a lot to do in Rome that children—and their parents —will enjoy.

Take them to a **pizzeria** with a wood-burning oven where they can see the chef work with the dough. Take a ride in a **horse and carriage**—it's fun and feels a lot less silly than it looks. Visit the **zoo** in Villa Borghese. Climb to the top of **St. Peter's Dome** (arduous but worth it for the incomparable views inside and outside the church). Spend some time in the city's many parks taking in, perhaps, a **Punch and Judy** show on the Pincio or on the Janiculum Hill where there is often a colorful stand selling puppets, too.

In December and early January, visit the big **Christmas bazaar** at Piazza Navona—then go to the huge **toy store** at the north end of the square.

An even greater spectacle (though not so grand as at Buckingham Palace in London) is the daily changing of the guard at the **Quirinale** palace, the residence of the president of Italy. Every day at 4 PM there's a military band and parade as the guards change shifts.

The well-run **Luna Park** amusement center in EUR is fun for the big Ferris wheel and roller coaster as well as other rides and games. In a residential suburb, it can be reached by bus 707 from San Paolo fuori le mura. (Via delle Tre Fontane, tel. 06/5925933; closed Tues.) There's usually a **circus** on somewhere in town—check billboards and newspaper listings. Also check listings for cartoon films that might be on at the **movies** and for **puppet shows** and other children's programs at theaters. Explore **Castel Sant'Angelo**. It's got dungeons, battlements, cannons, and cannonballs, and a collection of antique weapons and armor.

Rent **bicycles** and ride around Villa Borghese and through the center of town on Sunday when the traffic is lighter. In spring and September, take a **boat ride** to Ostia Antica and explore this Roman port city. The excursion is popular with school groups and is organized by **Tourvisa** (*see* Guided Tours in Essential Information). In the summer Tourvisa also runs **star gazing excursions** on the Tiber.

Downtown Rome is generally a safe city that swarms with thousands of teenagers on weekends. Your teenagers will probably feel at home hanging out at favorite gathering places— **Piazza della Rotonda** at the Pantheon, for example, or **Piazza di Spagna** and the **Spanish Steps**. There's a fast-food joint in each square. Or send them to a **disco**—some of them open at 4 PM on weekends.

Off the Beaten Track

Stop in to see the **Biblioteca Casanatense,** an impressive example of the hidden riches behind so many of the city's inconspicuous portals. Climb the stairs and tell the man at the desk that you want to see the *salone*. You pass through reading rooms lined with antique bookcases and shelves of rare volumes locked behind mesh screens. Then you come to the immense main hall, presided over by a larger than life statue of the library's 17th-century founder, Cardinal Girolamo Casanate, surveying the massed ranks of precious books and a series of antique globes. Among the collection are prints from the 16th, 17th, 18th, and 19th centuries, a 10th-century prayer book, thousands of early manuscripts of plays, and a number of early 19th-century musical scores. *Via Sant'Ignazio 52, tel. 06/ 6798988. Open July–Aug., Mon.–Sat. 8:30–1:30; Sept.–June, Mon. and Tues. and Thurs.–Sat. 8:30–1:30 and 2:30–6:30, Wed. 8:30–1:30.*

Another library, the **Hertziana,** near the church of Trinità dei Monti, is worth a look not for its collections but for its doorway, a grimacing stone monster. To get into the building you have to walk through the monster's mouth. It was designed by a painter, Frederico Zuccari (1540–1609), whose house this was. Zuccari sank all his money into this bizarre creation, dying in debt before his curious memorial, as it turned out to be, was completed. *Via Gregoriana 28.*

Explore the **Isola Tiberina,** the little island in the Tiber between the Ghetto and Trastevere. Descend the stone steps set into the side of the island to listen to the roar of the rapids; they mark the navigable limit of the river. Walk along the embankment. The Romans built a wall around the entire island, turning it almost into a ship, with prow pointed downstream.

Do as the Romans do. Stop in at an *enoteca*, a wine bar, for a glass of sparkling white prosecco, best served icy cold. Among the oldest of the city's many wine bars are those at Via dei Prefetti 15; Via della Croce 76; and Campo dei Fiori 15.

Browse among the objets d'art at the stunning **Apollodoro** art gallery. It was designed by leading Italian architect Paolo Portoghesi, and is run by his wife, Giovanna. Though it's small and tucked away in a corner of Piazza Mignanelli (behind the American Express office), you can't miss it: The entrance is a trompe l'oeil of Greek architect Apollodorus's Trajan's Market, hence the name. *Piazza Mignanelli 17.*

Go to **Lo Zodiaco.** It's a café on Monte Mario, north of the Vatican. The view from the terrace is stunning. Order one of the amazing ice creams. To get there take a taxi—it's about a 30-minute ride from downtown—or bus 913 (907 or 991 if you're going there from the Vatican). The café itself is located at the end of the road that winds through the park of Monte Mario. *Viale del Parco Mellini, tel. 06/3451032.*

Have lunch or dinner on the Tiber. There are several floating restaurants moored on the river. Two to try are **Isola del Sole,** near Piazza del Popolo (Scalo de Pinedo, tel. 06/3601400. Moderate prices) and **Il Canto del Riso,** near Ponte Cavour (*tel.* 06/ 361430. Moderate prices). They can be great for a long lunch when Rome sizzles in July and August.

For a terrific Roman taste treat, though only after 5 PM, make your way to **Er Filettaro** for a glass of Frascati and a plate of the house specialty: *filetti di Baccala*, batter-fried cod fillets, crispy hot and salty. *Largo dei Librai 88.*

5 Shopping

Introduction

Shopping in Rome is part of the fun, no matter what your budget. You're sure to find something that suits your fancy *and* your pocketbook, but don't expect to get bargains on Italian brands such as Benetton that are exported to the United States; prices are just about the same on both sides of the Atlantic. Shops are open from 9 or 9:30 to 1 and from 3:30 or 4 to 7 or 7:30. There's a tendency in Rome for shops in central shopping districts to stay open all day, but for many it's still in the experimental stage. Department stores and centrally located UPIM and Standa stores are open all day. Remember that in Rome most stores are closed on Sunday and, with the exception of food and technical supply stores, are also closed on Monday mornings from September to June, and on Saturday afternoons in July and August.

Most Italian sizes are not uniform, so always try on clothing before buying, or measure gift items. Glove sizes are universal. In any case, remember that Italian stores generally will *not* refund your purchases, and that they often cannot exchange goods because of limited stock. *Always* take your purchases with you: Having them shipped home from the shop may cause unlimited grief. If circumstances are such that you can't take your goods with you, and if the shop seems reliable about shipping, get a firm statement of *when* and *how* your purchase will be sent.

Gift Ideas

The best buys in Italy are still **leather goods** of all kinds—from gloves to bags to jackets—and **silk goods** and **knitwear**. Boutique fashions may be slightly less expensive in Rome than in the United States. Some worthy old **prints** and minor **antiques** can be found in the city's interesting little shops, and full-fledged collectors can depend on the prestigious names of some of Italy's top antique dealers. Genuine Italian **handicrafts** aren't so easy to find in these days of Oriental imports, but there are shops offering **pottery** and **handwoven textiles** made in Italy.

Leather Goods **Gucci** (Via Condotti 8) is the most famous of Rome's leather shops. It has a full assortment of accessories on the first floor, a fashion boutique for men and women and a scarf department on the second floor, and a full complement of Japanese customers, who line up to get in on busy days. **Roland's** (Piazza di Spagna) has an extensive stock of quality leather fashions and accessories, as well as stylish casual wear in wool and silk. **Ceresa** (Via del Tritone 118) has more reasonably priced fine leather goods, especially handbags and leather fashions. **Volterra** (Via Barberini 102) is well stocked, and offers a wide-ranging selection of handbags at moderate prices. **Sermoneta** (Piazza di Spagna 61) shows off a varied choice of gloves in its windows; there are many more inside. **Di Cori**, a few steps away, also has a good selection of gloves; there's another Di Cori store at Via Nazionale 183. **Merola** (Via del Corso 143) carries a line of expensive, top-quality gloves and scarves.

Nichol's (Via Barberini 94) is one of the few stores in Rome that stock American shoe sizes; it's in the moderate price range.

Shopping

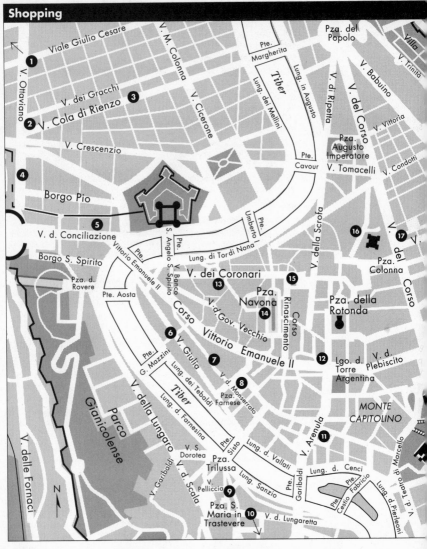

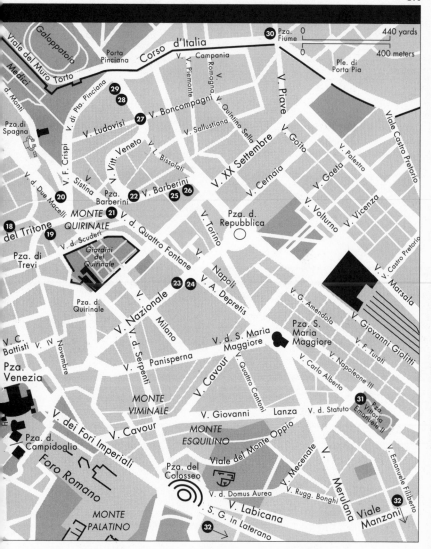

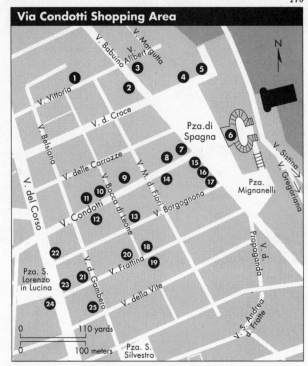

Via Condotti Shopping Area

Ferragamo (Via Condotti 73) is one of Rome's best stores for fine shoes and leather accessories; its silk scarves are terrific. You pay for quality here, but you can get great buys during the periodic sales. **Mario Valentino** (Via Frattina 58) is a top name for stylish shoes and leather fashions. **Magli** (Via del Gambero 1) is known for quality shoes at high-to-moderate prices and for attractive matching handbags. **Magli** at Via Veneto 70 is another branch of the same operation. **Campanile** (Via Condotti 58) has four floors of *dernier cri* shoes, classic models, and other quality leather goods.

Jewelry **Bulgari** (Via Condotti 10) is to Rome what Cartier is to Paris; the shop's elegant display windows hint at what's beyond the guard at the door. **Buccellati** (Via Condotti 31) is a tradition-hoary Florentine jewelry house, famous for silverwork; it ranks with Bulgari for quality and reliability. **Fornari** (Via Frattina 71) and **Frugoni** (Via Arenula 83) have tempting selections of small silver objects. **Bozart** (Via Bocca di Leone 4) features dazzling costume jewelry keyed to the latest fashions.

Silks and Fabrics **Galtrucco** (Via del Tritone 18), **Bises** (Via del Gesù 56), and **Meconi** (Via Cola di Rienzo 305) have the best selections of world-famous Italian silks and fashion fabrics. You can find some real bargains if you happen to be around when remnants (*scampoli*) are on sale.

Knitwear **Luisa Spagnoli** (Via del Corso 382, with other shops at Via Frattina 116 and Via Veneto 130) is always reliable for good quality at the right price and styles to suit American tastes. **Miranda** (Via Bocca di Leone 28) is a treasure trove of warm jackets, skirts, and shawls handwoven in gorgeous colors of wool or mohair, or in lighter yarns for the summer.

Household Linens and Embroidery **Pratesi** (Piazza di Spagna 10) is a Roman institution for fabulous trousseaux. **Cesari** (Via Barberini 1) is another; it also has less expensive gift items such as aprons, beach towels, and place mats. **Lavori Artigianali Femminili** (Via Capo le Case 6) offers exquisitely embroidered household linens, infants' and children's clothing, and blouses.

Boutiques All the big names in Italian fashion are represented in the Piazza di Spagna area. **Sorelle Fontane** (Salita San Sebastianello), one of the first houses to put Italy on the fashion map, has a large boutique, with a wide choice of ready-to-wear models and accessories. **Carlo Palazzi** (Via Borgognona 7) has elegant men's fashions and accessories. **Mariselaine** (Via Condotti 70) is a top-quality women's fashion boutique. **Camomilla** (Piazza di Spagna 85) has trendy young styles for women.

Antiques and Prints For old prints and antiques, the **Perera** shop (Via Babuino 92b) is a happy hunting ground. Early photographs of Rome and views of Italy from the archives of **Alinari** (Via Aliberti 16/a) make interesting souvenirs. **Nardecchia** (Piazza Navona 25) is reliable for prints.

Handcrafted Articles For pottery, handwoven textiles, and other handicrafts, **Myricae** (Via Frattina 36, with another store at Piazza del Parlamento 38) has a good selection. **Galleria del Batik** (Via della Pelliccia 29) in Trastevere is off the beaten track but well worth a visit; it has a wealth of handcrafted objects, beautifully displayed in a rustic setting. A bottle of liqueur, jar of marmalade, or bar of chocolate handmade by Cistercian monks in several monasteries in Italy makes an unusual gift to take home: They are on sale at **Ai Monasteri** (Corso Rinascimento, near Piazza Navona).

Shopping Districts

The most elegant and expensive shops are concentrated in the **Piazza di Spagna** area. That's where you'll find the big-name boutiques, too: Versace, Ferre, and Laura Biagiotti on **Via Borgognona**; Valentino on **Via Bocca di Leone**; Armani and Missoni on **Via del Babuino**. **Via Margutta** is known for art galleries and **Via del Babuino** for antiques. There are several high-fashion outlets on **Via Gregoriana** and **Via Sistina**. Bordering this top-price shopping district is **Via del Corso,** which—along with **Via Frattina** and **Via del Gambero**—is lined with shops and boutiques of all kinds where prices and goods are competitive.

Up from **Piazza Colonna, Via del Tritone** has some medium-priced and a few expensive shops selling everything from fashion fabrics to trendy furniture. Still farther up, on **Via Veneto,** you'll find a few more high-priced boutiques and shoe stores, as well as newsstands selling English-language newspapers, magazines, and pocketbooks.

In **Old Rome, Via dei Coronari** is lined with antique shops and some new stores selling designer home accessories. **Via Giulia** and **Via Monserrato** also feature antique dealers galore, plus a few art galleries.

In the **Pantheon** area there are many shops selling liturgical objects and vestments. But the place to go for religious souvenirs is, obviously, the area around **St. Peter's,** especially **Via della Conciliazione** and **Via di Porta Angelica. Via Nazionale** features shoe shops, moderately priced boutiques, and shops selling men's and women's fashions. **Via Cola di Rienzo** offers quality goods of all types; it's a good alternative to the Piazza di Spagna area.

Department Stores

Rome has only a handful of department stores. There's a **Rinascente** at Piazza Colonna; it sells clothing and accessories only. Another Rinascente at Piazza Fiume has the same stock, plus a good housewares and gadget department in the basement. **Coin** (Piazzale Appio near San Giovanni in Laterano) has fashions for men and women. The **UPIM** and **Standa** chains offer low-to-moderately priced medium-quality goods. They're the place to go if you need a pair of slippers, a sweater, a bathing suit, or such to see you through until you get home. In addition, they carry all kinds of toiletries and first-aid needs. Most Standa and UPIM stores have invaluable while-you-wait shoe-repair service counters.

Food and Flea Markets

Rome's biggest and most colorful outdoor food markets are at **Campo dei Fiori, Via Andrea Doria** (Trionfale), and **Piazza Vittorio.** There's a flea market on Sunday morning at **Porta Portese;** it now offers mainly new or secondhand clothing, but there are still a few dealers in old furniture and sundry objects, much of it intriguing junk. Bargaining is the rule here. All outdoor markets are open from early morning to about 2, except Saturdays, when they may stay open all day.

Bargaining and VAT Refunds

Prezzi fissi means just that: Prices are fixed and it's a waste of time bargaining unless you're buying a sizable quantity of goods or a particularly costly object. Most stores have a fixed-price policy, and most honor a variety of credit cards. They will also accept foreign money at the current exchange rate, give or take a few lire. Ask for a receipt for your purchases; you may need it at customs on your return home. Bargaining is still an art at Porta Portese flea market and is routine when purchasing anything from a street vendor.

It's theoretically possible to obtain a refund on the VAT, which is included in the selling price. In practice, however, the mechanism is so complex that it is hardly worthwhile worrying about it. To be eligible for a refund, you must spend more than 500,000 lire in one store and then endure a considerable degree of rigmarole at the airport when you leave.

6 Dining

Introduction

Our restaurant recommendations have been compiled under the direction of Eliana Cosimini, associate editor of Mondo Cucina, one of Italy's leading food and travel magazines.

There was a time when you could predict the clientele and prices of a Roman eating place according to whether it called itself a *ristorante*, a *trattoria*, or an *osteria*. Now these names are interchangeable. A rustic-looking spot that calls itself an osteria or hostaria may well turn out to be chic and expensive. Generally speaking, however, a trattoria is usually a family-run place, simpler in decor, menu, and service than a ristorante, and slightly less expensive. A true osteria is a wine shop, very basic and down-to-earth, where the only function of the food is to help keep the customers sober.

As the pace of Roman life quickens, more and more fast-food outlets are opening, offering tourists a wider choice of light meals. They are variations on the older Italian institutions of the *tavola calda* or *rosticceria* and offer a selection of hot and cold dishes, which you may take out or eat on the premises. A tavola calda is more likely to have seating. At both, some dishes are priced by portion, others by weight. You usually select your food, find out how much it costs, and pay the cashier. He or she will give you a stub that you, in turn, give to the counter person when you pick up the food. Snack bars and snack counters in coffee bars are catering to the new demand for fast food with heartier cold or toasted sandwiches. If you want to picnic, go to any *alimentari* store. *Pizza rustica* outlets sell slices of various kinds of pizza; there's one on practically every block in Rome.

You can have breakfast at your hotel, or at any coffee bar or café (where you can order such variations as *espresso*, *caffèlatte*, *cappuccino*, *latte macchiato*, or fruit juice and pastry, especially the typical Roman *cornetto*). Alternatively, try the few American-style luncheonettes in the center of Rome, all of which offer full breakfasts.

Mealtimes Lunchtime in Rome lasts from 1 to about 3, though you won't be turned away if hunger strikes shortly after noon. Dinner is served from 8 or 8:30 until about 10:30 or 11. Some restaurants stay open much later, especially in the summer, when patrons linger at sidewalk tables to enjoy the cool evening breeze, the *ponentino*.

Almost all restaurants close one day a week. Closing days are listed here, but they sometimes change; it's best to have your hotel *portiere* call ahead to check (and to book your table). Many restaurants and snack bars close for at least two weeks in August, a period when it can sometimes seem impossible to find sustenance in the deserted city.

Precautions Tap water is safe everywhere in Rome. Most Romans order bottled mineral water *(acqua minerale)*, either with bubbles *(gassata)* or without *(naturale* or *non gassata)*. It comes by the liter *(litro)* or the half-liter *(mezzo litro)*. If you're on a budget, keep your check down by ordering tap water *(acqua semplice)*. If you are on a low-sodium diet, ask for everything *senza sale*.

Ratings Always check the menu that's on display in the window or just inside the door. In all but the simplest places, there's always a cover charge *(pane e coperto)* and usually also a service charge *(servizio)* of 10% to 15%, only part of which goes to the waiter. These extra charges will increase your bill in all by 15% to 20%. A *menu turistico*—a fixed-price tourist menu—includes taxes and service, but usually not drinks.

Beware of dishes on à la carte menus, such as fish, Florentine steaks, or filets, marked "SQ" (meaning "according to quantity") or "L. 4,000 hg." They mean that you'll be charged according to the weight of the item you've ordered, or, in the second case, that the charge will be 4,000 lire per hectogram (about three and a half ounces).

The most highly recommended restaurants are indicated by a star ★.

Category	Cost*
Very Expensive	100,000 lire and up
Expensive	60,000–95,000 lire
Moderate	30,000–55,000 lire
Inexpensive	under 25,000 lire

*per person, for a three-course meal, including house wine and taxes

Credit Cards The following credit-card abbreviations are used: AE, American Express; DC, Diners Club; MC, MasterCard; V, Visa.

Downtown Rome

Very Expensive **La Cupola.** The elegant and opulent restaurant of the Hotel Excelsior serves classic regional Italian and international cuisine with flair. The empire decor is luxurious in keeping with the hotel's palatial atmosphere. Service is courteous and highly professional. Perfect pasta dishes, such as *bucatini all'amatriciana*, an earthy Roman specialty, and *gnocchetti di ricotta all'Excelsior* (small ricotta dumplings with tomato and basil sauce), are the other reason for eating here. *Hotel Excelsior, Via Veneto 125, tel. 06/4708. Jacket and tie preferred. Reservations not required. AE, DC, MC, V.*

Eden Panoramico Roof Garden. The Eden Hotel's rooftop restaurant is a favorite haunt of Italian politicians and other power brokers drawn by the classic regional Italian cooking and the breathtaking views. The decor, pink and green with gilt moldings and banks of flowers, is more than a little overblown but reflects the elegant garden ambience and sense of airy space. Try the deceptively simple *spaghetti alla carrettiera* (spaghetti tossed in hot olive oil, with grated pecorino cheese and black pepper). Regulars also love *piccata di vitello ai carciofi* (veal with artichokes). *Eden Hotel, Via Ludovisi 49; tel. 06/4743551, ext. 437. Jacket and tie preferred. Reservations advised for dinner. AE.*

Le Jardin. Le Jardin, located in the Parioli residential district in the exclusive Lord Byron hotel, itself a triumph of studied interior (and exterior) decoration, is one of Rome's classiest restaurants. The imaginative menu is a tempting compendium of seasonal specialties that are served with style. If they are on the menu, try the pasta with seafood and vegetable sauce or the subtly seasoned rack of lamb. *Hotel Lord Byron, Via Giuseppe De Notaris 5, tel. 06/3609541. Jacket and tie preferred. Reservations required. AE, DC, MC, V. Closed Sun.*

★ **Le Restaurant.** Le Restaurant, discreet haunt of Rome's classiest crowd, is the ultimate in elegance, as well it should be considering that it's the restaurant of the luxurious Grand Ho-

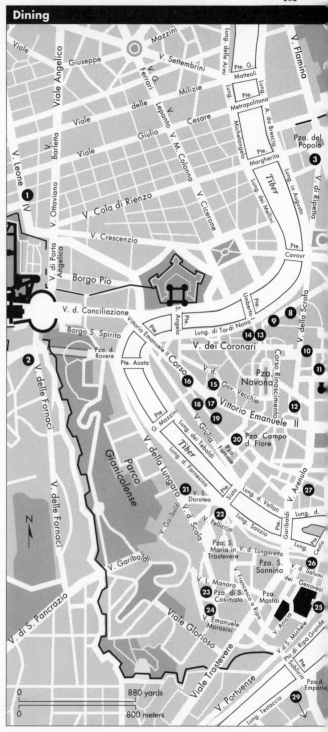

Dining

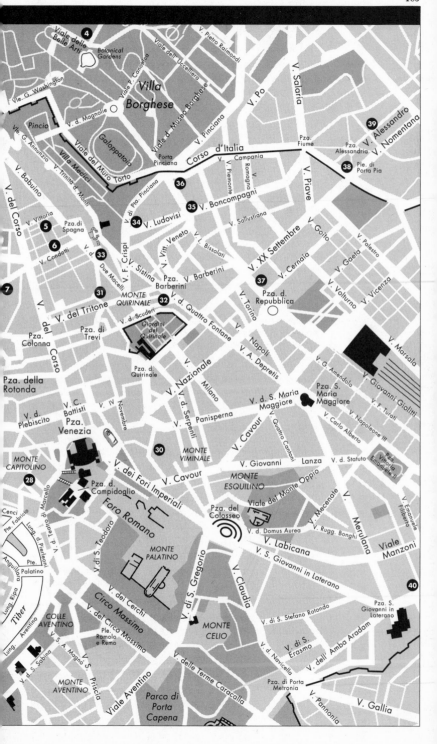

tel (*see* Lodging). The resplendent dining room is surely one of the most beautiful in Italy, the very model of 19th-century opulence, lavished with fine damasks and velvets in pale golden tones, crystal chandeliers, and fine oil paintings. The menu varies with the seasons; there is always a daily recommended menu. Among the specialties are *carpaccio tiepido di pescatrice* (brill with thin slices of raw beef) and *medaglioni di vitello al marsala con tartufo* (veal medallions with marsala wine and truffles). The wine list offers some majestic vintages. *Via Vittorio Emanuele Orlando 3, tel. 06/4709. Jacket and tie. Reservations advised. DC, MC, V. Closed Aug.*

★ **El Toulà.** On a little byway off Piazza Nicosia in Old Rome, El Toulà is one of a number of prestigious restaurants in Italy of the same name; all are spin-offs of a classy restaurant in Treviso in northern Italy. Rome's El Toulà has the warm, welcoming atmosphere of a 19th-century country house, with white walls, antique furniture in dark wood, heavy silver serving dishes, and spectacular arrangements of fruits and flowers. There's a cozy little bar off the entrance where you can sip a *prosecco*, the aperitif best suited to the chef's Venetian specialties, among them the classic *pasta e fagioli* (bean soup) and *fegato alla veneziana* (liver with onions). *Via della Lupa 29/b, tel. 06/6873750. Jacket and tie. Reservations required. AE, DC, MC, V. Closed Sat. lunch, and Sun., Aug., and Dec. 24–26.*

Expensive **Andrea.** Ernest Hemingway and King Farouk used to eat here;
★ Italian power brokers still do. A half-block off Via Veneto, Andrea offers classic Italian cooking in an intimate, clubby ambience in which snowy table linens gleam against a discreet background of dark green paneling. The menu features delicacies such as homemade *tagliolini* (thin noodles) with shrimp and spinach sauce, spaghetti with seafood and truffles, and mouth-watering *carciofi all'Andrea* (artichokes simmered in olive oil). *Via Sardegna 26, tel. 06/493707. Dress informal. Reservations advised. AE, DC, MC, V. Closed Sun. and most of Aug.*

★ **Alberto Ciarla.** Located on a large square in Trastevere, scene of a busy morning food market, Alberto Ciarla is thought by many to be the best seafood restaurant in Rome. In contrast with its workaday location, the ambience is upscale, with red-and-black decor. Bubbling aquariums, a sure sign that the food is superfresh, are set round the wall. Seafood salads are a specialty. Meat eaters will find succor in the house pâté and the lamb. Order carefully or the check will soar. *Piazza San Cosimato 40, tel. 06/5818668. Jacket and tie. Reservations required. AE, DC, MC, V. Dinner only. Closed Sun., Aug. 5–25, and Christmas.*

Coriolano. The only tourists who find their way to this classic restaurant near Porta Pia are likely to be gourmets looking for quintessential Italian food, and that means light homemade pastas, choice olive oil, and market-fresh ingredients, especially seafood. The small dining room is decorated with antiques, and tables are set with immaculate white linen, sparkling crystal, and silver. Although seafood dishes vary, *tagliolini all'aragosta* (thin noodles with lobster sauce) is usually on the menu, as are *porcini* mushrooms in season (cooked to a secret recipe). The wine list is predominantly Italian, but includes some French and Californian wines, too. *Via Ancona 14, tel. 06/861122. Jacket and tie preferred. Reservations advised. No credit cards. Closed Sun., and Aug. 1–25.*

Passetto. Passetto, located near Piazza Navona, has been a favorite with Italians and tourists for many years: It's a place you can rely on for classic Italian food and courteous service. If you can, eat on the shady terrace—it's especially memorable at night—as the mirrored dining room is staid. Roman specialties such as *cannelloni* (stuffed pasta tubes) and *abbacchio* (baby lamb) are always featured. *Via Zanardelli 14, tel. 06/6879937. Jacket and tie preferred. Reservations advised. AE, DC, MC, V. Closed Sun., and Mon. lunch.*

Piperno. Located in the old Jewish Ghetto next to historic Palazzo Cenci, Piperno has been in business for more than a century. It is *the* place to go for Rome's extraordinary *carciofi alla giudia*, crispy-fried artichokes, Jewish style. You eat in three small, wood-paneled dining rooms or, in fair weather, at one of a handful of tables outdoors. Try *filetti di baccala* (cod fillet fried in batter), *pasta e ceci* (a thick soup of pasta tubes and chickpeas), and *fiori di zucca* (stuffed zucchini flowers)— but don't miss the *carciofi. Monte dei Cenci 9, tel. 06/6542772. Dress informal. Reservations advised. No credit cards. Closed Sun. for dinner and all day Mon., Christmas, Easter, and Aug.*

Quinzi e Gabrielli. This small but bright locale near the Pantheon is the closest Rome comes to an oyster bar. Open only in the evening, it features a counter at the entrance where you can choose your own oysters or other seafood. These are served at little tables in the tiny dining rooms, decorated with garden-terrace motifs. Night owls stop in on their way to the many piano bars and discos in the neighborhood for an upscale snack. A full meal here nudges into the Very Expensive category. *Via delle Coppelle 5, tel. 06/6879389. AE, DC. Closed lunch and Sun.*

★ **Ranieri.** Ranieri, on a quiet street off fashionable Via Condotti near the Spanish Steps, is a historic restaurant founded by a one-time chef of Queen Victoria. It remains a favorite with tourists for its traditional atmosphere and decor, with damask-covered walls, velvet banquettes, crystal chandeliers, and old paintings. The Italian–French cuisine is excellent: Portions are abundant and checks remain comfortably within the lower range of this category. Among the many specialties on the vast menu are *gnocchi alla parigina* (souffléed gnocchi with tomato and cheese sauce) and *mignonettes alla Regina Vittoria* (veal with pâté and cream). *Via Mario de'Fiori 26, tel. 06/6791592. Dress informal. Reservations advised. AE, DC, MC, V. Closed Sun.*

Il Tentativo. Il Tentativo is one of a handful of restaurants in Rome that are setting the pace in new Italian cuisine; in fact, this sophisticated little spot in Trastevere has regularly won lavish praise from food critics. The decor is subdued and elegant, with small modern lamps over the tables creating pools of warm light and discreetly focusing attention on the real reason for coming here: the exquisite food—always presented with flair—and the carefully selected wines. The clientele ranges from classy to casual and doesn't mind lingering over dinner; but then food like this just can't be hurried. The menu changes seasonally, but you can usually find *ravioli di branzino bianco e nero* (freshly made pasta colored with squid ink and stuffed with bass) and veal fillet with a variety of sauces such as *astice e bottarga* (lobster and dried fish roe). *Via della Luce 5, tel. 06/5895234. Jacket and tie preferred. Reservations required. AE, DC, MC. Closed Sun. and Aug.*

Il Veliero. This is another of Rome's top seafood restaurants. It's in Old Rome, near Piazza Farnese. The attractive sailing-ship decor sets the scene for seafood feasts accompanied by fresh-baked bread from the wood-burning oven. There are many types of pasta and risotto with shellfish or squid to follow the splendid choice of seafood antipastos. For your main course, try grilled or baked fish, or succulent Mediterranean crayfish, scampi, or shrimp. Have the bluefish if it's on the menu. *Via Monserrato 32, tel. 06/6542636. Jacket and tie preferred. Reservations advised. AE, DC, V. Closed Mon.*

Moderate **Dal Bolognese.** Long a favorite with the arty crowd, this classic restaurant on Piazza del Popolo is a handy place for a leisurely lunch between sightseeing and shopping. While dining, feast your eyes on an extensive array of contemporary paintings, many of them by customers, both illustrious and not. As the name of the restaurant promises, the cooking here adheres to the hearty tradition of Bologna, tempting you with homemade pastas in creamy sauces and steaming trays of boiled meats. As if that were not enough, there's also *dolce della mamma*, a concoction of ice cream, zabaglione, and chocolate sauce. *Piazza del Popolo 1, tel. 06/3611426. Dress informal. Reservations advised. AE, V. Closed Mon.*

La Campana. This inconspicuous trattoria off Via della Scrofa has a centuries-old tradition: There has been an inn on this spot since the 15th century, and the two plain dining rooms occupy what were once stables. It's a homey place, with friendly waiters, a vigil light in front of a painted Madonna over the kitchen entrance, and good Roman food at reasonable prices. The menu offers specialties such as *vignarola* (sautéed fava beans, peas, and artichokes), *rigatoni* with prosciutto and tomato sauce, and *olivette di vitello con puré* (tiny veal rolls with mashed potatoes). *Vicolo della Campana 18, tel. 06/6867820. Dress informal. Reservations advised for dinner. AE, DC. Closed Mon.*

Cannavota. Cannavota, located on the square next to San Giovanni in Laterano, has a large and faithful following; indeed it has fed generations of neighborhood families over the years. Seafood predominates, but carnivores will be happy here, too. Try one of the pastas with seafood sauce, perhaps fettuccine with shrimp and scampi, and then go on to grilled fish or meat. The cheerful atmosphere and rustic decor make for an authentically Roman experience. *Piazza San Giovanni in Laterano, tel. 06/775007. Dress informal. Reservations advised. AE, V. Closed Wed. and Aug. 1–20.*

Da Checcho er Carrettiere. Tucked away behind Piazza Trilussa in Trastevere Checcho has the look of a country inn, with braids of garlic hung from the roof and an antipasto table that features some unusual specialties, such as a well-seasoned mashed-potato and tomato mixture. Among the hearty pasta offerings are *spaghetti alla carrettiera*, with black pepper, sharp cheese, and olive oil, and *linguine* with scampi. Seafood (which can be expensive) predominates but traditional Roman meat dishes are offered, too. This is a great place for genuine Trastevere color and hospitality. *Via Benedetta 10, tel. 06/5817018. Dress informal. Reservations advised. AE, DC. Closed Sun. evening and Mon.*

Colline Emiliane. Located near Piazza Barberini, the Colline Emiliane is an unassuming trattoria offering exceptionally good food. Behind an opaque glass facade there are a couple of plain little dining rooms where you are served light homemade pastas, a very special chicken broth, and meats ranging from boiled beef to *giambonetto di vitella* (roast veal) and *cotoletta alla bolognese* (veal cutlet with cheese and tomato sauce). Family-run, it's quiet and soothing, a good place to rest after a sightseeing stint. Service is cordial and discreet. *Via degli Avignonesi 22, tel. 06/4757538. Dress informal. Reservations advised. No credit cards. Closed Fri.*

Fortunato al Pantheon. Just two steps off Piazza della Rotonda in front of the Pantheon, Fortunato is a favorite of politicos from the House of Representatives a block or so away. With politicians around of course there's a back room, but you can happily settle for the larger of the three dining rooms, or even a table outside in good weather. For his faithful and demanding clientele, Fortunato varies his specialties, offering several pastas, such as *penne all'arrabbiata* with piquant tomato sauce, and *risotto alla milanese*, with saffron or with *porcini* mushrooms. He also serves many types of fish and meat dishes, some with expensive truffles. *Via del Pantheon 55, tel. 06/6792788. Dress informal. Reservations advised. AE. Closed Sun.*

Da Meo Patacca. Located on a picturesque square in Trastevere, this is a fun place for an evening of live music in an endearingly bogus Old-Rome atmosphere. Strolling musicians in folk costumes sing and play your requests; everybody joins in. The first-floor and downstairs dining rooms are strewn with an array of garlic, peppers, and antique junk. Dine outside in summer. The parchment-type menu may be too much for some, but you can't go wrong with the pasta and meat specialties "alla Meo." The food is surprisingly good. *Piazza del Mercanti, in Trastevere; tel. 06/5816198. Dress informal. Reservations advised. AE, DC, V. Closed lunch.*

Orso 80. This bright and bustling trattoria is located in Old Rome on a street famed for artisan workshops. In good weather the window doors of the two long and adjacent dining rooms are opened to catch the breeze. It's a popular place, known above all for a fabulous antipasto table. If you have room for more, try the homemade egg pasta or the *bucatini all'amatriciana;* there's plenty of seafood on the menu, too. If you can face dessert, the *ricotta* cake, a genuine Roman specialty, is always good. *Via dell'Orso 33, tel. 06/6864904. Dress informal. Reservations advised. AE, DC, MC, V. Closed Mon. and Aug. 10–20.*

Pierluigi. Pierluigi, in the heart of Old Rome, is a longtime favorite with foreigners resident in Rome and Italians in the entertainment field. On busy evenings it's almost impossible to find a table, so make sure you reserve well in advance. Seafood predominates—if you fancy a splurge, try the lobster—but traditional Roman dishes are offered, too: *orecchiette con broccoli* (disc-shaped pasta with greens) or just simple spaghetti. Eat in the pretty piazza in summer. *Piazza dei Ricci 144, tel. 06/6861302. Dress informal. Reservations advised. AE. Closed Mon. and 2 weeks in Aug.*

★ **Quattro Mori.** Quattro Mori is probably the best Sardinian restaurant in town, head and shoulders above the many mediocre Sardinian eating places that sprouted a few years ago. There's a tempting antipasto selection, then a choice between such Sardinian pastas as *malloreddus* (small shells made of semola), *culingiones* (vegetarian ravioli), and spaghetti *all'aragosta* (with lobster sauce). Second courses offer either meat or fish, including the Sardinian *maialino* (roast piglet) and the Roman *pajata* (baby lamb innards). For dessert, try *sebadas* (fried cheese-filled ravioli doused with honey). The restaurant is located near the Vatican. *Via Santa Maria delle Fornaci 8/a, tel. 06/632609. Dress informal. Reservations advised. No credit cards. Closed Mon. and Aug. 10–Sept. 4.*

La Rampa. A haven for exhausted shoppers and sightseers, La Rampa is right behind the American Express office on Piazza Mignanelli, off Piazza di Spagna. The attractive decor evokes a colorful old Roman marketplace, and there are a few tables for outdoor dining on the piazza. The specialties of the house are a lavish antipasto, *bombolotti alla vodka* (pasta with a tomato and vodka sauce), *pinturricchio* (veal escallopes with creamy sauce in a pastry shell), and *frittura alla Rampa* (deep-fried vegetables and mozzarella). La Rampa is popular and busy, and you may have to wait for a table. Get there early (or late). *Piazza Mignanelli 18, tel. 06/6782621. Dress informal. No reservations. No credit cards. Closed Sun., Mon. lunch, and Aug.*

★ **Romolo.** Generations of Romans have enjoyed the romantic garden courtyard and historic dining room of this charming Trastevere haunt, reputedly once home of Raphael's ladylove, the Fornarina. In the evening strolling musicians serenade diners. The cuisine is appropriately Roman; specialties include *mozzarella alla fornarina* (deep-fried mozzarella with ham and anchovies) and *braciolette d'abbacchio scottadito* (grilled baby lamb chops). Alternatively, try one of the new vegetarian pastas featuring *carciofi* (artichokes) or *raddicchio* (the fashionable reddish leaf). Meats are charcoal-grilled; there's also a wood-burning oven. *Via di Porta Settimiana 8, tel. 06/5818284. Dress informal. Reservations advised. AE, DC, V. Closed Mon., and Aug. 2–23.*

Tana del Grillo. Food from one of Italy's least-known gastronomic regions—Ferrara—is the draw here. Sausages and salami, *gnocchi* with a variety of sauces, and *pasticcio di maccheroni* are among the featured dishes. There is also a cart of steaming boiled meats. The family-run restaurant is located near the Forum in what were once the stables of a historic Roman palace. You dine under arched alcoves. Prices are at the top of the category. *Salita del Grillo 6, tel. 06/6798705. Dress informal. Reservations advised for dinner. AE, DC. Closed Sun. and Aug.*

Val di Sangro. Head here for heavy and substantial country-style pastas such as *tonnarelli Val di Sangro* (with mushrooms, bacon, sausage, and basil) or, in the evening, try one of the pizzas. Fish is featured Tuesdays. The restaurant is very much a neighborhood favorite and a great value. *Via Alessandria 22, tel. 06/861134. Dress informal. Reservations advised. No credit cards. Closed Fri., and July 15–Aug. 16.*

★ **Vecchia Roma.** The frescoed walls of this historic restaurant located in a one-time palace in Old Rome and the seafood specialties—among them *fettuccine verdi* (spinach-flavored pasta with cream sauce) and *petti pollo con gamberi di fiume* (chicken breasts with freshwater shrimp)—have long made this a classic choice of resident foreigners in Rome and sophisticated travelers. In summer you dine under white umbrellas. *Piazza Campitelli 18, tel. 06/6564604. Dress informal. Reservations advised. No credit cards. Closed Wed. and Aug.*

Inexpensive **Baffetto.** The emphasis here is firmly on good, old-fashioned
★ value: The food is much more important than the surroundings.

Baffetto is Rome's best-known inexpensive pizza restaurant, plainly decorated and very popular. You'll probably have to wait in line outside on the *sampietrini*—the cobblestones. The interior is mostly given over to the ovens, the tiny cash desk, and the simple paper-covered tables. *Bruschetta* (toast) and *crostini* (mozzarella toast) are the only variations on the pizza theme. Turnover is fast—this is not a place to linger over your meal. Expect to share a table. *Via del Governo Vecchio 114, tel. 06/6861617. Dress informal. Reservations not accepted. No credit cards. Open evenings only. Closed Sun., Aug.*

Bucatino. This is one of many popular pizzeria restaurants in the newly trendy Testaccio neighborhood. Eat as little or as much as you want. The pasta to order here is *bucatini all'amatriciana*, with a tangy tomato and bacon sauce. Note that if you only order pizza you'll have to pay the cover charge. Alternatively, if you order one of the meat or fish dishes, the check will nudge into the Moderate range. *Via Luca della Robbia 84, tel. 06/5746886. Dress informal. Reservations advised weekends. No credit cards. Closed Mon. and Aug.*

★ **L'Eau Vive.** This is an offbeat choice for an inexpensive lunch, but be aware that prices rise steeply in the evening. The restaurant is run by lay Catholic missionary workers, many of them from developing countries (national dress proliferates). The food is predominantly French though ethnic dishes are always offered. Order one of the fixed-price menus; they are among Rome's best-kept gastronomic secrets. You may have to hunt for the inconspicuous entrance, a little door by the entrance to Palazza Lante just off Piazza Sant'Eustachio near the Pantheon. If you haven't made a reservation, get there early. *Via Monterone 85, tel. 06/6541095. Dress informal (for lunch). Reservations advised. AE, DC, V. Closed Sun. and two weeks in Aug.*

Fiammetta. For an inexpensive meal at the Fiammetta, you have to order pizza and, perhaps, a vegetable dish or a salad; other dishes will send your check into the Moderate range. Near Piazza Navona, Fiammetta betrays its Tuscan origins in the frescoed views of Florence. In fair weather you can sit outdoors under an arbor. *Piazza Fiammetta 8, tel. 06/6855777. Dress informal. No reservations. No credit cards. Closed Tues.*

Hostaria Farnese. This is a tiny trattoria between Campo dei Fiori and Piazza Farnese, in the heart of Old Rome. Papa serves, mamma cooks, and, depending on what they've picked up at the Campo dei Fiori market, you may find *rigatoni* with tuna and basil, spaghetti with vegetable sauce, *spezzatino* (stew), and other homey specialties. *Via dei Baullari 109, tel. 06/6541595. Dress informal. Reservations advised. AE, V. Closed Thurs.*

Nello e Franco. With a menu that upholds the Roman tradition of a particular dish for each day of the week, this is a reliable and predictable place to dine. You're sure to find lasagne on Sunday, *gnocchi* on Thursday, and pasta *e ceci* (with chickpeas) on Friday. But there are other choices, too, such as *spaghetti alla carbonara* and *all'amatriciana*, both sturdy Roman favorites. Avoid the seafood if you want to keep the check low. *Via del Pellegrino 107, tel. 06/6569361. Dress informal. Reservations advised weekends. No credit cards. Closed Mon.*

Otello alla Concordia. The clientele in this popular spot—it's located off a shopping street near Piazza di Spagna—is about evenly divided between tourists and workers from shops and

offices in the area. The former like to sit outdoors in the courtyard in any weather; the latter have their regular tables in one
of the inside dining rooms. The menu offers classic Roman and
Italian dishes and service is friendly and efficient. Since every
tourist in Rome knows about it and since the shop-owners won't
relinquish their niches, you may have to wait for a table; go early. *Via della Croce 81, tel. 06/6791178. Dress informal. No
reservations. No credit cards. Closed Sun. and Christmas.*

Polese. On a charming square off Corso Vittorio in Old Rome,
Polese is best in fair weather, when you sit outdoors under the
trees. Like most centrally located, inexpensive eateries in
Rome, it is crowded on weekends and weekday evenings in the
summer. Straightforward Roman dishes are featured; specialties include *fettuccine alla Polese* (noodles with cream and
mushrooms) and *vitello alla fornara* (roast brisket of veal with
potatoes). *Piazza Sforza Cesarini 40, tel. 06/6861709. Dress informal. Reservations advised weekends. No credit cards.
Closed Tues., 15 days in Aug., and 15 days in Dec.*

Reali. This family-run enterprise, located on a main thoroughfare near the Vatican Museums, is short on decor but offers
good-value pastas, thick soups, and vegetable dishes, as well as
Roman specialties such as *abbacchio* (lamb chops) and *pollo con
peperoni* (chicken with peppers). Try the house wine, a very
dry white. *Via Leone IV 91, tel. 06/386744. Dress informal.
Reservations advised for groups. AE. Closed Wed. and Aug.*

Tavernetta. The central location between the Trevi Fountain
and the Spanish Steps and the good-value tourist menu make
this a reliable bet for a simple but filling meal. The menu features Sicilian and Abruzzo specialties; try the pasta with
eggplant or the roast suckling pig. Both the red and the white
house wines are good. *Via del Nazzareno 3, tel. 06/6793124.
Dress informal. Reservations required for dinner. AE, DC,
MC, V. Closed Mon. and Aug.*

Tulipano Nero. This bright and noisy Trastevere pizzeria is
very much a place for the under-25s. Unusual pasta dishes—
rigatoni with a walnut and cheese sauce—and a U.S.-style
salad bar are featured. *Via Roma Libera 15 (Piazza San
Cosimato), tel. 06/5818309. Dress informal. Reservations advised for groups. No credit cards. Closed Wed.*

Country Dining

**Along Via Appia
Antica**

L'Archeologia. In this farmhouse just beyond the catacombs
you dine indoors in cool weather beside the fireplace, or outdoors in summer in the garden under age-old vines. The
atmosphere is friendly and intimate, and specialties include
homemade pastas, *abbacchio scottadito* (grilled baby lamb
chops), and seafood. *Via Appia Antica 139, tel. 06/7880494.
Dress informal. Reservations advised for dinner and weekends. No credit cards. Closed Thurs. Moderate.*

Cecilia Metella. From the entrance on the Via Appia Antica,
practically opposite the catacombs, you walk uphill to a low-
lying but sprawling construction designed to cater weddings
and banquets. There's a large terrace shaded by vines for outdoor dining. Although obviously geared to handling larger
groups, Cecilia Metella also gives couples and small groups full
attention, good service, and fine Roman-style cuisine. The specialties are the searing-hot *crespelle*, served in individual
casseroles, and *pollo alla Nerone* (chicken à la Nero; *flambé*, of
course). *Via Appia Antica 125, tel. 06/5136743. Dress infor-*

mal. Reservations advised weekends. AE. Closed Mon. Moderate.

Sora Rosa. Quite a way off the Via Appia Antica (you need a car or taxi to get there), Sora Rosa is a delightful place, especially when you can eat outside under the eucalyptus trees. There's a pleasant, if plain, dining room for cooler weather. The cuisine is strictly Roman, with homemade fettuccine and *pollo alla diavola* (grilled chicken) the specialties. *Via Tor Carbone 74, tel. 06/7990453. Dress informal. Reservations advised weekends and dinner in summer. No credit cards. Closed Mon. Moderate.*

In the Castelli Romani

La Frasca. This is a traditional wine cellar in Frascati, that has been converted into a fine little family-run restaurant. The floor is paved with ancient cobblestones, while the beamed ceilings and rough plaster walls add to the rustic atmosphere. There's a terrace with a view of the town square and the plain below. Along with typical Roman dishes like *coda alla vaccinara* (oxtail stew), there are *gnocchetti verdi* (tiny potato-and-spinach dumplings) and *filetto alla Frasca* (filet of beef with port and fondue). *Via Lunati 3, Frascati; tel. 06/9420311. Dress informal. Reservations required Sun. MC, V. Closed Wed., and 15 days in Jan. Moderate.*

La Panzanella. Located on the lakeshore below the papal villa at Castel Gandolfo, this large, rustic restaurant is brightly decorated with orange accents and flowers on the tables. Come here to sample the creative cuisine including *tagliolini agli scampi* (homemade pasta with scampi) and classic *pappardelle alla lepre* (homemade noodles with hare sauce). The owner prides himself on his highly personalized cooking and inventive variations on Roman dishes. *Via Spiaggia del Lago 18, Castel Gandolfo; tel. 06/9360049. Dress informal. Reservations required. No credit cards. Closed Wed. and Aug. 15–30. Moderate.*

Pagnanelli. This Castel Gandolfo restaurant is a favorite for weekend outings and wedding parties. It features tiled floors and wooden ceilings, and there's a large veranda with a view over Lake Albano. The menu offers a choice of classic Italian and international cuisine; specialties include *fettuccine alla papalina* (homemade pasta with egg, ham, and parmesan cheese) and *trota compressore* (fresh breaded trout). *Via A. Gramsci 4, Castel Gandolfo; tel. 06/9360004. Dress informal. Reservations advised. AE, DC, V. Closed Tues. Moderate.*

7 Lodging

Introduction

Rome offers a wide range of hotels, all officially graded from five stars to one star. The top, deluxe hotels take their grading seriously: Most are positively palatial and offer service in the grand manner. There are disappointingly few inexpensive or even moderate hotels in the center of the city. A lot of formerly lower-priced hotels have taken advantage of their central locations and have upgraded their facilities and crossed over to the expensive category. Some of these still betray their roots in smallish rooms, however. With rare exceptions, all rooms in first-class hotels have bath or shower. In newer or recently renovated three-star hotels, most rooms have bath or shower, though the latter may well be the drain-in-the-floor type that floods the bathroom. Remember that you will always pay considerably less for a room without a private bath. The old-fashioned Roman pension no longer exists as an official category, but, though graded as hotels, some preserve the homey atmosphere that makes some visitors prefer them, especially for longer stays.

Rooms in all top hotels are soundproofed, but noise can be a problem in moderate and inexpensive hotels. Ask for an inside room if you're a light sleeper, but don't be disappointed if it's on a dark courtyard. In general, room quality in older hotels can be uneven; if you don't like the one you're given, ask for another.

Always book in advance. If you do arrive without reservations, try one of the following **EPT Information Offices** at: Via Parigi 5, tel. 06/463748; Termini Station, tel. 06/465461; Leonardo da Vinci airport, tel. 06/6011255; Roma-Nord Salaria service area on A1 autostrada, tel. 06/6919958; Roma-Sud Frascati service area on A2 autostrada, tel. 06/9420058. All can help with accommodations; there is no charge. Lines at the main office and at Termini Station can be long, however, especially in the summer. Students can try the **Protezione Giovanni** office at Termini Station; it specializes in finding low-cost accommodations for girls, but will help all students if the office isn't busy. **CTS** (Via Genova 16, tel. 06/46791) is a student travel agency by Termini Station. Don't rely on official-looking men who approach tourists at Termini Station: They tout for the less desirable hotels around the train station.

There are distinct advantages to staying in a hotel that is within easy walking distance of the main sights. With so much of downtown Rome closed to daytime traffic, the centrally located hotels are much quieter than they used to be. If you are visiting by car, park it in a garage and explore the city on foot or use public transportation. Parking space in downtown Rome is almost impossible to find, added to which you won't be able to use the car for much of the day anyway.

Residence Hotels If you plan to stay a month or more and want the independence offered by an apartment, look into the spate of residence hotels that have opened to satisfy the demands of long-stay visitors. Residence hotels have fully equipped kitchens, and offer linens, laundry, and cleaning services. Most are offered for monthly rentals; costs range from two million lire to four million lire. One of the most attractive, and expensive, is **Palazzo**

Lodging

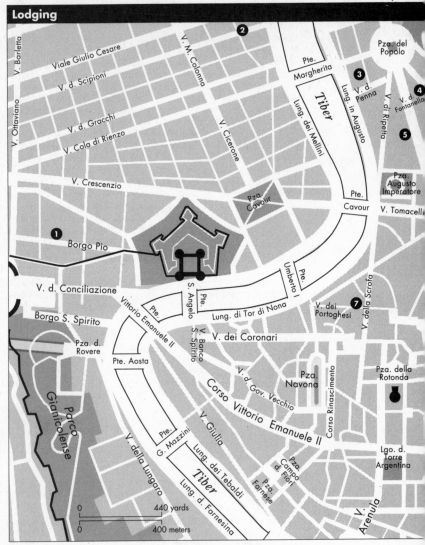

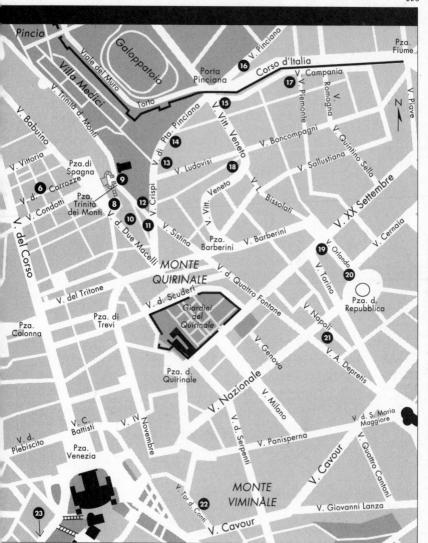

al Velabro, Via del Velabro 16, tel. 06/6792985. Alternatively, try **Residence Ripetta,** Via Ripetta 231, tel. 06/672141; it's centrally located and offers excellent facilities. Others to try are: **Residence in Trastevere** (Vicolo Moroni 35, tel. 06/582768) and **Mayfair Residence** (Via Sicilia 183, tel. 06/4814887).

Ratings Room rates in Rome are on a par with most other major European capitals. Rates are generally quoted inclusive of taxes and service. Some hotels will also quote separate rates for breakfast; these can vary from 25,000 lire per person in a deluxe hotel to 6,000 lire per person in an inexpensive hotel. If you object to paying extra for breakfast, remember that you're not obliged to pay, but make clear when you check in that you won't be having breakfast. Most hotels expect you to have breakfast in your room. You're not obliged to eat there, but again make clear when you check in that you prefer not to. Air-conditioning in lower-priced hotels may add an extra charge; in more expensive hotels it will be included in the room rate. All hotels are supposed to have rate cards on the room doors or inside the closet. These specify exactly what you have to pay and detail any extras. Rates in any given hotel can vary according to the standard of individual rooms.

The most highly recommended establishments are indicated by a star ★.

Category	Cost*
Very Expensive	350,000 lire and up
Expensive	250,000–300,000 lire
Moderate	150,000–220,000 lire
Inexpensive	under 100,000 lire

for two people in a double room, including tax and service

Credit Cards The following credit-card abbreviations are used: AE, American Express; DC, Diners Club; MC, MasterCard; V, Visa.

Downtown Rome

Very Expensive **Ambasciatori Palace.** This palatial hotel, opposite the U.S. Embassy on busy Via Veneto, has big, bright rooms and spacious suites. All are comfortably furnished and attractively decorated with radiant floral prints or damasks. All rooms are soundproofed and are equipped with color TV, radio, air-conditioning, and minibar. Linen sheets are standard; many doubles have twin baths. The hotel, built in the '20s, has a striking lounge decorated with stunning period murals of languid ladies with bobbed hair and dapper gentlemen in black tie; it's a great place to meet for drinks. The elegant *ABC Grill Room* on the first floor moves upstairs in summer to a cool terrace with a wall-length fountain. *Via Veneto 70, tel. 06/47493. 150 rooms and suites with bath. Facilities: sauna, massage, bar, restaurant. AE, DC, MC, V.*

★ **Eden.** The Eden celebrates its centenary in 1989 and has prepared for it by renovating three of its four floors. Just off Via Veneto, it combines a convenient location with discreet comfort and fine service, not to mention surprisingly low rates for its grading. From the cozy, wood-paneled lounge to the individually decorated rooms and suites, the hotel exudes a sense of well-appointed luxury. Service is polished. There's a touch of romance and fun in the uncluttered decor: a mixture of antiques, art deco, and streamlined modern, augmented by mirrors and marbles. All rooms have TV and minibar; those on the upper floors have terrific views. (The best view of all is from the penthouse bar and restaurant.) *Via Ludovisi 49, tel. 06/4743551. 93 rooms and suites with bath. Facilities: bar and restaurant. AE.*

Grand. A 100-year-old establishment of class and style, this CIGA-owned hotel caters to an elite international clientele. It's located between Termini Station and Via Veneto. Off the richly decorated, split-level main bar, where afternoon tea is served every day, there are a smaller, more intimate bar and a buffet restaurant. The spacious bedrooms are decorated in gracious Empire style with smooth fabrics and thick carpets in tones of blue and pale gold. Crystal chandeliers and marble baths add luxurious notes. The Grand also boasts one of Italy's most beautiful dining rooms, called, simply, *Le Restaurant* (*see* Dining). *Via Vittorio Emanuele Orlando 3, tel. 06/4709. 170 rooms and suites with bath. Facilities: 2 bars, 2 restaurants. AE, DC, MC, V.*

★ **Hassler.** Located at the top of the Spanish Steps, the Hassler boasts what is probably the most scenic location of any hotel in the city. The front rooms and penthouse restaurant have sweeping views over Rome; other rooms overlook the gardens of Villa Medici. The hotel is run by the distinguished Wirth family of hoteliers. They assure a warmly cordial atmosphere and ensure magnificent service from the well-trained staff. The public rooms are memorable, especially the first-floor bar (a chic city rendezvous), and the glass-roofed lounge with gold marble walls and hand-painted tile floor. The elegant and comfortable rooms are decorated in various classic styles; some feature frescoed walls. All have color TV, minibar, and air-conditioning. The Penthouse Suite has a bedroom with a mirrored ceiling and a huge terrace. *Piazza Trinità dei Monti 6, tel. 06/6782651. 101 rooms and suites with bath. Facilities: bar, restaurant. AE.*

Expensive **Flora.** With its slightly faded decor and old-world style, the Flora is less luxurious than some other Via Veneto hotels, but rooms are ample and comfortable and many have fine views of Villa Borghese. Potted plants are featured in the public rooms and marble-lined hallways. Period furniture, Oriental rugs, and old paintings add character to the rooms. All have minibar, and most have TV. Service is attentive, with a personal touch that's all too rare these days. And that, together with the unostentatious comfort, is what keeps the Flora's regular clientele coming back year after year. The management is especially proud of the lavish breakfasts, served either in your room or in the old-fashioned dining room, complete with crystal chandelier, oil paintings, and red-velvet chairs. *Via Veneto 191, tel. 06/497821. 200 rooms with bath. AE, DC, MC, V.*

★ **Forum.** A centuries-old palace converted into a fine hotel, the Forum is on a quiet street within hailing distance of the Roman Forum and Piazza Venezia. Although it seems tucked away out of the mainstream, it's actually handily located for all the main sights. The wood-paneled lobby and street-level bar are warm and welcoming. The smallish bedrooms are furnished in rich pink and beige fabrics; bathrooms are ample, with either tub or shower. All rooms have TV and air-conditioning. However, what's really special about the Forum is the rooftop restaurant: The view over to the Colosseum is superb. Breakfast on the roof or a nightcap at the roof bar can be memorable. *Via Tor dei Conti 25, tel. 06/6792446. 80 rooms with bath or shower. Facilities: bar, restaurant. AE, DC, MC, V.*

Giulio Cesare. An aristocratic town house in the residential but central Prati district, the Giulio Cesare is a 10-minute walk across the Tiber from Piazza del Popolo. It's beautifully kept and run, if rather sedate, with a quietly luxurious air. Rooms are furnished in classically elegant style with thick rugs, floor-length drapes, rich damasks in soft colors, and crystal chandeliers. All rooms have minibar and TV and are air-conditioned. Public rooms have Oriental carpets, old prints and paintings, and marble fireplaces. There is a garden terrace and bar where a wide range of snacks are offered in the evening (but no restaurant). *Via degli Scipioni 287, tel. 06/310244. 76 rooms with bath. Facilities: bar, terrace. AE, DC, MC, V.*

Jolly Via Veneto. If you're looking for contemporary efficiency and a classy location, the Jolly will fit the bill. It's at the top of Via Veneto, on the edge of Villa Borghese, in a striking steel-and-glass building. Off the sunken lobby are a large bar-lounge and a restaurant. Chocolate-brown carpeting and functional built-in white fittings are featured throughout. Try to get a room overlooking Villa Borghese; they are worth the extra charge. All rooms are soundproofed and air-conditioned and have minibar and TV. *Corso d'Italia 1, tel. 06/8495. 200 rooms with bath or shower. Facilities: bar, restaurant, garage. AE, DC, MC, V.*

★ **Valadier.** This sumptuous small hotel on an inconspicuous street in Rome's premier shopping district near the Spanish Steps promises to be a topic of conversation among those in the know. The result of a renovation of an existing hotel in a 300-year-old building once famous as an elite bordello, it will appeal to discerning guests with a taste for understated luxury. Bedrooms feature textured fabrics in light blue and beige with black accents. Mirrored walls, indirect lighting, and sleek bathrooms heighten the effect. Suite 308 and room 201 are among the larger rooms in what is bound to become one of Rome's classiest little hotels. Renovations are continuing on the first floor, where a new lobby is being built. A restaurant is planned for 1989. *Via della Fontanella 15, tel. 06/3610592. 40 rooms and 6 suites, all with bath. Facilities: bar, restaurant. AE, DC, MC, V.*

★ **Victoria.** Considerable luxury in the public rooms, solid comfort throughout, and impeccable management are the keynotes of this classy hotel near Via Veneto. Oriental rugs, oil paintings, welcoming armchairs, and fresh flowers add charm to the public rooms. American businessmen, who prize the hotel's personalized service and restful atmosphere, are frequent guests. Soothing combinations of peach, blue, or green characterize the homey rooms. Some upper rooms and the roof terrace overlook the majestic pines of Villa Borghese. There is a bar and a restaurant, the latter offering à la carte meals and a good-value fixed-price menu featuring Roman specialties. *Via Campania 41, tel. 06/473931. 150 rooms with bath. Facilities: bar, restaurant. AE, DC, MC, V.*

Moderate **Britannia.** Located near Termini Station and next to St. Paul's Episcopal church, the Britannia is a bright and compact hotel. Rooms are small, though well planned; 401 and 402 both have terraces. All rooms are decorated in blue-gray with red accents, and all have brand-new bathrooms. Guests—among them many Americans—meet in the handsome beige and peacock-blue lounge/bar/breakfast room. *Via Napoli 64, tel. 06/465785. 32 rooms with bath. Facilities: bar. AE, DC, MC, V.*

★ **Carriage.** You'll want to stay here for the location (by the Spanish Steps), the old-world elegance, and the reasonable rates. Totally renovated over the past few years, the hotel is decorated in soothing tones of blue and pale gold, with subdued Baroque accents adding a touch of luxury. Rooms have minibar and TV, plus antique-looking closets and porcelain telephones. Double room 402 and single room 305 have small balconies; elegant room 302 is spacious, with an oversize bathroom. Alternatively, try to book one of the two rooms giving onto the roof terrace. *Via delle Carrozze 36, tel. 06/6794106. 27 rooms and suites with bath. AE, DC, MC, V.*

Gregoriana. This is a place that will appeal to those with a taste for the bizarre. The 19 rooms are identified with fancy Erte letters (rather than plain numbers). Room decor is low key, but the owners have gone wild in the public rooms: Two floors have leopard-skin wallpaper; the third has a splashy floral print; the lobby is decked out in rattan. The building was originally a convent, and room C, the former chapel, preserves the altar niche and the original ceiling. Book well in advance: The Gregoriana is popular with the high-fashion crowd. It's located on a classy shopping street near the Spanish Steps. *Via Gregoriana 18, tel. 06/6994269. 19 rooms with bath or shower. No credit cards.*

★ **Internazionale.** With an excellent location near the top of the Spanish Steps, the Internazionale has long been known as one of the city's best mid-size hotels. It's in a totally renovated building on desirable Via Sistina, within easy walking distance of many downtown sights. Double-glazed windows ensure peace and quiet in the compact rooms, all of which have color TV, minibar, and air-conditioning. Rooms on the fourth floor have terraces; the fourth-floor suite has a private terrace and a frescoed ceiling. The decor throughout is in soothing pastel tones, with some antique pieces, mirrors, and chandeliers heightening the English country-house look. Guests relax in small, homey lounges downstairs and begin the day in the pretty breakfast room. *Via Sistina 79, tel. 06/6793047. 40 rooms with bath. AE, DC, MC, V.*

Locarno. In a central location off Piazza del Popolo, the Locarno has long been a favorite hotel among the arty crowd for its intimate mood, though some of its fine fin de siècle character has been lost in renovations. An attempt has been made to retain the hotel's original charm, however, while modernizing rooms; color TV and minibar are standard, bathrooms have chic tiles. The latest additions are electronic safes. Air-conditioning is still in the planning stage. The decor features coordinated prints in wallpaper and fabrics, lacquered wrought-iron beds, and some antiques. There is a large bar/lounge on the third floor. *Via della Penna 22, tel. 06/3610841. 38 rooms with bath or shower. Facilities: bar/lounge. AE, V.*

Sant'Anna. If there were any doubts that the picturesque old Borgo neighborhood in the shadow of St. Peter's was becoming fashionable, this stylish hotel goes some way toward dispelling them. Decorated with a flair that at times seems overdone, especially in the ample art-deco bedrooms, the mood here is nonetheless soothing and welcoming. There is a frescoed breakfast room; the courtyard terrace boasts a fountain. There's no elevator to take you up the four floors, but it's worth the climb to the top floor to stay in one of the spacious blue-and-white attic rooms, each with a little terrace. All rooms have TV, minibar, and air-conditioning. *Borgo Pio 134, tel. 06/6541602. 19 rooms with bath or shower. AE, DC, MC, V.*

Sitea. The Sitea has a lot going for it: a central location near Termini Station; spacious and well-decorated rooms, all of them double glazed to keep out noise; à la carte restaurant service any time of day; and, last but not least, an exceptional owner-manager, Signor De Luca, who combines attentiveness and efficiency in ample measure. There is air-conditioning throughout, plus a bar/lounge, and a tavern restaurant on the top floor. Rooms are individually furnished in classic style with fine fabrics; bathrooms are smallish. *Via Vittorio Emanuele Orlando 90, tel. 06/4751560. 40 rooms, most with bath or shower. Facilities: bar, restaurant. AE, DC, MC, V.*

Inexpensive **Ausonia.** This small pension has big advantages in its location
★ on Piazza di Spagna and in its helpful management and family atmosphere. Six rooms face the famous square (quieter now that most through traffic has been banished); all others face the inner courtyard. Furnishings are simple, but standards of cleanliness are high and rates are low. The hotel has many American guests; make sure you make reservations well in advance. *Piazza di Spagna 35, tel. 06/6795745. 10 rooms, none with bath. No credit cards.*

Brotzky. A family-run, pension-type hotel, the Brotzky has an excellent central location on Via del Corso. It's located on the top floor of an old building (it has its own elevator). Though long on charm in the public rooms—carved and polished wood abounds, and dried flowers are everywhere—bedrooms are basic to the point of austerity, with paper-thin walls. Nonetheless, the hotel has proved itself consistently popular with American and European guests, not least for the terrific location and low rates. Make your way up to the little rooftop terrace; you reach it up some steep and rickety iron stairs. *Via del Corso 509, tel. 06/3612339. 23 rooms, 13 with bath or shower. No credit cards.*

Dinesen. Near Via Veneto, the Dinesen is a longtime favorite for its old-fashioned comfort, roomy lounges, low rates, and location 10-minutes' walk from the Spanish Steps. It occupies the first and second floors of an old palace, but note that there is no elevator. Bedrooms are rather basic and can be noisy, but public rooms are homey, with flowered chintz, standing lamps, polished wood floors, and Oriental rugs. There is a small courtyard filled with potted plants. *Via di Porta Pinciana 18, tel. 06/4753501. 20 rooms, 18 with bath or shower. AE, V.*

Portoghesi. In the heart of Old Rome, facing the so-called Monkey Tower, the Portoghesi is a fine little hotel with considerable atmosphere and low rates for the level of comfort offered. From a tiny lobby an equally tiny elevator takes you to the bedrooms, all decorated with floral prints and handsome pieces of old furniture. All rooms are air-conditioned and quiet. There's a little breakfast room, but no restaurant. *Via dei Portoghesi 1, tel. 06/6864231. 27 rooms, most with bath. MC, V.*

Santa Prisca. This basic hotel in the quiet Aventine neighborhood is definitely off the beaten track. To some the restful location is the main attraction. Rooms are simple and beautifully clean; no surprise, perhaps, as the hotel is run by nuns. It makes a fine inexpensive base for a longer stay, but *not* if you want to be in the swing of things. Meals are provided, and there's a terrace where you can sit and take the sun. *Largo Manlio Gelsomini 25, tel. 06/5750009. 45 rooms with shower. No credit cards.*

★ **Suisse.** This homey and simple hotel has an unbeatable location five-minutes' walk from the Spanish Steps. Clean and comfortable rooms allied to reasonable rates make the Suisse an excellent value. The mood in the public rooms is old fashioned —the check-in desk is distinctly drab—but rooms are cheerful, with bright bedspreads, framed prints, and old furniture, though all are small. The lounge has large windows and well-upholstered armchairs. Some rooms face the (fairly) quiet courtyard. There's an upstairs breakfast room, but no restaurant. *Via Gregoriana 56, tel. 06/6783649. 28 rooms, half with bath or shower. No credit cards.*

8 Arts and Nightlife

The Arts

To many people, Rome itself is entertainment enough. The piazzas, fountains, and delicately colored palazzi make impressive backdrops for the living theater of vivacious Rome. Having said which, the city also offers a vast selection of music, dance, opera, and film.

Schedules of events are published in the daily newspapers, in the "Trovaroma" Saturday supplement of *La Repubblica*, in the *Guest in Rome* booklet distributed free at hotel desks, and in the monthly *Carnet* available free from EPT offices. Also, look for posters outside churches announcing free concerts and recitals of religious music. Depending on the venue, concert tickets can cost anything from 3,000 to 20,000 lire.

Rock, pop, and jazz concerts are frequent, especially in the summer, although even performances by big-name international stars may not be well advertised. Tickets are usually handled by **Orbis** (Piazza Esquilino 37, 00185 Rome, tel. 06/4814721).

Concerts Rome has long been a center for a wide variety of classical music concerts, although it is felt by many that the city does not have adequate concert halls or suitable auditoriums. The principal concert series are those of the **Accademia di Santa Cecilia** (offices at Via dei Greci; box office tel. 06/6541044); the **Accademia Filarmonica Romana** (Teatro Olimpico, Via Gentile da Fabriano 17, tel. 06/3962635); the **Istituzione Universitaria dei Concerti** (San Leone Magno auditorium, Via Bolzano 38, tel. 06/853216); and the **RAI Italian Radio-TV** series at Foro Italico (tel. 06/36865625). There is also the internationally respected **Gonfalone** series, which concentrates on Baroque music (Via del Gonfalone 32, tel. 06/68759527). The **Associazione Musicale Romana** (tel. 06/6568441) and **Il Tempietto** (tel. 06/5136148) organize music festivals and concerts throughout the year. There are also numerous small concert groups. Many concerts are free, including all of those performed in Roman Catholic churches, where a special ruling permits only concerts of religious music.

Opera The opera season runs from November to May, and performances are staged in the **Teatro dell'Opera** (Via del Viminale, tel. 06/461755). Tickets go on sale two days before a performance, and the box office is open from 10 to 1 and from 5 to 7. Prices range from 8,000 to 44,000 lire for regular performances; they can go up to 64,000 lire for special performances, such as an opening night or an internationally acclaimed guest singer. Standards may not always measure up to those set by Milan's fabled La Scala, but, despite strikes and shortages of funds, most performances are respectable, if not astounding.

As interesting for its spectacular location as for the music is the summer opera season in the ruins of the ancient **Baths of Caracalla.** Tickets are on sale in advance at the Teatro dell'Opera box office, or at the box office at the Baths of Caracalla from 8 to 9 PM on the evening of the performance. Take a jacket or sweater and something to cover bare legs: Despite the daytime heat of a Roman summer, the nights can be cool and damp.

Dance The **Rome Opera Ballet** gives regular performances at the Teatro dell'Opera, often with leading international guest stars.

Rome is regularly visited by classical ballet companies from the Soviet Union, the United States, and Europe; performances are at Teatro dell'Opera *(see* Opera), Teatro Olimpico, or at one of the open-air venues in summer. Small classical and modern dance companies from Italy and abroad give performances in various places; check concert listings for information.

Film Rome has dozens of movie houses, but the only one to show English-language films exclusively is the **Pasquino** (Vicolo del Piede, just off Piazza Santa Maria, tel. 06/5803622). Programs change frequently, so pick up a schedule weekly at the theater or consult the daily papers. Some film clubs and movie theaters occasionally show English-language films in the original language; consult the papers.

Nightlife

Although Rome is not one of the world's most exciting cities for nightlife (despite the popular image of the city as birthplace of *La Dolce Vita*), recent years have seen the opening of a wide variety of new places for after-hours entertainment. Discos, live-music venues, and quiet late-night bars have proliferated, both on the narrow streets of the old city and in far-flung parts of the town. Each night spot tends to attract its own clientele. However, the "in" places change like the flavor of the month, and many fade into oblivion after a brief moment of popularity.

The best source for an up-to-date list of late-night spots is the weekly entertainment guide, "Trovaroma," published every Saturday in the Italian daily newspaper, *La Repubblica.*

Bars Rome has a range of bars offering drinks and background music. Jacket and tie are in order in the elegant **Blue Bar** of the Hostaria dell'Orso (Via dei Soldati 25, tel. 06/6564221) and in **Le Bar** of the Grand Hotel (Via Vittorio Emanuele Orlando 3, tel. 06/4709). **Harry's Bar** (Via Veneto 150, tel. 06/4745832) is popular with American businessmen and journalists residing in Rome. **Little Bar** (Via Gregoriana 54a, tel. 06/6796386) is a relaxing place for cocktails after a shopping spree in the Piazza di Spagna area.

Young Romans favor **Calisé** (Piazza Mastai 7, tel. 06/5809404) in Trastevere, where sandwiches and salads, as well as drinks, are available until 3 AM. **Enoteca dell'Orologio** (Via del Governo Vecchio 23, tel. 06/6561904) is a popular wine bar; it's closed Sunday. The informal and cheerful **Bue Toscano** (Via Tor Margana 3, tel. 06/6798158), near Piazza Venezia, offers wine, cocktails, a cold buffet, and music from 8:30 PM until the wee hours; it's also open for lunch, but closed Monday.

"In" places around the Pantheon, a hub of after-dark activity, include **Le Cornacchie** (Piazza Rondanini 53, tel. 06/6564485), where Roman yuppies hang out, and **Hemingway** (Piazza delle Coppelle 10, tel. 06/6544135), which attracts a crowd from the worlds of movies, TV, and fashion. Both are open evenings only, until very late.

Irish-style pubs are popular with young Italians. Two of the best known are in the vicinity of Santa Maria Maggiore: **Fiddler's Elbow** (Via dell'Olmate 43, no phone) is open from 5 PM to midnight; closed Monday. **Druid's Den** (Via San Martino ai Monti 28, no phone) is open daily from 8:30 PM to 1 AM.

Music Clubs Jazz, folk, pop, and Latin-music clubs are flourishing in Rome, particularly in the picturesque Trastevere neighborhood. Jazz clubs are especially popular at the moment, and talented local groups may be joined by visiting musicians from other countries.

Alexanderplatz. Located in the Trionfale district near the Vatican, Alexanderplatz has both a bar and a restaurant, and features nightly live programs of jazz and blues played by Italian and foreign musicians. *Via Ostia 9, tel. 06/3599398.*

Big Mama. For the best live music, including jazz, blues, R-&-B, African, and rock come to Big Mama. There is also a bar and snack food. *Vicolo San Francesco a Ripa 18, tel. 06/582551.*

El Charango. South American food is dished up with the lively Latin music at El Charango. *Via di Sant'Onofrio 28, tel. 06/6879908. Closed Mon.*

Folkstudio. Founded a couple of decades ago, Folkstudio is a Roman institution. It presents both new talent and big-name performers of jazz, country, and folk music. Although currently under the threat of eviction, the club hopes to continue operating from the same premises. *Via Gaetano Sacchi 3, tel. 06/5892374.*

Music Inn. This is Rome's top jazz club, and features some of the biggest names on the international scene. *Largo dei Fiorentini 3, tel. 06/6544934. Open Thurs.–Sun. evenings.*

St. Louis Music City. Live performances of jazz, soul, and funk by leading musicians draw celebrities here. There is also a restaurant. *Via del Cardello 13a, tel. 06/4745076. Closed Thur.*

Discos and Nightclubs Most discos open about 10:30 PM and charge an entrance fee of around 20,000 lire, which sometimes also includes the first drink. Subsequent drinks cost about 8,000 to 10,000 lire. Some discos also open on Saturday and Sunday afternoons for the under-16s.

The Acropolis. There's deafening disco music for the under-30s crowd here, which sometimes includes young actors. Special events, such as beauty pageants, fashion shows, or theme parties, are featured, and there is a restaurant. Despite the official address, the entrance is actually on Via Luciani 52. *Via Schiaparelli 29–30, tel. 06/870504. Closed Mon.*

Club 84. With a disco and a piano bar, this club just off the Via Veneto has attracted a sophisticated crowd for many years. There is a live band on Friday and Saturday nights. *Via Emilia 84, tel. 06/4751538. Open nightly.*

Easy Going. You have the choice of a high-energy disco or a quieter cocktail bar at this gay club. There's no admission charge weekdays. *Via della Purificazione 9, tel. 06/4745578. Closed Sun.*

Gilda. This is the place to spot famous Italian actors and politicians. Formerly the Paradise supper club, this hot new nightspot now has two restaurants, as well as live and disco music. *Via Mario dei Fiori, near Piazza di Spagna, tel. 06/6784838. Closed Mon.*

Hysteria. TV stars and other celebrities come here to enjoy the variety of music: disco, funk, soul, and hard rock. It's located outside the center, off Via Salaria. *Via Giovanelli 12, tel. 06/964587. Closed Mon.*

Jackie-O. This spot has long been a favorite of the wealthy who party to disco music, dine in La Graticola restaurant, or sip drinks in the cocktail lounge. *Via Boncompagni 11, tel. 06/461401.*

The Open Gate. A glittering disco, piano bar, and restaurant attract the over-25s to the Open Gate. Dancing starts at midnight. *Via San Nicolo di Tolentino 4, tel. 06/4750464.*

The Piper. One of Rome's first discos, the Piper is currently the "in" spot for teenagers—though who can say if it will still be riding high in 1989? It has disco music, live groups, and pop videos. Occasionally there's ballroom dancing for an older crowd. *Via Tagliamento 9, tel. 06/854459. Open weekends at 4* PM. *Closed Mon. and Tues.*

Scarabocchio. Loud music and huge video screens make this another popular spot. *Piazza Ponziani 8, tel. 06/5800495. Closed Mon.*

Veleno. This is one of the few places in Rome to offer black dance music, including disco, rap, funk, and soul. Veleno attracts sports personalities and other celebrities. *Via Sardegna 27, tel. 06/493583. Open daily.*

For Singles Locals and foreigners of all nations and ages gather at Rome's cafés on **Piazza della Rotonda** in front of the Pantheon, at **Piazza Navona,** and **Piazza Santa Maria** in Trastevere. The cafés on **Via Veneto** and the bars of the big hotels draw mainly tourists and are good places to meet other travelers in the over-30 age group. In fair weather, under-30s will find crowds of contemporaries on the **Spanish Steps,** where it's easy to strike up a conversation.

9 Excursions

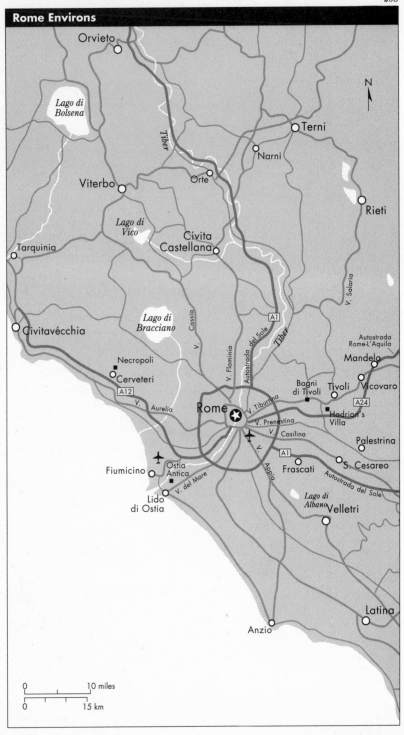

Rome Environs

Orvieto

Lago di Bolsena

Tiber

Terni

Narni

Viterbo

Orte

Rieti

Lago di Vico

Tarquinia

Cívita Castellana

V. Salaria

Civitavécchia

Lago di Bracciano

V. Cassia

A1

Tiber

Autostrada del Sole

Autostrada Rome-L'Aquila

Mandela

Necropoli

V. Flaminia

Cerveteri

A12

Bagni di Tivoli

Tivoli

Vicovaro

V. Aurelia

Rome

V. Tiburtina

A24

V. Prenestina

Hadrian's Villa

V. Casilina

Palestrina

Fiumicino

Ostia Antica

V. del Mare

Appia

Frascati

A1

S. Cesareo

Autostrada del Sole

Lido di Ostia

Lago di Albano

Velletri

Latina

Anzio

| 0 | | 10 miles |
| 0 | | 15 km |

N

Ostia Antica

The wind from the sea whispers through the tall pines at Ostia Antica, rustling the vines that clothe the ruins of ancient Rome's port city. Founded around the 4th century BC, probably by one Ancus Martius—he wished to secure control of the mouth of the Tiber for the growing town of Rome—Ostia Antica gives you an idea of what Rome must have been like. Here there are no medieval or Baroque encrustations. The ruins of the ancient city's streets, baths, theaters, and dwellings spread out on every side. Oleanders and creepers grow along mellow brick walls, as they did when the city was inhabited by a cosmopolitan populace of rich businessmen, wily merchants, sailors, and slaves. The great *horrea*, or warehouses, were built in the 2nd century AD to handle huge shipments of grain from Africa, and the *insulae*, forerunners of the modern apartment building, provided housing for the increasing population. Under the combined assaults of the barbarians and the anopheles mosquito, the port was eventually abandoned and silted up. Wind-borne sand and tidal mud covered the city and it lay buried until the beginning of this century. Now extensively excavated and excellently maintained, it makes for a fascinating visit, perfect for a mild day in winter, spring, or fall, or for a late summer afternoon. Ostia Antica conveys the same impressions as Pompeii, though on a smaller scale, but it is even lovelier, with its lush grass and vegetation.

Getting Around

By Car The Via del Mare leads directly to Ostia Antica. The ride from Rome takes about 35 minutes.

By Train There is a metro service to Ostia Antica from Termini Station. There are several morning departures, and three afternoon trips back to Rome. The ride takes about 25 minutes. There is also a regular train service from Ostiense train station (near Porta San Paolo). Trains leave every half hour and the ride takes about 30 minutes.

Guided Tours Tourvisa (tel. 06/4950284) runs all-day excursions by boat down the Tiber to Ostia Antica. A guided tour of the excavations is included. You return to Rome by bus.

Exploring

Near the entrance to the *scavi*, the excavations, is a **fortress** built in the 15th century for Pope Julius II. The little hamlet that grew up around it is charming. However, your visit to Ostia Antica itself starts at **Via delle Tombe**, lined with sepulchers of various periods. From it you enter the **Porta Romana,** one of the city's three gates. This is the beginning of the **Decumanus Maximus,** the main thoroughfare that crosses the city from end to end. On your right are the **Terme di Nettuno** (Baths of Neptune), decorated with black-and-white mosaics representing Neptune and Amphitrite. Directly behind the baths is the barracks of the fire brigade, which played an important role in a town where valuable goods and foodstuffs passed through its warehouses.

Next you'll see the beautiful **theater,** built by Augustus and completely restored by Septimius Severus. Behind it in the

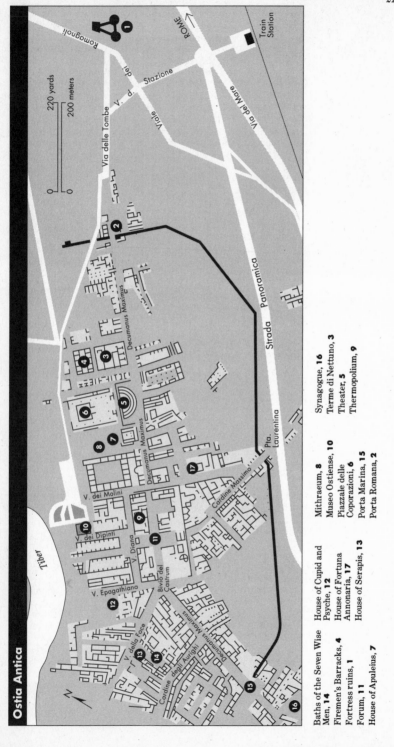

Ostia Antica

Baths of the Seven Wise Men, **14**
Firemen's Barracks, **4**
Fortress ruins, **1**
Forum, **11**
House of Apuleius, **7**

House of Cupid and Psyche, **12**
House of Fortuna Annonaria, **17**
House of Serapis, **13**

Mithraeum, **8**
Museo Ostiense, **10**
Piazzale delle Coporazioni, **6**
Porta Marina, **15**
Porta Romana, **2**

Synagogue, **16**
Terme di Nettuno, **3**
Theater, **5**
Thermopolium, **9**

vast **Piazzale delle Corporazioni,** where trade organizations similar to guilds had their offices, is the **Temple of Ceres.** Beside the theater you can visit the **House of Apuleius,** built in Pompeiian style, and the **Mithraeum,** with balconies and a hall decorated with the symbols of the cult of Mithras. On **Via dei Molini** there's a mill, where grain for the warehouses next door was ground with the stones you see there. Along **Via di Diana** you'll come upon a *thermopolium,* or bar, with a marble counter and a fresco depicting the fruit and foodstuffs that were sold there. At the end of **Via dei Dipinti,** the **Museo Ostiense** displays some of the ancient sculptures and mosaics found among the ruins. (Open 9–2.)

Retrace your steps along Via dei Dipinti to the **Forum,** with monumental remains of the city's most important temple, dedicated to Jupiter, Juno, and Minerva, and other ruins of baths, a basilica, and smaller temples. There's a **Round Temple,** a kind of pantheon of the emperors. At the crossroads, **Via Epagathiana** on the right leads to a large warehouse erected in the 2nd century. Off Via della Foce, on **Via del Tempio di Ercole,** the **House of Cupid and Psyche** is named for the statue found there; you can see what remains of a large pool in an enclosed garden with marble and mosaic decorations. On **Via della Foce** you'll also see the **House of Serapis,** a 2nd-century multilevel dwelling, and the **Baths of the Seven Wise Men,** named for a fresco found there. Take **Via del Tempio di Serapide** and the **Cardo degli Aurighi,** where you'll pass another apartment building, back to the Decumanus Maximus and follow it to the **Porta Marina.** Off to the left, on what used to be the seashore, are the ruins of the **Synagogue,** one of the oldest in the Western world. On your return, go right at the **Bivio del Castrum** past the slaughterhouse and the large round temple to the **Cardine Massimo,** a road lined with ruined buildings. From here, turn left to see the **House of Fortuna Annonaria,** the richly decorated dwelling of a wealthy Ostian. (Via dei Romagnoli. Admission: 4,000 lire. Open daily 9–4.)

Dining

Monumento. Handily located near the entrance to the excavations, this attractive trattoria serves Roman specialties and seafood. *Piazza Umberto I, tel. 5650021. Dress informal. Reservations advised in the evening. DC Closed Mon., Aug. 20 and Sept. 7. Moderate.*

Sbarco di Enea. Also near the excavations, this restaurant is heavy on ancient-Roman atmosphere with Pompeiian-style frescoes and chariots in the garden. On summer evenings you dine outdoors by torchlight, served by waiters in Roman costume. Come for lunch, which is blessedly lower-key, when you can enjoy *farfalle con granchio* (pasta with crab sauce) or linguine *con aragosta* (with lobster sauce), and other seafood specialties, without all the hoopla. *Via dei Romagnoli 675, tel. 06/5650034. Dress informal. Reservations advised in the evening. AE, MC. Closed Mon., and Feb. Moderate.*

Cerveteri

More and more is coming to be known about the Etruscans, the apparently peaceable and pleasure-loving people who inhabited the vast territory north of Rome long before the rise of the Roman Empire. One of the most interesting of the Etruscan sites in Italy is within easy reach of Rome by car or bus, a ride which gives you a look at the rolling landscape along the coast.

The nucleus of the old town of Cerveteri stands on the site of the Etruscan city of Caere, a thriving commercial center in the 6th century BC. Now the zone is overdeveloped with unattractive vacation villas, but you can concentrate on the serene beauty of the necropolis, or "city of the dead."

Getting Around

By Car Take either the Rome-Civitavecchia expressway or the Via Aurelia. The ride takes about 40 minutes.

By Bus Take the ACOTRAL bus from the Via Lepanto station on Metro Line A. It's about a 40-minute ride.

Guided Tours CIT, tel. 06/4794372.

Exploring

Start your visit in the 12th-century **castle,** which houses the **Museo Cerite** and contains some of the material found in the tombs. (Open May–Sept., Tues.–Sun. 9–2 and 4–7; Oct.–Apr., Tues.–Sun. 9–2.) Then either walk a mile or so, or take one of the special buses provided during the spring and summer, from the main square to the **Necropolis of the Banditaccia,** a park in which the Etruscan residents of Caere left a heritage of great historical significance. In this monumental complex of tombs they laid their relatives to rest, some in simple graves, others in burial chambers that faithfully reproduce the characteristics of Etruscan dwellings. In the round tumulus tombs you'll recognize the prototypes of the Augusteum, of Hadrian's Mausoleum in Castel Sant'Angelo, and of the Tomb of Cecilia Metella. The most interesting of the tombs are the **Tomba dei Capitelli,** the **Tomba dei Vasi Greci,** in which a great number of Greek vases were found, and the **Tomba dei Rilievi,** packed with detailed reliefs of household objects. Not all the tombs are open; opening is rotated to prevent deterioration. (Banditaccia. Admission: 4,000 lire. Open May–Sept., Tues.–Sun. 9–7; Oct.–Apr., Tues.–Sun. 9–4.)

Dining

La Necropoli. The walls of this restaurant are decorated with reproductions of Etruscan artistic motifs. If you prefer, eat on the terrace. Specialties include shellfish, which you can see in the aquarium, and *maltagliate mare e monti* (pasta with *porcini* mushrooms and fish). *Via Mura Castellane 54, tel. 06/ 9950123. Dress informal. Reservations not required. No credit cards. Closed Wed. Moderate.*

Tarquinia

This swing through Etruscan country takes you from Cerveteri north along the coast to Tarquinia, once a powerful Etruscan city and later an important medieval center. Tarquinia sprawls on a hill overlooking the sea north of Rome, beyond Civi tavecchia. Since both Cerveteri and Tarquinia require at least half a day to visit, you will want either to return to Rome late in the evening or stay overnight in Tarquinia. The latter gives you a chance to see some different Etruscan tombs the next morning, as the eight tombs are opened on alternate days. The town itself is charming, the surroundings green with woods and meadows. Below, sandy beaches stretch for miles along the coast.

Getting Around

By Car Tarquinia is about 90 kilometers (55 miles) from Rome. Take the Rome–Civitavecchia autostrada (A12) and the Via Aurelia. The ride takes about 90 minutes.

By Bus Take the ACOTRAL bus from the Via Lepanto station of metro line A; the ride takes about 90 minutes. (The bus is more direct than the train, which you take to Civitavecchia, where you have to make connections with a local bus.)

Guided Tours **Carrani** (tel. 06/460510) offers a one-day **"Etruscan Tour"** from April to October on Tuesdays and Fridays.

Exploring

Tarquinia offers unexpected visual delights as its narrow medieval streets suddenly open onto quaint squares dominated by palaces and churches. See the church of **San Francesco,** with its Romanesque rose window and massive 16th-century bell tower, and find your way to **Santa Maria di Castello,** a majestic medieval church, impressive in its simplicity. Walk down Via delle Torri and climb the hilly streets to the churches of **San Martino** and **Santissima Annunziata.**

Next make your way to **Palazzo Vitelleschi,** a splendid 15th-century building that contains a wealth of Etruscan treasures. One, perhaps the greatest, strikes you as you enter the main hall—the marvelous golden terra-cotta horses, a frieze that once decorated an Etruscan temple. Warm and gleaming against the gray stone background on which they've been mounted, they seem to come alive before your eyes, stepping and chafing at the bit. If you needed any proof of the degree of artistry the Etruscans attained, this is it. But there's more: The museum and its courtyard are full of sarcophagi found in the tombs buried under the meadows surrounding the town. The figures of the deceased recline casually on their stone couches, mouths curved in enigmatic smiles, in one hand a plate containing a few beans, Etruscan symbol of afterlife. Upstairs with more Etruscan artifacts are some of the most precious frescoes from the necropolis, the city of the dead. They were removed to keep them from deteriorating. You will be able to see others on the spot where they were painted in the tombs themselves. *Piazza Cavour. Admission: 4,000 lire (valid also for entrance to tombs). Open May–Sept., Tues.–Sun. 9–6:30; Oct.–Apr., Tues.–Sun. 9–2.*

A highlight of a visit to Tarquinia is the tour of some of the more recently excavated tombs. The admission fee includes a guide. The tombs are just outside town and can be reached on foot; ask at the museum for directions to the entrance to the necropolis. The tombs date from the 7th to the 2nd century BC and are decorated with lively frescoes depicting aspects of Etruscan life. The colors are amazingly well preserved, and the scenes testify to the great vitality and level of civilization of this mysterious and ancient people.

Of the thousands of tombs that exist throughout the territory of Etruria, only a small percentage have been scientifically excavated. Many more have been found and plundered by local "experts," called *tombaroli*. Yet, though these tombaroli dig illegally, many of them have a considerable familiarity with their delicate task and deep knowledge of their subject: Etruscan art. The valuable objects that they find cater to a thriving clandestine market. And what these enterprising individuals don't find, they make. Counterfeit copies of Etruscan antiquities that come out of hidden workshops in the area have been known to fool the experts. *Admission: 4,000 lire (includes museum admission). Open (access subject to formation of groups for guided tours) May–Sept., Tues.–Sun. 9–6:30; Oct.–Apr., Tues.–Sun. 9–2.*

Lodging and Dining

Hotel Tarconte. The rooms and lounges are modern and functional and the location is wonderful, with superb views. Try to get a room with a view even if you're here only overnight. *Via Tuscia 23, tel. 0766/856585. 53 rooms, with bath and balcony. Facilities: air-conditioning, restaurant, bar, garage. AE, DC, V. Moderate.*

Solengo Restaurant. The restaurant shares a modern building with the hotel in a hillside location in the newer part of town. From spring to fall you dine on a veranda with a sweeping view of the coastal plain. During the winter, the ambience is that of a rustic tavern, with plaid tablecloths and old utensils hanging from the rafters. Specialties include seafood and such local delicacies as *pappardelle al cinghiale* (homemade pasta with boar sauce) and roast boar. *Hotel Tarconte, Via Tuscia 23, tel. 0766/856585. Dress informal. Reservations advised. AE, DC, V. Moderate.*

Viterbo

Viterbo lies in the heart of Tuscia, the modern name for the Etruscan domain of Etruria, a landscape of dramatic beauty punctuated by thickly forested hills and deep, rocky gorges. Viterbo is a fine medieval city, excellently preserved and very picturesque. Like every other center in this area, it was founded by the Etruscans and later taken over by the Romans. Its moment of glory was in the 13th century when it became the seat of the papal court. The old town still nestles within 12th-century walls. Its old buildings, their windows bright with geraniums, are made of dark volcanic stone, known as *peperino*, which contrasts with the golden tufa rock of its walls and towers. Peperino is used in the characteristic exterior staircases that you see throughout the old town. Viterbo is the place to get a feel of the Middle Ages, to see a town where daily life is carried on in a setting that has remained practically unchanged over the centuries. You can also see a delightful Renaissance villa in the vicinity and, if you make the trip by car, visit the intriguing Monster Park at Bomarzo, a sort of Renaissance theme park.

Getting Around

By Car Viterbo is about 80 kilometers (50 miles) from Rome. Take the Via Cassia bis; the ride takes about 90 minutes. If you want to see Bomarzo, go via the Autostrada del Sole (A1), using the Orte exit. Again, it's about 90 minutes' driving time.

By Bus Take the ACOTRAL bus from the Via Lepanto station of metro line A. There are a few direct (*diretta*) bus departures from Rome between 7 and 9 AM; the *diretta* bus takes about 75 minutes. Slower buses leave every 20 minutes or so throughout the day. In any case, bus service is faster and more frequent than train service.

By Train Take the Ferrovia Roma Nord from the Piazzale Flaminio station. The ride takes about 90 minutes.

Guided Tours CIT, tel. 06/4794372.

Exploring

If you come by train you'll start your visit just outside the old town walls; the bus takes you right to the center of Viterbo. In either case, make your way to **Piazza San Lorenzo,** where the Gothic **Palazzo Papale** was built in the 13th century as a residence for the popes who chose to sojourn here. A conclave held here in 1271 to elect a new pope provided the people of Viterbo with a glorious moment of fame. The meeting had dragged on for months, apparently making no progress. Fed up with paying for the cardinals' board and lodging, the inhabitants tore the roof off the great hall in which the meeting was held and put the churchmen on bread and water. Sure enough, a new pope—Gregory X—was elected in short order. The fine Romanesque **cathedral** on the piazza has a Renaissance facade but its interior has been restored to its original medieval look. Inside you can see the chips that an exploding bomb took out of the ancient columns during World War II. To the left of the cathedral is a fine 15th-century town house.

Now walk down Via San Lorenzo and follow Via San Pellegrino through **the medieval quarter,** one of the best-preserved in Italy. It's a charming vista of arches, vaults, towers, exterior staircases, worn wooden doors on great iron hinges, and tiny hanging gardens—all in that lovely dark stone, occasionally accented with warm, rose-colored brick and golden tufa. You'll pass many antique shops along the way. At the end of Via San Pellegrino turn left toward Via delle Fabbriche and **Piazza della Fontana Grande,** where the largest and most original of Viterbo's quaint Gothic fountains spouts steady streams of water. Wander through the old streets, making your way toward **Piazza della Verità** and the **Museo Civico** (The Civic Museum), in the former **convent of Santa Maria della Verità,** which has a pretty cloister. The museum contains interesting archaeological finds, classical sculptures, and some fine old paintings. (Admission: 1,000 lire. Open daily 9–1:30.)

From the center of town take the bus for the 10-minute ride to **Bagnaia,** a picturesque hamlet that is the site of **Villa Lante,** which has twin 16th-century buildings, richly frescoed, in a jewel-like garden setting. One side of the estate is a park that was used as a hunting preserve. The terraces above and below the small but courtly residences are laid out in formal gardens with lovely fountains. *Admission: 2,000 lire. Open Tues.–Sun. 9 AM–30 mins. before sunset.*

If you have come by car, drive over to see the strange 16th-century **Monster Park at Bomarzo,** populated by weird and fantastic sculptures of mythical monsters and eccentric architecture. It was created for Prince Vicino Orsini for his wife Giulia Farnese. She is said to have taken one look at the park and to have died of heart failure. It's a remarkable place; children love it, too. There is a picnic area and a reasonably priced restaurant at the entrance. *Admission: 5,000 lire. Open daily 9 AM–one hour before sunset.*

Dining

Da Ciro. Ciro, located in the heart of the medieval quarter, has a huge hearth in gray peperino stone in which meat and sausages are grilled before your eyes. The decor is an incredible mixture of rustic-country style and kitsch contemporary; the effect is warm and inviting. In the summer you eat outdoors at sidewalk tables. The specialties are *ombrichelle di Ciro* (homemade pasta with tomato and mushroom sauce) and *maialino* (roast suckling pig). *Via Cardinale La Fontaine 74, tel. 0761/ 234722. Dress informal. Reservations advised on Sun. and for dinner from Sept. to Dec. AE, DC, V. Moderate.*

Tivoli

To get to Tivoli you pass through some unattractive industrial areas and burgeoning suburbs. You'll know you're close when you see vast quarries of travertine marble and smell the pungent and sulfurous vapors of the little spa of **Bagni di Tivoli.** This used to be green countryside; now it's ugly and overbuilt. But don't despair, for this trip takes you to two of the Rome area's stellar attractions: two villas—an ancient one, where the Emperor Hadrian built himself an idealized compendium of the most beautiful monuments in the then-known world; and a Renaissance one, where Cardinal Ippolito d'Este put a river to work for his delight. Ancient Tibur, as Tivoli was then called, has been a pleasure resort for a long time. The ancient Romans came here to take the waters in the hot springs of Aeque Albule on the plain before retiring to their fine country villas on the hill.

Fewer tourists, and fewer group tours, go to Hadrian's Villa. Both are outdoor sites, which entail a considerable amount of walking and, in the case of Villa d'Este, a lot of stair-climbing.

Getting Around

By Car Take Via Tiburtina or the Rome–L'Aquila autostrada (A24). There's likely to be heavy traffic on the former; the drive on the latter takes about 40 minutes.

By Bus ACOTRAL buses leave every 15 minutes from Via Gaeta, near Termini Station, but not all take the route that passes near Hadrian's Villa, which you should visit first. Ask for the bus that passes closest to Villa Adriana, and tell the driver as you get on to let you off at the villa; it's just a short walk from the bus stop. The ride takes about 75 minutes.

By Train There are trains to Tivoli from Termini Station, but they are less frequent and even slower than the buses.

Guided Tours **American Express** (tel. 06/67641) and **CIT** (tel. 06/4794372) offer half-day excursions to Villa d'Este. **Appian Line** (tel. 06/ 464151) has a morning tour which includes Hadrian's Villa.

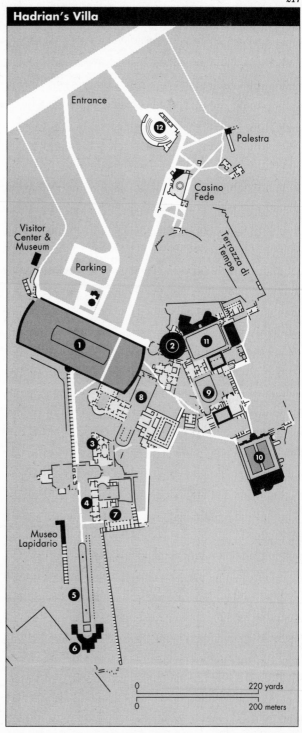

Hadrian's Villa

Entrance

Palestra

Casino
Fede

Terrazza di
Tempe

Visitor
Center &
Museum

Parking

Museo
Lapidario

0   220 yards

0   200 meters

Exploring

Visit **Hadrian's Villa** first, especially in the summer, to take advantage of the cooler morning hours; there's little shade in the afternoon. Then take the local bus up to town to enjoy the cool terraces of Villa d'Este and the refreshing waterfalls of Villa Gregoriana.

Hadrian built his villa over a vast tract of land below ancient Tibur; he needed the space, for he had a project in mind, inspired by a series of journeys to Gaul, Germany, and Britain—where he built his wall—and then to the Middle East, Greece, and Africa. He was a man of genius and intellectual curiosity, fascinated by the accomplishments of the Hellenistic world, a world he decided to re-create for his own enjoyment. From AD 118 to AD 130, architects, laborers, and artists worked on the villa, periodically spurred on by the emperor himself, newly returned from another voyage and full of ideas for even more daring constructions. After Hadrian's death in AD 138 the fortunes of his villa declined. It was sacked by barbarians and Romans alike; by the Renaissance many of the statues and decorations ended up in Villa d'Este. Nonetheless, it's still an impressive complex. Study the exhibits in the visitors' center at the entrance and the scale model in the building adjacent to the bar. They will increase your enjoyment of the villa itself by helping you make sense out of what can otherwise seem to be a maze of ruins.

Begin your visit at the **Poecile,** a vast portico surrounding a pool. Then turn to the little **Villa dell'Isola** (Island Villa), a small circular building surrounded by a canal where, it's said, Hadrian liked to shut himself off from the rest of the world by pulling up a drawbridge. Going back past the Poecile you come to the **Piccole e Grandi Terme** (small and large baths), where some fragments of ceiling stuccos are all that's left of what must have been lavish decorations. Now you can see the **Canopus,** an artificial valley in which Hadrian reproduced an ancient Egyptian canal on the Nile; this is one of the most beautiful spots in the entire villa. Columns and arches are reflected in the still water, a few statues evoke the time when the villa was full of them. (Some of the villa's original sculptures are displayed in a museum to one side of the Canopus.) The ruins at the end of the canal were once a **Temple of Serapis.**

Taking the path that goes behind the Grandi Terme, you come to the **Pretorio,** once believed to be the quarters of the Praetorian Guard, but probably used as warehouses. You pass the large **Nymphaeum** and turn right toward the **Imperial Palace.** On the right is the **Piazza d'Oro** (Golden Square), named after the precious statues and objects found there. There's a Doric atrium, followed by porticoes and the so-called **Cortile delle Biblioteche** (Courtyard of the Libraries), off which there are 10 small rooms with mosaic pavements; these were probably used by guests. Farther along is a wooded terrace and a **Greek theater.**

It's not the single elements but the peaceful and romantic effects of the whole that make Hadrian's Villa worth visiting. Oleanders, pines, and cypresses amid the ruins heighten their visual impact. *Villa Adriana. Admission: 4,000 lire. Open daily 9 AM–90 mins. before sunset.*

Time Out The **Adriano** restaurant at the entrance to Hadrian's Villa is a handy place for lunch and a rest before heading up the hill. The food is good and the atmosphere relaxing. *Closed Mon. AE, DC. Moderate.*

From Hadrian's Villa catch the bus up the hill to Tivoli. It stops in the town's main square, not far from the entrance to **Villa d'Este.** Ippolito d'Este happened to be a cardinal purely courtesy of his grandfather, Alexander VI, the infamous Borgia pope. To console himself for his seesawing fortunes in the political intrigues of the time, Ippolito tore down part of a Franciscan monastery that occupied the site which he had chosen for his villa. Then the determined prelate deviated the Aniene River into a channel that runs under the town to provide water for Villa d'Este's fountains—and what fountains! Big, small, noisy, quiet, rushing, and running, combining to create a late-Renaissance playground where sunlight, shade, water, gardens, and carved stone create a magical setting. *Villa d'Este. Admission: 5,000 lire. Open daily 9 AM–90 mins. before sunset.*

From Villa d'Este walk uphill through the narrow streets of old Tivoli toward Piazza Palatina and Ponte Gregoriano, beyond which you'll come upon the entrance to **Villa Gregoriana,** where, in 1835, Pope Gregory XVI ordered artificial waterfalls created, perhaps in emulation of his predecessor. They fall somewhat short of Villa d'Este's waterworks, but still are pretty spectacular. *Largo Sant'Angelo. Admission: 1,500 lire. Open daily 9 AM–90 mins. before sunset.*

Dining

Cinque Statue. The Cinque Statue, located opposite the entrance to Villa Gregoriana, offers a friendly welcome and good service. There's also a terrace for outdoor dining. The restaurant is family-run and serves local dishes. Start with the filling antipastos. The ricotta-filled crêpes and the pastas are good; other specialties include *abbacchio scottadito* (grilled baby lamb chops) and fillet *al pepe verde* (with green pepper). Let host Renzo suggest a good local wine. *Via Quintilio Varo 1, tel. 0774/20366. Dress informal. Reservations advised. No credit cards. Moderate.*

Del Falcone. On the main street leading off central Largo Garibaldi, near Villa d'Este, Del Falcone is popular and often crowded. In the ample and rustic wood-paneled dining rooms, try the homemade fettuccine and cannelloni. The country-style grilled meats—*abbacchio* and chicken—are excellent. *Via Trevio 34, tel. 0774/22358. Dress informal. Reservations advised. No credit cards. Inexpensive.*

Subiaco

This itinerary takes you on an excursion into the mystic past of Rome's rugged hinterland. Subiaco itself, a modern town built over World War II rubble, overlooking the narrow Aniene valley, is not the attraction. You come here to see a landmark in Western monasticism, the monastery where St. Benedict devised his rule of life in the 6th century, founding the order that had such an important role in transmitting learning through the ages. Even earlier, this was a refuge of Nero, who built himself a villa here, said to have rivaled that of Hadrian at Tivoli, damming the river to create three lakes and a series of waterfalls. As you walk up the sometimes steep footpath to the monastery of St. Benedict with the waters of the Aniene thundering deep in the gorge below, you can understand the attraction that this wild landscape had on both emperor and saint.

Getting Around

By Car Take the Rome–L'Aquila autostrada (A24) to the Vicovaro–Mandela exit, then continue on the local road to Subiaco. The ride takes about one hour.

By Bus ACOTRAL buses leave every 40 minutes from Viale Castro Pretorio, but not all take the faster route via the autostrada. If yours takes the autostrada, the trip takes about 70 minutes; otherwise the trip is about 1 hour 45 minutes. Either way, the bus is much faster and more frequent than the train.

Guided Tours Inquire at **Santa Susanna,** the American Catholic church in Rome, tel. 06/4751510.

Exploring

This excursion is best made by car as it's an almost two-mile walk from Subiaco to Santa Scholastica, and another half-hour by footpath up to San Benedetto. If you don't have a car, inquire in Subiaco about a local bus to get you at least part of the way. The first monastery you come upon is that of **Santa Scholastica,** actually a convent, and the only one of the hermitages founded by St. Benedict and his sister, Scholastica, to have survived the Lombard invasion of Italy in the 9th century. It has three cloisters, the oldest dating back to the 13th century. The library, which is not open to visitors, contains some precious volumes. This was the site of the first printshop in Italy, set up in 1474. *Open daily 9–12:30 and 4–6.*

Drive up to the **monastery of St. Benedict,** or take the footpath which climbs the hill. The monastery was built over the grotto where St. Benedict lived and meditated. Clinging to the cliff on nine great arches, the monastery has resisted the assaults of man and nature for almost 800 years. Climb the broad, sloping avenue and enter through a little wooden veranda, where a Latin inscription augers "peace to those who enter." You find yourself in the colorful world of the upper church, every inch of it covered with frescoes by Umbrian and Sienese artists of the 14th century. In front of the main altar a stairway leads down to the lower church, carved out of the living rock, with yet another stairway down to the cave where Benedict lived as a hermit for three years. The frescoes here are even earlier than those above; look for the portrait of St. Francis of Assisi, painted from life in 1210, in the **chapel of St. Gregory,** and for the oldest fresco in the monastery in the **Shepherd's Grotto.** Back in town, if you've got the time, stop in at the 14th-century **church of San Francesco** to see the frescoes by Il Sodoma. *Open daily 9–12:30 and 3–6.*

Dining

Belvedere. This small hotel on the road between the town and the monasteries is equipped to serve crowds of skiers on their way home from a day on the slopes of nearby Mount Livata, as well as pilgrims to St. Benedict's hermitage. The atmosphere is homey and cordial. Specialties include homemade fettuccine with a tasty *ragù* sauce and grilled meats and sausages. *Via dei Monasteri 33, tel. 0774/85531. Dress informal. No reservations. No credit cards. Inexpensive.*

Mariuccia. Close to the monasteries, this big, modern, barn-like restaurant caters to weddings, but is calm enough on weekdays. The view from the picture windows is good, and there's a large garden. The specialties of the house are homemade fettuccine with *porcini* mushrooms and *scaloppe al tartufo* (truffled veal escallopes). In the summer you dine outdoors under bright umbrellas. *Via Sublacense, km. 19.200, tel. 0774/84851. Dress informal. Reservations advised for lunch. No credit cards. Closed Mon. and Nov. Inexpensive.*

Palestrina

Palestrina, 37 kilometers (23 miles) outside Rome, is a town set on the slopes of Mount Ginestro, from which it commands a sweeping view of the green plain and distant mountains. It is surprisingly little-known outside Italy, except to students of ancient history and music lovers. Its most famous native son, Giovanni Pierluigi da Palestrina, born here in 1525, was the renowned composer of 105 masses, along with numerous madrigals, magnificats, and motets. But the town was celebrated long before the composer's lifetime. In fact ancient Praeneste, modern Palestrina, was founded much earlier than Rome. It was the site of the Temple of Fortuna Primigenia, which dates from the beginning of the 2nd century BC. This was one of the biggest, richest, and most frequented temple complexes of all antiquity. People came from afar to consult its famous oracle. Interestingly, no one had any idea of the extent of the complex until World War II bombings exposed ancient foundations that stretched way out into the plain below the town. It's since become clear that the temple was larger than the town of Palestrina is today. Now you can make out the four superimposed terraces that formed the main part of the temple; they were built up on great arches and were linked by broad flights of stairs. The whole town sits on top of what was once the main part of the temple.

Getting Around

By Car Take either Via Prenestina or Via Casilina to Palestrina, or the Autostrada del Sole (A2) to the San Cesareo exit and follow signs for Palestrina. The trip takes about one hour.

By Train Take an FS train from Termini Station; the trip takes about 40 minutes.

By Bus Take the ACOTRAL bus from Piazza dei Cinquecento (Termini Station) at the corner of Via Cavour; the ride takes about 75 minutes.

Exploring

Evidence of Palestrina's august past surrounds you as you approach the town on Via degli Arcioni. First you see the huge foundation stones of the temples; then the large arches and terraces that scale the hillside up to **Palazzo Barberini** come into view. The palace was built in the 17th century along the semi-circular lines of the original temple. It's now a **museum** containing a wealth of material found on the site, some of it dating back to the 4th century BC. The collection of engraved bronze urns is splendid, but the chief attraction is a 1st-century BC mosaic representing the Nile in flood. This delightful work is a large-scale composition in which form and color and innumerable details captivate the eye. It's worth the trip to Palestrina on its own. But there's more—a perfect scale model of the temple as it was in ancient times, which will help you appreciate the immensity of the original construction. The palace that you are standing in was the base of the Upper Sanctuary; the most sacred part of the complex was in the Lower Sanctuary, hidden under Palestrina's medieval buildings, perhaps in some grottoes near the cathedral square. They harbored the mysterious coded tablets which were the key to the interpretation of the oracle's pronouncements. *Museo Nazionale Archeologico, Palazzo Barberini. Admission: 3,000 lire. Open Tues.–Sun., spring and fall 9–6, summer 9–7:30, winter 9–4.*

When you've absorbed as much as you can of the museum–temple, make your way down the street staircases and explore the town. There's a very old **cathedral** built on ancient foundations, as well as a monument to composer Pierluigi. Shops sell handworked copper utensils and local embroidery in a stitch called *punto palestrina*.

Dining

Coccia. The dining room of a small, centrally located hotel on Palestrina's public garden, with views of the scenery through ample windows, Coccia offers a cordial welcome, lots of elbow room, and local dishes with a few interesting variations. The fettuccine are light and freshly made and are served with a choice of sauces. A more unusual item on the menu is *pasta e fagioli con frutti di mare* (thick bean and pasta soup with shellfish). *Piazzale Liberazione, tel. 06/9558172. Dress informal. Reservations not required. AE, DC, V. Moderate.*

Conversion Tables

Distance

Kilometers/Miles To change kilometers to miles, multiply kilometers by .621.
To change miles to kilometers, multiply miles by 1.61.

Km to Mi	Mi to Km
1 = .62	1 = 1.6
2 = 1.2	2 = 3.2
3 = 1.9	3 = 4.8
4= 2.5	4 = 6.4
5= 3.1	5 = 8.1
6= 3.7	6 = 9.7
7= 4.3	7 = 11.3
8= 5.0	8 = 12.9
9= 5.6	9 = 14.5

Meters/Feet To change meters to feet, multiply meters by 3.28.
To change feet to meters, multiply feet by .305.

Meters to Feet	Feet to Meters
1 = 3.3	1 = .31
2 = 6.6	2 = .61
3 = 9.8	3 = .92
4 = 13.1	4 = 1.2
5 = 16.4	5 = 1.5
6 = 19.7	6 = 1.8
7 = 23.0	7 = 2.1
8 = 26.2	8 = 2.4
9 = 29.5	9 = 2.7

Weight

Kilograms/Pounds To change kilograms to pounds, multiply by 2.20.
To change pounds to kilograms, multiply by .453.

Kilos to Pounds	Pounds to Kilos
1 = 2.2	1 = .45
2 = 4.4	2 = .91
3 = 6.6	3 = 1.4
4 = 8.8	4 = 1.8
5 = 11.0	5 = 2.3
6 = 13.2	6 = 2.7

7 = 15.4	7 = 3.2
8 = 17.6	8 = 3.6
9 = 19.8	9 = 4.1

Grams/Ounces To change grams to ounces, multiply grams by .035.
To change ounces to grams, multiply ounces by 28.4.

Grams to Ounces	Ounces to Grams
1 = .04	1 = 28
2 = .07	2 = 57
3 = .11	3 = 85
4 = .14	4 = 114
5 = .18	5 = 142
6 = .21	6 = 170
7 = .25	7 = 199
8 = .28	8 = 227
9 = .32	9 = 256

Liquid Volume

Liters/U.S. Gallons To change liters to U.S. gallons, multiply liters by .264.
To change U.S. gallons to liters, multiply gallons by 3.79.

Liters to U.S. Gallons	U.S. Gallons to Liters
1 = .26	1 = 3.8
2 = .53	2 = 7.6
3 = .79	3 = 11.4
4 = 1.1	4 = 15.2
5 = 1.3	5 = 19.0
6 = 1.6	6 = 22.7
7 = 1.8	7 = 26.5
8 = 2.1	8 = 30.3
9 = 2.4	9 = 34.1

Clothing Sizes

Men
Men's Suits
To change American suit sizes to Italian suit sizes, add 10 to the American suit size.
To change Italian suit sizes to American suit sizes, subtract 10 from the Italian suit size.

U.S. Size	36	38	40	42	44	46	48
Italian Size	46	48	50	52	54	56	58

Men's Shirts To change American shirt sizes to Italian shirt sizes, multiply the American shirt size by 2 and add 8.

To change Italian shirt sizes to American shirt sizes, subtract 8 from the Italian shirt size and divide by 2.

U.S. Size	14	14½	15	15½	16	16½	17	17½
Italian Size	36	37	38	39	40	41	42	43

Men's Shoes Italian shoe sizes vary in their relation to American shoe sizes.

U.S. Size	7½	8	8½/9	9½/10	10½/11	11½/12	12½
Italian Size	40	41	42	43	44	45	46

Women
Dresses and Coats To change U.S. dress/coat sizes to Italian dress/coat sizes, add 28 to the U.S. dress/coat size.

To change Italian dress/coat sizes to U.S. dress/coat sizes, subtract 28 from the Italian dress/coat size.

U.S. Size	4	6	8	10	12	14	16
Italian Size	32	34	36	38	40	42	44

Blouses and Sweaters To change U.S. blouse/sweater sizes to Italian blouse/sweater sizes, add 8 to the U.S. blouse/sweater size.

To change Italian blouse/sweater sizes to U.S. blouse/sweater sizes, subtract 8 from the Italian blouse/sweater size.

U.S. Size	30	32	34	36	38	40	42
Italian Size	38	40	42	44	46	48	50

Shoes Italian shoe sizes vary in their relation to U.S. shoe sizes.

U.S. Size	5/5½	6	6½/7	7½	8	8½	9
Italian Size	35	36	37	38	38½	39	40

Italian Vocabulary

Words & Phrases

	English	*Italian*	*Pronunciation*
Basics	Yes/no	Sí/No	see/no
	Please	Per favore	pear fa-**vo**-ray
	Yes, please	Sí grazie	see **grah**-tsee-ay
	Thank you	Grazie	**grah**-tsee-ay
	You're welcome	Prego	**pray**-go
	Excuse me, sorry	Scusi	**skoo**-zee
	Sorry!	Mi spiace!	mee spee-**ah**-chay
	Good morning/ afternoon	Buon giorno	bwohn **jor**-no
	Good evening	Buona sera	**bwoh**-na **say**-ra
	Goodbye	Arrivederci	a-ree-vah-**dare**-chee
	Mr.(Sir)	Signore	see-**nyo**-ray
	Mrs.(Ma'am)	Signora	see-**nyo**-ra
	Miss	Signorina	see-nyo-**ree**-na
	Pleased to meet you	Piacere	pee-ah-**chair**-ray
	How are you?	Come sta?	**ko**-may **sta**
	Very well, thanks	Bene, grazie	**ben**-ay **grah**-tsee-ay
	And you?	E lei?	ay **lay**-ee
	Hello (over the phone)	Pronto?	**proan**-to
Numbers	one	uno	**oo**-no
	two	due	**doo**-ay
	three	tre	tray
	four	quattro	**kwah**-tro
	five	cinque	**cheen**-kway
	six	sei	say
	seven	sette	**set**-ay
	eight	otto	**oh**-to
	nine	nove	**no**-vay
	ten	dieci	dee-**eh**-chee
	eleven	undici	**oon**-dee-chee
	twelve	dodici	**doe**-dee-chee
	thirteen	tredici	**tray**-dee-chee
	fourteen	quattordici	kwa-**tore**-dee-chee
	fifteen	quindici	**kwin**-dee-chee
	sixteen	sedici	**say**-dee-chee
	seventeen	diciassette	dee-cha-**set**-ay
	eighteen	diciotto	dee-**cho**-to
	nineteen	diciannove	dee-cha-**no**-vay
	twenty	venti	**vain**-tee
	twenty-one	ventuno	vain-**too**-no
	twenty-two	ventidue	vayn-tee-**doo**-ay
	thirty	trenta	**train**-ta
	forty	quaranta	kwa-**rahn**-ta
	fifty	cinquanta	cheen-**kwahn**-ta
	sixty	sessanta	seh-**sahn**-ta
	seventy	settanta	seh-**tahn**-ta
	eighty	ottanta	o-**tahn**-ta
	ninty	novanta	no-**vahn**-ta
	one hundred	cento	**chen**-to
	ten thousand	diecimila	dee-eh-chee-**mee**-la

| | one hundred thousand | centomila | chen-to-**mee**-la |

Colors	black	nero	**neh**-ro
	blue	azzurro	a-**tsu**-ro
	brown	bruno	**bru**-no
	green	verde	**vehr**-day
	pink	rosa	**ro**-za
	purple	porpora	**por**-por-a
	orange	arancio	a-**rahn**-cho
	red	rosso	**ros**-so
	white	bianco	bee-**ang**-ko
	yellow	giallo	**ja**-lo

Days of the week	Monday	lunedì	**loo**-neh-dee
	Tuesday	martedì	**mahr**-teh-dee
	Wednesday	mercoledì	**mare**-co-leh-dee
	Thursday	giovedì	**jo**-veh-dee
	Friday	venerdì	**ven**-air-dee
	Saturday	sabato	**sah**-ba-toe
	Sunday	domenica	doe-**men**-ee-ca

Months	January	gennaio	jeh-**nah**-yo
	February	febbraio	feh-**brah**-yo
	March	marzo	**mahr**-tso
	April	aprile	a-**pree**-lay
	May	maggio	**mah**-jo
	June	giugno	**joon**-yo
	July	luglio	**loo**-lee-o
	August	agosto	a-**goass**-to
	September	settembre	seh-**tem**-bray
	October	ottobre	o-**toe**-bray
	November	novembre	no-**vem**-bray
	December	dicembre	dee-**chem**-bray

Useful phrases	Do you speak English?	Parla inglese?	**par**-la een-**glay**-zay
	I don't speak Italian	Non parlo italiano	non **par**-lo ee-tal-**yah**-no
	I don't understand	Non capisco	non ka-**peess**-ko
	Can you please repeat?	Può ripetere?	pwo ree-**pet**-ay-ray
	Slowly!	Lentamente!	**len**-ta-men-tay
	I don't know	Non lo so	noan lo **so**
	I'm American/ British	Sono americano/a Sono inglese	**so**-no a-may-ree-**ka**-no/a **so**-no een-**glay**-zay
	What's your name?	Come si chiama?	**ko**-may see kee-**ah**-ma
	My name is . . .	Mi chiamo . . .	mee kee-**ah**-mo
	What time is it?	Che ore sono?	kay **o**-ray **so**-no
	How?	Come?	**ko**-may
	When?	Quando?	**kwan**-doe

Yesterday/today/tomorrow	Ieri/oggi/domani	**yer**-ee/**o**-jee/do-**mah**-nee
This morning/afternoon	Stamattina/Oggi pomeriggio	sta-ma-**tee**-na/**o**-jee po-mer-**ee**-jo
Tonight	Stasera	sta-**ser**-a
What?	Che cosa?	kay **ko**-za
What is it?	Che cos'è?	kay ko-**zay**
Why?	Perché?	pear-**kay**
Who?	Chi?	kee
Where is . . .	Dov'è . . .	doe-**vay**
the bus stop?	la fermata dell'autobus?	la fer-**ma**-ta del ow-toe-**booss**
the train station?	la stazione?	la sta-tsee-**oh**-nay
the subway station?	la metropolitana?	la may-tro-po-lee-**ta**-na
the terminal?	il terminal?	eel ter-mee-**nahl**
the post office?	l'ufficio postale?	loo-**fee**-cho po-**sta**-lay
the bank?	la banca?	la **bahn**-ka
the . . . hotel?	l'hotel . . . ?	lo-**tel**
the store?	il negozio?	ell nay-**go**-tsee-o
the cashier?	la cassa?	la **ka**-sa
the . . . museum?	il museo . . . ?	eel moo-**zay**-o
the hospital?	l'ospedale?	lo-spay-**dah**-lay
the first aid station?	il pronto soccorso?	eel **pron**-to so-**kor**-so
the elevator?	l'ascensore?	la-shen-**so**-ray
a telephone?	un telefono?	oon tay-**lay**-fo-no
Where are the rest rooms?	Dov'è il bagno?	doe-**vay** eel **bahn**-yo
Here/there	Qui/là	kwee/la
Left/right	A sinistra/a destra	a see-**neess**-tra/a **des**-tra
Straight ahead	Avanti dritto	a-**vahn**-tee **dree**-to
Is it near/far?	È vicino?/lontano?	ay vee-**chee**-no/lon-**tah**-no
I'd like . . .	Vorrei . . .	vo- **ray**
a room	una camera	**oo**-na ka-**may**-ra
the key	la chiave	la kee-**ah**-vay
a newspaper	un giornale	oon jor-**na**-lay
a stamp	un francobollo	oon frahn-ko-**bo**-lo
I'd like to buy . . .	Vorrei comprare . . .	vo-**ray** kom-**pra**-ray
a cigar	un sigaro	oon see-**ga**-ro
cigarettes	delle sigarette	day-lay see-ga-**ret**-ay
some matches	dei fiammiferi	day-ee fee-ah-**mee**-fer-ee
some soap	una saponetta	**oo**-na sa-po-**net**-a
a city plan	una planta della città	**oo**-na **plahn**-ta day-la chee-**ta**
a road map of . . .	una carta stradale di . . .	**oo**-na **cart**-a stra-**dah**-lay dee

a country map	una carta geografica	**oo**-na **cart**-a jay-o-**grah**-fee-ka
a magazine	una rivista	**oo**-na ree-**veess**-ta
envelopes	delle buste	**day**-lay **booss**-tay
writing paper	della carta da lettere	**day**-la **cart**-a da let-air-ay
a postcard	una cartolina	**oo**-na car-toe-**lee**-na
a guidebook	una guida turistica	**oo**-na **gwee**-da too-**reess**-tee-ka

How much is it?	Quanto costa?	**kwahn**-toe **coast**-a
It's expensive/ cheap	È caro/economico	ay **car**-o/ay-ko-**no**-mee-ko
A little/a lot	Poco/tanto	**po**-ko/**tahn**-to
More/less	Più/meno	pee-**oo**/**may**-no
Enough/too (much)	Abbastanza/troppo	a-bas-**tahn**-sa/**tro**-po
I am sick	Sto male	sto **ma**-lay
Please call a doctor	Chiami un dottore	kee-**ah**-mee oon doe-**toe**-ray
Help!	Aiuto!	a-**yoo**-toe
Stop!	Alt!	ahlt
Fire!	Al fuoco!	ahl **fwo**-ko
Caution!/Look out!	Attenzione!	a-ten-**syon**-ay

Dining Out

A bottle of . . .	una bottiglia di . . .	**oo**-na bo-**tee**-lee-ah dee
A cup of . . .	Una tazza di . . .	**oo**-na **tah**-tsa dee
A glass of . . .	Un bicchiere di . . .	oon bee-key-**air**-ay dee
Ashtray	Il portacenere	eel por-ta-**chen**-ay-ray
Bill/check	Il conto	eel **cone**-toe
Bread	Il pane	eel **pa**-nay
Breakfast	La prima colazione	la **pree**-ma ko-la-**tsee**-oh-nay
Cheers!	Cin cin!	cheen cheen
Cocktail/aperitif	L'aperitivo	la-pay-ree-**tee**-vo
Dinner	La cena	la **chen**-a
Enjoy!	Buon appetito	bwone a-pay-**tee**-toe
Fixed-price menu	Menù a prezzo fisso	may-**noo** a **pret**-so **fee**-so
Fork	La forchetta	la for-**ket**-a
I am diabetic	Ho il diabete	o eel dee-a-**bay**-tay
I am on a diet	Sono a dieta	**so**-no a dee-**et**-a

I am vegetarian	Sono vegetariano/a	**so**-no vay-jay-ta-ree-**ah**-no/a
I cannot eat . . .	Non posso mangiare . . .	non **po**-so man-**ja**-ray
I'd like to order	Vorrei ordinare	vo-**ray** or-dee-**nah**-ray
I'd like . . .	Vorrei . . .	vo- **ray**
I'm hungry/thirsty	Ho fame/sete	o **fa**-may/**set**-ay
Is service included?	Il servizio è incluso?	eel ser-**vee**-tzee-o ay een-**kloo**-zo
It's good/bad	È buono/cattivo	ay **bwo**-no/ka-**tee**-vo
It's hot/cold	È caldo/freddo	ay **kahl**-doe/**fred**-o
Knife	Il coltello	eel kol-**tel**-o
Lunch	Il pranzo	eel **prahnt**-so
Menu	Il menù	eel may-**noo**
Napkin	Il tovagliolo	eel toe-va-lee-**oh**-lo
Please give me . . .	Mi dia . . .	mee **dee**-a
Salt	Il sale	eel **sah**-lay
Spoon	Il cucchiaio	eel koo-kee-**ah**-yo
Sugar	Lo zucchero	lo **tsoo**-ker-o
Waiter/Waitress	Cameriere/ cameriera	ka-mare-**yer**-ay/ ka-mare-**yer**-a
Wine list	La lista dei vini	la **lee**-sta **day**-ee **vee**-nee

Menu Guide

English	Italian
Set menu	Menù a prezzo fisso
Dish of the day	Piatto del giorno
Specialty of the house	Specialità della casa
Local specialties	Specialità locali
Extra charge	Extra . . .
In season	Di stagione
Cover charge/Service charge	Coperto/Servizio

Breakfast

Butter	Burro
Croissant	Cornetto
Eggs	Uova
Honey	Miele
Jam/Marmalade	Marmellata
Roll	Panino
Toast	Pane tostato

Starters

Assorted cold cuts	Affettati misti
Assorted seafood	Antipasto di pesce
Assorted appetizers	Antipasto misto
Toasted rounds of bread, fried or toasted in oil	Crostini/Crostoni
Diced vegetable salad	Insalata russa
Eggplant parmigiana	Melanzane alla parmigiana
Fried mozzarella sandwich	Mozzarella in carrozza
Ham and melon	Prosciutto e melone
Cooked sausages and cured meats	Salumi cotti
Filled pastry shells	Vol-au-vents

Soups

"Angel hair," thin noodle soup	Capelli d'angelo
Cream of . . .	Crema di . . .
Pasta and beans soup	Pasta e fagioli
Egg-drop and parmesan cheese soup	Stracciatella

Pasta, Rice and Pizza

Filled pasta	Agnolotti/ravioli/tortellini
Potato Dumplings	Gnocchi
Semolina dumplings	Gnocchi alla romana
Pasta	Pasta
with four cheeses	*ai quattro formaggi*
with basil/cheese/pine nuts/garlic sauce	*al pesto*
with tomato-based meat sauce	*al ragù*
with tomato sauce	*al sugo*
with butter	*in bianco*
with egg, parmesan cheese, and pepper	*alla carbonare*
green (spinach-based) pasta	*verde*

Rice	Riso
Rice dish	Risotto
with mushrooms	*ai funghi*
with saffron	*alla milanese*
Noodles	Tagliatelle
Pizza	Pizza
Pizza with seafood, cheese, artichokes, and ham in four different sections	Pizza quattro stagioni
Pizza with tomato and mozzarella	Pizza margherita
Pizza with oil, garlic, and oregano	Pizza marinara

Fish and Seafood

Anchovies	Acciughe
Bass	Persico
Carp	Carpa
Clams	Vongole
Cod	Merluzzo
Crab	Granchio
Eel	Anguilla
Lobster	Aragosta
Mackerel	Sgombro
Mullet	Triglia
Mussels	Cozze
Octopus	Polpo
Oysters	Ostriche
Pike	Luccio
Prawns	Gamberoni
Salmon	Salmone
Shrimp	Scampi
Shrimps	Gamberetti
Sole	Sogliola
Squid	Calamari
Swordfish	Pescespada
Trout	Trota
Tuna	Tonno

Methods of Preparation

Baked	Al forno
Cold, with vinegar sauce	In carpione
Fish stew	Zuppa di pesce
Fried	Fritto
Grilled (usually charcoal)	Alla griglia
Seafood salad	In insalata
Smoked	Affumicato
Stuffed	Ripieno

Meat

Boar	Cinghiale
Brain	Cervella
Braised meat with wine	Brasato
Chop	Costoletta
Duck	Anatra
Lamb	Agnello
Baby lamb	Abbacchio
Liver	Fegato

Pheasant	Fagiano
Pork roast	Arista
Rabbit	Coniglio
Steak	Bistecca
Roast steak	Braciola
Sliced raw steak with sauce	Carpaccio
Mixed boiled meat	Bollito misto

Methods of Preparation

Battered with eggs and crumbs and fried	. . . alla milanese
Grilled	. . . ai ferri
Grilled (usually charcoal)	. . . alla griglia
Raw, with lemon/egg sauce	. . . alla tartara
Roasted	. . . arrosto
Very rare	. . . al sangue
Well done	. . . ben cotta
With ham and cheese	. . . alla valdostana
With parmesan cheese and tomatoes	. . . alla parmigiana

Vegetables

Artichokes	Carciofi
Asparagus	Asparagi
Beans	Fagioli
Brussels sprouts	Cavolini di Bruxelles
Cabbage	Cavolo
Carrots	Carote
Cauliflower	Cavolfiore
Cucumber	Cetriolo
Eggplants	Melanzane
Green Beans	Fagiolini
Leeks	Porri
Lentils	Lenticchie
Lettuce	Lattuga
Mushrooms	Funghi
Onions	Cipolle
Peas	Piselli
Peppers	Peperoni
Potatoes	Patate
Roasted potatoes	*Patate arrosto*
Boiled potatoes	*Patate bollite*
Fried potatoes	*Patate fritte*
Small, roasted potatoes	*Patatine novelle*
Mashed potatoes	*Purè di patate*
Radishes	Rapanelli
Salad	Insalata
vegetable	*mista*
green	*verde*
Spinach	Spinaci
Tomatoes	Pomodori
Zucchini	Zucchini

Sauces, Herbs and Spices

| Basil | Basilico |
| Bay leaf | Lauro |

Chervil	Cerfoglio
Dill	Aneto
Garlic	Aglio
Hot dip with anchovies	
(for vegetables)	Bagna cauda
Marjoram	Maggiorana
Mayonnaise	Maionese
Mustard	Mostarda
Oil	Olio
Parsley-based sauce	Salsa verde
Pepper	Pepe
Rosemary	Rosmarino
Tartar sauce	Salsa tartara
Vinegar	Aceto
White sauce	Besciamella

Cheeses

Fresh:	caprino fresco
	mascarpone
	mozzarella
	ricotta
Mild:	caciotta
	caprino
	fontina
	grana
	provola
	robiola
	scamorza
Sharp:	asiago
	gorgonzola
	groviera
	pecorino
	provolone
	taleggio
	toma

Fruits and Nuts

Almonds	Mandorle
Apple	Mela
Apricot	Albicocca
Banana	Banana
Blackberries	More
Blackcurrant	Ribes nero
Blueberries	Mirtilli
Cherries	Ciliege
Chestnuts	Castagne
Coconut	Noce di cocco
Dates	Datteri
Figs	Fichi
Green grapes	Uva bianca
Black grapes	Uva nera
Grapefruit	Pompelmo
Hazelnuts	Nocciole
Lemon	Limone
Melon	Melone
Nectarine	Nocepesca
Orange	Arancia
Pear	Pera

Peach	Pesca
Pineapple	Ananas
Plum	Prugna/Susina
Prune	Prugna secca
Raisins	Uva passa
Raspberries	Lamponi
Redcurrant	Ribes
Strawberries	Fragole
Tangerine	Mandarino
Walnuts	Noci
Watermelon	Anguria
Dried fruit	Frutta secca
Fresh fruit	Frutta fresca
Fruit salad	Macedonia di frutta

Desserts

Custard filled pastry, with candied fruit	Cannoli
Ricotta filled pastry shells with sugar glaze	Cannoli alla Siciliana
Ice cream with candied fruit	Cassata
Ricotta filled cake with sugar glaze	Cassata Siciliana
Chocolate	Cioccolato
Cup of ice cream	Coppa gelato
Caramel custard	Creme caramel
Pie	Crostata
Fruit pie	Crostata di frutta
Ice cream	Gelato
Flaked pastry	Millefoglie
Chestnuts and whipped cream cake	Montebianco
Whipped cream	Panna montata
Pastries	Paste
Sherbet	Sorbetto
Chocolate coated ice cream	Tartufo
Fruit tart	Torta di frutta
Apple tart	Torta di mele
Ice cream cake	Torta gelato
Vanilla	Vaniglia
Egg-based cream with sugar and Marsala wine	Zabaione
Ice cream filled cake	Zuccotto

Alcoholic Drinks

On the rocks	Con ghiaccio
Straight	Secco
With soda	Con seltz
Beer	Birra
light/dark	*chiara/scura*
Bitter cordial	Amaro
Brandy	Cognac
Cordial	Liquore
Aniseed cordial	Sambuca
Martini	Cocktail Martini
Port	Porto
Vermouth	Vermut/Martini
Wine	Vino

blush	*rosé*
dry	*secco*
full-bodied	*corposo*
light	*leggero*
red	*rosso*
sparkling	*spumante*
sweet	*dolce*
very dry	*brut*
white	*bianco*
Light wine	Vinello
Bottle	Bottiglia
Carafe	Caraffa
Flask	Fiasco

Nonalcoholic Drinks

Mineral water	Acqua minerale
carbonated	*gassata*
still	*non gassata*
Tap water	Acqua naturale
Tonic water	Acqua tonica
Coffee with steamed milk	Cappuccino
Espresso	Caffè espresso
with milk	*macchiato*
decaffeinated	*decaffeinato*
lighter espresso	*lungo*
with cordial	*corretto*
Fruit juice	Succo di frutta
Hot chocolate	Cioccolata calda
Lemonade	Limonata
Milk	Latte
Orangeade	Aranciata
Tea	Tè
with milk/lemon	*col latte/col limone*
iced	*freddo*

Index

Personal Itinerary

Departure *Date*

Time

Transportation

Arrival *Date*　　　　*Time*

Departure *Date*　　　　*Time*

Transportation

Accommodations

Arrival *Date*　　　　*Time*

Departure *Date*　　　　*Time*

Transportation

Accommodations

Arrival *Date*　　　　*Time*

Departure *Date*　　　　*Time*

Transportation

Accommodations

Personal Itinerary

Arrival *Date*   *Time*

Departure *Date*   *Time*

Transportation

Accommodations

Arrival *Date*   *Time*

Departure *Date*   *Time*

Transportation

Accommodations

Arrival *Date*   *Time*

Departure *Date*   *Time*

Transportation

Accommodations

Arrival *Date*   *Time*

Departure *Date*   *Time*

Transportation

Accommodations

Personal Itinerary

Arrival *Date*   *Time*

Departure *Date*   *Time*

Transportation

Accommodations

Arrival *Date*   *Time*

Departure *Date*   *Time*

Transportation

Accommodations

Arrival *Date*   *Time*

Departure *Date*   *Time*

Transportation

Accommodations

Arrival *Date*   *Time*

Departure *Date*   *Time*

Transportation

Accommodations

Addresses

Name	Name
Address	Address
Telephone	Telephone
Name	Name
Address	Address
Telephone	Telephone
Name	Name
Address	Address
Telephone	Telephone
Name	Name
Address	Address
Telephone	Telephone
Name	Name
Address	Address
Telephone	Telephone
Name	Name
Address	Address
Telephone	Telephone
Name	Name
Address	Address
Telephone	Telephone
Name	Name
Address	Address
Telephone	Telephone

Addresses

Name

Address

Telephone

Name

Address

Telephone

Name

Address

Telephone

Name

Address

Telephone

Name

Address

Telephone

Name

Address

Telephone

Name

Address

Telephone

Name

Address

Telephone

Name

Address

Telephone

Name

Address

Telephone

Name

Address

Telephone

Name

Address

Telephone

Name

Address

Telephone

Name

Address

Telephone

Name

Address

Telephone

Name

Address

Telephone

Fodor's Travel Guides

U.S. Guides

Alaska
American Cities
The American South
Arizona
Atlantic City & the
  New Jersey Shore
Boston
California
Cape Cod
Carolinas & the
  Georgia Coast
Chesapeake
Chicago
Colorado
Dallas & Fort Worth
Disney World & the
  Orlando Area

The Far West
Florida
Greater Miami,
  Fort Lauderdale,
  Palm Beach
Hawaii
Hawaii *(Great Travel
  Values)*
Houston & Galveston
I-10: California to
  Florida
I-55: Chicago to New
  Orleans
I-75: Michigan to
  Florida
I-80: San Francisco to
  New York

I-95: Maine to Miami
Las Vegas
Los Angeles, Orange
  County, Palm Springs
Maui
New England
New Mexico
New Orleans
New Orleans *(Pocket
  Guide)*
New York City
New York City *(Pocket
  Guide)*
New York State
Pacific North Coast
Philadelphia
Puerto Rico *(Fun in)*

Rockies
San Diego
San Francisco
San Francisco *(Pocket
  Guide)*
Texas
United States of
  America
Virgin Islands
  (U.S. & British)
Virginia
Waikiki
Washington, DC
Williamsburg,
  Jamestown &
  Yorktown

Foreign Guides

Acapulco
Amsterdam
Australia, New Zealand
  & the South Pacific
Austria
The Bahamas
The Bahamas *(Pocket
  Guide)*
Barbados *(Fun in)*
Beijing, Guangzhou &
  Shanghai
Belgium & Luxembourg
Bermuda
Brazil
Britain *(Great Travel
  Values)*
Canada
Canada *(Great Travel
  Values)*
Canada's Maritime
  Provinces
Cancún, Cozumel,
  Mérida, The
  Yucatán
Caribbean
Caribbean *(Great
  Travel Values)*

Central America
Copenhagen,
  Stockholm, Oslo,
  Helsinki, Reykjavik
Eastern Europe
Egypt
Europe
Europe *(Budget)*
Florence & Venice
France
France *(Great Travel
  Values)*
Germany
Germany *(Great Travel
  Values)*
Great Britain
Greece
Holland
Hong Kong & Macau
Hungary
India
Ireland
Israel
Italy
Italy *(Great Travel
  Values)*
Jamaica *(Fun in)*

Japan
Japan *(Great Travel
  Values)*
Jordan & the Holy Land
Kenya
Korea
Lisbon
Loire Valley
London
London *(Pocket Guide)*
London *(Great Travel
  Values)*
Madrid
Mexico
Mexico *(Great Travel
  Values)*
Mexico City & Acapulco
Mexico's Baja & Puerto
  Vallarta, Mazatlán,
  Manzanillo, Copper
  Canyon
Montreal
Munich
New Zealand
North Africa
Paris
Paris *(Pocket Guide)*

People's Republic of
  China
Portugal
Province of Quebec
Rio de Janeiro
The Riviera *(Fun on)*
Rome
St. Martin/St. Maarten
Scandinavia
Scotland
Singapore
South America
South Pacific
Southeast Asia
Soviet Union
Spain
Spain *(Great Travel
  Values)*
Sweden
Switzerland
Sydney
Tokyo
Toronto
Turkey
Vienna
Yugoslavia

Special-Interest Guides

Bed & Breakfast
  Guide: North America
  1936...On the
  Continent

Royalty Watching
Selected Hotels of
  Europe

Selected Resorts
  and Hotels of the U.S.
Ski Resorts of North
  America

Views to Dine by
  around the World

Reader's Survey

Join us in updating the next edition of your Fodor's guide

Title of Guide:

1 **Hotel** ☐ **Restaurant** ☐ *(check one)*

Name

Number/Street

City/State/Country

Comments

2 **Hotel** ☐ **Restaurant** ☐ *(check one)*

Name

Number/Street

City/State/Country

Comments

3 **Hotel** ☐ **Restaurant** ☐ *(check one)*

Name

Number/Street

City/State/Country

Comments

Your Name *(optional)*

Address

General Comments

Business Reply Mail

First Class   Permit N⁰ 7775   New York, NY

Postage will be paid by addressee

Fodor's Travel Publications

201 East 50th Street
New York, NY 10022